SLIM HARPO

Slim Harpo's first publicity shot, late 1950s (Courtesy Bear Family Records)

SLIM HARPO
BLUES KING BEE
OF BATON ROUGE

MARTIN HAWKINS

 LOUISIANA STATE UNIVERSITY PRESS   BATON ROUGE

Published by Louisiana State University Press
Copyright © 2016 by Martin Hawkins
All rights reserved
Manufactured in the United States of America
First printing

Designer: Barbara Neely Bourgoyne
Typeface: Minion Pro
Printer and binder: Maple Press

Library of Congress Cataloging-in-Publication Data

Names: Hawkins, Martin, author.
Title: Slim Harpo : blues king bee of Baton Rouge / Martin Hawkins.
Description: Baton Rouge : Louisiana State University Press, [2016] |
    Includes bibliographical references and index.
Identifiers: LCCN 2016008119| ISBN 978-0-8071-6453-2 (cloth : alk. paper) | ISBN
    978-0-8071-6454-9 (pdf) | ISBN 978-0-8071-6455-6 (epub) | ISBN 978-0-8071-6456-3
(mobi)
Subjects: LCSH: Harpo, Slim, 1924–1970. | Blues musicians—United
    States—Biography.
Classification: LCC ML420.H163 H39 2016 | DDC 781.643092—dc23 LC record available at
http://lccn.loc.gov/2016008119

For the King Bee, wherever he may buzz,
for all the worker bees, keeping the music alive,
and for the Gambler and Moore families

CONTENTS

Illustrations follow pages 124 and 208.

FOREWORD

A biography of Slim Harpo, the Baton Rouge swamp-bluesman? The possibility never occurred to music writers during Harpo's lifetime. In fairness, blues research was still in its comparative infancy then. For example, in the United States, *Living Blues* magazine was not founded until 1970, the year that Harpo died and took his memories with him. A couple of short latter-day interviews were all Martin Hawkins had to work with as prime sources for this long-overdue book.

Those early overseas researchers from *Blues Unlimited*—Mike Leadbitter, Bruce Bastin, and Rick Milne—had traveled the South in the 1960s, to be joined by Robin Gosden and myself in 1970. But in those days, everybody was looking at a virtual blank slate in blues-research terms, and wanted to fill in the big picture first, so individual artist biographies were not a priority.

Even today, the Louisiana blues bookshelf is hardly groaning with publications. Through Leadbitter, such a visionary, there were trailblazing *Blues Unlimited* pamphlets: *Crowley, Louisiana Blues* (1968), devoted to J. D. "Jay" Miller and his artists, and *From the Bayou,* a study of Goldband Records with Eddie Shuler (1969). Then Leadbitter edited *Nothing but the Blues* (1971), a compendium of *Blues Unlimited* articles with swamp-blues content. In 1975, Harry Oster, who had recorded Robert Pete Williams among other old-style bluesmen, contributed *Living Country Blues* (first published locally in 1969), followed by Jimmy Beyer's local pamphlet *Baton Rouge Blues* (1980). I stepped into the fray with the book *South to Louisiana: The Music of the Cajun Bayous* (1983), giving historical overviews of Cajun, zydeco, swamp-blues, local hillbilly, and swamp-pop music on phonograph record. Since then, the zydeco element has been covered in Michael Tisserand's *The Kingdom of Zydeco* (1998) and *Zydeco!* by Rick Olivier and Ben Sandmel (1998). Also, swamp-pop artist Johnnie Allan's *Memories* (1988), a pictorial history of South Louisiana musicians, includes several Baton Rouge blues and rhythm-and-blues (R&B)

artists. Then Shane Bernard's *Swamp Pop: Cajun and Creole Rhythm and Blues* (1996) studied the rock 'n' roll music of Cajun teenagers with several references to Slim Harpo's big hit, "Rainin' in My Heart," which was as much swamp-pop as swamp-blues.

This biography by Martin Hawkins, which incorporates a history of the comparatively under-researched Baton Rouge blues scene, is therefore more than welcome. It joins a list of biographies featuring top post–World War II bluesmen such as Muddy Waters, B. B. King, Little Walter, Jimmy Reed, Elmore James, Howlin' Wolf, John Lee Hooker, Ike Turner, Lightnin' Hopkins, and Buddy Guy. That's quite an exclusive club. Hawkins's book follows hot on the heels of his supervision of a well-received five-CD box set on Bear Family Records, *Buzzin' The Blues: The Complete Slim Harpo*.

What is swamp-blues? To me, it is a sound that is rooted in the Excello Records releases of artists such as Harpo, Lightnin' Slim, Lonesome Sundown, Lazy Lester, and Silas Hogan, produced and engineered by Jay Miller in Crowley, Louisiana.

The term "swamp-blues," as with "swamp-pop," relates directly to its South Louisiana origins, and was possibly influenced by the usage of those hip record reviewers in the *Cash Box* trade magazine to describe records aimed at the Deep Southern markets. As I noted in *South to Louisiana*, "By the late 'fifties many Louisiana bluesmen had begun to forge their own warm, recognizable style from the borrowed sounds, mainly Chicago-based. The style was the swamp-blues, and Baton Rouge became its spiritual home." Among the artists who influenced the local bluesmen were Jimmy Reed, Muddy Waters, Little Walter, and Sonny Boy Williamson II. It is interesting how young South Louisiana bluesmen Guitar Jr. and Buddy Guy settled easily into the Windy City environment. The impact on the swamp-blues artists of Lightnin' Hopkins and Lil' Son Jackson, both from Texas, should not be forgotten.

A major swamp-blues stylistic feature is the high caliber of the backing musicians with an unhurried approach, always with time to spare and never seeking the limelight. Slim Harpo's King Bees in the early 1960s "Rainin' in My Heart" era were a model in this respect, as were Silas Hogan's Rhythm Ramblers and Jimmy Anderson's Joy Jumpers.

Martin Hawkins explains that other blues and R&B men would take the comparatively short road trip from Baton Rouge to Crowley into Jay Miller's studios, including Tabby Thomas, Schoolboy Cleve, Lester Robertson, Eddie Hudson, Sonny Martin, and Whispering Smith. Fortunately for them (and us), Miller had an excellent ear for the music and was a recognized songwriter and a talented recording engineer. Let us not forget, too, that he operated mixed-racial sessions in a highly segregated part of the country. A controversial character to some, including to Harpo, Miller always received me well and was a favorite interviewee. In the final analysis, he has left a marvelous body of work for posterity. Without the Crowley record man, would there have been a swamp-blues style as we know it?

Harpo's post-Miller sound was markedly different, taking in experimental soul-tinged and rock excursions recorded at Royal Studios in Memphis; Fame in Muscle Shoals, Alabama; Woodland Sound in Nashville; and studios in Los Angeles. It makes one wonder where Harpo's career would have led him if he hadn't died too young. The wider rock markets—and international trips—were already beckoning.

As a young English bank clerk in the early 1960s, I became entranced by the output of Excello Records and started importing those striking orange-and-dark-blue 45s from Ernie's Record Mart of Nashville. The ordering process was made relatively easy because Ernie's was a division of Nashboro-Excello, although I still had to surmount the Bank of England's arcane currency restrictions of the time. Among the many gems that knocked me out were Slim Harpo's double-siders "Rainin' in My Heart" / "Don't Start Cryin' Now" and "I'm a King Bee" / "I Got Love if You Want It," plus the record collectors' favorite, "Blues Hangover." After sending letters to Excello owner Ernie Young and Miller—and getting responses—I felt able to write about Excello, Young, and Miller in the very first issue of *Blues Unlimited* in April 1963; there were just six Harpo singles and one LP available at the time. At the time of my first Excello purchases, I had no idea that Harpo's records would soon emerge as an inspiration for the British R&B boom, and I was ignorant, too, of the drama that erupted between Harpo and the two record men close to him, Miller and Young, as deftly explained by Hawkins.

The author's work spurs inevitable personal questions: How did Miller come to have such an affinity for the blues? Why was there no Louisiana blues legacy to speak of before the Miller recordings? How was it that Texas pre–World War II street musician Blind Lemon Jefferson was a favorite among so many postwar blues artists, including Harpo? Exactly which band members and session men were used in Miller's recordings? Who influenced Harpo on harmonica in his early days, and whom did Harpo influence? Why didn't Miller record other Baton Rouge artists such as Big Papa, Clarence Edwards, and Raful Neal? What influence did New Orleans music have on Harpo and the swamp-bluesmen? Who was bigger in Baton Rouge: Lightnin' Slim or Slim Harpo? Such teasers, and more, are tackled head-on by Hawkins.

There are the intriguing lesser-known players: bandleader and record-shop owner Buddy Stewart; record men Sam Montalbano and Lionel Whitfield; and Boe Melvin, who impressed me greatly as a guitarist when accompanying Tabby Thomas at a New Orleans Jazz & Heritage Festival appearance. All added color to the Baton Rouge scene, as Hawkins notes. Then there are the Baton Rouge and Port Allen club scenes, which the author brings alive through interviews and local newspaper research. In some instances, the hunt for more information goes on.

It was my privilege to bring a longtime appreciation of Excello Records to a wider public—and not just in magazine articles or books—by supervising the reissue deal with Ace Records of London from 1993 through 2000. I was like a kid in the proverbial candy store when I was sent to Woodland Sound Studios in Nashville to make digital transfers of the master tapes for CD release. You can imagine my delight at handling the original Harpo tape boxes of "I'm a King Bee," "Rainin' in My Heart," and "Baby Scratch My Back," and finding high-quality previously unissued tracks like "Yeah Yeah Baby" and "Boogie Chillun." A series of three Harpo CDs ensued from issued and unissued Excello recordings, plus a renegade originally unissued session for Imperial Records from 1961. Starting in the 1970s, my good friend Bruce Bastin had made a similar trawl of Miller's non-Excello Crowley tapes that were licensed to his Flyright label.

Through the years, a lot of work has been done in researching the swamp-bluesmen, but I still marvel at this Harpo biography. It's taken a tenacious, dedicated researcher like Martin Hawkins to bring this book to fruition. He comes with an impressive track record that extends back to documenting the famous Sun label of Memphis with Colin Escott—resulting in the definitive Sun book, *Good Rockin' Tonight: Sun Records and the Birth of Rock 'n' roll*—and includes *A Shot in the Dark: Making Records in Nashville, 1945–1955*, bringing alive the untold story of the early days of the music business there—right up to the recent Harpo box set. Please read on and, like me, be impressed by Hawkins's championing of a swamp-bluesman who deserves a royal biographical treatment: Slim Harpo *is* a King Bee.

—JOHN BROVEN
East Setauket, New York, July 2015

PREFACE

THE REASONS

For numerous reasons—not least because he never got to tell it himself—the story of Slim Harpo and his music is among the most fascinating in all blues and R&B. Slim Harpo seemed to come out of nowhere in 1957 to make his impressive entrance into the world of blues recordings and the American independent record business. Here was a man with a memorable name, a strong song in "I'm a King Bee," and a finely crafted minimalist style, at once familiar and novel. In 1961 he emerged again after years of local scuffling to make an even more impressive entry into the American R&B and popular music charts; his "Rainin' in My Heart" became one of those barely categorizable hits that just couldn't be ignored. He scored for a third time in the mid-1960s with some equally individual and memorable blues-based dance numbers.

By many benchmarks, Harpo's career was a success, and for periods in his life he was in the spotlight, yet very little detail of his life and career became known while he was alive. Born in 1924, he was among the last of the original down-home bluesmen, but also one of the first to register pop music hits. He was among the first wave of artists, black and white, who developed the swamp-pop sound in the late 1950s and early 1960s, but he would have been the last to say he was anything other than a bluesman. He was a brilliant harmonica player and yet was often seen in later promotional photos as a guitar slinger. He or his wife wrote many of his own blues songs, but when he gained wider recognition, it was for a ballad and several dance grooves. Harpo was at odds with his main record producer and sometime song collaborator—Jay Miller—much of the time, but together the two men crafted a memorable sound and style that merged down-home blues with other familiar sounds in Louisiana music. Harpo lived, worked, and performed most of his life in and around Louisiana, but he was feted in the rock music circles of New York and Los Angeles when he did appear there in his last few years. He remained based in his hometown of Baton Rouge all his life and had the opportunity to give very few interviews. Apparently an unassuming and mainly calm man, he nevertheless developed a very polished and slick stage appearance. He died young, aged forty-five, just as his career was taking off for the fourth and potentially most lucrative time at home and abroad. He died young enough to avoid the pressures that would probably have adulterated his music. His legacy remains one of the most consistently good and coherent bodies of blues recordings of all time.

Harpo's successes, measured in sales charts, were modest. His first recording and signature song, "I'm a King Bee," was never more than a regional hit when issued in 1957, and it was not until 1961 that he registered a national hit. That year, "Rainin' in My Heart" went to number 17 on the *Billboard* R&B chart and number 34 on the pop chart; in 1966, "Baby Scratch My Back" went to number 1 R&B and number 16 pop, and both "Shake Your Hips" and "I'm Your Bread Maker, Baby" were "bubbling under" the popular Hot 100; in 1967, "Tip on In" made number 37 R&B and created small pop bubbles; and finally, in 1968, "Te-Ni-Nee-Ni-Nu" registered at number 36 on *Billboard*'s R&B chart. But in the four and a half decades since his death in 1970, Harpo's music has achieved greater recognition than his chart placings would dictate. In 2008 he received a post-humous Grammy Hall of Fame Award for "I'm a King Bee" as a "recording of lasting qualitative or historical significance." His music has been revered by successive generations of blues aficionados and fans of Louisiana swamp-pop. Much of it has been reissued down the years, and his name continues to appear on the lips of those he influenced and in the works of blues researchers and writers.

There is an interesting accord among writers and commentators that, as Louisiana music expert John Broven wrote, Harpo was "one of the most accessible" of the down-home bluesmen and that "his recordings have a timeless and mellow quality." Singer and broadcaster Paul Jones felt this was because "Harpo was a paradox, a downhome bluesman who sounded like a city slicker." Jones was part of the early 1960s wave of British groups playing in an R&B style. As singer with the group Manfred Mann, he admitted that, initially, as the R&B boom was gathering pace, Slim Harpo was too pop for him: "Blues were characterized by words like harsh and brooding, agonised, or even tortured. . . . words like relaxed and subtle made rare appearances, pleasing and melodic were distrusted, and entertaining was almost an insult. Yet Slim Harpo warranted all these and was no less a pure bluesman." New Orleans music expert Jeff Hannusch wrote that Harpo was the most successful and celebrated Louisiana-based blues artist of all time: "Known in pop circles for two massive chart successes, the swamp-pop ballad 'Rainin' in My Heart,' and the hypnotic 'Baby Scratch My Back,' he was one of the toughest blues artists of his generation, but he was also comfortable embracing rock 'n' roll, pop and even country music." Music writer and cultural historian Peter Guralnick described how Harpo's singing was "as if a black country and western singer or a white rhythm and blues singer were attempting to impersonate a member of the opposite genre." Pete Welding, writing in *Rolling Stone* magazine, considered Harpo "a stylist who's carved out his own niche and within the relatively narrow confines of that approach, he's unbeatable—and, of course, immediately recognisable. . . . the emphasis is on forceful, direct rhythm, tight and simple arrangements that work beautifully with Slim's sly, laconic singing and harmonica playing and, above all else, feeling." Musician and writer Hank Davis said, "When Slim is on, he is utterly delightful. Most of all, he is melodic. Actually quite country. Both are qualities that make him very special. When he is not on, he is undistinguished." Fortunately Slim was often "on," and another musician and researcher, Steve Coleridge, wrote, "Slim Harpo stands out [from other bluesmen] in his depth of texture, his non-reliance on the 12 bar format . . . the complexity of the bass and guitar parts, and, above all, he could write the best tunes." Sam Charters noted on an LP sleeve that "his harmonica kept its Louisiana blues tinge whatever style he played. . . . there is a kind of understated emotionalism to what he does" and that, in a talented generation of bluesmen, "he was one of the best of them." In a booklet promoting Baton Rouge blues, researcher Jimmy Beyer concluded that "tracing Slim Harpo's influences isn't easy. . . . Mostly, one hears a unique type of rural blues that is distinctively Slim Harpo." One of the few people who ever interviewed Harpo, Jim Delehant, quoted Slim admitting that he made some "attempt at rock 'n' roll, but I'd much rather do the blues. That's my favorite because I can get more feeling out of it."[1]

So, Slim Harpo made music that was pure blues in a number of forms but also borrowed from and wandered into other styles without losing face. It's easy to listen to, easy to love, but real. It's music that has been recorded by a wide range of artists down the years. The first was Sun Records' rocker Warren Smith ("Got Love if You Want It"), followed by, among others, soul man Otis Redding

("Baby Scratch My Back"), country men Hank Williams Jr. ("Rainin' in My Heart") and Marty Stuart ("Shake Your Hips"), rock groups the Grateful Dead ("I'm a King Bee"), the Doors ("I'm a King Bee"), and George Thorogood and the Destroyers ("Tip on In"), blues maestro Muddy Waters ("I'm a King Bee"), blues pianist "Ironing Board Sam" Moore ("Rainin' in My Heart"), and artists of a much newer persuasion like the Cramps ("Strange Love"). In 2012 a Jack Daniels whiskey ad included "I'm a King Bee" by the Stone Foxes band, in 2013 Little Jonny and the Giants recorded Harpo's "Hey Little Lee," and at the end of 2015, former ZZ Top member Billy Gibbons opened his first solo album with a reinvigorated Harpo song ("Got Love if You Want It"). And then, of course, Harpo has made his posthumous impact on both the small and large screens. Before the fictional Blues Brothers carried their strange blend of musical influences around the world in blockbusting movies of the 1980s, Dan Ackroyd and John Belushi had started their act wearing, not shades and black hats, but bee costumes. They first appeared singing "I'm a King Bee" on national TV in a comedy sketch for *Saturday Night Live* in 1976.

Most American artists, though, came late to the Harpo appreciation party. The recording of his songs really started in England in the early 1960s during the R&B boom there. At the forefront were the Rolling Stones ("I'm a King Bee" and "Shake Your Hips"), the Kinks ("I Got Love if You Want It"), the Yardbirds ("Baby Scratch My Back" retitled as "Rack My Mind"), the Pretty Things ("I Got Love if You Want It" reworked bizarrely as "13 Chester Street," and "Rainin' in My Heart"), Them ("Don't Start Crying Now"), Love Sculpture ("Shake Your Hips"), and Pink Floyd ("I'm a King Bee"). Nearly fifty years later, in 2010, Rolling Stones guitarist Keith Richards was telling *Rolling Stone* magazine that Harpo's "Blues Hangover" was among his personal top-10 songs—and that one was never any kind of hit for Slim. Mick Jagger, when asked by the same magazine back in 1968, said: "You could say that we did blues to turn people on, but . . . what's the point in listening to us doing 'I'm a King Bee' when you can listen to Slim Harpo doing it?"[2] Well, exactly.

Except, actually, music evolves, and with each new generation of musicians more of the previous generation are forgotten than are remembered. Only the music of the very best and most original, or lucky, artists will endure long and have their music recreated by others. The fact is that Slim Harpo has his name in the record books, his songs in the repertoires of successive generations, and an annual music-awards festival named after him in his hometown. Now, finally, there is this biography of Harpo, too.

THE QUESTIONS

Piecing together the Harpo story has not been easy; in fact, it's been strangely difficult considering the man died only forty-six years ago. Had Harpo lived just a couple more decades, we would probably know more about him than we need; as it is, we'd like to know more than we now possibly can. In the 1980s and 1990s, if he'd lived to continue working nationwide blues and rock venues and made it to the international blues festivals, there would have been in-depth articles in publications from the nationals down to the most obscure of collectors' magazines. We'd have known everything about what Harpo did and thought, or at least what he cared to say. But as it was, his death took all that away with him. *Rolling Stone* published only a small obituary instead of a major article, noting his recent-found fame among the rock audience and concluding, "[his songs] were marked by his sly, almost tongue in cheek vocal style, which made him seem like an easy-going guy, probably something of a character."[3]

Just what kind of a "character" is what this book is about. In it, I present new information about his life, his personality, his career, and the challenges involved in taking an essentially rural black music to a new audience in a time of racial segregation. I also review the careers of other local blues musicians—because what they did and did not do throws light on Harpo's career and achievements and his life and times in Baton Rouge. There is no attempt to analyze Harpo's music in anything beyond a basic manner. I am not a musician. Like most of us, I just "know what I like." So what you'll read here is more personal and social history than musical scrutiny. It's based on my review of practically every word ever written about Harpo and his colleagues in the specialist music press, and everything of relevance in the Louisiana newspapers and the national and international press during and beyond Harpo's lifetime. It's based, too, on unpublished video interviews with his wife and some of his band members by Steve Coleridge and later by Johnny Palazzotto, and on my own interviews with Harpo's musicians, friends, acquaintances, and family members.

The sum of all this is, I think, a fascinating story, but one that has not been artificially embellished. It's a story I've tried to tell straight, based on facts rather than opinion and theory. But it's a "story" nonetheless because the facts have to be linked together and presented in context, and those links can never be fully known. To an extent, the fixed points in Harpo's life story are an accumulation of fragments of information and opinion, and these may not have been the things to which Slim himself would have attached most significance. Certainly some of the fixed points have been set by white authority and later by white record collectors. The events that occurred and the causes and effects of Harpo's actions throughout his life cannot all be known, even to Harpo's family and friends, even if those people were disposed to give an account of them. Most people were but, frankly, some of them were not.

The tragedy, of course, is that no one asked Harpo himself in his lifetime. He gave very few, brief interviews in his career, only one of which was published, and he died just too soon to see the major expansion of rock journalism and blues journals that would surely have led to key one-on-one interviews and answered some of the frustrating questions I now have to leave partly solved and partly unresolved. Some of these questions are: What did Harpo do during the 1940s when he left home; what happened to him in those years? When did he actually start to play harmonica in a semi-serious way; was it 1944, say, or 1954? Who truly influenced him the most? What did he really think of record producer J. D. Miller and the white bookers and promoters within whose world he had to carry on his career? What were his social and political views; did he vote, and if so for whom? And what sort of changes was he planning for his music and his career, if any? A decade after Harpo died, local researcher Jimmy Beyer wrote, "Harpo would play the Apollo Theater [in New York] one night and two days later he'd be seen driving a sugarcane truck. Then, in a couple of days he'd play the Acadian club, a youth club on Jefferson Highway, or a small nightclub on the Airline Highway in Baton Rouge. The people who knew him said that success never changed Slim Harpo. He never took the success too seriously, and was quite content to drive a truck."[4] Was that really so?

THE TALE

In telling Harpo's story, I've had to consider this thorny issue of the extent to which history, at least oral history, belongs to the last man standing. What the next generation remembers or takes as given is often the gospel according to the final person to tell the tale. For example, the late Rudy Richard, as great and important a guitarist as he was, has for many years been written up in local newspapers and on websites promoting Baton Rouge music as "the man who played guitar on all Harpo's records" or "the man who put the sting in the King Bee." But it just wasn't true. Slim Harpo recorded "I'm a King Bee" well before Rudy joined his band, and Rudy was gone from the band by the

time of "Baby Scratch My Back." Rudy was happy to give interviews, but
he didn't often put people straight unless they asked, and why would he? A
different example, a small point but still a distortion of history: Buddy Guy
described in his autobiography how in 1951 he was impressed by a guitarist
who wandered into a local store and played for tips. He asked someone who
it was and was told "that's Lightning Slim." But that wasn't possible, because
Otis Hicks didn't take on that name, for recording, until 1954.[5] No doubt the
guitar man in the store was Otis Hicks, but that doesn't mean he had started
his professional career three years early. A more general example: because
of the lack of written logs for many of Harpo's recording sessions where the
musicians might have been identified clearly, there is often a conflict between
lack of knowledge, the knowledge imparted by musicians in the past, and the
knowledge offered by musicians in more recent years. If the last man standing
is correct, there was only one drummer on "Rainin' in My Heart"; if everyone
else is correct, there were about ten drummers on the session!

Some of the unresolved questions about Slim Harpo's life reflect the nature
of local newspaper coverage in his time. The main papers, principally the
Baton Rouge Advocate and *State-Times* and the *New Orleans Times-Picayune,*
focused on national and international news in general and local events of interest principally to their white readership, taking little interest in the exploits
of local musicians who mainly appeared as bit-part players in the dances and
social events described in the entertainment or society pages. There was an
unacknowledged bias against the African American community evidenced in
the almost total lack of coverage of black people and events and the devotion
to pointing out when the perpetrator of a criminal offense or scandalous act
was a "Negro." The national and local papers produced by and for the black
community covered general national news too, nearly always with a view
on how it affected the black race, but the society pages of all black papers,
from the national *Chicago Defender* to the *Baton Rouge News Leader* serving
the local black community, followed the aspirational and refined tone of the
white papers with never-ending lists of courtly debutantes, civic occasions,
visiting dignitaries, and suchlike. The religious sections were more strongly
presented because of the slightly different role of black church leaders in the
struggle for racial advancement.

Newspapers for blacks and whites were equally scathing about the lower
forms of life, of which bluesmen were apparently considered a part until after
Harpo's day. As one of the earliest black directors of a folk or arts festival,

Edgar Clark of Fort Valley College, Georgia, wrote in a festival program of 1940: "People look down on some of the folk music. This type of music may be what polite society calls gutter songs. Often these 'gutter songs' or blues, as they are rightly called, are the very essence of Negro life; songs that men and women sang in their America." Interestingly, through Harpo's era, white and black papers alike covered R&B and rock 'n' roll far more in their entertainment pages than they did the blues. The list of bluesmen associated with Baton Rouge that will come easily to the minds of blues fans worldwide will not contain many, if any, of the people who actually gained local coverage at the time in their home community.

Although I have written about musicians and singers who came up with Harpo or carried on in his tradition, this is not intended as a definitive history of Baton Rouge blues, least of all in the years that predate Harpo or in the modern era. My aim has been to examine Harpo's life, music, and legacy in the context of his contemporaries and his immediate successors—but there is much more that could be told about each of them. I have alluded, too, to some of the musicians who picked up the baton, as it were, in the wake of Harpo's generation. There probably should be a definitive history of Baton Rouge blues up to the present day, but I must leave that to someone who is both an ethnomusicologist, or at least a musician, and a devotee of rock-era barroom blues of the post-Harpo era. For now, readers of this book might want to get out their Harpo records and their swamp-blues CDs and dip into them now and again, or check them out on iTunes or other modern media, as they go through this story, remembering always that each recording was first made as a separate two- or three-minute slice of the blues to be heard on a jukebox or played on a little home record player.

I first became aware of Slim Harpo sometime in the mid-1960s when I developed a habit of buying rock 'n' roll, country, and blues records rather than the latest chart sounds nearly all of my schoolmates listened to. I found Slim when I lighted on the music of Louisiana as captured by recording engineers like Jay Miller of Crowley, issued on Excello Records of Nashville, and imported into England by dealers in American discs who fed the growing enthusiasm for "real" blues and R&B to offset the recycled versions popular with British beat groups. By the mid-1970s, I was making annual spring trips to the United States to buy obscure old records, but by the time I ended a swing through Mississippi, Texas, New Orleans, Lake Charles, and Crowley by finding myself busted flat in Baton Rouge, traces of Slim, who was already five years under the ground, were hard to find. Forty years on, when I told people I was writing a book about Harpo, the usual response was one of encouragement and "about time," although one blues collector responded smartly, "Oh, bad luck," and went on to say he found Harpo's music too repetitive.

Leaving aside such personal opinions and preferences, summarizing and categorizing Louisiana's music is not that easy. One man's repetition is another's groove. Down the years, the music of Louisiana has been filed in many ever-loosening categories (much the same as 1950s rock 'n' roll, which, once so frightening and new, can even be seen listed within an easy-listening category today). Beyond the local folk, Cajun, zydeco, and blues niches, whenever any of that music looked toward the music charts and became to an extent "popular," it has ended up being recognized as either swamp-pop or swamp-blues, both terms being coined after the event.[6] In Slim Harpo's lifetime, some sixty or so records out of Louisiana made the national bestseller charts for R&B, country, or popular music. Most of these were swamp-pop, the likes of white artists Dale and Grace, Rod Bernard, Warren Storm, Jimmy Newman, or Jimmy Clanton, and black artists including Barbara Lynn and Cookie and the Cupcakes. In fact, only six swamp-blues songs made the national record-sales charts. Clarence Garlow hit with "Bon Ton Roula" in 1950 and Lightnin' Slim with "Rooster Blues" in 1959, but Slim Harpo had four times as many chart successes as anyone—"Rainin' in My Heart," 1961; "Baby, Scratch My Back," 1966; "Tip on In," 1967; and "Te-Ni-Nee-Ni-Nu," 1968—and his songs went pop as well as R&B.

Two things started to happen on either side of Harpo's death in 1970. For one thing, white blues fans and collectors of regional records began to spread the word through specialist magazines, and to visit places like Baton Rouge, seeking the music and the artists they heard on obscure, often faraway records. For another, there was an increase in the number of local music festivals across America, and these wanted, probably needed, to keep alive the music people knew from their youth.

Down the years, there have been quite a few people who took real interest in documenting and promoting the bluesmen of Baton Rouge. These include Dr. Harry Oster of Louisiana State University, who made "field" recordings for his Folk-Lyric Records in the late 1950s and early 1960s, as well as Chris Strachwitz of Arhoolie Records in California and Mike Vernon of Blue Horizon in England, who both recorded Baton Rouge musicians around 1970. Mike Leadbitter and John Broven, among others, championed the blues of

Louisiana through the pages of *Blues Unlimited* magazine from the early 1960s on, and in the 1970s Bruce Bastin's Flyright Records issued many hitherto-unknown recordings by Harpo and other local artists. Jimmy Beyer was commissioned by Nick Spitzer and the Louisiana State Division of the Arts to write a booklet about Baton Rouge blues in 1980; Steve Coleridge relocated from Europe in 1989 to play with local bands and to film and interview them. *Blues & Rhythm* magazine took a valuable interest in his work and that of another musician, Julian Piper, around that time, publishing stories about several Baton Rouge bluesmen. Jim O'Neal and others founded *Living Blues* magazine to help keep the music alive, and have carried a number of features on music in Baton Rouge. There are many folks who have contributed to the Baton Rouge Blues Foundation, Blues Society, and Blues Festival committees in recent years, not least Johnny Palazzotto, who produced his first recording session in 1970 and has been producing and promoting Louisiana music ever since, including establishing the annual Slim Harpo Awards.

The notion that I should write a biography of Slim Harpo came to me gradually during 2013 when I was asked to produce a boxed set of five CDs containing every known recording made by Harpo during his relatively brief recording career from 1957 to 1970. I realized I was acquiring way more information than even the large booklet within that box could hold, and not just information about Harpo the recording artist. I was gathering more and more details about his band musicians and his other musical acquaintances and friends and relatives in Baton Rouge. It seemed important that someone should put all of that information together and tell Harpo's story, but tell it within the context of the society and the blues music scene from which he emerged. Very few people from Harpo's community had the education or opportunity to express themselves in work and life. Instead, those who could used song making and music making as the means to channel their creative abilities.

I started to write the book even before I finished the CD set, and the further I got into it, the more I realized it was a far more worthwhile project than it first appeared. Strangely, although Harpo's music had been collected on LP albums and CD retrospectives for four decades since his death and his basic story had been told and rehashed many times, it soon became clear that the basic story was all there was out there—and some of that was wrong. I came to see that little, really, was known of Slim Harpo, as a person, beyond his fading circle of musicians, friends, and family. And less still was known about his life and times in Baton Rouge.

ACKNOWLEDGMENTS

Before acknowledging people who have helped, I should first expose the guilty party who set me off down this trail; if Richard Weize of Bear Family Records had not asked me to produce his CD set of Slim Harpo some years ago, then I wouldn't have reintroduced myself to the Baton Rouge blues and become so fascinated by Harpo's story and realized this book was necessary.

Throughout the planning and writing of this book, the expert chronicler of Louisiana's music, John Broven, has been incredibly encouraging and helpful, volunteering information and ideas for no reason other than that Harpo has always been one of his favorite artists. He was also persuaded to write the foreword and to read a draft of the manuscript. My colleagues from the days of our Sun Records research, Hank Davis and Colin Escott, both supportively read and helped improve this text. So too did Barbara Sims, a contact from the Sun days who also had many years' residence in Baton Rouge to draw upon.

The person who produced the greatest volume of information, in the form of filmed interviews with Harpo's wife and musicians, and with Jay Miller, was Steve Coleridge, who also provided analysis in his "Musical Appreciation," included at the end of this volume. Steve planned to write a book about Harpo in 1989, but didn't. I'm happy he's been so keen to see mine come to fruition.

A number of music promoters, fans, and movers and shakers in Louisiana have been enthusiastic and informative. Johnny Palazzotto, who started the annual music shows and awards in Slim Harpo's name and who is a great enthusiast for the King Bee, let me see footage from his interviews and projected documentary film and has been supportive in providing names and numbers of other folks who could help. Several musicians who worked the white music world back in Harpo's day provided useful context about Harpo and the Baton Rouge music scene, in particular Lynn Ourso, who also recorded with Harpo and other blues artists. Writer and producer Cyril Vetter shared his memories of the club scene in 1960s Baton Rouge. Songwriter Roy Hayes spoke about his work with Slim Harpo. Photographer and writer Gene Tomko contributed many snippets of vital information from local musicians, and Becky Owens shared her work with John Broven concerning recording studios in Crowley.

Considerable thanks are due to David Kearns, who has been exceedingly encouraging and who is responsible for our being able to hear a live show played by Harpo in 1961, an incredibly valuable record in both senses of the word.

The past writings and current memories of Fred Reif, Peter B. Lowry, and Peter Guralnick proved invaluable, as did other information from Donn Fileti and Rob Santos. Mike Vernon provided an account of his recordings of Baton Rouge bluesmen. Bruce Bastin helped clarify some aspects of his invaluable work in the 1970s researching and issuing Jay Miller's recordings of Harpo and many others. Bill Millar, as always, was enthusiastic and opened up his invaluable archive of records and memorabilia. Dave Booth at Showtime Archives in Toronto also sent memorabilia and provided his radio interviews with Jay Miller. Bob Eagle was consulted about the fascinating biographical data on Louisiana bluesmen in a section of the book by Eric S. LeBlanc and Eagle, *Blues: A Regional Experience* (Praeger, 2013).

Feature articles about Harpo's music have been written down the years by Mike Leadbitter, Bruce Bastin, Todd Everett, Jeff Hannusch, Steve Coleridge, Bill Dahl, and others. Through their original interviews, the lives and views of Jay Miller, John Fred Gourrier, Lazy Lester, and many others have become real. In recent years the local press in New Orleans and Baton Rouge has covered the Harpo-related awards and music festivals—principally in the writings and interviews of John Wirt of the *Advocate,* Ruth Laney in *Country Roads* and *225,* and Chelsea Brasted in the *New Orleans Times-Picayune.*

Among the local folks in Baton Rouge who provided memories of Harpo or his community were David Couvillon, Connie Dents, Arlene Batiste, Brian Falcon, Joanne Bourgeois, and Margaret Canella. Lee Smith and Justin Nystrom of Tulane University also provided information about life in Mulatto Bend and New Orleans. Julie Rose and Angelique Bergeron of West Baton Rouge Museum opened their files on Harpo and related topics.

At the various libraries in Baton Rouge, Lee Bareford, Andrew Tadman, and Melissa Eastin went out of their way to help at East Baton Rouge Public Library, as did Angela Proctor at Southern University Library and Germain Bienvenu, Judy Bolton, and Tara Laver at Louisiana State University Libraries.

Genealogical researcher Judy Riffel provided invaluable assistance from Baton Rouge, helping conclude some puzzling questions, as did Jari Honora in New Orleans.

Through library reading rooms and online research sites such as the Newspaper Archive, I was able to look comprehensively at the relevant past editions of the following newspapers and journals: *Baton Rouge Advocate* and *State-Times, Baton Rouge Post, Baton Rouge News Leader, New Orleans Times-Picayune, Louisiana Weekly, Chicago Defender, New York Amsterdam News, Memphis World, Nashville World, Atlanta World, Houston Times, Los Angeles Times, Billboard, Cash Box, Record World,* and many other local papers. Laurie Lee Moses at the Columbia College Center for Black Music Research in Chicago was also most helpful in connection with an unpublished interview with Harpo.

At LSU Press, there are a number of people who turned my manuscript into this rather good-looking book. When offered my work, acquisitions editor Rand Dotson was immediately enthusiastic as was the director, MaryKatherine Callaway. External editor Stan Ivester made many helpful and knowledgeable interventions, and Mary Lee Eggart turned my envelope drawing into a proper map. Then, in-house editor Catherine Kadair and designer Barbara Bourgoyne saw the process expertly through to conclusion. Erin Rolfs and the marketing team took it from there to you, and I hope everyone involved found the end product as worthwhile as I do.

Finally, but most importantly, I want to thank several people who knew James Moore best either as a member of their family or as the musician Slim Harpo. James Johnson, Otis Johnson, and Leslie Johnson (not related) are among the few musicians left from Slim's day, and their insights were valuable to set alongside filmed interviews with Lovell Moore, Rudy Richard, Jesse Kinchen, and others. Ray Moore, Harpo's nephew, gave an informative account of his family life, and William Gambler, Slim's stepson, shared memories and memorabilia from the life and times of James Moore. William and Dorothy Gambler and their family members, including Alonzo Gambler and Tynita Howard, were most welcoming to me, and William provided a fascinating drive around Red Stick to view the houses, clubs, and streets that were home to Slim Harpo, many of which I would not have found otherwise.

SLIM HARPO

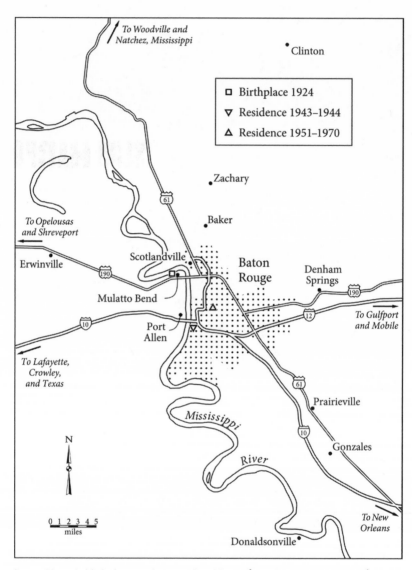

James Moore's birthplace and areas of residence (Map by Mary Lee Eggart)

1. SOMETHING INSIDE ME

Early Life and Times | The Death of Clyde Moore | Going to New Orleans
Postwar Blues | The Red Stick Blues | Ms. Lovell | Lightning Strikes

EARLY LIFE AND TIMES

The various mysteries about the life of Slim Harpo start right at the beginning, with his name. For most of the first thirty-three years of his life, the man who would become the musician "Slim Harpo" was known as James Moore, just another hard-working Louisiana man born in hard times and a tough environment. However, when midwife Hester Green signed his birth certificate, she recorded him instead as Isiah Moore, born at 7 p.m. on February 11, 1924, on Bellmont (now Belmont) Plantation in the farming community known as Mulatto Bend. This was tucked into a bow on the west side of the Mississippi River, just east of the tiny town of Lobdell, a few miles north of the town of Port Allen, and northwest of Baton Rouge, on the other side of the river. "Isiah" was a name the boy apparently never used and one that nobody has ever recalled being used. By the time he was six years old, his mother told the US Census of 1930 that he was James Moore, as he was again in the census ten years later. Possibly he had taken against the name Isiah as a child, possibly someone in the family took to calling him James, possibly there had been a disagreement or confusion about what name to register, or possibly the birth certificate, filed a month after the event, had been completed incorrectly. "Back in those days," said Connie Dents, longtime resident of Mulatto Bend and daughter of Menty Dents who, local people said, was born on the same day as James Moore, "the midwives took a little while to turn their information in, from out in the country. Folk was told that he or she was born on one day but when receiving his or her birth certificate it is totally different. For instance my mother was told that her birthday was February 10, 1924, but when she received her birth record then it said February 11, 1924, because of how the midwives turned in the information. In those days folk didn't receive his or her birthday records until they were much older."[1]

For the purposes of this book, we'll call our man "James." He was the son of Clyde Moore and Pearline Emerson. His father, Clyde, was born in Milam near San Augustine, Texas, on May 1, 1892, according to US Army records, or February 1891 according to the US Census of 1900. His mother was born Pearline Brown in Port Hudson, Louisiana, some twenty miles north of Baton Rouge on Highway 61. According to her gravestone, she entered the world in 1889 and apparently on the same day and month, May 1, as her future husband, Clyde Moore.[2] When James was born in 1924, Pearline already had three children, and she would have a fifth when James was three years old. She had also given birth to six other live children who had died in infancy. In the 1910 census, Pearline was recorded as twenty-two years old and living in Police Jury Ward Four of west Baton Rouge.[3] At that time, she was the wife of Frank Emerson, a "hostler" working for a private family. It is not clear whether he worked with horses as denoted by the traditional meaning of the word, or with trains or trucks. Frank and Pearline had a one-year-old son, Herbert, but it was noted that Pearline had already given birth to two other children who had not survived. Both Frank and Pearline, sometimes known as Pearlie or Pearl, were recorded as natives of Louisiana. In 1913, they had a daughter together, Lillie Emerson, but by the time of the 1920 census, while Pearline was still living in Jury Ward Four, she was now recorded as the "wife" of Clyde Moore, and Frank was missing. Pearline and Clyde would not in fact be married for some years to come, but Clyde had taken on both Herbert and Lillie as stepchildren, and his household now also contained Pearline's brother-in-law, Zuke Emerson.

The community of Mulatto Bend originated in the 1700s when the area that would become Louisiana was ruled by the French. It was first called Mulatto Point sometime after 1774 when two "free men of color" named Paul and Julien settled there, and later it was known as "free negro point." Land transfer documents from 1790 show further tranches of land owned by six free men of color in the area of Port Allen. The term "mulatto" then referred to people of mixed race, some of whom were free, though many others were slaves during the colonial period. Those at Mulatto Bend were property-owning, French-speaking Catholics. When the French settlers had first arrived with their slaves, they operated a social system known as "Code Noir," under which the landowner would take care of everyone on his land. Although interracial marriage was not allowed, the result nevertheless was a group of mixed-race offspring of French men and African women who were freed by their fathers and often given financial assistance. Their names are recorded in a property map from 1799 by Vicente Sebastian Pintado when the Spanish took control of the area from the British, who had briefly taken Louisiana from the French during the years 1763 and 1779. Free people of color fitted with Spain's colonization approach, being native and Catholic, so many obtained Spanish land grants and others purchased property. One Mulatto Bend resident, Jean Baptiste Bienville, became very wealthy, and at his death in 1802 he owned property that included nineteen slaves. After a period of land treaties, purchases, and rebellions at the start of the new century, eventually, in 1812, both sides of the river at Baton Rouge became part of the renamed American state of Louisiana. By then, the people living there were a mix of British, American, French, Spanish, Native Americans, and African Americans both free and enslaved.

Baton Rouge was named for the "red stick" the founder of the French colony of Louisiana, Pierre Le Moyne d'Iberville, first saw on March 17, 1699, sticking out of the ground near the river, "a maypole with no limbs, painted red, several fish heads and bear bones being tied to it as a sacrifice" by the local Houma people. It, or probably several such trees stripped of bark, marked the boundary between the Houma and Bayou Goula native tribes, but soon the red stick was being used as a landmark for French travelers indicating where the east-side bluffs began. Gradually a settlement grew up there, and in 1718 when Bernard Diron received a land grant at Baton Rouge, he arrived to find "two whites and 25 negroes on the land." By 1722 there were 30 whites, 20 blacks, mainly enslaved from Senegal and Gambia, and 2 native Indian slaves. As late as 1809 a visitor, Fortescue Cuming, described the settlement as "a dirty little town of 60 cabins crouded [sic] together in a narrow street on the river bank." Nevertheless, Baton Rouge was incorporated as a town in 1817, and in 1846 it was named the capital of Louisiana. Although only 2,500 people lived there, it was already a center for the steamboat trade and an agricultural and transport hub. Government offices were erected there along with a capitol building later derided by celebrated writer Mark Twain as "an architectural falsehood . . . a whitewashed castle with turrets and things."[4] Zachary Taylor, a soldier who had settled there in 1821, held considerable sway in the developing town, where he lived until 1849 when he became president of the United States.

On the western side of the Mississippi, opposite Baton Rouge, was the settlement of St. Michel, named in 1809, and renamed Port Allen in mid-century for Henry Watkins Allen, a planter and soldier who became the Confederate governor of Louisiana during the Civil War, the seventeenth man to hold the governorship of the state. In the period leading up to the Civil War, the emancipation laws of the French and Spanish were toughened under American rule, and the ownership of land by mulatto people was made illegal. At the same time, because the river near the bend was treacherous, periods of flood and levee setback meant that during the nineteenth century some of the original homes at Mulatto Bend were lost to the course of the river and their land swallowed up by the Baton Rouge Bayou.

The Civil War affected economic progress in the area. Baton Rouge was at first under Confederate rule, but in August 1862, after three battles, Union forces occupied the town. Many whites left the town, which was badly damaged during the war, and the government was moved to Shreveport, but nevertheless the capitol building was rebuilt in time for the business of government to return to Baton Rouge in 1882. With the arrival of the first railway, the New Orleans and Mississippi Valley, later the Illinois Central, the town saw significant industrial development linked to its strategic location for the production of petroleum, natural gas, and salt, as well as agricultural goods. In 1909, Standard Oil of New Jersey decided to build a major refinery at Baton Rouge. This led to expansion of the port to international trade and the creation of a shipping and industrial center on a scale previously unenvisaged.

In its natural state, the Mississippi River created levees along its banks and flowed over them through crevasses during times of high water, swamping the backland areas. Once the European settlers started controlling the levees, though, the original landscape changed, so that first indigo and then sugarcane could be grown on large plantations, each with its own landing area. In *Life on the Mississippi,* Mark Twain found in 1883 that, at Baton Rouge, "both banks for a good deal over a hundred miles are shorn of their timber and bordered by continuous sugar plantations."[5] By then, many plantations had developed commercial landing stages, including one at Mulatto Bend. Growing sugarcane was a labor-intensive business and relied before the Civil War on slave workers and afterwards on a sharecropping system that continued into James Moore's day.

In 1855, across West Baton Rouge Parish as a whole, there were to be found 1,782 white residents, 106 free people of color, and 4,808 slaves. Among the plantations in west Baton Rouge were the Belle Vale, Anchorage, and Catherine plantations, established by Abraham Lobdell in the years after he arrived from New York; Bellmont Plantation, established by John Bird; and Poplar Grove Plantation, established in the 1820s by James McCalop, bought in 1885 by Joseph Harris of New Orleans, and developed into the Poplar Grove Planting and Refining Company by Horace Wilkinson after 1903. These were the plantations that covered the area either side of the original Mulatto Bend settlement to the south and west of Free Negro Point. The point itself was owned by Mrs. Von Phul of Bel Air Plantation at the time of an 1879 map produced by the Mississippi River Commission. To the west of the point was William Carey's Viola Plantation, then Bellmont Plantation owned by Mr. A. Guesnard, and farther west the Belle Yale Plantation owned by J. L. Lobdell. To the south of the point was the Poplar Grove Plantation, facing, over the river on the eastern side, Scot Bluffs and Scotland Landing just north of Baton Rouge itself. All of these plantation lands were devoted to the production of sugarcane. Individual houses were marked on the map, with the Bellmont and Quornor roads on the Bellmont Plantation having some twenty-five dwellings in total in the area that would become home for James Moore.[6]

By the time of the 1890 census, Lobdell, two miles west of Mulatto Bend, had a population of 42 people and a post office. Port Allen had 250 people, compared with over 5,000 today, and a railroad service. Across the river, the city of Baton Rouge had over 10,000 people, compared to a quarter of a million today, and had become a railroad hub. Above Baton Rouge, now-populous places like Baker and Zachary had populations of 150 people only.

It is not known when and why Clyde Moore moved the two hundred or so miles from Milam, Texas, to Bellmont Plantation sometime before 1920 to set up family with Pearline Emerson. In 1910 the US Census had located him living at Brazos River Road near Milam with his father, fifty-eight-year-old farm laborer Larkin Moore, described in the census as a "mulatto," born in South Carolina of parents also from that state, and his mother, forty-six-year-old Margaret M. Moore, also described as a "mulatto," born in Texas but whose parents both came from Alabama. According to the 1900 census, Larkin Moore was born in May 1851 and Margaret in June 1862. They had married in 1878 and seem to have had at least eleven children: Willie, Johnnie, Pearlie, James, Lulu, Clyde, Lillie, Ozella, Callie, Conway, and Roazavelt.

It is likely that Clyde and Pearline met sometime after June 6, 1917, the day Clyde's draft card showed him entering the Pioneer Infantry as an unmarried man. He was noted to be tall, as his son James would also be, of medium build, having black hair and eyes, living in Port Allen, and working as a farmhand for the Poplar Grove Cutting and Refining Company. Clyde was home from the Army by 1920, when the census for West Baton Rouge Parish found him living with Poline [*sic*] Emerson and her children, Herbert and Lillie Emerson, aged eleven and seven, and Pearline's brother-in-law Zuke Emerson. Clyde was now a laborer on the "steam rail road," and Pearline was a farm laborer "working out." By now, a rudimentary River Road ran alongside the levee up from Port Allen, and the occupied areas were concentrated on such unmade roads as South Mulatto Bend Road, North Riverview, Bellmont Road, and Plantation Road, which all ran inland from the river. Clyde and Pearl lived on Bellmont Road in the area known as Bellmont Farm, formerly Bellmont Plantation, near Quornor Landing and Bellmont Landing.

James Moore first appears in public records as a six-year-old in the 1930 census, living on "River Road and Quornor" in West Baton Rouge Parish with his parents, Clyde and Pearl, his stepsister Lillie Emerson, and two natural sisters, Tilda, born in 1921, and Doris, born in 1927.[7] Pearl's brother was also living with the family but this time recorded as Felix Emerson.[8] James's apparent given name of "Isiah" does not appear in this or other public documents, and it is clear that he was known as James almost from the beginning of his life. Just possibly he was named after Clyde's older brother, James.

James Moore arrived in the world in the early days of 1924, when life was very different from that experienced by anyone born in the Baton Rouge area in the second half of the last century or the present day. It was a world where some people still living had been born into slavery or had owned slaves, and many people were aware of how the West was won from known experience rather than the movies. In fact, moving pictures were then still a relatively new phenomenon. The year started colder than many in one of the warmest states of the Union. In the second week of January, the local evening newspaper, the *State-Times Advocate,* reported that "King Winter has been indulging in another prank, and Baton Rouge folks awakened to a temperature of 32 degrees" with the frost so heavy it resembled snow. Five days earlier the thermometer had dipped to minus 17.

It is not recorded whether the cold and ice contributed to the death of George Fredericks at the wheel of his automobile on his way to work at Standard Oil at 6:30 on the morning of Friday the eleventh, but it would certainly have been unwelcome to the heavily pregnant Pearline. The weather did not cool the temper of populist politician Huey Pierce Long, one of three candidates (with Hewitt Bouanchaud and Henry Fuqua) in the imminent election to decide the governorship of the state that month. Long's often-admired style included attacks on utility industries and private corporations, New Orleans–focused politicians, and other "wealthy parasites" whose success worked against the poor, particularly the rural poor who made up over half the state's population. Huey Long, "the Kingfish," would not be elected governor until the next election, in 1928, when Louisiana still had only three hundred miles of paved highway, a frighteningly high illiteracy rate approaching 75 percent, and a very low percentage of people registered as voters, particularly among the black community. In 1924, Long was engaging in a continuing debate threatening, if he were elected, to move the state capital "out of the Standard Oil offices" in Baton Rouge and over to Alexandria, a town favored by the Ku Klux Klan. News from Atlanta that January saw the ousting from power within the Klan of founder William Simmons in favor of current leader Dr. Hiram Evans. In February the Klan was reported conducting raids on liquor premises in Herrin, Illinois, with a constable killed and a deputy sheriff shot after riots between "wets" and "drys," resulting in US Army troops taking control of the town. Meanwhile, automobile mogul Henry Ford was reported in Massachusetts, "playing the fiddle and calling off some old country dances, jollying with the girls," at a party there. Ford, like all businessmen, was awaiting February policy statements by the recently installed president, Calvin Coolidge. On Tuesday February 12, in news from Atlanta, newspapers had a field day with the arrest of Mrs. Asa Candler, the wife of the millionaire Coca-Cola capitalist, found in a room with an empty whiskey bottle and "two prominent men."

Nearer to home, from New Orleans the news during January and February featured the refitting of Mexican gunboats to help quell the revolution there, but investors from Louisiana were assured that their money in Mexico was safe. There was excitement about the commencement of huge export orders of cotton to Russia, ten thousand bales at a time. In the local *Advocate* newspaper, it was reported that the redevelopment of Third Street had seen property values climb so that "today Baton Rouge faces as bright a future as any town in the South." The good folks of Baton Rouge were also advised in the small ads that Marmola tablets were a simple, harmless, effective remedy for "overfatness" while Aspironal elixir would give relief from colds and flu within two minutes. While a new Studebaker coupe was advertised at $545, Davis Chevrolet could deliver a new sedan model for just $258 and pointed out that "it's an ideal car for the weather we're having now."

The main local papers, the *Morning Advocate* and the *State-Times Advocate*, carried little news of the activities of Baton Rouge's large population of Americans of African descent, for whom the term "Negro" was then normally used. Although there had been short-lived newspapers aimed at the black community in the Baton Rouge area, the likes of the *Grand Era*, the *Crusader*, and the *Observer* had all closed by 1900 and would not be replaced until the *Post* emerged in 1937 and the *News Leader* in the years after 1952. In 1924, news came mainly through the *Advocate*, where reports about the black community largely concerned things the newspaper found unusual or threatening. The most prominent such feature during January concerned Melvin Payne under the heading "Negro gets five days in jail for theft of 70 cents."[9] Other convictions were Garfield Hutchinson, thirty days for stealing a wristwatch, and Joe Woods, who got twenty days for hitting his wife a "love lick" with a brick even though he insisted "he was only playing." Another Negro, Henry Germany, was arrested for robbing telephone pay stations and electric pianos. The *Advocate* revealed, "He had on his person a cigar box full of nickels, a pistol, a flash light, a hammer and a pair of pliers. He is being held as a dangerous and suspicious character."[10] A further report concerned Alex Potter, "an aged negro," who had deposited eighty dollars in the Freedman's Bank in Shreveport between 1873 and 1878 when his race was newly liberated during Reconstruction. Potter had been warned there would be "a delay in paying off" as the money had been loaned to a railroad project but, with some fifty years having elapsed, he "figured payment was due." Federal officials, it was reported, "were able to give the old man scant encouragement." As James Moore entered the world, his parents might well have made a note to advise him sometime soon that he'd come to a tough place.

As far as is known, James and his siblings were brought up in the Bellmont Road area continuously. However, when James was four years old, in 1928, his mother was in Houston, where on April 28 she informed the Bureau of Vital Statistics in Harris County that Herbert Emerson, James's older stepbrother, had died there three days before of pulmonary tuberculosis and pneumonia. Pearline, who gave her maiden name as Brown and her current name as Emerson, not Moore, was living at 2 Trenton Street in Houston at the time, just a matter of months after James's younger sister Doris was born. Herbert's birthplace in 1909 was given as Lobdell, Louisiana (actually mistyped as "Loddell"), and so it is most likely that Pearline was in Houston temporarily while Herbert was in a TB sanitarium toward the end of his life, but it is just possible that the whole family had been in Texas at some point, perhaps even for Clyde Moore to obtain work in the booming oil-drilling business. Near Milam, his hometown, the Minerva Oil Field was discovered in 1921 during a major oil boom. Herbert was recorded by the bureau as having been a "common laborer" who had lived all his life in the city where death occurred, which is apparently incorrect.

Either way, the entire Moore/Emerson family was back on Bellmont Road at the time of the 1930 census, and it was only after then that James's parents actually married. Their license was dated June 9, 1931, and both were declared to be aged thirty-nine and resident at Mulatto Bend. Clyde stated this was his first marriage, and Pearline Emerson, recorded as Pauline, was described as a widow. They were married on July 9, 1931, by Reverend E. D. Billoups. The witnesses were Steve Dickerson, Sam Winston, and Ed Lewis. Neither the bride nor the groom could sign their names, and where Pauline made her mark, the clerk wrote her name as "Pearline," which is how she was known by her family despite the plethora of spellings of her name in official documents. Her precise age remains more of a mystery, her birth date having been given variously in public records as 1888, 1892, or 1893 as well as the unsubstantiated date of May 1, 1889, on her gravestone.

By the start of the 1930s, the Moores were among some fifty thousand people living in the greater Baton Rouge area. Apart from being Louisiana's capital city, with all the government and administration services that entailed, the area was known for its petroleum products, metalworks, lumber and rice mills, and sugar and syrup refineries. It was a developing industrial hub rising up amid an agricultural community. The Mississippi River and six railroads carried goods and people to all parts. The annual city directories for Baton Rouge boasted that labor conditions were ideal and strikes were unknown, but that didn't make life any easier for the homegrown farming families like the Moores living out in the country in houses with no electricity and precious few other amenities. Many families lived in log houses not too dissimilar from the former slave cabins peculiar to the area with their saddlebag style, one room deep and two wide, often with two front doors and housing two families. There was no electricity in west Baton Rouge until 1925 and then not out in the country areas. There were few automobiles and fewer telephones, and people in small communities like Lobdell had started to move into Port Allen or across into Baton Rouge.

By the time of James Moore's birth, the general expansion of the city had led to the building of some improved facilities specifically for the black community. From 1914, Baton Rouge had even been home to one of the few prestigious black universities in the South, Southern University, having moved from New Orleans to the developing area of Scotlandville on land granted for the purpose on the east side of the Mississippi, just a stone's throw from Mulatto Bend. Downtown in Baton Rouge, one of the remaining monuments to this time is the Prince Hall Masonic Temple at 1335 North Boulevard, now on the Register of National Historic Places. Built in 1925 by local black building company Conner, Bryant, and Bell for the Grand United Order of Odd Fellows, it was a neoclassical building of brick and concrete, its four floors housing the Odd Fellows Lodge, a large meeting place, various offices for black businesses and professionals, and the Temple Theater and Temple Roof Garden. The Roof Garden, later the Grand Ballroom, was the glamour spot for black Baton Rouge social functions. The *State-Times* of October 16, 1925, welcomed the new addition to the city's entertainment options: "Grand Opening of Temple Theater (Colored)." The paper noted that the theater would show movies with "program changes daily" and that musical events were under the direction of C. L. Porter, the former head of the Music Department at Southern University. With its built-in heating and cooling systems and an inclined floor, the paper noted that "no amount of money or pains has been spared to make it one of the most complete and best appointed amusement houses in the country." The Temple booked entertainment for the Negro population, but that did not mean the white populace had no interest in black performers.

Soon after it was opened, the Temple Theater threw its doors open to white patrons for a separate show once a week, just as other large venues did in most southern cities, including the theaters on Beale Street in Memphis, "The Main Street of Negro America," where "Midnight Ramble" shows were hugely popular. At the Temple, the first visiting blues show seems to have been on January 4, 1927, when the *Advocate* carried a large advertisement for a "Midnight Frolic 11.30 pm, invitation performance for white persons only—Mamie Smith and her Colored Players." Mamie Smith was one of the most prominent of the wave of female blues singers who had emerged from the black vaudeville circuits, singing and moaning big-voiced blues to the backing of a small jazz orchestra. Her 1920 recording of "Crazy Blues" is reckoned to be the earliest "proper" blues recording by a black artist, and it allegedly sold over a million copies in its first year. She was followed into the Temple on March 17 by "Wilie and Wilie—Okeh record artists—with 5 vaudeville acts." A year later, there was a *State-Times* boxed ad for the "Midnight Ramble (White Only) at Temple Theater . . . Ida Cox and Company, famous record artist and blues singer."[11] Soon there would be well-remembered appearances by national big-name bands such as Cab Calloway, Fats Waller, Louis Armstrong, and Duke Ellington. When they played in the spring and summer months, people recall, the huge windows of the Roof Garden were thrown open, and the music reverberated throughout the neighborhood.

It is unlikely that any of this city-center entertainment touched the early life of James Moore. His was a rural existence, and money was probably very tight. People gained their money and goods as best they could and, as James said years later to interviewer Jim Delehant: "In the country, when you get to be 12 you're like a grown man, and you have to go to work."[12] Other musicians have told their own stories about growing up in rural Louisiana. One said, "Life in the country is set by the seasons. . . . we grew the greens, we picked the cotton, we planted the corn. It was a cycle that didn't stop."[13] Another said, "I started out when I was a youngster, thirteen years old. I used to skin cows, sell the hide. Sell the bones for fertilizer. I worked at a dairy, I'd get up at two o'clock in the morning to go to work."[14] Those who couldn't or wouldn't work had other means; a year before James's birth there was a report in the *State-Times* of the burglary of the store run by G. W. Ory in nearby Lobdell.[15] When James was ten years old, he'd have heard about, probably even known, "11 year old Isidore Landry who was hit over the head with an iron bar for attempting to steal shrimp." The local paper reported that his body fell into the river and was washed up at Scotland.[16] James may also have known or been related to a fisherman, Preston Moore, who was protecting his shrimp and who, according to the press reports, "has lived in Lobdell several months." These were times of economic depression, and many people were on the move from town to town in search of work or at least some kind of living, often competing with the local people.

Although the city of Baton Rouge was shielded from the worst of the Great Depression because of its range of industries and businesses and the activity surrounding the government buildings downtown and Louisiana State University on the south side of town, there was still the need for several initiatives to improve the lot of workers in and around the area in those years. In 1932, the local press reported that firms were urged to retain their present employees: "By retaining the staff they already have Baton Rouge firms will not only be helping those in need of work but at the same time will be holding their organizations intact against the time when a full force or staff will be needed."[17] Frank Kean was chairman of the local Share the Work Committee, linked to a national initiative by Standard Oil, and he asked, "If a firm has 20 employees but an actual need for only 16, why not by a system of rotation give a weeks vacation without pay to each employee? I believe the employees would be willing to cooperate [in such times]." Among the targeted companies locally were sugar refiners, including the Poplar Grove Planting and Refining Company, which had numbered Clyde Moore among its employees before he went to work on the railroads that carried its refined sugarcane off to market. Each October the local news contained reports on the commencement of the sugarcane grinding season, emphasizing that West Baton Rouge Parish had four major mills, including Poplar Grove, and a sugarcane area of eighteen thousand acres supplying 250,000 tons for sale.

It is clear that James Moore's early life included work in the sugar fields. He later said, "I had a pretty rough childhood. . . . I worked in the fields for a long time. I'd go right from school out into the field every day until I went on my own."[18] The Moores formed part of a small yet close community. "I grew up under James Moore at Mulatto Bend Road, about a half a mile from Bellmont," remembers his neighbor, Connie Dents, who said it was a good place, a family-oriented place, and "everybody knew everybody well, everybody was related to somebody. James was the same age as my mother, and he went to school with her under the teacher who was the pastor of our church. In that time there were no public schools for black people. The building where they had school is now the United Benevolent Society Building of Lobdell."[19] Musician Buddy Guy came from another rural area a little north of Baton Rouge, and he might have been describing James Moore's life when he talked about the isolation, the lack of material things—news, running water, radios—and the plentiful, blistering heat that drove him down under his wooden cabin to play and rest up. He remembered Baptist school, too: "That's where I was taught to use utensils and read little books about white children. . . . black people weren't in those books. Blacks weren't part of history. All we knew was the present time. . . . and today meant shuck the corn and feed the pig."[20]

Port Allen had its first school in 1887, opened in the Episcopal Church building, but this was for white people only. A state rural schools inspection of 1915 noted there was now a "colored school" in Lobdell with one room, sixty-one pupils, and four grades. Even if there was such access, black pupils in west Baton Rouge attended school just five months in the year, January to May, until 1936, and then six months, leaving the rest clear for agricultural work. The first high school for blacks in Port Allen was Cohn High, opened in 1949. In Baton Rouge, a Colored High School was built on today's Myrtle Street in 1914, and in 1926 McKinley High was opened; but back in the country, west of the river, education was sparse.

James Moore's schoolteacher was the man who had conducted his parents' marriage ceremony, Edward Doyle Billoups. He had been born locally and from 1922 pastored the New St. John Baptist Church, founded in 1872 in Mulatto Bend, up to 1970 when the church was taken over by his son, Leo Billoups. Edward Billoups became a regional vice-president of the National Baptist Convention and an active member of the National Association for the Advancement of Colored People as well as a local educator. He was apparently a good man to have as a mentor and role model.

By the time James was in his teens and already a veteran worker in the fields, several local and national initiatives had been taken to improve the education of rural Louisianians. On May 18, 1935, the *Advocate* reported, "Eleven hundred negro boys and girls representing the 14 negro schools of west Baton Rouge parish dressed in their Sunday best gathered at Port Allen school Friday for their annual 'field day' program. Tests were given in reading and arithmetic and prizes were given by J. N. Moody, supervisor of West Baton Rouge negro schools." Exhibition rooms also showed for each school the best of the girls' handicrafts and the boys' woodwork, underlining the vocational nature of the Negro educational programs at that time. Probably James was there on that day. Three years later, the *Morning Advocate* described a new school building project under way in Port Allen: "Pending completion, adult negro schools are being held throughout the parish. Six negro teachers from New Orleans are instructing the classes because no qualified teachers were on the relief rolls in West Baton Rouge parish."[21] The report described the eleven current makeshift venues being used, including those at Mulatto Bend, Lobdell, Westover, Chamberlin, and Choctaw. Local officials were pleased that "about 400 adult negroes have enrolled, one half of whom have never attended school before." It is not known whether James Moore attended any of these classes. Two years further on, the newspaper was reporting the success of Works Progress Administration projects locally, saying: "Colored teachers will hold an achievement day program tonight at Mulatto Bend in west Baton Rouge parish. Various musical and literary numbers will be offered by the adult students and there will also be a spelling bee. . . . white people interested to attend will be welcome." The report went on to say that east and west Baton Rouge now had 45 paid instructors and 3,489 adult students, black and white, studying basic school subjects, commercial subjects, driving safety, piano, "and classes for alien adults wishing to speak the English language."[22]

In contrast to these reports of social improvements, the pages of the local newspapers were also full of the "large number of cases being brought before the West Baton Rouge parish grand jury" by the close of the 1930s. In one report alone, the jury was asked to consider twenty-five cases, including two murders, five alleged assaults with intent to kill, disturbing the peace, robbery, larceny, reckless driving, cutting and wounding, and carrying concealed weapons. It is not known, and perhaps unlikely considering his age, whether the court report in the *State-Times* of March 6, 1936, about "James Moore, charged with possession of stolen property and converting the same to his own use," relates to our James Moore, but if it does then we can only hope that the property was a musical instrument. James did later say that he took up the harmonica at age twelve. The person in question pleaded not guilty, and a hearing date was set but never reported, so it is just possible that the court realized they had arrested a minor. James grew into a tall man and by all accounts was a tall teenager too. It is equally possible that references to Matilda Moore in the newspapers of July 1937 were to James's seventeen-year-old sister, who had moved to a lodging house at 712 North Fifteenth Street in Baton Rouge. The court reports included "State v Matilda Moore, larceny: Two negresses are held for theft of $5 dress. Matilda Moore, 712 North Fifteenth Street, took dress and other items from Mrs. Curtin of Istrouma for whom she worked. Julia Smith of Gayoso Street was seen wearing the dress." Both women pleaded guilty and were sentenced to jail.[23]

In 1937 Baton Rouge saw the opening of the *Post* newspaper, claiming to bring to black Baton Rouge "all the news about all the people," local, national, and international, from the opening of a black bathing beach in New Orleans to the work of the NAACP in Louisiana, the progress of an antilynching bill in the Senate, and the abdication of Haile Salassie in Ethiopia. Through 1938 the society and entertainment pages were full of seasonal weddings and black society balls, the performance in Baton Rouge at the Temple Roof Garden of an all-female dance band, the Harlem Play Girls, and the eager anticipation of the arrival of the orchestra of Andy Kirk, the "Sultan of Sophistication." William Byrd's activities promoting local orchestras including the Louisiana Stompers, Toots Johnson, and the Victor and Roseland bands were noted with approval. There was no coverage of blues music in any form, however, let alone the daily life of ordinary working folks out on Mulatto Bend.

The censuses and news reports of the 1930s make it clear that James Moore was living in a family and a community that comprised established, hardworking families alongside a shifting population of migrants. It was a community with a churchgoing tradition but also one where people were never far from the temptations of the devil. We do not know how often James participated in church or whether spiritual or gospel music was any real influence on him, but he did once say that, when he was a little-schooled and hardworking teenager, "Music was the only thing I had, and no contact at all with music outside my area. The music I knew was blues and I got it from the people I lived and worked with. When I sing the blues, I can tell about the hard times I've had and the places I've been living; the things I'll never forget."[24] From this distance, we can only imagine what those experiences were and how they would shape his approach to life.

James talked occasionally in later life about listening to music from outside his local experience and how he'd parlay what he'd heard into his first faltering steps toward becoming a musician. He told one interviewer: "I liked music but there was no money for instruments. I thought my best was to get something I could afford, which was a harmonica—all I had was a dime, you know. I listened to records. I'd listen to songs, mostly blues, and the next day I'd try to play them on the harmonica. Blind Lemon Jefferson was my favorite blues player. And also Howlin' Wolf. I'd listen to their songs and try to play. This was when I was living in the country. Back at home I played mostly all blues, like at house suppers, fish fries. People with guitars and harmonicas would play. No electric instruments then. If I would make two or three dollars a night, that was a lot of money then."[25]

Lemon Jefferson was from the Wortham area of East Texas, some four hundred miles from Baton Rouge. He worked the streets and clubs of towns like Dallas and Shreveport but also had elements of the cotton-field holler in his call-and-response vocal and guitar style. Lemon sang with deep feeling but in a high voice that had a real edge to it, and he accompanied himself with music that would not keep one beat but would adapt to fit the speeding or slowing of the words and phrasing. His recordings for the Paramount and Okeh labels in the late 1920s became very popular, and his fame and influence, based on songs like "Matchbox Blues," "Black Snake Moan," "Jack 'o Diamonds Blues," and "Low Down Mojo Blues" lasted for some years after his early death in 1929. James Moore would have been well aware of Lemon even ten years after his demise. On the other hand, his reference to Howlin' Wolf is ambiguous. In later years he is known to have admired Chester Burnett, the Howlin' Wolf who made hits on Chess Records, but it seems that James was talking of Blind Lemon's era and the Wolf he'd more likely have meant would have been J. T. "Funny Papa" Smith from Texas, who recorded in the 1930s and was known for his melodic and well-composed songs like "Howling Wolf Blues" on Vocalion. Jefferson and Smith were guitarists, but it is possible to hear their overall stylistic influence in the vocal and harmonica music James Moore would make later on. Still talking of the 1930s, James told another interviewer:

> My first listening experience was on the radio. All I heard was the blues. I always did like music and I wanted to play an instrument. Back then nobody had any money but a harmonica only cost ten cents. I couldn't play anything else. I guess I was about 12 years old when I got a harp. When I got my harp I'd listen to songs real close on the radio and learn them, then I'd play it on the harp. The only live contact was at house suppers. In fact I started playing music when I was very young at picnics and house parties. Every Friday and Saturday night we'd have off from work and every weekend we'd have a big supper at somebody's house. There'd be a couple of guys there with guitars and drums. That was a lot of fun. We played music for dancing called the "Slow Drag." It was for holding each other real close. It's just a one step or two step when you dance to slow blues.[26]

Unfortunately, James did not go into detail about where he might have heard blues on the radio in the 1930s. Until WJBO started in Baton Rouge in 1934, those with radios could only hear stations from New Orleans or East Texas. The daily schedules for WJBO in 1936 list mainly dance orchestras and popular-music concerts, nothing remotely blues—and it's possible James meant to say that he learned folk and popular tunes off the radio and blues songs at house parties. He did, though, tell about when he first heard blues music played live outside his own community, along with Cajun and country music—"I remember we'd walk seven or eight miles into Baton Rouge on a

Saturday night." If he meant Baton Rouge, rather than Port Allen, then he'd have had to take a ferry too because there was no bridge across the Mississippi until 1940. By all accounts, both Baton Rouge and Port Allen contained a number of clubs and joints supporting live music and were a magnet for people of all races and economic circumstances when they were looking for a good time. In the late 1930s and early 1940s, the "Colored Bars" in the city included the Easytown Bar and the Five Crown Tavern on Thirteenth Street, the Green Parrot Night Club at 1520 Reddy, Perry's on Butler, Waldo's on South Thirteenth, Browns Night Club on Margaretta, and the Paradise Night Club and Edgar Seals on Scenic Highway.[27] In addition to the clubs that featured jukebox music and local musicians whose names are long lost to us, the core black area of Baton Rouge of the 1930s and 1940s was home to at least three professional "colored bands": those of Toots Johnson based at South Twelfth Street, Kid Dimes of South Fourteenth, and Victor's Dance Orchestra of South Sixteenth.

When James mentioned learning his music from local players and from the radio, it is likely that those mentors in turn took some influence from recorded music. In the 1930s, the recording industry was in depression, but some blues singers were still popular in homes and on jukeboxes. Men such as Blind Lemon Jefferson from Texas and John Lee "Sonny Boy" Williamson from Tennessee had both moved to Chicago to live and record but retained a strong following in the South. Records were available from furniture stores where record players and radios were sold, such as those on Main Street and North Boulevard—Capital, Globe, Star, Kornmeyer, Joubert's, and Werlein's— and music shops such as Causey's and Fourrier's on Main Street. Some of the many lunchrooms and bars contained jukeboxes and also sold records, such as John Germany's, the Railroad Café, the Lincoln Café, and Kate Kelley's, all for black clientele only. Such establishments acquired their amusement machines and music boxes from dealers such as the Standard Amusement Company of South Thirteenth Street or the Louisiana Amusement Company on Lafayette and the Baton Rouge Amusement Company on North Boulevard.

Although James's life in the farming communities was tough during the Depression years of the 1930s, the Baton Rouge economy was better placed than most to gear up for increased production as the war years approached. The controversial Governor Long, who had been elected in 1928 by a large majority, and who became a US senator in 1931, worked enthusiastically in Baton Rouge to encourage and develop public facilities until his combative style led to his being assassinated inside the new State Capitol Building in 1935. The area remained in work through World War II when Baton Rouge produced over three-quarters of the nation's aviation fuel, for instance, making use of the rapid development of the petrochemical industry, which also led the way in the production of synthetic rubber and other products of importance before, during, and after the war.

By the time of the April 1940 census, greater Baton Rouge had enlarged to some seventy-five thousand people, many employed at Standard Oil's largest refinery, and an increasing number from outside the immediate area were employed in professional, academic, or governmental pursuits. The Moore family, though, was recorded in the census on April 5 as living in the "same house" as they were in five years earlier, the place being now described as Bellmont Farm Road, Lobdell Village, West Baton Rouge Parish.

At the time of the 1940 census, a twenty-eight-year-old man from North Dakota had given up his pharmaceutical practice and his part in the family-run drugstore and was studying for a master's degree at Louisiana State University in Baton Rouge. Hubert Humphrey was interested in political science and preparing for a career in politics. Some of what he found on his first trip to the South stayed with him through his career, during which he worked to ensure a civil rights plank at the Democratic Party Convention in 1948 and, as vice-president of the United States, to help secure the Civil Rights Act of 1964 and the Voting Rights Act of 1965. Back in 1939, he said, he was "dismayed" by the living conditions for black people he observed in Baton Rouge, contrasting "the white, neatly painted houses of the whites, the unpainted shacks of the blacks; the stately homes on manicured lawns of the white sections, the open sewage ditches in black neighborhoods." When he first saw the "White" and "Colored" signs posted above water fountains and toilets, he said he found them "both ridiculous and offensive," and Louisiana taught him something about American life that he barely knew in fact or in theory. As a conventional northern white liberal, he had never been exposed to black Americans, and said, "I had never been truly aware of institutionalized white paternalism. . . . Everything you did in Louisiana—study or work—was, in a sense, conditioned by that environment of often corrupt, usually bizarre, southern politics and race relations."[28]

In 1940 only 3 percent of black Americans were registered to vote in the South, largely because of the stringent, almost impossible, literacy tests applied to blacks registering to vote. After the Civil War and the optimism of the freed slaves, the registration of black voters in Louisiana rose to 45 percent by 1896. That year, though, Louisiana had passed a law disallowing any former slave or descendant of slaves to vote, and this "grandfather clause" ensured the percentage of registered black voters fell to just 4 percent in 1900.[29] It was not until after the 1965 Voting Rights Act that these barriers to registration were removed in the South.

One of the biggest events of 1940 for the residents of Mulatto Bend was the opening of the first road and rail bridge across the Mississippi at Baton Rouge, a truss cantilever construction over a mile long funded through President Roosevelt's New Deal initiative and built by the Public Works Administration at a cost of over $8 million. Previously, the Third Street ferry had been the only way of linking people, goods, and businesses from Baton Rouge to Port Allen. The ferry had been opened in 1820 by C. Hubbs in the days when the town on the west bank was still called St. Michel, and it served for over 150 years until the last ferry operated in 1971, three years after a newer bridge was opened and Highway 1 rerouted in Port Allen. In 1940, the first bridge, named for Huey P. Long, soared above the water and deposited both trains and the traffic on Highway 190 back to earth in the middle of the cane fields not more than a mile and a half from the Moore residence at Bellmont Road, now increasingly spelled "Belmont." Airline Highway, as it was also known, greatly increased the possibilities of access to Baton Rouge for the people of West Baton Rouge Parish and, among other things, eased the passage of musicians from communities and bars on one side of the river to the other.

THE DEATH OF CLYDE MOORE

Two days before Christmas 1940, the *Morning Advocate* carried this story: "Old Negro Struck By Car; Succumbs: A 60 year old negro was fatally injured yesterday when he was struck by an automobile on Highway 71 near the west approach of the Mississippi river bridge, police reported last night. The negro, Clyde Moore of Lobdell, was brought to Our Lady of the Lake sanitarium for treatment of a fractured left leg and internal injuries shortly after the accident happened at 3 pm. He succumbed about 8.30 pm."

It is likely that James and his sisters were there to witness this traumatic event because it happened on the occasion of a local funeral. It was all the more upsetting because it was not a straightforward accident their father had. As the newspaper reported on Christmas Eve:

Involuntary Homicide Charged In Death Of Aged Negro: Charges were led yesterday against Henry Brown, negro of Kahns, who was being held in the West Baton
Rouge parish jail in connection with the death of Clyde Moore, 60, negro, who
died Sunday as a result of injuries received when he was struck by a car driven by
Brown. Death was attributed to a fracture of the left leg and rupture of the kidney
as a result of the accident by Coroner Harry Johnston who conducted an inquest
here yesterday. State police who arrested Brown on the west side approach of the
Mississippi river bridge said that Moore was standing on the north side of the
highway halting traffic to enable a funeral procession to cross the road. Brown,
they said, struck Moore when he drove his car on the shoulder in an effort to pass
a car in the funeral procession.

The details of this report all appear to be perfectly clear, apart from the
lifespan of the "aged" Clyde, who was actually nearer to forty-eight years old
than sixty. The census returns for 1920–1940 show Clyde having been born in
1891 or 1892. Unless the returns were off by ten years, the apparently erroneous
newspaper report probably stemmed from confused witness statements at
and after the time of the event. On December 31, 1940, Clyde's wife, Pearline,
made an application to the US Army for a headstone marker to be provided
to her at no cost since Clyde was a war veteran. Her application, signed by
a mark, gave his date of death as December 21, his Army enlistment in the
801st Pioneer Infantry as July 28, 1918, and his discharge as June 21, 1919.

Clyde's death left James as the male head of his family at the age of sixteen
and, as far as is known, he continued for some time to work on Bellmont
Farm and to do what he could to help his mother and his three sisters. In
the 1940 census, taken the April before Clyde Moore died, James was listed,
like his father, as a "farm laborer" at Bellmont, an "unincorporated place"
that had become part of Lobdell Village. The former Belle Vale Plantation,
owned by the Lobdell family, had apparently been broken up and was in the
process of being developed for housing as part of the wider expansion of
the area around Port Allen and of Baton Rouge itself. Across the Mississippi
River from Bellmont Farm, above Baton Rouge in East Baton Rouge Parish,
other areas of expanded population were emerging, including Scotlandville,
Baker, and Zachary. The area just northeast of the Moore household and near
the oil refineries of east Baton Rouge was originally known as Scot's Bluff but
became Scotlandville as it developed from a collection of nineteenth-century
shacks among established tall oaks and willows into a residential and business district in the wake of the grocery store established there by the Drago

family and the new campus for Southern University. For black residents, by the 1940s, it had become "a country-in-the-city community . . . agrarians who had come to town, and it was a place of barbeque and church suppers and blues honky tonks," according to Louisiana folklorist Nick Spitzer.[30]

James's oldest (step)sister, Lillie, had married by 1940 and was living with Dan Collins in the household next to the Moores. Dan worked on the construction of roads and had possibly been part of the WPA teams that built the new Huey P. Long Bridge. According to the census, the values of the Moore and Collins houses were $250 and $150, respectively. Felix Emerson, James's mother's older brother, still lived with the family at this time. His name was apparently misheard, and he was recorded in the census as Felix "Amos." James's youngest sister, Doris, was at home in 1940, aged thirteen, although she became Mrs. Doris Robertson at some point prior to November 22, 1943, when she filed a Lost Notice in the *Advocate* as part of the process to recover her rights to the wartime rations that had been introduced in 1942. The clerk of court confirmed that Doris had "duly sworn that the War Ration Book number 3 belonging to her husband George Robertson and her uncle Felix Emerson has been lost or destroyed, that she is making application for two new books, that none of the stamps had been used from either book, and that she had never received War Ration Book number 4." George was apparently away in the service at this time, and certainly the *Advocate* of December 7, 1940, had listed a George Robertson of 614 South Fourteenth Street among those men due to receive their "questionnaires," the first step in the Army enrollment process. James's middle sister, Tillie, was no longer living at home but was listed at a lodging house on North Fifteenth Street as a "farm laborer."

It is likely that James stayed at home for a time after his father died, although it is also possible he was the man named James Moore listed in the city directories of 1941 and 1942 living at 975 River Road, employed as a laborer at the Baton Rouge Lumber Company, and the man fined for running a stop sign near there in May 1941.[31]

GOING TO NEW ORLEANS

Suddenly, in 1942, James Moore moved away from home altogether. He said later, "When I was 18, I took a job as a longshoreman on the riverfront in New Orleans."[32] There is no documentary record or family memory of this, but it is very likely to be true. The Baton Rouge Lumber Company job may have been somehow connected with shipping goods to New Orleans, and may have opened up an opportunity down there. Possibly James just wanted to get away from the farming life, or even from his newly enhanced family responsibilities, but it is equally as likely that he saw the move as a way to earn better wages and to send some money home. His stepson, William Gambler, said, "[He] never talked to me about his early life, before he met my mother. But I can understand how he'd go to New Orleans because there would have been better work opportunities there. There were companies in Baton Rouge where they didn't employ black workers." The exact time period in which James was away from Baton Rouge is not known because he may not have left right at the start of 1942, when he literally turned eighteen, and he moved between the two cities at least twice. He once said, "After I worked there [New Orleans] for a while, I came back and took a job as a contractor," but the building contract work came after a later, second spell in the Crescent City.[33]

New Orleans was continually developing its role as a port for freight and passengers, and between 1903 and 1940 some eighteen new wharves were built to help compete with road and rail companies and to enable an increase in trade. So, jobs were plentiful there by the early 1940s, with the many thousands of longshore jobs divided almost equally between black and white workers, each with their own union organization. Assuming James did go to New Orleans in 1942, his stay there, or at least his first stay, had ended by September 1, 1943, when he was living at 168 Mary Street in the south part of downtown Baton Rouge and next door to Robert Causey, a musician from the same family as Clyde Causey, also known as "Harmonica Nose."[34] That was the day he was interviewed by the clerk of court in East Baton Rouge Parish about a license to marry Verna Mae Murrell, also of 168 Mary Street, the twenty-one-year-old daughter of Clara Murrell of 1124 St. Joseph Street, some half a mile away. Clara later became Clara Johnson but had been Clara Hills from Napoleonville when she married Noah Murrell from Livingston Parish just east of Baton Rouge. Verna had been born some forty miles south of Baton Rouge in her mother's town, Napoleonville, Louisiana, on June 23, 1923, according to her marriage records, or June 2, 1922, according to her Social Security records. The Murrell family had been in Baton Rouge at least since 1937, and by 1943 Verna was working as a maid while Clara was a cook, living with her other daughter, Elva, and a younger son, Rehula. Possibly James had just returned from New Orleans and was between work when he applied to be married because he described his occupation as "none." The marriage license was granted on September 10, 1943, and witnessed by Doris Robertson and Dan and Lillie Collins, James's sister, brother-in-law, and stepsister.

The background to James's marriage to Verna is unknown, and no one has been able to say how and when he met her or how and why the marriage ended. If James did go to New Orleans in 1942, at age eighteen, then he probably did not know Verna before that. Or, maybe they ran off together and used New Orleans as an escape until the Murrell family persuaded him back to marry her? If so, there is no record of any children ensuing. Back in Baton Rouge in 1943, James took a job at the Ethyl Gas Company. In both the 1943 and 1944 city directories of Baton Rouge, James and Verna are listed as living at 745 North Fourteenth Street, north of central downtown, with James employed by Ethyl Gas.[35] Verna Moore's Social Security record was commenced in January 1944. By 1945, though, references to James and Verna Moore had disappeared from the public records of Baton Rouge, and James does not reappear for certain in any records there until 1951. He had returned again to New Orleans for part of those six years.

Years later, he told his booking agent that he took a job in the New Orleans area, but he "only stayed in New Orleans for three years because he wanted to return to Baton Rouge where he had a pad."[36] Civil District Court records from Orleans Parish show that James and Verna Mae were living in New Orleans by April 1944 and that they separated some two years later.[37] The reasons are unknown. Maybe they just didn't get along, either or both being to some extent volatile. A Veral [sic] Mae Murrell, aged seventeen, had been placed in the East Baton Rouge Parish Jail in 1940 and received ninety days for "cutting and wounding," according to newspaper reports.[38] The city directory for New Orleans in 1947 shows that Verna M. Moore was living at 2917 Piety Street and working as a machinist at the American Sheet Metal Company at 331 North Alexander. James is not listed at that address, though he is later listed as a longshoreman, resident at 3926 Laurel, a shotgun-type house just three blocks back from the riverfront docks off Tchoupitoulas Street near the Port of New Orleans. This was not far from Harmony Street Wharf, where musician Bill Webb has described working with James.[39]

While James was in New Orleans, it is likely that he had plenty of access to music. "All along the streets that run parallel to the Mississippi River, from Tchoupitoulas above Canal Street to the central business district and Decatur Street in the French Quarter, one could find seaman's bars and corner joints

that catered to the around-the-clock work routine of the docks," according
to longshore historian Justin Nystrom.

> Dockworkers dominated the first several blocks in from the waterfront where they
> lived in the ubiquitous shotgun double houses situated within hailing distance of
> the ships' horns. The Longshoremen tell of the tedium of loading 250-pound sacks,
> the oppressiveness of the heat working inside a ship's hold in the summer, and the
> relentless pace. But they also tell of the camaraderie of life on the docks, steady
> work, good wages, and a responsive union. "You're hired and fired every day,"
> explained retired longshoreman Robert Blake. Once a ship was fully loaded or un-
> loaded, it meant finding more work at the hiring offices of shipping lines that used
> to be located at the foot of Canal Street. At first blush, this suggests employment
> uncertainty, but the opposite was true. With over 150 shipping companies operat-
> ing during the midcentury heyday of breakbulk cargo, work was plentiful. [Before
> the container era] . . . "they had a lot of mens, and everything, and I just liked
> to be in that number," explains longshoreman John McSwain, who came to New
> Orleans from rural Alabama in 1959 at the age of nineteen to work on the river.[40]

When James Moore was first on the docks, he would likely have worked
as a "rabbit," who had to get up around five in the morning and go to the
dock to try for hire on a casual basis. Longshoreman Mark Ellis said, "That
means they are not registered, they are not part of the permit work force, and
that term 'rabbit' came about as a way of describing them 'cause they had to
hop, run, and jump to make a living and try to get their foot in the door."
After a while, a man might be accepted enough to buy a registration card,
an SG card, from the union office, that allowed him to work regularly. Ellis
explained that there were two local longshore unions, "Local 1418, which was
the predominantly white local, and 1419, which was the predominantly black
local, and you know, every company and every foreman had their corner or
their bar, and many cases at the foot of Canal Street where they were hired."
Depending on the company hiring and the ships in port, a longshoreman
would unload or load anything from steel to cotton to grain or sugar, or vehicles and machinery. Longshoreman Robert Blake remembered: "Everything
was on the floor. We had to pick it up and put it on pallet or in a sling, a rope
sling. Then we had to pull it out to the ship. And then hook it up, put it on a
ship, and then pull the wagon back and reload it. It was a good day's works.
All day . . . it was dangerous and we worked in gangs, and you had to rely on
your partners. It was nicknames." Most men had a nickname that was used
regularly and often didn't know their gang members' real names.[41]

Sometimes the longshoreman's day ended at a bar as well as starting there. James McClelland went to the docks in 1949 and remembered that there were "a lot of them. Frankie and Johnnies, Murées, just the neighborhood bars that were closest to the docks sometimes. . . . Some of the typical fun barrooms. Most probably had a back room you could make a bet on racehorses, or the football games, or play poker. Things of that nature."[42] It is possible that James Moore picked up his longtime enjoyment of gambling at cards in such an environment.

James's time in New Orleans probably came to an end around the time his marriage to Verna Mae failed irretrievably. On April 18, 1949, Judge J. J. Yarrut signed a divorce judgment in Civil District Court in New Orleans following receipt of a petition from Verna Mae Moore dated March 8 that year. Her petition against James Moore stated that the couple had been married in Baton Rouge on September 10, 1943, that "the matrimonial domicile has been in this city [New Orleans] and this state since the month of April 1944," and that the "petitioner has lived continuously in this city and state, separated and apart and under separate roof from said defendant, from and after the seventeenth day of April 1946, without reconciliation." It was also stated that "there are no children issue of said marriage." The divorce papers were addressed to James at Box 70, Route 1, Port Allen, and served there by hand to the defendant by the deputy sheriff on March 11, 1949, giving him fifteen days to respond. Apparently, there was no response from James, and on April 4 Verna Mae attended district court to swear that "she is well acquainted with the defendant . . . and she knows he is not in the Military, Naval or Armed Force of the United States of America." The court had recorded James as being in default at the end of March and, having covered off the only legitimate reason for a delay in proceedings, Judge Yarrut ruled on April 18 that "the default entered on the twenty ninth day of March . . . be confirmed and made final" and, "accordingly, let there be judgement in favor of the plaintiff."[43]

There must have been some urgency to obtain the divorce because, just nineteen days after her divorce from James, Verna Mae Murrell married again, in New Orleans, on May 7, 1949. She was married by Rev. F. P. Jackson to Carroll Vaughn, originally from Woodville, Mississippi, who had moved to New Orleans in 1936. Verna and Carroll were both living at 3041 Clouet Street in New Orleans at the time of their marriage. Verna gave birth to a daughter, Carol, in August, a mere four months after her divorce from James, and she also bore twin daughters the following year.[44] By 1952 the Vaughns were living at 2128 Lafitte, a mile or so out from the French Quarter and downtown, when Carroll was listed as a laborer at the American Sheet Metal Company, where evidently he had first met Verna Moore sometime either side of 1947 when Verna was known to be working there.

James Moore's return to the Baton Rouge area came sometime before or during early 1949. He was there when the divorce papers were served, but he may have only recently returned and, indeed, he may have moved between the two locations for a year or two if the city directories are accurate. Among the other still uncertain things about James Moore's life in the 1940s is whether the World War II draft board ever came looking for him. If they did, he seems to have avoided them, either on account of his farming and family responsibilities or his working on the river. At James's age, it is likely he would have been called by the Army, and the *Advocate* regularly published lists of names of men who were being sought for military service and who had been sent "questionnaires" to establish their identity, eligibility, and availability for induction interviews. James's remaining descendants have been unable to say whether he was ever contacted, and there is no for-certain military record relating to him. There were several James Moores who enlisted in the services in Louisiana, Mississippi, or Texas during the 1940s, but none seem to be our man due to their age, color, or location. If he was not exempt by virtue of being a farmer or a docker, he was possibly lost to the authorities because he had changed location both within Baton Rouge and then to New Orleans.[45]

The war years had brought rationing of tires, gas, and other essential supplies to Baton Rouge residents including, ironically, sugar, for which there developed a black market. The war also brought many thousands of military personnel stationed at camps around the area, and Port Allen was home to a prisoner-of-war camp also. Many of the prisoners worked on plantations such as Poplar Grove at this time. During 1945, though, the thoughts of people in Baton Rouge turned away from the war and the fifteen years of relative depression since the Wall Street crash of 1929. There was an increasing mood of optimism after the war, and the *Advocate* started to run ads for better leisure opportunities, including the wares carried by Filiberto's Music Store, 839 Main Street, which not only offered "the finest selection of popular, classic, jazz and blues records available" but enabled customers to "make a record on our new modern recording system." It is unlikely that James Moore ever took up this challenge but, again, we don't know for sure. Possibly he would have been unable to do so on the grounds of his color. Certainly he would have been unable to attend many of the venues that were increasing their ads for bigger and better dining experiences, floor shows, and dances.

The accent was on small orchestras and big bands, jazzy pop songs. Between 1946 and 1949, the regular bands included Victor's Orchestra at John's Playhouse, Flivver Ford at Penders, Ovide Leonard's Orchestra at the Lighthouse, Billy Clayborne at the Tropicana, and the Tune Toppers at Lucky's Club. The Ray Barrios Band was popular among whites following an April 1946 show at the Recreation Center that drew 200 local girls to a dance with 1,800 men from Camp Polk—just some of the 20,000 servicemen stationed around the Baton Rouge area. Out-of-town bands included Chuck Foster from Memphis and Jimmy Dorsey from New York. Hillbilly bands were advertised occasionally, including a major Grand Ole Opry touring show in 1949, which featured Ernest Tubb, Hank Williams, and Minnie Pearl. By far the most intriguing ads, though, were for the May 1948 dances at Louie's Bar B Q to "the toe tangling tunes" of Charles Ball and His Swinging Jigs. The jig kick was a key move in swing dancing of the period, and so the band's name may not have been as provocative as it would later have been.

POSTWAR BLUES

In the postwar years, local bars, clubs, general stores, and other venues continued to rely on the jukebox business to generate interest and custom. Over half the records sold in America were to jukeboxes via a national network of local "coin operators," who supplied jukeboxes as part of the amusement-machine industry. In Baton Rouge, the main ops were the Baton Rouge Amusement Company and the Louisiana Amusement Company. Before World War II, the large national recording companies based in the North had always relied on furniture-store dealers, who sold records, and on coin-machine men to help channel the right kind of music to local jukes—for instance, Jewish records in New York, Mexican in the Southwest, blues and hillbilly across the South, and Cajun in Louisiana. Now, postwar, the main companies could not keep up with the new demand for musical entertainment, and many local and regional recording companies emerged. There were none in Baton Rouge, but there were companies recording blues, R&B, hillbilly, and Cajun music in Houston, New Orleans, and Crowley, Louisiana. These companies in turn fed into the radio business, where there was an increasing trend to program the sounds of local preference as well as nationally networked music. In addition to clubs and dance venues, records, and radio, there was continuing buoyant attendance at theaters and cinemas. In Port Allen, that meant the Magic Theater and the Edith Theater. In Baton Rouge, it meant many more, among which the black community attended the Temple, the East End, and the McKinley theaters.

Although there was an increase in economic and personal enthusiasm for postwar life, through 1946 the politicians and the press were increasingly concerned with how society would evolve. In both world wars there had been conscription of black soldiers, albeit often confined to maintenance and support roles—including the man who would become blues singer Howlin' Wolf, one of James's favorites, who was on maneuvers in Louisiana in 1941 and photographed cleaning horses' hooves as part of a horse-drawn artillery unit. Postwar, there was mounting pressure on white-led society to recognize and resolve the problems faced by their black neighbors. In 1944 several black leaders in Louisiana had formed the Louisiana Progressive Voters League to help prepare more black people to register as voters and to push for better public and recreation facilities. On April 17, 1946, the *Advocate* reported: "Race Relations Committee is formed in EBR: A permanent committee for the purpose of furthering better understanding between the negro and the white people of this area was formed at a meeting between leaders of the two races at McKinley High School Monday night." It was agreed there was need for a long-range program to benefit both, although their starting points and motivations were clearly different. The white judge, J. S. Favrot, who chaired the committee, thought better control of delinquency and the setting up of a juvenile court were important, as was increased involvement from school and church leaders. Favrot said, "White juveniles are more prone to commit acts of malicious mischief and negro youths commit, in the main, acts of theft." The Rev. Gardner Taylor, pastor of Mt. Zion Baptist Church, explained, "All the negro wants is to be looked upon as an ordinary human being. . . . one of the main needs of the local negro is better police protection and understanding . . . and for the vision to deal with problems of the races without resort to the courts. Another desire is to lessen incidents of friction on the public bus system."

Some problems were generated by the natural world rather than by inequalities in society. One was the perpetual battle to control the Mississippi River at times of high water, and it is possible that James would have played a part in resolving a disaster that befell his home community at the end of the 1940s. On the morning of Thursday, March 24, 1949, just thirteen days after service of his divorce papers, the *Advocate* carried news of the great Mulatto Bend flood: "Levee Break: 12,000 acres inundated by flood waters. The levee broke in the pre-dawn hours Thursday at Mulatto Bend, five miles north of Baton Rouge and on the opposite side of the river. . . . The waters have spread to cover some 20 square miles and the damage estimated at least $100 an acre in the rich sugar cane lowlands." The break in the levee bank occurred at Horace Wilkinson's Bel Air Plantation, just north of the Mississippi River Bridge, and rescue operations were coordinated from Wilkinson's Poplar Grove Plantation, both right next to Bellmont Road and the Moore family base. "Army engineers were soon mobilized and by Friday had almost completed a dike ringing the break. Unable to get mechanical pile-drivers, they set laborers to work hammering huge pilings into the soft mud." It is possible that James Moore would have been drafted in or volunteered to help as the crisis took hold. He may even be one of the workers pictured in the various reports given by the *Advocate* that month. Highways 71 and 190 had become blocked, and through traffic was rerouted via Natchez some one hundred miles north. Every ferry from Port Allen was loaded with the vehicles of people trying to get away. As the newspaper reported, "About 70 negro women and children from Belmont Plantation and Mulatto Bend sought refuge at Port Allen Community Center." Water had entered houses in Mulatto Bend and was starting to do so at Belmont. A resident named Pearl Young was quoted describing the ingress of water as she left her home.

The newspaper examined the causes of the flood and concluded that it was caused by cuts in funding for levee repair as part of flood-control planning. The paper noted that the only previous break on this scale had occurred in 1927, and that was principally because the US Army Corps of Engineers had deliberately dynamited the levee below Baton Rouge to protect New Orleans. Crevasses were natural escape routes for floodwaters and led to annual submersion of land in the days before planters arrived. As late as 1890 there was a big crevasse at Lobdell, and in 1912 large parts of west Baton Rouge were covered by water, including the area around Port Allen. The Great Flood of May 1927, which extended to a width of sixty miles at some points and displaced nearly a quarter of a million people, was memorialized in prose by Richard Wright and William Faulkner. It followed a year of sugarcane virus, and when the Depression hit soon after, the only way many plantations could survive was through consolidation. The 1927 flood inspired many blues and gospel songs, starting with Lonnie Johnson's "Broken Levee Blues," Charley Patton's "High Water Everywhere," and Memphis Minnie's "When the Levee Breaks." After 1928 new levees were constructed all along the west Baton Rouge riverfront, and the river road was rerouted in 1932, leaving Poplar Grove's plantation house between the levee and the river.

By the time of the Mulatto Bend flood, James was either back living in that area with some of his sisters, as the address for service of legal papers implies, or he was living somewhere in Baton Rouge itself. If little is known of his whereabouts and his life in general at this time, this is equally true of his musical life through the 1940s. His only known comment on the period after he returned from New Orleans was that he started working in construction as a contractor and that "during that time, I was still playing music."[46] If he was keeping up with postwar trends, he would have heard the jump blues of T-Bone Walker and Louis Jordan and some of the new R&B styles emerging from the plethora of small record companies then starting up. He would have known, too, that there were new names coming to prominence among the men who continued to play blues of the down-home style.

The influential guitar-boogie technique of John Lee Hooker may have been forged in the South, but by 1949 Hooker's recording of "Boogie Chillun" was selling strongly in the northern cities where he and more and more southerners swelled the market for blues that would soon be captured by the likes of Muddy Waters, Little Walter, and Howlin' Wolf. It was a really influential record that led to a number of juke-joint blues records.[47] In Texas, Lightnin' Hopkins and Little Son Jackson were among the down-home stylists whose music would have been familiar at house parties and on jukeboxes in towns like Baton Rouge. Apparently James Moore was also playing music as a sideline in small clubs in his local area. Leslie Johnson, who would later be known as the musician Lazy Lester, recalls seeing James around Baton Rouge when Leslie was a teenager: "This was way back in the last of the '40s, in these little clubs, you know. I wasn't playing then, didn't play with him, but I knew him, along with the other musicians. He started to call himself 'Harmonica Slim.' He had a little band playing in those clubs, this was before we made any records."[48] The assertion that James had a band that far back is not supported by any other testimony, but it is of course possible that he did. Assuming he was mainly playing harmonica, it is likely that he was following the styles of John Lee "Sonny Boy" Williamson, who recorded in Chicago for Bluebird, and Jazz Gillum, an influential Mississippi-born recording artist and backing musician active in Chicago.

THE RED STICK BLUES

At the time of the Mulatto Bend flood, which incidentally put paid to several small local music venues, James Moore was twenty-five years old, just returned from New Orleans, and apparently still very much an amateur musician. As far as is known, he listened to the radio, heard the jukeboxes, and took part in local house parties, playing harmonica. It has not been possible to establish whether there was any real tradition of music-making in the Moore family, but it is clear that he was not the first or only local musician in and around Baton Rouge who provided music for parties and neighborhood clubs and bars, mostly on a casual basis.

Some of the local musicians of the 1930s and 1940s are known by name though not through recordings; others are now lost to us entirely. The few small waves of folk-song collection and private recordings made in the early part of the twentieth century largely passed over the black music of Louisiana. There was some jazz-band blues and a little solo blues recorded in New Orleans and later some recording of blues singers in Shreveport, but nothing in Baton Rouge. Interestingly, when folklorist John Lomax made his pioneering trips of 1933 and 1934 to record folk music "in the field" for the Library of Congress, he had a portable recording machine made especially for the purpose, and he collected the machine from Baton Rouge where it had been delivered. There it had to be tested in a laboratory on the Louisiana State University campus due to a number of malfunctions. Once working, it seems not to have been used at all in Baton Rouge, Lomax recording instead mainly traditional French folksongs in the surrounding areas. He did record a very few black singers in English around New Iberia and Morgan City, and in Lafayette the mysterious, highly regarded blues of Wilson Jones, from Opelousas, known as Stavin' Chain. Had he dug around just a little in Baton Rouge and surrounding areas, it is likely he would have found a number of black string bands and folk singers of interest and possibly of originality. Instead, he preferred to seek out old black songs in the Louisiana State Penitentiary at Angola, discovering among others the soon-to-be-renowned Louisiana folk-blues singer Lead Belly.[49]

In the rural communities of James Moore's youth, many local people played an instrument in their spare time, and the most local of these to James was Willie B. Thomas, born May 25, 1912, in Lobdell and raised on the same Bellmont Plantation. Thomas remembered working on the farm from age ten, scrapping, picking up sugarcane that had not been collected properly by the harvesters. A year after James Moore was born, Thomas's family moved across the river to a cotton farm in Zachary, and Willie was apparently injured when crushed by some furniture during the move, suffering a twisted back and other health problems. He said he learned to play kazoo as a teenager and the guitar and banjo in his twenties while working odd jobs as a caretaker, messenger, water boy for construction crews, and the like. In the 1930s and 1940s, he played at Saturday suppers and developed a repertoire of blues, spirituals, hillbilly, and popular songs. Working at the Ethyl Gas plant on Scenic Highway in 1947, just possibly alongside James Moore, who was certainly there in 1944, Willie Thomas said he "heard a voice calling" him to teach the gospel, and he spent many years working the streets as a singing preacher.

It is almost certain that James would have known Thomas but difficult to know whether Thomas was any kind of musical influence. What is clear, though, is that the two men shared some musical vocabulary. Thomas once said, "We had a string band, you know, guitars, fiddle, such as that. . . . we just called them blues and some of them breakdowns. . . . the achin' hearted blues is slow, breakdowns is fast. . . . This is the thing about it: we didn't know nothin' *but* blues. And we—we thought it was common."[50] Years later, James Moore talked about his music being played "commonly."

By the 1930s Willie Thomas had occasionally teamed up with a fiddle player, James Cage, known as "Butch," born on March 16, 1894, near Roxie in Franklin County, Mississippi, where his parents were sharecroppers. He said he picked up music from two local fiddle men, Frank Felters and Carol Williams, and said he had mastered the fiddle and the fife, both well-established instruments in the folk music of black Mississippians, by the time he was seventeen years old. "All of my folks was some sort of musician," he remembered. He recalled playing church songs, field songs, and popular songs at dances for both black and white gatherings. In 1927, after the great flood, Cage joined his brother in Zachary. He played music at local parties and events while by day he worked odd jobs on the farms, the railroads, and in the trash-collection service in Baton Rouge. He retired in 1960 from his day jobs, at a point when he and Willie Thomas had come to the attention of a local folklorist, Harry Oster, who described Cage as "a great representative of the now virtually extinct nineteenth century negro fiddle tradition."[51]

Far from celebrating Butch Cage or Willie B. Thomas's prowess with blues music, the local newspapers chronicled Thomas's regular brushes with the law. On May 9, 1940, the *Morning Advocate* said: "Negro stabbed in altercation: Willie B. Thomas, 24 year old [*sic*] negro of 130 Allen Street was being held by Police last night following an altercation with Crawford Griffith, 40 year old negro of 180 Allen Street in which the latter was stabbed. During an argument between the two men at 130 Allen Street, Thomas stabbed Griffith four or five times in the back. His condition is regarded as serious." Thomas was in court again on March 29, 1946, for being disorderly and was fined five dollars. He was back on July 12, 1947, for reckless driving and fined fifty dollars or thirty days. On January 22, 1951, there was an *Advocate* story about Willie B. Thomas, "tried and found guilty on a theft charge of an overcoat." He was sentenced to sixty days in the parish jail, but if he was preaching on the streets and in need of a warm coat, this may not have been too unwelcome.

Apart from the portion of West Baton Rouge Parish where James Moore came from and extending west of the Mississippi up through New Roads and Pointe Coupee Parish, the latter being the point at which explorer Pierre Le Moyne d'Iberville "cut off" his 1699 foray up the Mississippi River, the most abundant areas for folk and blues musicianship seem to have been those in east Baton Rouge north of the city through Scotlandville and stretching up Highways 61, 19, and 67 to Zachary, Slaughter, Jackson, and Clinton. To the southeast, down the Mississippi, there were also some musicians associated with the areas around Donaldsonville and Gonzales.

Another of the musical generation above James Moore was Herman E. Johnson, born in Zachary on August 18, 1909, according to his Army draft card. Johnson later talked about his early life, when "times was hard for a poor man," and about his conversion to the blues: "I had a good religious father, a good religious mother. They both was members of the Baptist church. I was the onliest jack of the family. I don't belong to any church. . . . So my life was just that way, to keep out of trouble, drink my little whiskey, an go and do little ugly things like that, but always on the cu-tee." When Johnson heard his first blues singers on records in the 1920s, he was sufficiently impressed by the likes of Blind Lemon Jefferson—"wasn't nobody could play the guitar like Lemon"—to try to follow suit. He took up the guitar, playing sometimes with the instrument flat on his knees, later remembering: "In 19 an' 27 I taken up the habit of playing the guitar. . . . I was raisin' cotton, plowin' the mule, and from that milkin' in milk dairies, from that driftin' on to larger cities, workin' on barge lines where there was ship docks, workin' at scrap metal companies . . . construction jobs, an' then we worked pourin' concrete and whatsoever other things was necessary. Sometime we would cut sugar cane in the winter months, such as we could to get a dollar. . . . Didn't have the education to afford a better job, so we had to use it manually and we worked through many hard trials. We endured many things we didn't want to endure, but that was our onliest way."[52] He could almost be describing James Moore's work experiences in his teens and twenties as well as his own.

Herman Johnson was living on Route 1 in rural Zachary when he received his Army call-up. His military questionnaire, dated October 24, 1940, indicated that he and his wife, Elizabeth, were living in Zachary and that he was employed at the chemical plant of the E. J. du Pont de Nemours Company. At some point, Johnson took a job at the Esso Refinery in Baton Rouge, which lasted for fifteen years. When he was let go, he became a janitor at Southern University but always rued the loss of his better-paying job. He may well have been the Herman Johnson of Route 4 Hooper Road who applied for a liquor license for Alma's Cafe and Bar at Route 1 New Hammond Highway in 1956. If so, his nightlife as a bluesman counted against him, as described by the parish clerk: "Application denied because the character and moral condition of the applicant is not sufficient for operating a beer and liquor establishment—March 4 1955, guilty of speeding fined $15; April 12 1955, guilty of drunk driving, having no driving license, carrying a concealed weapon, $50 or 30 days."[53]

Also from Zachary, and also of the generation above James Moore, was Robert Williams, known as "Pete" or "Robert Pete," born into a sharecropping family on March 14, 1914. He also later described to folklorists how he worked in the fields in Baker and then moved to Scotlandville, where he did farmwork before finding employment in a lumberyard in the mid-1930s. He liked to listen to records by Blind Lemon Jefferson and Peetie Wheatstraw, and at age eighteen he was inspired to make his own crude guitar out of a sugar box—"It didn't hold up so I bought an old guitar for $1.50 . . . an old box, strings about an inch from the neck."[54] When he was twenty-one, he bought a good guitar cheaply from a white woman whose son wouldn't play it—"White folks started having me to play at their parties. I got to rappin' good with the guitar. They used to call me [after] Peetie Wheatstraw because I could play all his tunes."

He said his older brother played piano and guitar and two sisters also played, but he honed his own style with instruction from two older guitarists, Frank and Robert Meddy, and later spoke about other local men, including Henry Gaines, Silas Hogan, his uncle Simon Carney, and Lacey Collins.

He also mentioned Solomon Bradd, Dan Jackson, Walker Green, and Willie Hudson as players he liked hearing locally, though he always confirmed, "but Blind Lemon Jefferson was my man," admiring his speed, flexibility, and range. Of the local players, apparently Carney, Bradd, and Jackson all played at times with a bottle or knife on the frets, making a slide sound, but their inspiration or their originality is not known. Neither is the style the Meddy brothers played, although Robert Pete recalled that they used both finger picking and slide approaches to their instruments.[55] Williams has described how he used to sing at house parties, all-night parties, and Saturday fish fries in the 1930s even though his wife, Ella, would become jealous. One night he found she had burned his guitar and his shoes so he couldn't go out. He married for the third time in 1948 and eventually had a dozen children. Musically, Williams seems to have changed his style in the 1940s, "when I see where I could find more notes on a guitar." In the 1950s, when folklorist Harry Oster first heard Robert Pete Williams, he felt he was an innovative artist, raw and spontaneous, "as close to pure folk tradition as anyone of his generation."[56] This spontaneity also extended to whether he would play at all. He later described how "during the '40s and '50s I used to practice for a month or two and then lay up my guitar for six months."

Robert Meddy was born in Louisiana around November 1878 and at the time of the 1900 census was farming in Bienville, some two hundred miles north of Baton Rouge. He possibly came originally from Boutte in St. Charles Parish just west of New Orleans but had moved into the Baton Rouge area at least by the 1920s. His brother Frank does not appear in publicly available records but was remembered clearly as the better musician by Silas Hogan, another protégé of the Meddys.

Born in Westover in west Baton Rouge on September 15, 1911, Silas Hogan was raised in Irene, north of the city. He described the family's twenty acres of cotton and potato land: "I had four brothers and sisters and we all had to work on the land. It had to be that way—we had no money to pay anybody." Hogan's father had a reputation as something of a musician in the local community: "My daddy played guitar, cross tuning and Spanish, and used a knife. Nobody could play much like that except the man that taught my father—

Frank Meddy. I don't know where he got the idea of using the knife; we didn't see too many people passing through." Robert and Frank Meddy were his uncles, and Hogan recalled that in the mid-1920s, aged about sixteen, he started to learn guitar from them. Hogan initially played along with church songs, "but I still preferred to play them blues. I used to kinda play the tune on the guitar as I was singing, used to play in cross note, because it sounded better that way. . . . the first things I learnt was things like 'When The Saints' and a [Simon Carney] song called 'Gambling Man.' . . . I used to play them old house parties. A dollar and a half was what you got. Start early and play all night. Course it wasn't electric then."[57] Hogan has recalled local musicians variously using stringed and wind instruments including homemade things like a jazzhorn, "a trumpet mouthpiece with cigarette paper stretched across." Some of the music he heard probably originated with the musicians he knew but, like most bluesmen starting out after the mid-1920s, he took much of his music from the Victrola or the jukebox. "I'd take them old records, Blind Lemon [Jefferson] and Kokomo [Arnold] records, and put 'em on. I learned a lot from them records."

In 1930 Hogan was working at a fruit farm in Independence, Louisiana, but returned to the Irene area. When Irene started to be covered by chemical factories, Hogan moved in 1939 to Scotlandville five miles nearer town, nowadays an integral part of Baton Rouge between the airport and Highway 61 near the river but then a less developed, wooded area with a down-home atmosphere. At the 1940 census he was living with his wife, Lubertha. In October 1940 he registered for Army service, and in March 1941 he was called up to begin a year's military training at Camp Shelby,[58] but he may not have gone because in January 1944 he was listed again among "the following named negroes selected for induction and report at the Municipal Auditorium in New Orleans."[59] In the early 1940s he took a job at the Esso Refinery, keeping it until his retirement in 1974. As the area first known as Scotland developed into the much more planned residential area of Scotlandville, gradually various venues appeared where Hogan and his friends could make their music on a regular if not exactly professional basis. He described how "there was clubs all over there, and downtown, back in the '50s. Used to play up in St. Francisville, Clinton, Jackson. . . . I would play [downtown] Friday on a street off north Acadian and also Saturday evening, 4 to 8 o' clock. Then go to Clinton and play from 9 to 1." Sundays were often spent playing at Parker's bar—"but a man got shot, killed. Scared a lot of people off, but we got em back."[60]

Hogan featured in one of the more bizarre court cases in Baton Rouge in February 1951. He had been in an auto accident, but before he could give evidence, the case got off to an unusually bad start due to a strange identity mix-up. The *Advocate* of February 21 reported: "A clerk in District Court this morning called the case of State v Elbert Thomas charged with operating a vehicle while under the influence of liquor and asked the defendant to come forward. A man came to the front and was told to sit down in the seat for defendants. Officers who investigated the case then testified that the truck driven by Thomas was in collision with a vehicle driven by Silas Hogan. Judge Holcombe asked the man in the defendants chair whether he wished to ask any questions. 'I don't have anything to do with this case,' the man replied. 'I'm a witness in another case and I just came up to ask the judge a question.'"

When he was around forty-five years old, in the mid-1950s, Silas Hogan formed his own regular band for the first time. His Rhythm Ramblers were Sylvester Buckley on harp, Jimmy Dotson on drums, and guitarist Isaiah Chattman. They played in Baton Rouge clubs at night, while Hogan maintained his day job at Esso Standard Oil Company and later took to wearing his hard hat on his music jobs as well as by day, a move that became his trademark in later years. They played in the city and at clubs in towns up to the Mississippi line, according to Dotson, who later described those days: "I was playing with Silas Hogan and the Rhythm Ramblers for about six years, we never did change musicians." This stability meant a solid understanding between the players, and Dotson said, "That was the Rhythm Ramblers' trademark, we would copy a record note for note."[61] If Silas Hogan had ever learned any kind of original, unrecorded style of playing from the Meddy brothers or others, it is clear that he had long since ditched that for the more commercial forms of blues heard on records.

One of the other local musicians Hogan became associated with in the 1950s was Arthur Kelley, born on November 14, 1921, in Clinton, some thirty miles above Baton Rouge.[62] One of a farming family of nine, Kelley said he was twelve before he saw his first guitar, in the hands of Arthur Gerald, his future brother-in-law, who came calling on one of Kelley's sisters. Another branch of the Gerald family lived next door to them. Kelley managed to persuade Gerald to give him some lessons, including how to splice broken strings together with hay wire, and eventually to give him the guitar. By age sixteen, Kelley was playing guitar in church, but "Mama and them wouldn't let me play no blues." By the time of the 1940 census, Arthur was listed as a farmer and the head of a family with a wife, Fannie, and two daughters living on Greenberg Road. When he was called to the Army registration office in 1942 at twenty-one years of age, he said he was employed by Conrad Hooge in Clinton. The Kelleys lived not far from Fritz Hooge, a German immigrant farmer, who presumably was related to Conrad.

A few years later, Arthur moved to Baker, the community just north of Scotlandville. According to Kelley, he had had enough of the farm life and he "just picked up and left." He was increasingly interested in the music he heard from other musicians, saying, "When I'd go in a beer joint and hear a record I'd go back home, take out my guitar and play it. . . . Everybody was either gambling or drinkin' or something else and I didn't want to do none of that so I just played guitar." He was influenced at first by the playing of a neighbor, Nance Williams, at house parties, but increasingly he liked Lightnin' Hopkins and said he bought an electric guitar in 1946 to better create a style based on Hopkins. This is probably so, but the date of 1946 is unlikely as Hopkins had barely started to make records. Hopkins's Gold Star label discs out of Houston in 1948 are more likely influences. Sometime in the early to mid-1950s, Kelley started working with Silas Hogan on rhythm guitar and a drummer who was added when Kelley saw another Hopkins devotee, Otis Hicks, playing in Hopkins's style with a drummer and another guitarist playing bass strings. Hicks was "the first man I saw that used a drummer and guitar player. I used to go around with [him], played while he rested."[63]

Another part-time bluesman with a big reputation in the local black community was harmonica player John W. Tilley, known as "Big Papa." A contemporary of James Moore, Tilley came from the Clinton area, and was born on July 11, 1924. He maintained a band for many years in the 1940s and 1950s. Their activities remained unrecognized in the press though the *Advocate* did report on July 12, 1947, that the District Court fined John Tilley fifty dollars or fifteen days in jail for disturbing the peace and resisting arrest. By then, Tilley had moved to Baton Rouge. In 1939 he was living with his wife, Ora, at 130 North Seventeenth Street and working at Guss Simonizing Shop. By 1942 he was a porter living on South Seventeenth, and in 1944 he had become an attendant at Florida Street Service Station. After the war, he moved to North Twenty-Third Street and worked as a driver for Dunbar Taxi Service. He became a laborer living on Zion Street by 1950 and married again, to a woman named Bessie. By 1956 they were at Valley Street, east of downtown and some three miles south from James Moore. Tilley listed himself then in the city directory as a "musician, Big Papa and his Country Boys." Tilley's band featured an ever-changing lineup of young and unknown musicians.

As a youngster in the mid-1950s, budding guitarist Philip Guy often watched his older brother playing with Papa: "Big Papa was a big guy in weight, about 350 pounds. He wasn't known, he was just a local, [but] that's who started Buddy [Guy] off playing with the bands. Big Papa was a harmonica player; he used to play one and play [another] one through his nose and stuff like that. . . . He was a nice easy old chap to be around, a jolly guy. He liked to dance and talk and do music and he would never be late on a gig. He had a big old Oldsmobile and he would put everything in that. . . . he was the only guy that I knew who was getting the blues guys together around there at that time."[64]

Apparently Papa's band based its style on recent and current songs by the likes of Howlin' Wolf, B. B. King, John Lee Hooker, Muddy Waters, and Lightnin' Hopkins. In the 1950s, Papa played most regularly at a place called the Rockhouse in Innis, way out in the country some forty-five miles north of Port Allen. It is not clear when he first ventured into Baton Rouge to play music or whether he knew James Moore back in the 1940s. As a harmonica player himself, Big Papa would not likely have had occasion to use James in his band. However, they certainly knew each other well by the late 1950s, when Tilley passed some of his musicians over to James. One of them remembered Papa having a regular spot at the Alligator Bar on Perkins Road in Baton Rouge.[65]

There is virtually no testimony about which, if any, of the older generation of musicians were known to James Moore in the late 1940s and into the early 1950s. It is very likely that he knew Willie Thomas, Arthur Kelley, and Silas Hogan in the 1940s, and on that basis he probably knew most of the others as well, and indeed probably spent some time playing in jam sessions at parties and barrooms in both west and east Baton Rouge and up through Scotland-ville and Zachary. After leaving Mary Street in 1944, James had traded in his work at Ethyl, first for life on the longshore in New Orleans and then for life as a general builder back in Baton Rouge, and by the close of the 1940s it seems that he was more focused on making a living in construction work than as a musician.

MS. LOVELL

While working on construction projects at the end of the 1940s, James Moore met the woman who would become his life partner and help him manage his transformation from part-time musician to touring performer and song-writer. She was Lovell Jones, born on May 7, 1924, on Bayou Goula Road in Dorseyville, near White Castle, some thirty miles and five bends of the Mississippi south of Port Allen. Lovell was the daughter of laborer Job Jones, known as "Shine," and Edna Henderson, one of their eight children. Lovell was the same age as James, but she already had two children, William and Betty Ann, from an earlier marriage to William James Gambler. By 1950, she was living in Baton Rouge at 906 North Thirty-Sixth Street with her mother and working as a cook at the Blue Jay Sandwich Shop at 434 Louisiana Avenue, a mile or two downtown.[66] Her son, William Gambler, was born in Independence, Louisiana, in 1942. He remembers: "I was nine years old [in 1951] when my mother met James. We were living on Thirty-Sixth Street in Baton Rouge, where I was with my mother and grandmother. Apparently, so she said to me, my mother was going to work one day and James was doing roofing work on a church on Acadian Thruway which was on her route. He spoke to her while she was waiting for a bus. Several days in a row he would speak with her and they established a rapport. He made a pass at her, I guess, and that's how they met."[67]

Lovell told a little more of the story to Johnny Palazzotto, emphasizing her religious upbringing. "James kept asking me to meet him, to go out, and I said 'no.' He asked me to meet him at a club, a nightclub. Well, I wasn't that sort of person. I did agree to go, but I didn't go, I couldn't. Next day, he asks me why, and continued asking, and eventually, well, I did go to meet him, I went along with it."[68]

Lovell's mother, Edna, was listed in city directories as a laundress, resident at 906 North Thirty-Sixth Street through the early 1950s. Lovell spoke about those days forty years later, remembering a move at age fourteen from Dorseyville to Donaldsonville with her mother and then another move to Baton Rouge: "When we moved here my mother had to find a job because I was the youngest of eight kids. Baton Rouge was just like the country then, no paved streets, just mud and gravel where we were. I got my first job as a dishwasher, but I didn't know anything about [city] work because before that we were living out on a farm."[69] In Lovell's own accounts she often gave 1948 or 1949 as the year she met James, when William would have been six rather than nine years old, and it could be that William was not aware of James until James moved into their house a little later, probably in 1951. North Thirty-Sixth Street was a couple of miles east of downtown Baton Rouge, and James is first listed as resident there living with Lovell in 1951, as "Jas I. Moore," a laborer at Michelli's Esso Servicenter. Michelli's was owned by W. J. Babin and known locally for its successful ten-pin bowling team as well as its service to vehicle owners.

The 1951 directory was apparently the only place where James was accorded a middle initial or referred to in any manner that might reflect his original given name of Isiah. In later years, a different middle initial of "H" was included when his song copyrights were registered with Broadcast Music Inc., and this was quoted by Lovell's solicitor after James died. Later still, one writer described his middle name as Isaac, and this has been erroneously used by several subsequent writers and spread around the Internet. The fact is that none of his personal certification includes a middle name at all, and William Gambler doesn't recall James ever using one. Strangely, in 1952 James was shown as still working for Michelli but living at 1262 North Thirty-Sixth Street while the house at 906 North Thirty-Sixth showed "Lovel" living with "Gamble, Jas." This was probably a data-collection error that assumed James had the same surname as Lovell. Thereafter, the city directories listed James as a laborer with the J. M. King Company, a construction firm handling medium-sized jobs. In the early to mid-1950s, King built the concrete radio tower of WLCS on Groom Road, extensions to schools and hospitals, improvements to Goudchaux's Store on Main Street, and a number of churches, including the Weller Baptist Church on Prescott Road on a contract worth a quarter of a million dollars in 1952. By then, Lovell was working at Howard's Café on North Twenty-First Street and riding the bus to work just as she had when she and James first met.

Because of the relative lack of bus services to the black community in the 1940s, by the end of that decade, independent black-owned buses were being operated around the city, buses that acquired such colorful names as the Jelly Bean or the Blue Goose Bus. Early in 1950, however, the operation of private buses was declared illegal in Baton Rouge, and at the same time city bus fares were raised from ten to fifteen cents. This did not much impress the Reverend Theodore Jemison, who had arrived in Baton Rouge from Selma, Alabama, to become pastor of Mt. Zion Baptist Church in 1949. As a leader in the black community, he approached the City Council in February 1953 to point out that black people had to stand in the overcrowded back of the buses while there were usually empty seats in the white section further forward. He said later, "I watched women who had cooked and cleaned in houses of white folks all day having to stand up on the long ride back home." Others supported him. Willis Reed, who had owned the black newspaper the *Baton Rouge Post* in the late 1930s, said "what led me to get involved . . . were the attitudes of the policemen and the attitudes of bus drivers. They were very uncourteous to people, they talked to them as if they were unhuman."[70]

In response to Jemison and his followers, at the end of February 1953 the City Council approved an ordinance stating that black people could fill up the bus from the back to the front, and white people could fill the bus from front to back based on a first-come, first-served basis. In the main, this was ignored by bus drivers until they were ordered in June to comply. Reverend Jemison tested the law by taking a front seat on June 13, and the next day two bus drivers were suspended for noncompliance. On June 15 the bus drivers briefly went on strike, but by the time they returned, Jemison and the United Defense League had organized a boycott of city-run buses and set up a free-ride system provided by members of the black community and supported by collections to purchase gasoline for their carpool. A mass meeting took place at the Municipal Auditorium, and by June 24 a new ordinance was passed allowing all people to sit anywhere on buses apart from two rows at the front and back reserved for white and black people respectively. It was a compromise, but it was a significant improvement, and it pointed a way forward. Although the Baton Rouge boycott lasted for only eight days, it did bring Martin Luther King Jr. to visit Reverend Jemison, and he was able to take away a blueprint for future use. Historian Douglas Brinkley noted that all of the people in Montgomery studied Baton Rouge: "It became their case study. What did the people of Baton Rouge do right? What did they do wrong? Rosa Parks told me how important it was, what went on in Baton Rouge. In her NAACP office in Montgomery, they were monitoring what was happening there, daily."[71] On a more local level, Eddie Johnson, later a community leader but then a thirteen-year-old on a bus, remembered:

> Segregation was a part of life at the time. You didn't like it, you knew that, but you try to overcome it. You knew you had to be better to get certain jobs. So we prepared ourselves to be better. It was just that some of the community leaders thought that it was time that we were able to sit anywhere on the bus, so that's what led to the bus boycott. At the time, Churches were the main source of communication and that's where we basically heard it from. I remember the community coming together, pulling their financial resources to finance the boycott. So the whole community was behind the bus boycott. I think it was a hundred-percent

involvement with the city and with the community. Nobody rode the bus. There were many, many conflicts as we were growing up. That was during the era of segregation. After high school, we [African Americans] did the manual labor whereas the students of the other race had jobs as clerks and secretaries in the department stores. We did janitorial work, construction work that kind of thing. Of course promotions, you weren't promoted, because of your race. There were certain things that we knew, there were places we couldn't go, things that we couldn't do because of our color.[72]

Maxine Crump was a young girl in Maringouin outside of Baton Rouge at the time of the boycott, who later moved to the city and made her name as a pioneering black broadcaster. She later described "growing up in a town where the police are white, everyone of any position was white. The mail carrier is white, the postal workers were white, the store owners were white. Everybody was white but the undertaker because whites didn't want to handle black bodies, and the nightclub owners, because they did not want to socialize with them. Other than that . . . and the hairdressers were black because they didn't want to do our hair. That's it. You could only have the jobs they didn't want."[73] As James Moore said in one of his very few interviews, when he sang the blues he could tell of the hard times he'd had, "the things I'll never forget."[74]

All the while, though, there was music to brighten his day and the desire to play nagged inside him, and it's unlikely James would have forgotten the big blues event of 1952 when a harmonica player, "Little Walter," Marion Jacobs from Marksville, Louisiana, but now living in Chicago, hit the R&B charts with his swinging instrumental tune "Juke" and kept it there for over five months, staying at number 1 for two months. Jacobs was six years younger than James but had spent years traveling to New Orleans, Memphis, and eventually Chicago, before hooking up with Muddy Waters and helping define the Chicago blues. Though he never listed Walter as an influence, it seems likely that James spent a good part of the early 1950s playing that song and wondering whether Ms. Lovell would mind him going out just one more night to demonstrate his prowess on the harp somewhere where musicians gathered.

Just exactly what James's prowess was, and what his style was, in the early 1950s we'll probably never know. It is clear that other musicians remember him first and foremost as a harmonica player in the days before he started making records. At some point, he even took on a name that indicated he had some degree of proficiency on the instrument. Lovell always told interviewers that James "used to be as skinny as a rail, so . . . we called him Slim. He used the name 'Harmonica Slim' at the time."[75] But who influenced his harmonica method? The most popular blues harp players in the 1940s were John Lee Williamson from Tennessee, who recorded as "Sonny Boy" Williamson, and Jazz Gillum from Mississippi, both of whom moved to Chicago and made regular and sometimes popular discs there for RCA/Bluebird. When Little Walter threw down a new level of challenge to blues harp men in the early 1950s, Walter nevertheless said, "On the harp, well, I heard them all, and I give Sonny Boy Williamson the credit as a creator. I was crazy about his records. He had a true balance. He was the only man I really admired, but I didn't model myself on him."[76]

Jazz Gillum's influence, and his high notes, appeared in the music of another Mississippi musician who had moved north during the early 1950s—Jimmy Reed, a man from the same town as Gillum. Reed is often seen as "a pivotal overall influence" on the man who was just starting to ply his trade as Harmonica Slim.[77] And then there's the "Louisiana factor," the French Cajun or Creole influence. Speaking of Little Walter, Mississippi bluesman David Edwards, known as "Honeyboy," noticed the slightly different element in his early harp playing: "[Walter] had that Cajunly sound on harmonica, like a pushbox (accordion)."[78] If Harmonica Slim already had this inflection, too, which he certainly did later on, then the local popularity of recordings such as Nathan Abshire's "Pine Grove Blues" from 1950 may have had some relevance. In truth, though, the fully fledged style Slim would later display is as close to being his own as anyone else's. Like most musicians, he would say, when asked later, that he didn't follow anyone's style, but he did say that when he played someone else's tunes he would try to replicate their style faithfully.

In 1954, someone named James Moore appeared in the local press three times in unfavorable circumstances. There were at least six black people living in the Baton Rouge area with the name of James Moore that year, and in the absence of addresses in the court records, it is anybody's guess whether our James Moore was responsible for any of the following misdemeanors. On May 11, 1954, fined in the City Court $15 or ten days for being disorderly; on May 27, 1954, subject of a personal suit filed by a William Armstrong for auto damages totaling $154; and on June 8, 1954, sentenced by Judge Coleman

Lindsay to serve ninety days for aggravated assault on Willie Scott of Zachary with a pocketknife. William Gambler is sure the latter was not his stepfather. "No, it was definitely not him. No. There was another man named James Moore who lived near us. He was kinda rowdy." It was probably the other James Moore who got sixty days or a $100 fine for another aggravated assault on May 18 two years later.[79]

Through most of the 1950s, James was better known on the 900 block of North Thirty-Sixth Street as a family man rather than as a harp blower. Lovell's mother, Edna, had become ill and moved to her sister's house in Dorseyville in 1954 before she died, leaving James and Lovell, William, and Betty Ann in Baton Rouge. William Gambler remembers the early years when James moved to Thirty-Sixth Street with Lovell: "It was my grandmother's house actually, where we lived. Slim came there when I was about nine years old, in third grade [in 1951]. In those days, I just accepted him as a man, and as one my mother liked. He was a nice person, you know. He was friendly. Matter of fact, he and I had a good relationship. I didn't know anything about him playing music at that time. He mainly worked construction, and also he was always interested in engines and so on, and working on them was one of his skills." William was less clear about his sister's attitude to her stepfather: "I guess she and James got on OK. Betty was a little different than me, though. I was easier to get along with! And she never knew our real father. He worked at sharecropping, whatever. I was about two when he left and that was right after Betty was born. She was a baby. I was in the Air Force when I ever heard any more about him. He didn't want to know us. So James was the only father we knew."[80]

Gambler described how Moore would stay close to his own family across the river, too. "He would go all the time to his sisters and nephews, to visit them at Mulatto Bend. Slim had a normal relationship with his sisters, you know, like families do. He didn't have any favorites. He'd take us over there sometimes. I remember when we first knew him, he took our family over the river to his family's side on a picnic. There were no proper picnic grounds we could go to back then, so Slim parked under the old trestle bridge there for shade, and we had a fine picnic then. I spent the night over there a couple of times. Slim's mother Pearline, she was just like a grandmother to me." Gambler was a little more circumspect in talking about Slim's sisters. By the time the Gamblers were visiting the Moores with James in the mid-1950s, Lillie, married to Dan Collins, had gained a son-in-law, Henry Collins, from Dan's earlier marriage and a foster-son, Ray Anthony Moore. Ray was born in 1952 to James's sister Doris, who already had another son, Otis Kelly, born in 1946, and would have a third son, Herbert, in 1956. Gambler explained, "Ray is Doris's son, but Lillie raised him. Doris was a little—well, she used to 'enjoy' life a little bit, we'll say. She was married but she lived with her mother when I knew them. Lillie, who raised Doris's son, she enjoyed life too. Dan Collins had a job over there but I don't know what they all did." Gambler had even less contact with Matilda Moore: "I only ever met James's other sister, Tillie, once or twice. She was not around so much."[81] According to Mulatto Bend resident Arlene Batiste, James's nephew, Otis Kelly, is her first cousin: "His father is my uncle, Marshall Collins, my mom Annie's brother. He is right here in Mulatto Bend, but he don't say much to nobody."[82]

Although Otis has been reluctant to talk about those days, another of James's nephews, Ray Moore, remembered them clearly: "I lived at 4255 Mulatto Bend Road, Port Allen. Doris Moore was my mother and Lillie Collins was her sister and they lived next door to each other. The two houses was about six feet or so apart from each other. My Aunt Lillie and Uncle Dan had an extra bedroom, so one day while in first grade I spent the night with them, they spoil me and I stay there until I finish college." These houses were almost next to St. John Baptist Church in Mulatto Bend, and they were the same ones occupied by Clyde and Pearline Moore and Dan and Lillie Collins at the time of the 1940 census. Otis Kelly still lives on Mulatto Bend Road today, next to the now-vacant lot where James Moore lived as a youngster.

Ray Moore remembered his visits as a child to his uncle's house across the river in Baton Rouge: "[During the 1950s] uncle James and aunt Lovell would come over seems like at least once a week. I would go and spend the weekend with them from time to time throughout my childhood. My younger brother Herbert would come sometime too, and my older brother Otis would come sometime too. They would take us to the movies from time to time. I loved staying with them on weekends, and they would bring us back home on Sunday night so we could go to school on Monday. This was on North Thirty-Sixth Street in the old house, the old wooden shotgun house. Later in my childhood they build a new house there and knock the wooden one down."[83]

William Gambler described the house on North Thirty-Sixth Street as "a little raised-frame shotgun house" with a double fireplace with one chimney facing two rooms. It was hot in summer and cold in winter, and there was no indoor bathroom. He told local journalist Ruth Laney, "At night, we used chamber pots. When James moved in, my grandmother, my mom, me and Betty and two older cousins lived there. All three rooms were used as bedrooms." Grandma Edna did most of the cooking while James and Lovell were working. A neighbor, "Miss Bert across the street, was the neighborhood security; she'd say, 'all right William, don't do that, I'm gone tell.' We lived between two families who were mentally disturbed. Mr. Gray would throw water at us and we'd throw rocks at him. The same the other side."[84]

Apart from his two families, after a while it became clear to Lovell, William, and Betty Gambler that James had this other love, too. William said, "When I first realized James played music, I guess in the early '50s, he played very occasionally. Harp only. He would play locally, basically just in small juke joints, clubs, between Thursday to Saturday. He just picked up with other bands." Lovell, too, has described James's early faltering attempts to become a musician. "He could play guitar before I met him, and he could also play the harmonica at the same time. He was self taught. Before James started making records, he used to go to all the clubs, you know, and he started to sit in with different musicians. That's how he got started, because he liked music." Lovell was quick to point out, though, that "he was still working regularly, you know, regular jobs, like construction, hauling sugarcane."[85]

We'll probably never know which bands and musicians James Moore picked up with in the ten or so years before he started making records, or exactly when he started using the name "Harmonica Slim." Of his music activities in the early 1950s, his stepson remembers: "Well, he would only play in town and around. He was just a sideman then, at first. He'd go out to Baker and maybe as far as Zachary. He knew all the musicians from everywhere." From what other people have said and implied, it is fairly certain that by the mid-1950s he had played with local blues and R&B musicians Silas Hogan, Willie Thomas, Arthur Kelley, Herman Johnson, Clarence Edwards, John Tilley, and possibly Robert Pete Williams, Butch Cage, "Schoolboy" Cleveland White, and others. There must have been several other now-forgotten players living very close to the Moores with whom he would have honed his skills at local joints and house parties. The one person James himself confirmed he knew in the early days, and who in turn has spoken about playing with James, was singer, guitarist, songwriter, and ex-convict Otis Hicks, who came to Baton Rouge sometime after 1948 and who became known as Lightning Slim in 1954. Years later, James talked about his early amateur days, saying,

"I ran across a guitar player called Lightning Slim and we worked all those parties together." More precisely, he told interviewer Sue Cassidy Clark, "I met Lightning Slim who was recording in Crowley. He was doing a gig at a little place called The Lucky Mule, and I went up and talked to him, and told him I was interested, and he carried me over to Crowley."[86]

LIGHTNING STRIKES

Although he told some interviewers he came from St. Louis, Otis Verries Hicks was apparently born in Good Pine, Louisiana, on March 13, 1913, some eighty-five miles north of Baton Rouge. He was raised with his stepparents, Clyde and Savannah Floyd, in Bienville, a further seventy-five miles northwest toward Shreveport and the Texas border. He was there at age seven when the 1920 census was taken, as was his older brother, Layfield Bo Hicks. They may have lived with relatives in St. Louis for a time, but at some point, probably in the late 1920s, the family moved to St. Francisville, a small town that hugged the east side of the Mississippi some twenty-five miles north of Baton Rouge up Highway 61.[87] There, Otis said, he began his working life as a field hand. He said that he was fascinated by the songs some of the laborers sang, and which it seemed to him were sometimes composed spontaneously. He said that he would occasionally "borrow" a guitar from someone and take off to the riverbank to try to play and sing while fishing.[88] He said, years later, "I went as far as the tenth grade and my father died so I had to quit school and go to work to help the family. Before my daddy died, he taught me what he knew on guitar. He showed me where my fingers should be to make chords. I'd take that old guitar with me fishing and set under a tree and play it all day. At the time I listened to Lonnie Johnson, Blind Lemon Jefferson, and Ma Rainey. My folks got the records and I listened to them. They made me want to play music too. My biggest influence on guitar would be Blind Lemon Jefferson."[89]

Further details of his early life are sparse and sometimes contradictory, but it seems that his brother Layfield moved back to Bienville in the 1930s and Otis was then in charge of his two other siblings and running their farm near St. Francisville. He said, "I growed cotton, corn, sweet potatoes. I wasn't wanting for anything but the sun to go down so I could knock off."[90] Then, sometime in the late 1930s, Otis got into some trouble and was sent to the Louisiana State Penitentiary at Angola Farm near St. Francisville for, he said, ten years. Certainly, he was there at the time of the 1940 US Census and still on October 25, 1941, when the US Army's local Recruitment Board Number 3 had him fill in his questionnaire about availability for war service. Hicks gave his home mailing address as Route 4, East Baton Rouge Parish, and his occupation as a laborer. The penitentiary officials confirmed his unavailability for service.

It is not known exactly when Hicks returned from Angola—he gave differing accounts suggesting both 1946 and 1948—but it seems that it was only then that he learned to play guitar properly, being taught in part by his brother, who had returned from Army service. He enjoyed playing informally at country suppers and house parties and said he learned his first songs when he sat in with local players such as guitarist "Left Hand" Charlie or a harmonica player from Clinton named Monro Doddy.[91] Soon Hicks took a job at a fertilizer plant near Baton Rouge, but he enjoyed far more the opportunity to listen and play at the many small bars and clubs around the area. He remembered, "There was a lot of music going on there and I got interested in it. So I learned to play pretty good and me and a friend got together and went down to a little town called Gonzales, it was just me and him on drums. That old boy owned an electric guitar besides his drums so I played it sometimes. We played house parties and dances for two years."[92] The "old boy" Hicks mentioned may have been drummer Robert Murray, who also played informal gigs with other local men, including "Guitar" Taylor, "Schoolboy" Cleve, and James Moore. Then Otis Hicks acquired his own electric guitar and started playing more seriously, at first sitting in with groups organized by Papa John Tilley at places such as Johnny's Cafe at 1219 East Boulevard and other venues around Baton Rouge. It was in these clubs that musicians like Hicks started to make their own interpretation of the electric-guitar blues sounds being recorded in Texas by Lightnin' Hopkins, in Detroit by John Lee Hooker, and in Chicago by Muddy Waters and Jimmy Reed.

In 1952 the entertainment trade paper *Billboard* noted the increase in southern-styled blues being issued by northern and West Coast record companies like Chess and Modern, saying, "A wide gulf sometimes existed between the sophisticated-type city blues and good-rocking novelties waxed for the northern market, and the country or delta blues that were popular in the South." Gradually the two forms intermingled, and "some exclusively country artists have achieved popularity of late, including Howlin' Wolf, B. B. King, Muddy Waters and others."[93] Otis Hicks and others started focusing on guitar and harmonica leads backed by a languid and muted drumbeat, a style that would eventually become known as the swamp-blues.[94] Teenaged Buddy Guy had a glimpse of the future, he said in his autobiography, sometime around the spring of 1950 at Artigo's General Store up in Lettsworth when a skinny man got out of a car with a guitar and a black box. He asked the skinny man about the box and was told, "When this here electrical guitar starts to buzzing, folks gonna be flying in here like bees to honey."[95] He set up his amplifier in the store and, sure enough, soon drew a crowd for his blues playing. Then he packed up and lit out of town like the Lone Ranger. In Guy's memory it was Lightning Slim, but in reality it was Otis Hicks, still four years shy of a record deal and a catchy name.

By 1954, Otis Hicks was known to work with John Tilley's group off and on, and it was probably Papa Tilley's Country Boys that Hicks was playing with when the opportunity arose for them to audition at a local radio station with a view to getting onto records. The man responsible was a black disc jockey on a new radio station, Ray Meaders of WXOK, Baton Rouge.

Ray Charles Meaders was a twenty-nine-year-old from Mississippi when he joined WXOK from WMPA, Aberdeen, Mississippi, where he had worked as Ray "Blues Boy" Meaders. He had started an R&B program there called *Red Hot and Blue*, though it is not clear whether his show copied or predated the famous program of the same name by WHBQ Memphis disc jockey Dewey Phillips, the man who later broke Elvis Presley's first record. There was a movie of the same title starring Betty Hutton and Victor Mature in the cinemas late in 1949, and this might have inspired either or both announcers in the naming of their shows.[96]

On February 15, 1953, the *Advocate* carried a big advertisement for the opening of radio station WXOK: "A new sound is born tomorrow—WXOK 1260—many solid hours of good listening . . . jive, hillbilly, spirituals, folk, pop . . . the music the people of Baton Rouge told us they prefer." The station was to feature a range of music and a cast of "personality" announcers, disc jockeys with names like "Diggy Doo" Meaders, "Cornpone" Bishop, "Golden Boy" Griffith, and "Buzzy Fuzz" Lynch. The station was one of four owned by Jules Paglin, who opened WBOK in New Orleans in 1950 and followed with OK stations in Lake Charles, Louisiana, and Houston as well as in Baton Rouge, adding WLOK in Memphis to the chain in 1956. The stations were all geared to providing wall-to-wall music between the hourly news updates and to garnering as much locally based advertising as possible aimed at specific audiences. Paglin was interviewed after WXOK had been running for a year and a half, and he confirmed, "Hillbilly music and jive draw more mail than any other kind." An *Advocate* feature on October 10, 1954, titled "WXOK: Backbeat Boogie and Barnyard Bop," confirmed this focused approach—"There's a western twang from the announcers of folk music and the negro discman Diggie Doo will soon have a female counterpart to run a religious show for negro housewives." It confirmed that Meaders played "a solid two and a half hours of jive, blues and what-not, straying occasionally into popular music but never, never using a script, whatever comes up. Like the hillbilly jockeys, Meaders takes it out of the mailbag and off the top of his head, saying between records whatever comes to mind."

Diggie Doo Meaders was popular immediately, and as early as January 1954 the *Morning Advocate* was running big ads for "The Town's Top Jive Man . . . sponsored by Sun Gold Wine." Meaders was on from seven to eight in the morning and again between two and five in the afternoons, sponsored by Budweiser—"Be A Buddy, Drink Bud." His shows intermingled with the gospel show *Stars of Faith* and the country shows *Hillbilly House Party* and *Barnyard Frolic*. WXOK was up against WIBR's show *Blues and Jive* in the afternoons and their *Platter Party* in the mornings. There were also three larger stations in Baton Rouge with affiliations to the main national networks: WJBO had local news and advice programs and pop music fed from NBC, while WCLS took popular music and theater from ABC, and WAFB ran news, hillbilly, and pop music as part of the Mutual network. Although WXOK was not a black-only station like WDIA in Memphis or WERD in Atlanta, it nevertheless quickly became the station of the majority of black radio listeners in Baton Rouge.

If James Moore was inspired as much by recorded music he heard on the radio as he was by local musicians, it's likely that he was one of many devoted listeners to Diggie Doo. Then, one day in the spring of 1954, he would have heard Diggie play a deeply impressive blues record titled "Bad Luck," made by an artist named Lightning Slim on the Feature Records label out of Crowley along Highway 90. He would quickly have realized, if he didn't know already, that this was none other than locally based musician Otis Hicks. On the back of his first disc, Hicks soon decided to make music his main occupation, booking himself out as "Lightning Slim" from 1954, changing to "Lightnin' Slim" a few years later. The money he made apparently came at a good time because Hicks made his debut in the District Court default reports of the *Advocate* on July 2, 1954, when he was sued by Parliament Loan Corporation, a payday loan company also called Asco Loans, operating at 237 Main Street. At some point, James and Otis met, but quite when is not known. Lovell said James knew Hicks "before he met me. I think he met him at a club across the river in Mulatto Bend,"[97] and she has quoted 1948 as a possible date. Her son William thinks that it was some time after Hicks started to make records in 1954.

Irrespective of when they met, William Gambler remembers how "James started to play more frequently after he met Lightning Slim," and he was certainly playing jam sessions and some regular gigs with Lightning by 1956. Lightning said, "Harpo, me and a drummer teamed up in Baton Rouge. We'd just play for friends at a birthday party or wedding or something like that. We never really made any money at it; we had a lot of fun. I taught him how to play music. In fact I gave him his first set of instruments to play with. He could play one number and that was 'Blue Suede Shoes.'"[98] If that's true, then their early collaborations must be dated to 1956 because Carl Perkins's song was a hit in the first half of that year, crossing over from the country and popular charts to the R&B chart as well. Lightning referred to his meeting James in several interviews, saying: "[James] played harmonica with me a while. When I met him he could only blow one little tune, 'Blue Suede Shoes.' I'd let him play it kinda fast, then let him walk around a while, then when he came back he'd blow it slow, blues style. He was doing construction work [then]."[99] In another interview Hicks said James played the tune slowly at first, left the bandstand for a while, and then came back playing it fast. Either way, unless Hicks has quoted the wrong song in all his several tellings, it seems that James Moore did not play with him in any kind of formal sense until 1956. The other interpretation could be that, even though he said James could only "blow" one tune, perhaps Lightning was referring not to his harmonica playing but to a new desire James had to sing or to play guitar. In that case, it makes sense that his early steps as a vocalist could have come in 1956, and that the instruments Lightning said he gave James were guitars.

What is very clear is that James Moore took his harmonica playing seriously and had collected a number of different instruments for his use as Harmonica Slim. This obviously did not go unnoticed in his local community, and on October 20, 1956, the *State-Times* ran this report: "Eight harmonicas are reported stolen here: An apparently musically inclined thief yesterday took eight harmonicas, valued at $18, from the front seat of an auto parked in the driveway of the residence of James Moore, 906 North 36 Street. According to police, Moore reported the theft and said the thief broke a window from the auto in order to get the harmonicas." The reporter made no connection with Harmonica Slim, his career having only just begun.

The loss of harmonicas was as nothing compared to the travails of another Baton Rouge musician. Robert Pete Williams was tried for murder. The *State-Times* reported on February 29, 1956: "Baton Rouge murder trial begins: Robert 'Pete' Williams went on trial for his life today in the pistol slaying of another local man, last December 17. . . . Williams, 41, of Blount Road is accused of murdering Alonzo Spurlock, 49 of North 36 Street in the barroom of Bradley's Grocery at Baker Road following an argument between the pair. . . . Dr Chester Williams, parish coroner, said cause of death was two .45 caliber bullet wounds in the chest and abdomen."

Years later, Robert Pete told a different version: "See, I didn't get into trouble on my own. I got in trouble by a smart guy that taken me for the wrong man. . . . This fella, Jackie Lee . . . he came up to where we was sitting, my sister and brother and me, and he cursed at me . . . and I saw that he meant to kill me. So the first time I shot him in the stomach. He kept coming, and the next shot hit him in the heart. So I just beat him up to the draw. And that's how I was misused, 'cause I was sent to prison all for the sake of that one I referred to was paid to go against me."[100]

On March 2 the headline read: "Robert 'Pete' Williams was saved from the electric chair last night when a 12 man jury found him guilty of murder without capital punishment. The verdict shortly after 8 pm, followed some four hours of deliberation by jurors to climax a two day trial. Williams, father of seven, now faces a life sentence in the state penitentiary. Judge Holcombe commented: 'I thoroughly agree with this verdict. This man was certainly guilty.'" Interestingly, the front page of the *Morning Advocate* on the day of the verdict carried a large photograph of the trial in progress and a story that was less focused on Williams's fate than it was on groundbreaking legal process. The caption read: "Local murder trial: these sixteen millimeter motion picture photographs of a murder trial were taken by a WBRZ cameraman yesterday after district judge Holcombe granted permission for pictures to be taken on an experimental basis only. They are the first photographs ever to be taken at a local trial. The pictures were taken from a telephoto lens from the rear of Division A courtroom. The trial was that of Robert Pete Williams."

Just as Robert Pete was on his way to the pen at Angola, a former inmate there was on the up. By the end of 1956, Lightnin' Slim had already seen seven

records issued and used several different harmonica players at his recording
sessions, including "Schoolboy Cleve" White and Henry Clement. To promote
his records, Lightnin' Slim took to the road in the local area and at some point
started taking James Moore with him as Harmonica Slim. By the time of his
next recording sessions in 1956 and 1957, Lightnin' had decided that James
Moore was more reliable as an accompanist than the other harp players, and
so it was that Harmonica Slim started to go along with Lightnin' Slim to the
recording studio of J. D. Miller in Crowley.

2. SWAMP RECORDS AND RADIO SALES

Jay Miller: The Swamp Records Man | Ernie Young: Excello Records and
Nashville Radio Selling | Miller Style

JAY MILLER: THE SWAMP RECORDS MAN

In Crowley, some eighty miles west along the highway from Baton Rouge, the former country and Cajun musician and currently successful songwriter, Jay Miller, was starting to widen his search for musical talent. He was recording musicians for his own Feature Records label and for Excello Records in Nashville, where he had a production deal.

Joseph Delton Miller, known as Jay or J.D., was born in Iota, Louisiana, on May 5, 1921. He was the son of Leo Miller, a shipping clerk in a rice mill whose work took the family variously to El Campo, Texas, back to Iota, and then to Lake Charles, Louisiana, in 1933. There Jay took to studying his new Gene Autry songbook and guitar, and he was soon able to play folk songs. He said, "One of my first attempts at playing in public was when my parents entered me in a local ice-cream company's talent contest," and this led to his own radio spot every Saturday on KPLC in Lake Charles, where "my repertoire was mostly cowboy songs or what would come to be called Country and Western."[1]

In 1937 the Miller family moved to Crowley, the center of Louisiana's rice production, which hyperbolically marketed itself as the "rice capital of the world." Miller became fascinated with the local bands playing a mix of western jazz and folk and Cajun music. Miller remembered playing with the Breaux Brothers band at a remote dance hall in Kaplan where there was no electricity—"I'd never seen an accordion before," he admitted. "When [Amidie Breaux] pulled that thing out of the box, I didn't know what I'd gotten into!"

Soon he formed a band with his brother-in-law, confirming, "That's how I really got started. We called ourselves the Musical Aces. Then I joined a band called the Daylight Creepers. Later on I played with the Four Aces, and also Harry Choates."[2] Miller said his next influence was the western swing of Cliff Bruner and the Texas Wanderers, who were on local radio every day and whose spot he took when the popular band moved back to Texas. After the war, Miller married Georgia Sonnier, the daughter of Livaudais "Lee" Sonnier, a fine exponent of the local Cajun accordion style. Miller soon went into business with Sonnier, remembering, "When I came out of the service, I think it was 1946, I went into electrical contracting. My wife and I cashed $500 worth of savings bonds, at that time they were known as war bonds. And the building I leased in Crowley was $150 a month."[3] Miller told John Broven, "My father in law, Lee Sonnier, was doing electrical contracting work. We founded the M&S Electric Co., and we were doing industrial work in the rice mills. I rented a building to house our company but it was such a large building it looked bare . . . [so] I took an idea to put a little music and record shop in it." Miller soon found that many of his customers wanted Cajun records, but there were not enough on the market. So, "I got the idea I'm gonna make some."[4]

Miller went to Cosimo Matassa's fledgling J&M Recording Studio in New Orleans in June 1946 and recorded singer Happy Fats with fiddler Doc Guidry and singer Louis Noel—"we did a French thing and a country thing," he told radio interviewer Dave Booth—and arranged for their records to be pressed in California on a label he named Fais Do Do Records. "When I got them back," he told Broven, "I was so proud you wouldn't believe." Having seen Cosimo's studio, Miller soon got the idea that it would be faster, cheaper, and more interesting to put in his own recording studio. In October 1946 he set up his studio at the back of the M&S Electrics Store at 218 North Parkerson Avenue in downtown Crowley, a few blocks from Miller's home on East First Street. Taking time and effort to get a good recorded sound, he said, "I went to Houston to the Gates Radio Supplies. They had just received three Magnecord tape recorders, it seems like it was the PT-6 model. You could carry it around, so I bought that, three microphones and a three volume mixer. I think I was helped by my electrical background. . . . I had a sense of something. I didn't go by the book because I went by these two things . . . my ears."[5]

As well as Fais Do Do, Miller soon established a new label, Feature, de-signed to draw attention to the increasing number and range of musicians who sought him out. As well as Cajuns like Amidie Breaux, Chuck Guillory, Happy Fats, and Lee Sonnier and the Acadian Stars, Miller started recording young Cajun boys who sang in the hillbilly style. These included Bill Hutto and then Al Terry and Jimmy Newman, who would both go on to be very successful, and a female country singer named Alice Montgomery. Miller had long since started writing songs, first for himself to play and later for his artists to record. The hillbilly singers also gave him an entree into Shreveport's influential *Louisiana Hayride* radio program and stage show and, briefly, Miller took on a managerial role for the hottest country singer to emerge in the early 1950s, Lefty Frizzell. For Alice Montgomery, Miller wrote "Did God Make Honky Tonk Angels?" a song that gave the woman's view in response to the wave of honky-tonk songs like Hank Thompson's big hit, "The Wild Side of Life." Miller mentioned his song to Lefty Frizzell, who put him in touch with a song plugger in Nashville, Troy Martin, who visited Miller, took away a copy of Montgomery's disc on Feature (credited on the label to Al Montgomery), and arranged for Kitty Wells to record it within a few days. He telephoned Miller: "I got a call at seven in the morning from Troy Martin. He says 'I want you to listen to something. We got ourselves a hit.' . . . it was the first time a female singer had a number one country hit." Wells's version on Decca, retitled "It Wasn't God Who Made Honky Tonk Angels," went to the top spot in August 1952, and soon Miller started attending Nashville's annual late-fall business bash, the disc jockeys' convention.

He quickly cemented his reputation as a songwriter and made a deal with Fred Rose, Nashville's premier songwriter and publisher, to have his country songs considered by Acuff-Rose and rerecorded on their Hickory label. Miller explained, "I was under contract to Acuff and Rose as a writer and I brought the first Cajuns over there to record. I had to take my artists over to Nashville to record them in a Union studio, so I'd go to Nashville every four to six weeks."[6] Through Hickory and other labels he enabled country artists including Al Terry, Jimmy Newman, Rusty and Doug Kershaw, and Tommy Hill to join the big time in Tennessee from 1954 onwards. Apart from the concern of the Nashville musicians' union to have country music recorded in their town rather than elsewhere, Hickory would also have had doubts about the quality of Miller's studio. While Miller was content to go along with his Nashville colleagues and take country artists there to be recorded, he was also keen to improve his own recording facility, and around 1955 he put in a new studio at premises he'd acquired at 116–118–120 North Parkerson. Now his studio, office, and warehouse could be located together. It was in his new studio that Miller would develop the classic echo-laden Excello sound with discs like Guitar Gable's "Congo Mombo" in 1956.

Miller was an energetic and enthusiastic businessman whose recording activities took place alongside his interests in property, in nightclubs, in managing and acting as a booking agent for singers, and in running a local jukebox business. His management role with Lefty Frizzell, who had four number-one country hits to his name, lasted for about one year in 1952. Miller said Lefty ran him ragged through his drinking and unpredictability. Miller was also part-owner of the El Toro Club on Highway 90, where many country and Cajun artists played, and he had a radio program, *Stairway to the Stars*, on KSIG in Crowley. He was involved, too, in the *Louisiana Jamboree*, a program networked by four stations from the Chief Theater in Crowley. He was soon an established force in his town, well known to most people who mattered, but always operating on his own terms. He was not afraid of a little conflict now and again.

When the state police raided his jukebox business, possibly as a by-product of a targeted clampdown on slot-machine gambling, he hit back in an unusual way, as described in the *State-Times* of October 31, 1953: "Col. Francis Grevemberg, State Police Superintendent, had a warrant issued to him by the Crowley City Judge delivered by one of his own troopers. . . . J D Miller, Crowley business man, charged Grevemberg yesterday with simple criminal damage to property. Miller said that State Troopers broke up phonographs and parts worth more than $500 in a raid on the Welcome Club near Crowley. Miller operates an electric store in Crowley and owned the phonographs and parts."

Grevemberg retorted that when he took office he had realized he "would incur the disfavor of a certain minority within the state who would suffer either financially, politically or otherwise from the strict enforcement of state laws." He added that his troopers had found the jukeboxes already broken. On November 26 the case was dismissed by the district judge on the basis that there were no witnesses to the alleged destruction. Miller disagreed, saying, "We should have our day in court just like I am giving Grevemberg his day in court." Grevemberg replied, "Miller hasn't given me anything." Perhaps that was at the root of the argument.

It was early in 1954 when J. D. Miller started to take a serious interest in the possibilities that the black music of Louisiana might provide for his Feature Records label, issuing discs by Wesley Brown and Clarence Garlow from the Lake Charles area, although he said, "My first blues artist was a local boy from Crowley here, called Richard King. It was called 'In My Darkest Hour.' It didn't come out too well [but] . . . I learned to love blues, just like the country music."[7]

Miller at first dabbled in a sound closer to rhythm-and-blues, hoping to revive the career of Clarence Garlow, who had already scored a Cajun-influenced R&B hit with "Bon Ton Roula" on Macy's Records of Houston in 1950, and having big hopes for the R&B band of "Guitar" Gable and King Karl, who were working in the Opelousas area. However, he soon found that the black music he particularly liked was the blues played by people like Otis Hicks, who were coming to the attention of disc jockey Ray Meaders in Baton Rouge and who Meaders felt could make records that in turn would feed local interest in his *Diggie Doo* show on WXOK.

There are two versions of how Miller and Hicks got together. Hicks told interviewers that he was playing guitar outside his house in Baton Rouge one day in 1954 when Meaders drove past in his car, stopped to listen to some blues, and told him he could make a connection with someone who might record him. Miller, though, always maintained that he went to Meaders's radio studio to audition a group and that Hicks was the guitar player in that group. The two accounts are not impossible to reconcile because Miller would not have known how the group was assembled before he encountered them. He said,

> [Diggie Doo] called me one day. He wanted me to go over [to WXOK] and listen to a band. . . . After the station closed there, this band played. We listened to them through the night. They were about seven or eight pieces, but in my judgment they wasn't too much of a band. And I was just walking out the hall when I heard a guitar playing some of these low-down blues. So I just turned round, I said "who in the world is that?" I hadn't heard the guitarist, you see the room wasn't very large and with 7 or 8 musicians, they had three horns, I had never heard the guitar once. I just thought he was so great I turned round and went back in there, started talking to him. I asked him if he did any singing. He said "I knows a few numbers," you know how he talked, real slow and everything. So he sang two or three songs and I tell you what, they did things to me. I just knew right then and there we had somebody that would sell.[8]

Miller wasted no time in arranging a session back in Crowley and then issuing Otis's songs "Bad Luck" and "Rock Me Mama" on Feature, renaming the artist Lightning Slim in reference to Hicks's slow pace and relaxed manner:

"Lightning" with a "g" at the end. Miller said, "I loved him from the start. I thought his music was just so real, you know. He was exactly what I wanted."

For those first recordings in the spring of 1954, Meaders drove Hicks to Miller's studio, and it was agreed that Miller would provide a harmonica player and drummer. Miller didn't know of any blues harp players, but he had been told by a disc jockey friend of his, J. P. Richardson (later better known as the "Big Bopper"), about a man named "Wild Bill" Phillips, so Miller drove to Beaumont, Texas, to pick him up. Phillips was in jail and had to be bailed out, and when they finally got to the studio, Miller said, he gave Hicks and Phillips a bottle of wine and asked them to rehearse some songs. "They'd never met before but in two hours they looked like brothers." Unfortunately the drummer had not shown up at all, so Miller pressed Ray Meaders into service even though his grasp of percussion was fairly rudimentary. Miller said he recorded the drums way back and focused on Lightning Slim's guitar and vocals, and it's true that Lightning carried the performance of "Rock Me Mama" almost on his own. The wailing harmonica was more to the fore on "Bad Luck," in which Miller saw Lightning's style cemented. He loved the forlorn lyrics such as "if it wasn't for bad luck / poor Lightning wouldn't have no luck at all" and his telling how he was born so late in the year that "to tell you the truth about it / I was lucky to get here at all." He also encouraged Lightning's signature call to his support player, "blow your harmonica, son." Both of Lightning's first tunes were adapted from songs he'd probably heard for years on jukeboxes and in the mouths of other singers, but his expressive voice and hangdog style made the songs almost his own. Lightning was clearly influenced by Lightnin' Hopkins, a man like John Lee Hooker who carried some of the prewar blues-guitar styles and songs into mid-century, and to an extent by Muddy Waters and the other emerging Chicago blues stylists, but at the same time he had the ability to make it clear to his listeners that he was the one singing and playing for them. Miller loved the personalized nature of Lightning's songs, both in his storytelling and in his intense, brooding, conversational voice, and both Miller and Ray Meaders agreed to promote Lightning's first Feature disc as hard as they could.

With the radio promotion of the Feature label by Meaders on his *Diggie Doo* show, Miller started to sell his blues discs locally and in New Orleans, across Louisiana, and in Texas, but his distribution arrangements were rather limited and, by December 1956, Miller wrote to a distributor acknowledging that, "at the time of [first] release, we had no distribution" for "Bad Luck" and his other blues discs. He knew that, as with country music, he would make better money if he had a deal where he could produce blues records for release on a label with more extensive distribution. He had met Ernie Young at an annual hillbilly disc-jockey convention in Nashville, and in 1955 he decided to approach Young, who issued discs on his Nashboro and Excello labels and also ran Ernie's Record Mart, a successful retail, wholesale, and mail-order business.

Ernie Young, in response, called Miller, who explained: "He wanted to buy some records of Lightning Slim's first Feature disc, 'Bad Luck' and 'Rock Me Mama.' I sold him those and two or three titles and then he had me go over to Nashville and we got together a deal on a lease basis. I would record the master tapes and pass them on to him and he'd get them pressed and pass back a royalty, you know. . . . After [Lightning] Slim we recorded others, a lot from Baton Rouge. They had oodles of bluesmen over there, and good ones too. We couldn't possibly record them all [on Feature] because we didn't have the money to get them pressed."[9] The pair agreed that Young would issue any new blues or R&B recordings by Miller on his Excello label, starting with Slim's "Lightnin' Blues" in the fall of 1955. Up to the time he struck the deal with Excello, Miller had released three blues discs by Lightning Slim on Feature, "Bad Luck," "New Orleans Bound," with its incredibly forlorn flipside "I Can't Live Happy," and "Bugger Bugger Boy," a take on Muddy Waters and "Hoochie Coochie Man." Miller had also fought off an attempt by Jackson, Mississippi–based record man Johnny Vincent to poach Lightning from him. Vincent had pressed "Bad Feeling Blues" on his Ace Records label in 1955, probably believing or hoping Lightning was out of contract after one year. But, Miller said, "I think he intentionally misled Slim. I told Johnny personally that if he ever caused trouble to me or my artists again I would give him a whipping he'd never forget."[10] The Ace disc was announced in *Billboard* that August, along with the launch of the Ace label, but it was quickly withdrawn. Vincent also issued hillbilly discs by Miller's artists Lou Millet and Al Terry.

On Feature, Jay Miller also issued discs by two other Baton Rouge men, Tabby Thomas and Schoolboy Cleve. Tabby Thomas must have heard about Miller from Lightning Slim or Ray Meaders because he appeared on Feature later the same year as Lightning. Thomas said, "I went to his [Miller's] house early one Sunday morning and knocked on the door. I told him I was from out of town and wanted to record. He told me to meet him at his studio at 10 o clock." Miller had a song called "Tomorrow" he wanted someone to sing, and Tabby apparently recorded it that same day along with "Mmmmm, I

Don't Care," a New Orleans R&B-styled call and response tune with riffing saxes and an out-of-control piano that was far from the down-home blues of Lightning Slim. Thomas was backed by the Bob Johnson Orchestra, containing musicians from Southern University. Cleveland White had become Lightning Slim's most regular harmonica player during 1955, and he was soon in Miller's studio with him. On one Lightning session, Miller gave Cleve his own vocal debut on "She's Gone" and "Strange Letter Blues," the former a jumping blues where the excellent harp playing takes precedence over the perfunctory lyrics exhorting a leaving woman to come back, and the latter another familiar tale about news from far away, enlivened by harmonica sounds right out of the book of the second Sonny Boy Williamson, Rice Miller, whose discs on Trumpet Records of Jackson, Mississippi, were influential along with his radio broadcasts out of Arkansas. Miller was delighted to find that Cleve already had a quirky, marketable name, and the disc came out as by Schoolboy Cleve. It was to be the last blues on Feature before Miller turned his attention to his Excello pact.

Miller told John Broven about the Excello deal: "Ernie Young was paying me [to produce] but at a nickel a record and no publishing you're not going to make money. . . . Ernie and I would argue about the rate [but] the most I got Ernie to do was 6 and a half cents [per disc]."[11] This was actually quite good considering that the mechanical rate was 2 cents per disc and the standard artist royalty was around 2 to 3 cents a disc. Nevertheless, Miller observed to writer Bill Dahl, "Ernie was a strange fellow. He was an oddball. A nice man, a good man. As far as I know he always treated me right. We had a lot of terms in our agreement—it was just a handshake."[12] In reality, Young and Miller were both too businesslike for a handshake agreement alone, but they were both the type to regard a deal made as a deal to be kept—even while both men strove to improve their profit margins.

ERNIE YOUNG: EXCELLO RECORDS AND NASHVILLE RADIO SELLING

In the entertainment and music trade press of the mid-twentieth century, the people who ran independent recording companies were often collectively known as "record men," just as Billboard and Cash Box called those who ran amusements companies or jukebox businesses "coin men." They came in all forms, from the flamboyant Miller to the more circumspect Ernie Young.

Excello's founder, Ernest Lafayette Young, was born in Giles County, Tennessee, on December 2, 1892, and was in his fifties by the time he got into the record business. He was in the grocery business originally, then restaurants, and he set up a jukebox operation to avoid having to pay someone else to supply music to his eateries. By 1944, he had set up a record-and-phonograph store on Second Avenue in downtown Nashville, and by 1946 he had moved all his business to the larger Record Mart, established at 177–179 Third Avenue North. At an age when someone else might be contemplating retirement, Ernie Young found new purpose in the record business. Nashville disc jockey Cal Young, Ernie's nephew, observed: "Ernie was a guy who never clicked with anything very much until he found the record business. That was his forte, his niche if you like. Ernie was a good businessman. He had the foresight to see the market for black music in Nashville."[13]

And not just in Nashville. Ernie was soon involved in selling records by mail clear across large parts of America by advertising his wares on high-power radio stations, principally WLAC. Like other Nashville record men, he would sponsor particular radio shows: "You'll find your favorite records at Ernie's Record Mart / Listen to Ernie's Record Parade on WLAC and on WSOK each afternoon at 3 p.m." His main pitchman was WLAC disc jockey John Richbourg, a white radio announcer who reinvented himself for black radio as "John R." Richbourg remembered, "Ernie's averaged, for years, better than three or four hundred orders per day, of anywhere from one record to twenty-five. That's a lot of records." Cal Young confirmed the scale of the business: "Back in those days of radio selling, the first thing Ernie Young would do was to weigh the morning mail, not open it. He wanted to get an estimate of what the daily take was going to be and he had a formula down to an art."[14]

In June 1951, Ernie Young and his wife, Roberta, launched Nashboro Records, and Young set about turning seven years' experience with Ernie's Record Mart into a successful recording business. He had been around long enough to know that there was a large market for gospel music, and he made this his main business, dabbling with blues and hillbilly releases occasionally. Soon he realized the Nashville area had many fine blues and R&B bands too, and in August 1952 he started Excello Records, which, he explained, developed for pragmatic reasons into a mostly blues label: "When I started Ernie's," he said later, "it seemed like everyone was a singer or musician or knew someone else who was. People came along to the store and would ask to record." Young soon found that recording songs in his record store after hours was limiting, and so converted his third floor into a studio. "It was easier to audition performers that way. People like Louis Brooks, Arthur Gunter, Kid King, they just were around. All I had to do was to try to pick who was going to do some good in sales."[15]

He had some success with Louis Brooks, the Marigolds, Earl Gaines, and others across a spectrum of R&B styles, and Excello went on to have significant national chart action with the Gladiolas' "Little Darlin'," Lillian Offit's "Miss You So," and the Crescendos, whose "Oh Julie" came out on Nasco, the teen-oriented label Young launched in 1957. But Young recorded some more basic blues too. In 1954 he recorded an acknowledged blues classic, Arthur Gunter's "Blues after Hours," which introduced Gunter's pleasing, dry voice and his laconic, back-porch style. "Baby Let's Play House," initially the flipside of Gunter's debut, was a romping mix of country and blues shuffles that reworked the old blues lyric about finding the right girl—"I'd rather see you dead little girl, than to be with another man." Released right at the end of 1954, "Baby Let's Play House" was a simple, primitive, even sloppy, recording but another classic nonetheless making number 12 on the R&B charts by January 1955. It was a style that Young found echoed in the economical style of Lightning Slim, and he soon embraced the lazy, swampy music of Louisiana provided by J. D. Miller. Once Young and Miller had agreed that the blues output from Miller's studio would appear on Excello, Miller quickly made more recordings with Lightning Slim, and three discs were issued on Excello in quick succession, following "Lightnin' Blues" with "Sugar Plum" and "Goin' Home" early in 1956. Young changed Miller's spelling of Lightning's name to "Lightnin'" for Excello releases, and Otis Hicks became generally known as Lightnin' from that point on.

The secret of Ernie Young's success was not cutting-edge record production (his discs varied considerably in their styles and in the quality of their arrangements) but marketing—specifically the marketing of his six-pack specials by mail order through WLAC radio shows. John Richbourg's *Midnight Special* show and *Ernie's Record Parade* generated a large percentage of Excello's sales. Ernie had the WLAC spot down to an art, continually putting together new specials with catchy names; listeners would be seduced by, for example, "Ernie's Whiz-Bang Blues Special" or "Ernie's White Cross Spiritual Special," selling at five for $3.98 or whatever price Ernie chose. The packs always included the R&B hits of the day with at least one record from the

Excello group. It's telling that many Excello recordings, particularly those by one-shot artists, had loose arrangements at best and slightly chaotic openings and endings, as if Young wanted to give the artist a chance but at the same time knew that well over half the resulting discs would be giveaways with radio packages and so didn't rate hours and hours of studio time. In those circumstances he was equally willing to issue anything half-decent that Jay Miller might record. He knew that some would be gems, and the others he would shift anyway. He also knew the value of a big catalog and the possibility of one of his copyrighted titles being recorded elsewhere. He was always proud of the long-term income generated by "Baby Let's Play House" after Elvis Presley recorded it for Sun in 1955.

Almost uniquely for a local independent record producer, Young was always recalled favorably by the musicians who came and went through his studio. One, Al Garner, called him "my man. Anything I asked for, he would let me have—a little money, an advance for car repairs, whatever. And not just me. He was giving dudes breaks who couldn't get a break in a china shop." Another bluesman who got a break with Young was Earl Gaines, who was adamant in his praise: "I never did hear anyone who ever had a bad word to say about Ernie Young. He was a Christian man; he didn't believe in taking advantage of people. He was a sharp businessman, but he always paid you your three cents a disc. And he would help people. Many musicians would sell songs to him for cash, but often he would sell them back if the song got to be a hit. He'd say: 'You have it, it's your song!' And he didn't have to do that."[16]

MILLER STYLE

Although the sort of accolades that came Ernie Young's way flowed less frequently toward Jay Miller, in his own dealings with performers and songwriters Miller felt he also operated in a way that treated people right even when the margins were small. Firstly, when someone recorded for him, Miller always put a lot of effort into producing a distinctive disc—and he soon developed a recognizable studio sound, with characteristic echo and unusual percussion. He said, "See, we didn't even have a set of drums in my studio, and [if] the people we recorded didn't have [their own] drums—we used percussion. We improvised, and that wasn't all bad—because it gave us a different sound. I've used everything from a coke bottle, beating a newspaper, a saddle from my horse."[17] Next, Miller put effort into tidying up songs, just as his former contact in Nashville, Fred Rose, had done for years for Hank Williams, though Rose didn't take a cowriter's percentage. Miller wrote country songs in his own name, but when he started working on blues songs he normally used the name "Jerry West" so as not to violate his writing deal with Acuff-Rose. He also put effort into promoting the artists he felt could go somewhere, often changing their name to something more memorable, and acting as a kind of booking agent in many cases. He tried to help his artists any way he could, and he was quick to point out that, when some of them complained about lack of payment, this was normally because their records had not sold. Then, too, he had a music store, which came into the equation because many performers coveted an item or two from his window. He described how "[the artists] they had to have a guitar, but they didn't have money. You put it on the books tip-top, [but] you'd never collect it. They said 'I'll pay for it out of royalties.' . . . they got the thing and I got the bills."[18]

Perhaps in order to keep a tighter rein on Lightnin' Slim, who was already proving elusive on occasions, Miller started to manage bookings for him and Schoolboy Cleve in the towns around Crowley. At some point in 1956, Miller also financed Lightnin's first touring band, comprised of Baton Rouge players: guitarist Larry Keyes, "Kingfish" Johnson on bass, Roosevelt Sample on drums, and Leslie Johnson or Moses Smith on harmonica. They traveled in a truck Miller provided for them, swinging through a circuit of gigs for both black and white crowds focused on Beaumont and Port Arthur, Texas, and Opelousas, Lake Charles, and Church Point in Lousiana.[19] Leslie Johnson had moved to Rayne near Crowley at this time, and remembers, "When we was working together, Lightnin' Slim would live with me in Crowley. The whole band would stay there. Lightnin' would stay over, he and his wife, or somebody else's wife most of the time." At that time, Lightnin' had no rival locally, either as a musician or as a traveling lothario. Another guitarist, Matthew Jacobs, said, "Lightnin' Slim was the king of the blues in Louisiana. He influenced everybody."[20]

In reality, Lightnin' Slim was mainly channeling and recreating songs he'd heard elsewhere. His "Mean Old Lonesome Train" was based on Muddy Waters's "Still a Fool," though with a much more powerful backbeat, and "It's Mighty Crazy" was taken from Lightnin' Hopkins (a man whose epithet started to sometimes gain a "g" just as Hicks would lose his). He memorably reworked John Lee Hooker's "Boogie Chillun" as "Just Made Twenty-one," as always overlaying his own presence and peculiarities. According to Slim, his blues were composed down by the river. He said, "I'd take me a fishin' pole and go on the fishin' bank and sit there. . . . I'd have my guitar, try to learn somethin' new. That's the only way I could—get off by myself. Go down on the fishin' bank and sit all day. As long as I'm by myself, I can think more better—when I don't have nobody to cut me off. And when I come back I'd have somethin' together. . . . I be ridin' around, talkin', seein' this, hear somethin' . . . and then I'd take it up afterwards from there. I'd get the sound of it, then maybe as I ride along I'd sing me a song of it. Then I'd go get my guitar."[21]

When Lightnin' Slim took his guitar and his song into Jay Miller's studio, though, something else happened. Miller found a way to turn the down-home blues into swamp-blues. As one writer summarized Miller's sound, "its characteristics were a steady walking bass, four solid beats to the bar; a cool, rough, slurred, almost detached delivery; and the wedding of electrified instruments to an ethnic, down home style."[22] In Lightnin's case, the bass line was normally played on guitar and the solid beats were made with a serious thump on the drum kit.

As Lightnin' Slim commenced spreading this muddy sound of Louisiana via Excello discs and his personal appearances spread the name of Excello around Louisiana, it became clear to Miller that he needed to find a continuing supply of similar talent to feed Ernie Young's production machine. In 1957 he provided Excello with recordings by several mid-Louisiana artists, including Gabriel "Guitar Gable" Perrodin, then living in Opelousas and whose group became a sort of R&B house band for Miller; Vince Monroe, originally from Woodville, Mississippi, but now in Louisiana; Cornelius "Lonesome Sundown" Green from Donaldsonville; Joe Hudson and the Rocking Dukes from Baton Rouge; Leslie "Lazy Lester" Johnson, based in Baton Rouge and Rayne near Crowley, and who would become a regular session man and general helper at Miller's studios during the next ten years; and—Slim Harpo.

3. I'M A KING BEE

Recordings, 1956 and 1957 | The Baton Rouge Club Scene | Recordings,
November 1957 | Catholic Blues | Baton Rouge Bluesmen | Recordings,
May 1959 | The King Bees | Recordings, November–December 1959 |
The Social Whirl | Recordings, Summer 1960 | The Beach Blues |
The Rise of Swamp-Pop

RECORDINGS, 1956 AND 1957

It is likely that James Moore's first appearance on records came when Lightnin'
Slim made his seventh disc, his third for Excello, in the spring of 1956. Until
then, Lightnin' had recorded first with two session men as harp players, Bill
Phillips and Henry Clement, and then he normally used Schoolboy Cleve
through 1954 and 1955. He would go on to use Lazy Lester and Moses Smith
from 1957 onward, but his sessions recorded in 1956 and early 1957 have a
different harmonica sound. The chances are that it is James "Harmonica
Slim" Moore playing on songs including "Goin' Home," "Wondering and
Goin'," with understated and under-recorded harp, and "I'm Grown" and
"Bad Luck and Trouble," all with a tone similar to that soon to be heard on
records by Slim Harpo.

In the spring of 1957, Jay Miller called Lightnin' Slim to Crowley for a
new session, when he was again accompanied by "Harmonica Slim," who,
Lightnin' told Miller, would also like to make some records in his own right.
In his only account of that day, years later, James described how he played
harmonica for Lightnin' and, "after I helped him with his session, the man
listened to what I could do. I played 'King Bee' and 'Moody Blues' and he
liked it."[1] By Miller's accounts, although he liked James's harp playing, he
didn't see him as a potential singer and leader. Miller confirmed:

James Moore came here with Lightning Slim. He was playing harmonica with Lightning . . . and Lightning kept after me and said, "James wants to make a record," so I said, "we'll listen to him after your session." [When we did] it sounded horrible, you know. . . . I said, "that won't fly." Lightning said, "Mr. Miller, man, I'm afraid James will quit me if you don't record him." So I said, "Tell him to try to get a good song. Bring him over again if he can get a good song." So sure enough he did come back in two or three weeks. And he had this *great* song, "I'm a King Bee," . . . but he sounded terrible on it, you know. I was trying to search my mind on how to pacify him into letting one of the other artists record it, but he didn't want that. I said to myself "I've got to do something," and I don't know why or how it happened, but what I did, I told him "I've got an idea." I would change his voice. I told him, "James, I want you to sing, but I want you to sing nasal." He said, "Mr. Miller, what do you mean—nasal?" He looked at me like I was crazy, and I kinda felt like I was crazy. [I said] "Sing through your nose." But that was it. It wasn't great singing, but it was so unusual, unique. That's what sold the records he sold.[2]

In another interview, Miller said that the nasal idea came to him when thinking of Hank Williams's style in country music. In truth, although it has been often told and repeated that James sang *through* his nose, the fact is that Miller meant James to sing with his nasal passages *partly closed,* creating a more pinched, conversational sound. The extent to which James actually changed his voice is unclear since his speaking voice naturally displayed similar characteristics, but it's a good and enduring story. The more likely reality is that James came into the studio trying to sing like someone else, perhaps Muddy Waters or Howlin' Wolf, and was helped to revert to his more normal voice and then to boost elements of it.

It was sometime early in 1957 when James Moore auditioned as a singer, was rejected, and then given a reprieve. We don't know the exact dates as Miller didn't keep a recording log, and the information given on the boxes in which his tapes were kept was insufficient to enable researchers and record companies to piece the full story together in later years. Using some notes made on tape boxes along with clues within the tapes themselves, it has been possible for discographers to figure out that he made about fifteen sessions for Jay Miller between March 1957 and September 1966. Some were genuine single-day sessions; others took place over several days, with the output aggregated onto "session" tapes. Miller recorded several takes of most songs and normally cut out from the session tapes the versions he thought were best to send to Excello, retaining whatever other takes were on the original tape.

The alternative versions that have survived have been issued down the years, and it is very rare for Jay Miller ever to have chosen the "wrong" version of a song for commercial purposes or for Ernie Young to have complained about the quality of the music offered to him. Both men had a solid understanding of their music and its marketplace.

Jay Miller often said that, while he did not like James Moore's voice too well, he did like some of the ideas he had for songs. From the outset, Miller especially liked the two songs that he would soon release as a single, "I'm a King Bee" and "I Got Love if You Want It." When the disc came out, it was credited on the record label to "Slim Harpo" rather than to Harmonica Slim or James Moore. This seems to have been Jay Miller's decision. Miller was well aware that an artist needed a clear and memorable name—and he had already shortened the Cajun names of many of his country singers. When he first recorded Otis Hicks, he had persuaded Hicks to adopt the name "Lightning Slim." Then he persuaded Leslie Carswell Johnson to become "Lazy Lester" and Cornelius Green that he should be known as "Lonesome Sundown." Now he told James Moore that he needed a snappy name, something that reflected his abilities, the prime one in Miller's eyes being his prowess on the harmonica. Miller was very likely to have known there was already a recording artist called Harmonica Slim— he was Travis Blaylock from Texarkana, who moved to California in 1949 and whose mid-1950s recordings on Aladdin and Vita were very much current in 1957—and so Miller lit upon the slang word "harp" for inspiration. Or someone did. Lovell Moore has said she came up with the name because "the Harpo is for mouth-harp you know, with an 'o' on the end." Maybe the naming was a group effort, but anyway Miller said: "We called him 'Slim Harpo,' just like we gave many of the other blues singers a distinctive name. Not a one of them balked at their name. Most of them were real proud, and if they introduced themselves to someone, that was the name they'd use."[3] Lazy Lester was always the first to agree he had a laid-back style to match his new name, and he agreed that Miller had no choice but to rename James: "When I was growing up, Slim Harpo called himself Harmonica Slim. Now at that time, there must have been a hundred of them across the country."[4] James Moore never said what he thought about this, but "Slim Harpo" was the name he went by for the rest of his career.

Opening with little more than a muffled drumbeat of the type Jay Miller had established as a signature sound on Guitar Gable's "Congo Mombo," and a repeating bass-guitar buzz-note, Harpo's recording of "I'm a King Bee" was taken at a medium pace, enabling Slim to almost talk his way into his double-entendre lyric about the hive he wants to enter. Two or three sparse guitar "stings" follow, and there is a low-key harmonica solo. It's a real illustration of the sum being greater than the parts. One of those parts was Miller's use of his trademark echo to enhance the sound. The song has the well-recognized blues form of three-line verses, making a statement, a restatement, and a further comment. In this case,

> Well I'm a king bee, buzzing around your hive
> Well I'm a king bee, buzzing around your hive
> Well I can make honey baby, let me come inside.

Then the clear sexual image is developed, the King Bee forcefully boasting, "I'm young and able, to buzz all night long / Well when you hear me buzzin' baby, some stinging is going on." Next verse, it becomes a love song when the King Bee explains he wants a queen, so that "Together we can make honey / The world have never seen." Finally it changes again, into a back-door-man song: "Well I can buzz better baby, when your man is gone."

"I Got Love if You Want It" opened with a harp solo floating above a deceptively simple Latin rhythm. Slim's song asks his girl to quit teasing him with other men, and reminds her of what he's got to offer, if she wants it. It's a low-key pitch, and the outcome is left unresolved. There is one surviving alternative take of "I'm a King Bee" and of "I Got Love if You Want It." These may be the very earliest of Harpo's recordings to survive on tape, along with the slow blues "This Ain't No Place for Me," but it is possible that another song, "One of These Days," is even earlier, maybe even an example of Harpo's pre-nasal vocal style recorded at the end of a Lightnin' Slim session. In an interview years later, he talked about working with Lightnin' and added, "He was on my first records, too."[5] "One of These Days" has a "deeper" blues sound than many of the sides Harpo would later record. Found on the same tape, but not recorded at the same time, was the rocking "That Ain't Your Business," which in contrast does have an exaggerated "pinched" vocal on lines like "toined up her nose." Another early recording, "Things Gonna Change," unissued at the time, included a piano part for the first time. The pianist is unidentified but could be Theodore "Sonny" Martin from Ethel, Louisiana, who moved to Scotlandville and was a member of the same teenage band as Lazy Lester back in Baton Rouge. Martin later recorded in his own right for Miller and appeared on the Rocko and Excello labels as well as working in the local band of Buddy Stewart.

The musicians who played with Harpo on the "King Bee" session and other dates in the late spring of 1957 have been a matter of some debate. It would have made sense for them to have been Lightnin' Slim's group, but people have remembered it differently. Jay Miller told several interviewers that he had brought in Guitar Gable's band to back Harpo at his early sessions, but Gable told people that he only played on one of Harpo's discs a little later, though he could not recall what it was.[6] Another guitarist, Matthew Jacobs, from Marksville, Louisiana, a second cousin of the star blues-harp player of the 1950s, Little Walter, and playing then in Baton Rouge as "Boogie Jake," told Gene Tomko: "I played with Slim Harpo on 'King Bee.' I did the 'sting' [guitar part]."[7] This could be so because Jake had been introduced to Miller by Lightnin' Slim and Lazy Lester in 1957, and Miller did record him playing "Early Morning Blues," though nothing was issued at the time because, according to Jake, they could not agree on royalty payments. Lazy Lester was not present at Harpo's first session, but he was in and around Miller's studio regularly and, as a friend and sometime band member with Boogie Jake, he was aware of the recordings. He remembers: "The ones who made that record with Slim were Matthew Jacobs and James Taylor with Pee Wee Johnson on drums. Taylor, he got killed. Johnson, he was a little guy. People say it was Guitar Gable and [drummer] Jockey Etienne, but no, no, no, that's all wrong. It's as wrong as two left shoes. I played percussion on 'King Bee.' I took a drum brush and played a rhythm on a cardboard box. I dubbed it on after the session because I was out playing somewhere else when they recorded."[8]

Harpo's later guitarist, James Johnson, agrees: "Slim always told me the man who played guitar on 'King Bee' was Guitar Taylor. There's other people given the credit but that's who it was."[9] "Guitar" Taylor, also known as "J.T.," was Andrew James Taylor, born in 1925, who later played with Jimmy Anderson and other local artists. Certainly Guitar Gable's own recordings have a smoother, more melodic sound than the more basic sound of "I'm a King Bee." Of drummer Pee Wee Johnson, little is known save a report in the *Advocate* of April 6, 1954: "Lonnie Pee Wee Johnson, 1605 Bynum Street, a delivery boy for the State Drug Store 803 Main Street, was arrested last night for stealing from his employer, city police said." It is easy to believe that Harpo's first session was a fairly impromptu one as it features mainly bass-string guitar runs and drumming and percussion played on who-knows-what. Jay Miller often described how he used rolled-up newspapers or maracas to make percussion sounds, and Lazy Lester's memory of the cardboard box sounds about right. Lester told Becky Owens, "After everyone was gone, Miller asked me to listen to it. We agreed it needed something else. Miller put the tape on and I went to the microphone with that cardboard box and played on it at certain parts of the song. Miller said, 'That's it!'"[10] In that case, Miller must for some reason have had Lester do the same thing on the inferior alternative version that survives on tape.

Musician Jimmy Dotson, who briefly played gigs with Lightnin' Slim and Slim Harpo, has also spoken about James Moore's preparations for his first record release, saying, "The demo to 'King Bee' was made in my grandmother's living room. I'm playing drums. I know very little about Slim Harpo but we were truck drivers together there, early on, and I made some gigs with him."[11] How and when James Moore or Grandma Dotson acquired a tape machine is not known.

Jay Miller probably taped the master version of "I'm a King Bee" in March 1957. The tape boxes indicate that he sent the master to Ernie Young around April 8, and the disc appeared as Excello 2113 at the end of June. It was well received for review by the trade paper *Billboard* and was given a "Spotlight" notice on July 15, 1957: "Harpo comes on strong with his insinuating Southern stylings. 'King Bee' gets a flavorsome chant with clearly defined intent, humor beat and market potential. Flip also gets a great performance by the artist with colorful primitive support. Fanciers of this delta style should go for either side." *Billboard* listed it as a Territorial Tip for Chicago on August 12, 1957. While it did not go on to be a national chart hit, it gained much attention from disc jockeys in certain territories over a wide period of time, and it sold well via the Ernie Young–sponsored radio show on Nashville's WLAC. Looking back, it is easy to see what a wondrous, original thing Slim's first disc was, well worth the purchase price of eighty-nine cents.

So the style and sounds we hear on Harpo's first session or sessions belong to whom? Partly to James Moore, Slim Harpo, for sure—and partly to Jay Miller, who had a sense that he needed to record sounds that were "different." As for Harpo's influences, he said some ten years later, "My favorites are B. B. King, Howlin' Wolf, Muddy Waters, and, most of all, the old blues singer Blind Lemon Jefferson." Echoing the comments of Robert Pete Williams, Herman

Johnson, Silas Hogan, and Lightnin' Slim, he also said, "I never saw Lemon but I heard his records. He sounded better than anybody else I heard."[12] It is intriguing that so many Baton Rouge musicians of Harpo's age should have cited Blind Lemon Jefferson as an influence, but ultimately there is little of his style to be heard in musicians from the Red Stick area apart from Robert Pete Williams. Blind Lemon, Peetie Wheatstraw, and Sonny Boy Williamson seem to have influenced musicians through their popularity rather than more specifically. Although Slim never said it himself, many commentators have taken the view that his main influence was singer and harp player Jimmy Reed, who had his origins in the South before making laid-back Chicago blues recordings on Vee-Jay Records. Reed and his guitarist, Eddie Taylor, came from the Mississippi Delta, born within a year or two of James Moore, and on the back of middling hits like "You Don't Have to Go," an R&B top-5 hit early in 1955, Reed was touring extensively that year. He did not start to tour regularly in the South at this time, but his biographer has written that "Jimmy's laconic harp blowing rang a bell with the South, and with Louisiana in particular. The so-called swamp-blues artists seemed to take Jimmy Reed's music and use it as a launch pad for their own styles." He cites the lazy vocal style, laconic harp delivery, and Reed's "lump" beat."[13] It's true that Lightnin' Slim's recordings contain something of the style of Reed's first discs such as "High and Lonesome," and after Reed hit the R&B chart again in 1956 and 1957 with "Ain't That Lovin' You Baby" and "You Got Me Dizzy," a number of blues harp players took notice.

However, Reed's first really "swampy"-sounding disc was not yet released, and by the time "Honest I Do," with its loping beat and plaintive harp playing, hit the pop music Hot 100 at number 32 at the end of 1957, Slim Harpo already had made his own mark with "I'm a King Bee" and had made a second session for Miller in his own style. Harpo's rhythms were more complex than Reed's from the outset, and there is little real similarity in their voices or harp playing.

Reed's intoxicatingly infectious music was picked up by young white record buyers as well as blacks, and there is no doubt that Reed would soon start to influence many southern white musicians. Cajun rocker Johnnie Allan has reported seeing Reed at the Southern Club in Opelousas, Louisiana, in the late 1950s, and bluesmen from the Baton Rouge area also remember seeing Reed in Opelousas, a Cajun town with a large black population and a reputation for its wide-open music scene every day of the week. With Reed's unlikely underground white popularity, music promoters started to describe many performers as being like Reed, including Slim Harpo. Nevertheless, the view that it was Reed who most strongly influenced Harpo did not become prevalent until the white "blues revival" of the 1960s after Reed registered crossover hits with "Baby, What You Want Me to Do" and "Big Boss Man," both of which took elements of their sound from the swamp-blues. There is some of the sparseness associated with Reed's style in "I'm a King Bee," along with elements of Harpo's favorite artists like Muddy Waters, but far more than that, the recording owes a debt to Harpo's swamp-blues contemporaries and to his own abilities, including the voice that gave Harpo such an insinuating delivery. Then there's the sparse, brooding sound created by the bass and drum parts. It is the guitar sounds, though, with the contrasting bee-like buzzes and stings, that are vital. Jay Miller said: "The contrast between the high notes on the guitar and the bass line was what made it different. That was his song. He had the melody but we put the arrangement together in the studio. Lazy Lester and Lonesome Sundown had their own sounds, but Slim Harpo was more unusual, he did more unusual things, almost country songs."[14] The reality is that, while Reed and Harpo both had styles that were deceptively simple and catchy and both played harmonica, there really was little direct stylistic influence from one to the other.

As to the genesis of the King Bee song, there are differing versions here too. Lovell always said, "It was me who wrote 'King Bee.'. . . I don't know where we were, but we were on our way somewhere and passed some beehives and he said 'go get your paper and pen' and he started humming 'I'm a king bee, baby.'"[15] In Slim's own, more likely version, he and Lovell were working together in their own yard "one summer," perhaps meaning spring 1957, and happened to bother a nest of bees; after the stings wore off, they laughed about it and wrote "I'm a King Bee."[16] In Jay Miller's account, Harpo came in with the bones of the bee song, and it was finished and arranged in the studio. This may be borne out by the fact that Harpo left a fragment of a slightly different lyric, "I Love to Be Your Honeycomb," on one of his early tapes.

The theme of the buzzing, stinging bee was not a brand-new one in the blues, but the concept of a nature-defying "King" bee was. Muddy Waters had released a blues about a "Honey Bee" on Chess in 1951, which may have been at the back of Harpo's mind if not Memphis Minnie's earlier hit "Bumble Bee." Minnie recorded her song several times for different labels either side of 1930, with its distinctive "buzz buzz buzz . . . sting me, bumble bee, until

I get enough." Back in her day, there was also the Georgia bluesman Amos Easton, who recorded as "Bumble Bee Slim." Stylistically, his "Honey Bee Blues" on Paramount and "Queen Bee Blues" on Vocalion were not any kind of influence on Harpo, but the song titles and Easton's nom de disque all add to the weight of precedent for the bee allegory in the blues. Slim Harpo may also have had in the back of his mind the catchphrase of a black disc jockey, Clifton "King Bee" Smith, who broadcast on KCOH in Houston every day at noon. Smith had taken over the title from a Cajun, Lonnie Rochon, who had established a show called *The Beehive* on the pioneering black station in 1950. Then, too, Slim, as a smoker, may have been paying homage to the "King Bee" brand, one of several made in New Orleans by the influential Liggett and Myers Tobacco Company, headquartered in Durham, North Carolina, and who used the phrase "buzzin" among their publicity lines. In Baton Rouge, Boy Scouts had handed out King Bees to victims of the great flood of 1927. Whatever the genesis and connotations of the song, its effect was considerable, particularly on female listeners who enjoyed the notion that Slim could "buzz all night long." Chicago disc jockey Herb Kent remembered a girl he seduced with Slim Harpo's record: "Something that really happened to me . . . there was a girl that was really in love with me and all I had to do to get her to kiss me was play this record [Slim Harpo] and she would just jump in my lap."[17]

On the strength of his first record, Harpo and Miller both thought that the formula they'd stumbled upon could be a winning one. Slim started touring the local area on weekends in addition to performing at his established haunts. William Gambler confirmed: "The music there was mostly blues—it was Lightnin' Slim, Silas Hogan, Guitar Kelley. He'd be at the Green Parrot, the White Eagle, Richard's Club in Lawtell, other clubs in Baton Rouge and surrounding cities like Lafayette. He didn't ever have a band until after he started making records." Lovell agreed: "He didn't have a band immediately, he toured with Lightnin' Slim." Jay Miller obtained work for him in the Crowley region, and Harpo spent time developing a stage act and working on new songs. After he met Miller, he played a lot at a Crowley bar, the Ace of Clubs, owned by Shirley Jackson, cousin of singer Big Joe Turner, and Miller has described how he wrote a lot of songs there.

Encouraged by becoming Slim Harpo on records, James Moore decided to spend less time working in construction and more as a musician. William Gambler remembered that day: "He told my mother, 'I'm not going to work anymore.' He was making maybe a dollar an hour doing construction. He told her, 'I'm going to play music.' She kind of went berserk a little bit to herself, but she didn't say anything. It was a struggle. As a matter of fact, we was considered poor. The funny thing about it, we was living in this old raggedy house, but Slim had a [big] car. He needed the car to get to where he could make some money. People didn't understand that. If I needed something and he had it, he would give it to me. Actually, sometimes he would find a way, even if he didn't have it himself. He was good like that."

Lovell confirmed their struggles: "Sometimes it was hard to begin with. Sometimes he wouldn't work at all for a week and we would get out and start looking for work."[18] This entailed calling in at venues, making deals, putting up posters locally, and hoping for the best. Musician Tabby Thomas recalled seeing Harpo for the first time after his first records came out, when he joined the patrons at Ed Salmi's club, the Blue Moon. "[Slim] was tall, his hair processed, wearing a suit and tie, dressed real nice." His records were on the jukebox, but apparently Slim was not able to play on stage, "because all those guys were into the Dixieland school. . . . They were into jazz, and jazz musicians don't respect no harp player."[19]

The week Slim Harpo first hit the music press as a charting record artist, his life was still very much the same as it had been for some years. The *Morning Advocate* of August 13 confirmed that much was the same in the wider world, too. The headlines were about the efforts of southern politicians to block the reading of the Civil Rights Bill in the Senate. Passed a month later, the bill sought to enforce the ruling for the desegregation of schools three years earlier and to ensure all Americans could exercise their right to vote. In 1957, only about 20 percent of black Americans were registered to vote, and it would take another seven and eight years respectively for anti-discrimination and universal voting rights to begin to be properly implemented. The paper also reported the death of Slim Webb, the fireman in the "Cannonball Express" train crash as it sped south from Memphis that spawned the legend of driver Casey Jones. It is not recorded in the local paper where Slim was that night, but R&B veteran Dave Bartholomew was at the Town and Country Club in Donaldsonville while the big band of Claiborne Williams was at Cal's Club and R&B pianist Robert Milburn was at the Club Carousel. Jimmy Clanton, a white teenager who grew up in Baton Rouge as an R&B fan, and whose moody ballad "Just a Dream" had entered the national pop charts the month before, was also at the Carousel. His thin-voiced throwaway teen lyric would be a surprise number-one R&B hit and one of the first swamp-pop hits, but even so it seems strange that he was billed by the Carousel as "Jimmy Reed" Clanton.

THE BATON ROUGE CLUB SCENE

The live-performance venues in and around Baton Rouge were divided between the dinner-and-entertainment and society clubs, normally with white patrons, and the separate clubs and bars catering to the black community, which ranged from the aspirational to the everyday.

The main music clubs for whites included the Candlelight Inn on Highway 190, "one mile, west end of bridge," which offered "tonite and every nite" a floor show and revue; Kelly Shaw's Carousel Club, in west Baton Rouge; the Bellemont Motor Hotel, the Golden Spur, and the Wagon Wheel, all on Airline Highway; the Club Major, five miles west of the city; the Ogden Inn, on Government Street; the Pink Elephant, on South Boulevard; the Wagon Wheel Bar, on East Boulevard; and many, many more. There were some significant clubs located in the smaller towns ringing the city itself, principally Cal's Club, in Prairieville, where the top New Orleans band of Dave Bartholomew was resident on weekends for many years; the Bantam Club, in Prairieville; the Town and Country, in Donaldsonville; and the H&H Club, in Zachary off Scenic Highway. Baton Rouge also had, like most cities, an "across the tracks" section of town with sophisticated middle-class black clubs.

In some contrast to the clubs patronized by white music lovers, James Moore's routine daily habitat to date had been in the clubs and bars of the black areas of Baton Rouge. Some had a degree of prestige, like the Tropicana or Wishadell's Dream Club, run by Willie Palmer at 10283 Scenic Highway. The Blue Light and the White Eagle were important gathering places for musicians in Port Allen, too. In the main, though, Slim would have been playing in smaller clubs and bars like the Dew Drop Inn, owned by Gilbert Whitfield (North Thirty-Ninth at 10060 Scotland Avenue), the Black Cat, the Green Parrot (1100 North Thirty-Fourth Street), and In The Hole. Musician and sometime radio repairer Harvey Knox moved to Baton Rouge from Tallulah near the Mississippi border, and he remembers playing with Harpo and others in local bars. "Everywhere you looked they had bars. Wishadell's Dream Club used to have bands. Anderson's bar used to have bands. In The Hole used to have bands. That was a little bitty place, but it used to have bands. Tropicana had bands. That was a big old place right around the corner from Miss Sally Jenkins. They had a liquor store downstairs and a nice nightclub upstairs." He also talked about Whitfield's, the Dew Drop, the Black Cat, and local stores where music was played, including Field's Grocery.[20]

Such clubs were characterized in the local press, when mentioned at all, by the unfavorable aspects of their existence. They were places where the police were called often to a brawl of some kind only to find a number of men disappearing out the back with stolen money and goods as the police entered from the front. The owner of the Green Parrot, Albert Christenberry, apparently had problems keeping staff and was forever advertising positions for a "negro waitress, clean, efficient." On December 26, 1956, the *Advocate* carried the story of a brawl on Thirty-Fourth outside the Green Parrot, when Frank Haynes beat, stabbed, and attempted to murder Ernest Andrews of New Orleans, who had danced with a girl in the club. On September 11, 1957, police "arrested a negro carrying a loaded 12 gauge shotgun near the Green Parrot Saloon, [who was] looking for a negro named Campeye who had compared and then switched watches with him, taking his $127 watch." The next year, on September 9, 1958, the trial date was set for Thomas Ramsey, who shot another Negro, Robert Collins, in a restroom dice game in the White Eagle club, four miles west of Port Allen. The Bonanza Club in the 1500 block of North Boulevard featured in a number of reports of Negro stabbings. Then, too, on February 4, 1961, the *Advocate* had this story: "Negro woman arrested for stabbing: an 18 year old negro woman was arrested and charged with aggravated battery here Friday morning after she admitted stabbing another negro at Wishadell's Dream Club, 10283 Scenic Highway. Barbara Jean Davis stabbed Edward Hudson Jr., 23 of 1221 North Acadian Thruway because he had allegedly cursed her." Eddie Hudson was a twenty-four-year-old budding singer in Baton Rouge whose sister had married harmonica player Cleve White and whose two-year-older cousin, Joe Hudson, led an R&B band called the Rocking Dukes. Both Hudsons had by this time recorded for Excello Records.

In the days when James Moore was starting to take music more seriously with Lightnin' Slim, there was no trail of their movements, even in the black paper, the *News Leader,* published at five cents weekly in Baton Rouge. Through the early and mid-1950s, the entertainment pages contained no ads or stories about local music and were more occupied with the social diary of the black middle classes, ranging from operettas to mystery dramas, barbecues, baby contests, and church gatherings. There was, however, often the exhortation to "Listen to Diggie Doo Daily 4 to 5 pm." A number of radio announcers and especially Diggie Doo had a major profile in the black community, linking all kinds of commercial and social ventures together. Taking August 1954 for example, when Lightnin' Slim was first making some waves on disc, he rated no mention in the paper while much was made of the new Dig 'N Gold Record Room on Scotland Avenue owned by disc jockeys Ray "Diggie Doo" Meaders and Herman "Golden Boy" Griffith. Meaders also featured in a story celebrating the current craze for mambo music, among other Latin trends. Louisiana-based R&B singer Ivory Joe Hunter had featured at the Temple Roof in July 1954 while jazz vocalist James Moody starred at the Miss Baton Rouge Ball that month, and the paper was looking forward to seeing out-of-town black stars Nat King Cole and Buddy Johnson's Orchestra in September.

Far from promoting local blues musicians, the paper found space for black singers in the pop, jazz, and current R&B veins, although the latter were sometimes disparaged along with the bluesmen when it came to lyrical content. The November editions ran a campaign to "Outlaw Suggestive Recordings," citing the Midnighters and Big Joe Turner as artists whose songs like "Work with Me Annie" and "TV Mama" should have no place in the home. Among the local citizens polled for their opinion, several Scotland residents decried the awful effect suggestive lyrics would have on teenage radio listeners, including Olevia Nelson of Fourteenth Street, who confirmed, "I don't listen to those lowdown bluesy recordings. I like sweet music and hymns." Reader Datis Holmes said that the disc jockeys should be made to clean up their programs, but the paper was happy to take ads for Diggie Doo promoting Sungold Wine, TNT Wine, and several other intoxicants, probably because he was also prominent in supporting Bible quizzes and church fundraisers.

Into the next year, the editions for May 1955, for example, were concerned with the forthcoming Freedom Day rally organized by the NAACP and with steps in the state legislature to look into the desegregation of schools in light of the recent *Brown v. Board of Education* ruling. The paper also carried news of a ruling of the East Baton Rouge Medical Association against allowing black doctors to treat their own patients in local hospitals, alongside news of two very serious cutting incidents, one at the Harlem Bar on East Boulevard and another at Fillups Tavern on Government Street. The thirteenth block of Government Street was singled out for blacks to support a clean-up initiative by State Police Superintendent Francis "Get Em" Grevemberg against violence, gambling, excessive drinking, and admittance of minors. Fillups and the Big Four bar were held to be "a disgrace to the city and to the Negro community and should be closed in the interest of good morals and community betterment." Such reports were far from uncommon and were just a part of the environment in which James Moore and other musicians operated. At the same time, the paper was offering "a word to the wise," having heard that "cocktail lounges and beer parlors are doing so bad and crying about it, all except Oscar Vince's, Percy's and the Ebony Lounge who all advertise in the *News Leader.*"

The following month, there was a story about a local black-university musician made good, Jimmy Vaughan, a drummer whose Rhythm and Blues Orchestra was said to be recording in Houston for Peacock Records and who was to tour Texas and the West that summer. If he did record for Peacock, though, nothing was released under his name. Diggie Doo was pictured downing a bottle of booze, sponsored by T&T Wine. In the main, the music stories related to nationally known stars like Lionel Hampton, Lena Horne, and Al Hibbler. Although an anonymous columnist, the Stroller, did cover entertainment venues in his "Midnight Stroll," there was little or no blues interest, with coverage going to the "out of this world floor shows and bands" at Kleinpeter's Apex Lounge and the attempts of Sam Johnson to book ever bigger and better stars for the Temple Roof. In July 1955, the Stroller did get out to Scotlandville—"always nice to get away from the smell of the big city to inhale some of those aromas of the big industries"—but if he encountered any blues music he didn't think to say. He did give a name check to the local establishments, though, including the Club Crystal, where he took a gander at the two fine chickens there; the Six O Clock, where there was a big crowd; Ike Brown's new Triangle Club; Land's Drive-In; and the Club Canal across the pond.

On July 2, 1955, the *News Leader* was campaigning against a plan to redecorate the "cullud" waiting room at Baton Rouge General Hospital, on the grounds that effort would be better spent on getting rid of such a room, but it found space too for a huge ad for a forthcoming Diggie Doo show, "Pop, Rhythm, Blues," at the McKinley High School auditorium, featuring northern-based artists Sarah Vaughan, Nappy Brown, the Muddy Waters Quintet, the Moonglows, the Cardinals, and Red Prysock's Big Band. When interviewed years later, James Moore credited Muddy Waters as a major influence, and just maybe he was in attendance at shows such as this. In September, the *News Leader* carried an ad for appearances by Ray Charles, adding a little bit about another singer, "a local boy who is known widely as a blues vocalist." This was James "Streamline" McNeil, just back from the West Coast with his five-piece band and due to appear at the Apex Club to play his recording of "I've Got a Mind to Ramble." In fact, McNeil and his music soon disappeared from view.

In the first week of 1956, when Carl Perkins's groundbreaking rockabilly song "Blue Suede Shoes" made its debut on the radio on its way to being a crossover R&B hit as well as a country and pop hit, and James Moore was perhaps starting to try to sing it with Lightnin' Slim's group, the *News Leader* was preoccupied with advising its black readership about the best strategy for achieving racial equality. Columnist W. G. S. Gordon, a local minister, gave the message every week that "the only solution to this, our most important problem, is to continue registering to vote or, as our editor says, becoming ten feet tall." He referred to the "wave of terrorism and six martyrs on the altar of white supremacy" in Mississippi and concluded, both literally and tongue-in-cheek, that "by voting only can we get to the point where we can assist our public officials in their governmental functions." He noted that, when Baton Rouge had over 15,000 Negro voters and Louisiana had 200,000, then "plenty of people will want to fight our battles for us." A week later Gordon explained the message this way: "Until we get more Negroes registered to vote in this parish and state, we'd better keep our mouths shut. I hear our Louisiana lawmen have taken a page from our sister state's book and we now have a crime called 'Mouth Riot.' So keep your mouths shut and all you registered voters show an unregistered person how to get registered."[21] Gordon also regularly peddled the line that "we are not interested in racial equality but we are tired of the discrimination and prejudice that make up second class citizenship."[22] In July, Gordon opined that "between integration and segregation lies equal opportunities and equal justice, and those two must come first. So, register to vote." He regularly railed against the corruption of public officials but felt that church leaders could do more; "ministers should lay off the fire and brimstone and preach civic pride, registration and arbitration instead."[23] He was ambivalent toward Governor Earl Long, who when elected in 1948 had supported an extension of black voting but had since proved to be a master at keeping all sides content.

W. G. S. Gordon's column was called "I Heard," and he regularly rounded up the local information he'd been given or had seen for himself, telling it in the words of the mythical Ole Bodidly Brown, a character who hears it all—"Jes remember, I know nothing, nobody tells me nuttin' . . . I only heard." Gordon painted pictures of his stroll across parts of town each week, encountering characters like William "Commander" Byrd at his hotel and café, and whose son little Willie played drums with Slim Harpo; the Spot on Government Street; Sis Ida Ross at her Lincoln diner and hotel on Twelfth Street; the folks at Steve's Bar and Lounge on East Boulevard; the Purple Circle Auditorium on South Boulevard; and Mr. Salmi and Ora Lee at the Blue Moon cocktail bar at Texas and Harrison. He regaled readers with the doings of characters called "Stone" and "Cotton" and business folks like Charlie Holmes and George Reed; "them guys had all the fun." Further out from the center, he recommended the life at Ethel's Snack Shack in Scotland-ville, the Cosmo Inn and Grill on Scenic Highway, and James Henderson's Club Tropicana on Scotland Avenue, the town's finest nitery "where the elite meet" with dancing nightly. In contrast, one day he "went on down through Battlefield—Thirteenth Street. Do you know, more folks have been shot and stabbed in four blocks of 13 than any other sector of Baton Rouge, and do you know, we are not going to get any Negro police; not until we have at least 15,000 Negroes registered to vote!"[24]

Andrew Lee Jones was the music reviewer for the *News Leader*. For the most part, he featured nationally known black artists like Sammy Davis Jr., Nat King Cole, Sarah Vaughan, and Harry Belafonte. He was keen on getting a modern jazz club going in town, and he reviewed plenty of R&B discs by New Orleans artists like Fats Domino and Smiley Lewis, but there was relatively little coverage of the very local musicians unless linked to some local good works. In July 1956 he passed on a message from Diggie Doo, who had orga-nized the March of Dimes benefit dance at the Temple Roof recently: "Ray gives most sincere thanks to the bands of Joe Hudson, Buddy Stewart and his Top Notchers, Tabby Thomas, Papa Lou, Sugar Boy, George Williams."[25] Even here, the focus was on R&B rather than the bluesmen of the town. The leaders of the African American community, whose views were represented in the papers, were focused on enhancement, and blues played against that, even then being seen as downtrodden, unsophisticated music.

In the years immediately after World War II and through the early 1950s, the Baton Rouge clubs booked relatively little space in the entertainment pages of the local papers. Those ads were focused on promoting the distinctive aspects of an establishment's food offerings or any unusual comedy acts or visiting dance bands. There was little promotion of local bands and musicians as a main attraction themselves. These artists and venues relied mainly on word of mouth, local advertising bills, and just knowing that their regular clientele were aware of what was happening and when. Thus, there are no surviving newspaper ads for performances by James Moore, Harmonica Slim, or Slim Harpo up until the middle of 1958.

Nevertheless, once he had a record out in mid-1957, Harpo was able to develop some kind of a name for himself locally and to play at better local venues, including those patronized solely by whites. These included the Glass Hat Lounge at 8342 North Boulevard and an even more regular gig Harpo found at the Acadian Club, Jefferson Street, which lasted most Saturday nights on and off for the next seven years. Even so, it would be 1960 before James Moore had himself listed for the first time in the local city directory as a "musician."

The timing of Harpo's emergence just after the first flush of rock 'n' roll was significant. He was playing the blues, but white teenagers as well as black were starting to take an interest in R&B and black rock 'n' roll—including New Orleans music, following hits like Lloyd Price's "Lawdy Miss Clawdy" from 1952—and to seek out black entertainers for their own venues. In this, the emergence of the teenage rocking nights put on at several venues was important. The first such shows were put on by the Capitol Athletic Club at 3812 Scenic Highway and starred Joe Hudson and the Rocking Dukes. But the most important for Harpo were the shows at the Catholic Youth Organization Center (CYO) at 2245 Florida Street. As early as June 1958, the CYO was advertising dance nights for white teenagers featuring R&B artists such as Sugar Boy Crawford, Big Boy Myles, and Lester Robertson, and white rockers including Frankie Ford, Jimmy Clanton, Dick Holler, and John Fred's Playboys. The first mention in the *Advocate* of a show by Slim Harpo came on November 27, 1958. Other dates there followed, and for the next few years the CYO was advertising performances by Slim Harpo regularly.

Harpo's wider white following also began in 1957 and 1958. Many of the people who bought Excello discs by mail order after hearing the radio-advertised deals from Ernie's Record Mart in Nashville were white kids enjoying R&B and blues. One of these was budding Cajun and blues musician Burton Gaar, later a bandleader in his own right, who as a teenager hitched into Baton Rouge to the Glass Hat lounge to listen to Harpo and to hope Slim would let him stand in for any musician who did not turn up. He recalled, "Blues artists performed at various social clubs and community centers . . . [and] I had a strong desire to become a blues musician." As Johnny Palazzotto, a Baton Rouge native who much later would set up an annual awards show in Slim's honor, said: "I have been a Slim Harpo music fan since 1958 when I first heard 'I'm a King Bee' on local radio station WXOK. He lived on 36th St and I was on 38th. I remember I'd see him outside his house on the driveway sitting on a coke case playing guitar with the harmonica harness. I didn't know who he was then, and later I realized that was Slim Harpo."[26] Up in Memphis, country and rockabilly singer Warren Smith had never seen Harpo perform either, but he liked the raw power that could be generated on a song like "I Got Love if You Want It." In Slim's hands, the song was a mid-paced, almost plaintive, offering—come and get it *if you like*. When Warren Smith took his band into the Sun Records studio in October 1957, he and Sam Phillips changed the rhythm into a rocking disc that *insisted* you come and get it. Smith added a little of "King Bee" into the song too for good measure. The Sun disc was the first to carry another artist's version of a Harpo song, but it would be four or five years before there was a trickle of such tributes leading to an eventual deluge.

RECORDINGS, NOVEMBER 1957

By the time Warren Smith's unlikely cover of "I Got Love if You Want It" was issued, Jay Miller had taken Harpo back into his Crowley studio to make a second single. This may have been around November 5, 1957, according to the original tape boxes, and coupled "Wondering and Worryin'" with "Strange Love," both songs continuing some of the rhythms and themes of Harpo's first disc. Both the session and the resultant disc came after some delay. This may be because "King Bee" continued to sell steadily over a lengthy period, or it may reflect either Miller's or Harpo's concern that they should not record until they had a strong song. It may even have been linked to some early concerns by Harpo about his likely remuneration.

This time the session probably did feature Guitar Gable's group, as Jay Miller remembered, with Lazy Lester providing extra percussion. "Guitar Gable" was twenty-year-old Gabriel Perrodin, from a farming community in Bellevue near Opelousas, Louisiana, who first recorded for Miller in 1956 and whose group, the Swing Masters, later known as the Musical Kings, was briefly used by Miller as a kind of house band. Gable had been one of the first black artists Miller pitched to Excello after Lightnin' Slim, and he saw six singles issued between 1956 and 1959. His first disc made a big impact, and "Congo Mombo" helped cement Gable's reputation as a guitarist who could work within any kind of rhythm. He was featured in a picture ad in the *Baton Rouge News Leader* for a performance at Sandy's Big 6 Palace on Harrison Street in February 1957, where he was billed as a "Sensational new Rock & Roll Artist" rather than a blues player. Gable had "Guitar Rhumbo" out at the time he was called upon to work with Harpo and would follow with "Gumbo Mombo." His usual band members were his fourteen-year-old brother, John Clinton Perrodin, on bass guitar; pianist Tal Miller from Opelousas, not heard on this session; and drummer Clarence Joseph Etienne, from Broussard. Born in November 1933, Etienne was working at a service station in Lafayette when he was drafted in 1951—his draft card recording him as five feet four inches and weighing 128 pounds. He rode racehorses after his service years and was often known just as "Jockey" by the time he became a musician. It is likely that there was another guitarist on this session, too—Leroy Washington, born in 1932 in Palmetto near Opelousas, who had started to record for Miller with the Gable band and whose own disc "Wild Cherry" would soon appear on Excello. *Living Blues* writer Gene Tomko has chronicled Washington's career with Miller, during which he recorded with what Tomko describes as an "aggressive attack, with signature strong, sharp bends, recognizable turnarounds and almost sentence-like solo phrases."

In "Wondering and Worryin'," Slim again casts himself as the supplicant, offering his wares and hoping his baby will change her mind about getting together. The sparse sound is there again, the unassuming bass notes and drums mirroring Slim's vocal approach. "Strange Love," which started out as "I Love to Be Your Honeycomb," also has the trademark Harpo sound and imploring lyric, though it employs an unusual line for a down-home blues song; Slim probably didn't hear "can I take you out to dinner?" in a Blind Lemon Jefferson song, even if this is a prelude to some stinging going on. There are several alternative takes of "Wondering and Worryin'" at a slower pace but arguably with better harmonica playing.

Jay Miller was not looking for a perfect sound—he was looking for different sounds—but he was a perfectionist when it came to making the most of the raw material, the singers, players, and songs that came through his studio.

He understood that, although the market was unpredictable, something that was average rarely sold well. The business thrived on recordings that could be marketed for their newness, their quality, their quirkiness. He knew that in this he had a role just as much as the artists did, both as producer and songwriter: "On many occasions these blues artists wanted to record, and the first thing a producer is going to ask is have you got any material, recent material? Usually they start playing or singing something I've heard on record before, so I kinda got used to writing new lyrics. Slim would get some good ideas, and several of the songs he and I wrote together."[27] According to Miller, this process started in earnest with Slim's second disc, and the vast majority of the songs recorded by Harpo in the next three years had "J. West," Jerry West, Miller's blues-writing name, as cowriter with James Moore.

Issued as Excello 2138 at the end of April 1958, "Wondering and Worryin'" failed to gain the same attention as the bee song with its buzzing, stinging guitar. It probably sold well enough in certain markets, including the still strong jukebox market, but failed to find the charts. It was a good blues record, but it did not have the originality, flair, and impact of Slim's first disc. However, it did give Slim more radio exposure, and his local one-night appearances continued to increase—so much so that at some point Slim and Lovell came to the conclusion, rightly or wrongly, that they really should be seeing more money than they were from Miller's deal with Excello. Matthew Jacobs apparently had refused to let Miller issue his recordings because it had been suggested he give up part of his songwriting credits. Miller would have been more used to artists taking the approach Guitar Gable has described: "Back then, all we wanted was a little fame, getting played on the radio, and working regularly six days a week. [Songwriting credit,] that was like honey in the butter. And, to tell the truth, I forgot about the royalties. We all did."[28] Except James and Lovell; they apparently decided they were being cheated, and Harpo refused to make another recording session for Miller. The standoff appears to have lasted for over a year, right through 1958, and Harpo's next datable session did not come until May 1959.

Jay Miller once explained how he felt he looked after his artists well, all in all, but that as a strategy to help him survive in the cutthroat independent record business he would "never pay royalties or advances in a lump sum." If he did, his experience was that the artists, whose careers Miller paternalistically believed he was helping develop for their mutual benefit, often just vanished with the money or went off to record somewhere else. So Miller's style was to "give them a taste of the money every now and then."[29] Whether this applied in Harpo's case is uncertain. It appears, though, that Slim first set up his small trucking business during this recording lull in 1958. Lazy Lester remembers that "Slim was a business guy. He was a great musician, but he was always working at something. He ran three trucks at one time, making money. He asked me to drive one, but I wouldn't." Lester sympathized with Slim's stance against his record producer but took a longer-term view: "Jay Miller, he was a self guy. He didn't pay anybody, and Slim didn't like that. But I got on well with Jay Miller, as far as you could back in those days, and I profit from that now. I'm still working after all these years [2014] because of those Miller recordings."[30]

Miller had two reasons not to be overly worried about any problems with Slim Harpo. He had been trying to move and improve his studio during 1958, but an attempt to build a better echo chamber backfired and Miller said he "had no active studio for several months."[31] He remembered this ruefully because in that time he had to turn down the option to record white singers Johnny Preston and the Big Bopper, who both made pop hits elsewhere with the songs they had brought to Miller. Also, when he could record, he was busy taping budding Cajun rockers and zydeco bands for his new Zynn and Rocket/Rocko labels, as well as his blues favorites Lightning and Lester and new bluesmen including Leroy Washington for Excello.

CATHOLIC BLUES

Through 1958, Harpo was concentrating on building up his reputation as a live performer. His preferred music was strictly blues, but he would have been increasingly aware of the march of R&B and rock 'n' roll into the better venues in and around Baton Rouge. In the spring of 1957, just when he was making his recording debut, he would have known that Little Joe Carl, another Jay Miller artist, and his band had performed at the annual Catholic Key Club ball on March 7 and that the annual Baton Rouge High School ball had drawn the cream of local R&B acts: "Rock 'n' roll / rhythm 'n' blues— Sugar Boy, Big Boy Myles, Billy Tate, Tabby Thomas, Cy Holley's Dukes of Blues, Buddy Stewart's Top Notchers—stars of Imperial, Chess, Choyce, and Peacock Records."[32] The Club Carousel had booked New Orleans–born R&B singer Larry Williams three times that May and June on the back of pop hits like "Short Fat Fannie." Then, on November 1, Harpo would have seen the hoopla advertising the "Jimmy Clanton Day" parade and show in Baton Rouge in honor of the hometown white teen idol who was presented with a Gold Record by Johnny Vincent of Ace Records for sales of his top-selling pop hit "Just a Dream" that summer.

Harpo would have known that the CYO had been booking rock 'n' roll singers regularly in recent months, but on Friday, July 18, 1958, they branched into the blues for the first time, booking a touring show from Vee-Jay Records: "Tonite—The King Of The Blues—Jimmy Reed . . . Honest I Do . . . I Know Its A Sin—with the great Al Smith orchestra,"[33] in reality a group of Chicago session musicians. It was billed as Reed's first appearance in Baton Rouge playing the lazy Mississippi blues he had adapted for the Detroit and Chicago nightclubs. Harpo would likely have felt that Reed wasn't doing anything he couldn't do, although Reed's music was deceptively simple with a "feel" that was hard to replicate. Someone among the teenage fans at the CYO must have started to see a link between Reed and the Harpo style because they booked Slim Harpo as the joint headliner of their annual Battle of the Bands on November 27, 1958. The show ran from 2 p.m. until midnight, starting with local rock 'n' roll acts, including John Fred and the Playboys playing "Shirley," Baton Rouge's current number-one song; Lenny Capello and the Dots; Vic Wilder and the Royals; and Wally Jeffries.

In the evening, there was a blues/R&B battle between Slim Harpo and his King Bees and Lester Robertson and his Upsetters. The one-dollar admission covered all of this, but the downside for those attending was that the event, the ads in the *Advocate* said, "will be well-chaperoned." The event was trailed on the "Teenage Party Line" page, along with a photo of two white Baton Rouge teens, Buddy Ronaldson and Bo Bowling, wearing "appropriate attire" in support of the "no blue jeans allowed" standing rule at dances in Baton Rouge, where "neatness is necessary." This was probably another convention that Harpo had to adjust to after years of blowing harp at house parties, juke joints, and bars. It is not recorded who won the battle of the bands. If it was Harpo, he had to overcome the fact that Robertson was on the record label owned by the organizer of the CYO events, Sam Montalbano. Robertson had previously been on Excello as vocalist with Joe Hudson and his Rocking Dukes on the swampy R&B disc "Baby, Give Me a Chance." Nevertheless, Slim might have overcome the odds, as a report on forthcoming CYO events published two days later made a point of promoting further shows by "Slim Harpo, south Louisiana's answer to the famous Jimmy Reed." Note that the

CYO sought to underline that Harpo was a bluesman to compete with Reed, not someone to copy him.

The deep involvement of a church-related organization such as the CYO in supporting the careers of local rock 'n' roll singers and blues bands was unusual—"only in Catholic Louisiana" as one resident, Barbara Sims, later observed. In 1958, Sims, then Barbara Barnes, was working in Memphis as Sun Records' publicist, helping promote another Louisianian who had an unusual relationship with religion and rock 'n' roll, Jerry Lee Lewis. Moving to Baton Rouge to teach, she met Buddy Ronaldson in later years. "[He] and many others recalled their youth and enjoying all this talent at CYO but also in the clubs, some black ones across the river. They would tell their folks they were going to the movies and go to those clubs, which often had entertainment on Sunday afternoon."[34]

BATON ROUGE BLUESMEN

While Harpo was enjoying the patronage of the CYO and other venues oriented to rock 'n' roll and R&B in the late 1950s, there was a wave of other bluesmen and blues-based bands looking to make their mark in the Red Stick. The number and scale of entertainment venues was expanding throughout the 1950s, and so were the opportunities for other would-be musicians. Blues players included Cleveland White, Buddy Guy, Phil Guy, Clarence Edwards, Moses Smith, and Raful Neal, in addition to Silas Hogan and the older generation of players. More uptown in their styles were Robert Milburn, Matthew Jacobs, Tabby Thomas, Buddy Stewart, and others. Some managed to find their way to a record label too, at around the same time James Moore became Slim Harpo. None would realize the same level of success as Harpo during his lifetime, but their lives and careers in Baton Rouge all help to set Harpo's achievements in context.

Cleveland White was born in Baton Rouge on June 10, 1925. He said he was self-taught on guitar and harmonica and that he enjoyed particularly the music of Sonny Boy Williamson, the harmonica player and singer from Tennessee who had some influential blues discs on Bluebird Records, notably "Good Morning, School Girl." White said that he attended local music venues when he was underage and would always ask any visiting musicians whether he could play with them, eventually gaining the name "Schoolboy" when musicians, apparently including Sonny Boy himself, remembered him and would ask, "Where's that little schoolboy today?" He was in the Army at the end of the war and afterwards continued working in Baton Rouge by day and making the bars at night. He played guitar and harmonica with Lloyd Renaud's band in the Opelousas area, some sixty miles west of Baton Rouge, in the early 1950s, and then he fell in with Lightnin' Slim for a couple of years and made a record in his own name for Feature Records. By that time he had clearly been studying the second Sonny Boy Williamson, who worked in Mississippi and Arkansas and recorded for Trumpet Records in Jackson, Mississippi.

White was one of the best of the local down-home blues players, but he always tried to balance his passion and his daily existence, saying years later, "Music, deep in my heart, is my life, but I had to carry a day job too. I was determined to have a good family life and still do my music. It took a lot of heart and pain and discipline to do that."[35] From the Baton Rouge court reports down the years, it seems that White also had other ways of making money, including gambling and pilfering. In the *Advocate* of August 28, 1947, Cleveland White was fined twenty-five dollars or twenty days in jail for carrying a concealed weapon. On June 6, 1948, the *Sunday Advocate* said: "Held for investigation: Cleveland White, alias Schoolboy, was arrested at Giles Tavern on Louise Street 1.30 pm yesterday by sheriff's deputies. He is being held for investigation for burglary." In 1954 he was twice caught in betting raids. In March it was reported from Port Allen that there was "a double-barrelled raid against alleged handbook operators."[36] White was among five men charged, including Kelly Shaw, owner of the Carousel Club in west Baton Rouge. "Simultaneous raids on homes and the club Carousel by state troopers discovered evidence that [illegal] horse race bets were being taken in the club."[37] On August 7, 1954, there was another story about the culmination of a two-week police operation and the arrest of thirteen men in a gambling raid on South Thirteenth, one of them Cleveland White of 2552 Tennessee Street. Police seized gambling paraphernalia, cards, dice, several knives, and a model pistol. Against this, White's fine from the city court of five dollars or three days in jail for running a stop sign in June 1955 was relatively tame.

In March 1949, Cleve White had married Dorothy Hudson, who was related to singer and drummer Joe Hudson with whom he played music on occasion, particularly after he left Lightnin' Slim's group. In 1957, White recorded for Ace Records of Jackson, Mississippi, along with Hudson, but nothing was issued and he apparently became disillusioned with music. On

December 9, 1958, a sheriff's notice advised that the property of Cleveland and Dorothy White on Tennessee Street had been repossessed by the LaSalle Mortgage Corporation and sold by auction. The Whites moved to Los Angeles in 1959.

Cleve White was under-recorded in his heyday, but another important local bluesman did not get onto records at all at this time. This was Clarence Edwards, born in 1933 in Linsey, Louisiana, but resident since the early 1940s in Alsen on Highway 61 just out from Scotlandville. He was self-taught on guitar, listening to his grandmother's blues records of Charley Patton and Sonny Boy Williamson. He said, "I'd just sit down and listen to those records and pick on it until I could play it. No-one ever taught me nothin'. It was just something I wanted to do real bad. . . . It was just in me to play."[38] His brother, Cornelius, had a guitar, though, and he later said that was what inspired him to start playing at around age seventeen. By the mid-1950s, Clarence was proficient enough to be jamming in Zachary with Butch Cage and others. He and Cornelius started a band in 1952 with bass player Landry Buggs and drummer Clyde Causey, who had been a neighbor of James Moore some years before. Working the joints and bars could be a hazardous business, though, as Edwards found out on August 14, 1953. The *Morning Advocate* reported the trial of West Hilton, who shot and wounded two brothers, Eddie and Clarence Edwards, both of Route 4 Scenic Highway, outside of McClure's nightclub in Alsen.[39] Clarence Edwards was shot in the leg and wore a cast over his fractured bones at the trial. The jury heard that "Hilton had hit Eddie Edwards, leading to a tussle and two shots. Earlier, in the club, Hilton had knocked beer out of the hand of Hazel Williams, age 23. Hilton says he apologized but four men jumped him outside." When Clarence Edwards recovered, he went back to a day job and to music part-time. Like most of his contemporaries, he was by no means a professional. He said, "See, we couldn't make no living from playing music so I worked at the scrapyard and did a little farm work. I worked at the scrapyard since 1955. Pete [Robert Pete Williams] used to bring stuff in, so did Slim Harpo, he had a truck and he used to bring stuff in."[40] In the evenings, Edwards said, "I joined a band called the Boogie Beats and we played at a place called Joe D's across the river down on the bayou. We just played the [old] blues, like Charlie Patton."[41] Joe D was Joseph DiGerolamo, who ran a grocery and market at 672 Jefferson Highway.

Another man with a big local reputation but who didn't make records was "Papa" John Tilley, the man whose band had once harbored Otis Hicks and would encourage others too. Blues star Buddy Guy remembered as a young man working at a service station, fooling with his guitar in a quiet moment, when "a big mountain of a man drove up to the station just when I was trying to play." He said he was Big Papa and was looking for a guitarist to play at a barroom called Sitmans that night. Later, "Papa took me to all the roadhouses in and around Baton Rouge, the Lakeland Lodge, Rockin Lucky, Joe Bradley's Dew Drop Inn. We went in his Oldsmobile 98. He was so big he took up the whole front seat." According to Guy, Papa had a jealous wife. "She wouldn't let no other woman go with us."[42] Jimmy Dotson remembered a rivalry between Big Papa and the Silas Hogan band. "One day we had a 'battle of the blues' contest out from Donaldsonville with Big Papa and the Cane Cutters."[43] "The place was Champ's Honeydripper Club, they were looking for a regular band to play on Sundays. . . . Big Papa had a way of blowing two harmonicas at once, he could blow one with his mouth and one with his nose. He had a six-piece band and they were sounding really good." So the Hogan band decided they needed to play a very popular song, a hit of the day, to stand a chance of winning. They settled on a song just released by Jimmy Reed, "Honest I Do," played note for note. "Sylvester [Buckley] hit the harmonica—squeak squeak squeak—and I hit the drum rolls. And we got the show just from the first few notes."[44]

This was a rare setback for Papa Tilley, remembered fondly by most musicians down the years. Papa was known for encouraging several local guitarists within his Country Boys band. As well as Buddy and Phil Guy, guitarists included Matthew "Boogie Jake" Jacobs, Boe Melvin, and James Johnson. Johnson was eighteen when he joined up with Tilley in 1958 and recalled when Papa quit the blues: "I was playing with him and he said he wanted to change his life, go to church and everything. He said 'I ain't gonna be playing no more, let me hook you up with someone.' And it turned out Slim Harpo needed a bass player so he took me over and I talked with Slim and I said, 'yeah I'll give it a try.'"[45] Phil Guy recalled that shortly after, Big Papa "got real sick and he passed on."[46] John Tilley died in February 1961.

Like many of the musicians of Harpo's generation, newer players like the two Guy brothers, Buddy and Phil, were also inspired by listening to their family's old 78-rpm discs, but they had access to a more current style in the early 1950s through their father's collection of Muddy Waters, Sister Rosetta Tharpe, and John Lee Hooker records. The Guys came from Lettsworth in Pointe Coupee Parish, a dot on the map some sixty miles northwest of

Baton Rouge. Buddy Guy was born there on July 30, 1936, and has recalled more about assembling a homemade guitar at the age of fourteen than any other aspect of his early life in a sharecropping family. Philip Guy was born on April 28, 1940. He remembered his brother Buddy's self-help guitars and how they would sing gospel and doo-wop songs with their cousins on the riverbank late at night. They listened to the late-evening R&B disc-jockey shows from Nashville's WLAC and soaked up all the guitar music especially.[47]

Buddy Guy described some of his background with older blues musicians from Baton Rouge in his autobiography: "In 1949 . . . 'Boogie Chillen' [sic] was the biggest hit in the country among black folk." Simple, one guitar, didn't even rhyme, "but the groove got to me." Guy came in to Baton Rouge from Lettsworth at age fifteen to attend McKinley High and live with his sister, saying, "I see it [now] as a kicked-back rural kind of a city, but when I arrived fresh off the farm there was an adjustment to make." After school, he worked for a couple of years in a beer factory, a service station, and as a maintenance man at Louisiana State University. The evenings belonged to the jukeboxes, listening to Muddy Waters and Little Walter. According to Guy, Big Papa played good harp, but "he was no Little Walter. . . . Before Little Walter, harmonicas cost a dime. Folks looked at them as toys. After Little Walter, harmonicas cost $5." Guy also witnessed the guitar showman out from New Orleans, "Guitar Slim," Eddie Jones, walking into the Temple Theater from outside as he played using "a 300 foot cable." Before then, "my idea of a guitarist was Lightnin' Slim, who sat when he played."

When the Guy brothers and their cousins heard the first few discs by Jimmy Reed, his raw Mississippi blues being channeled back south from Vee-Jay Records up north, Phil said, "That's where we all learned to play what we call the lump-de-lump, that Jimmy Reed stuff. [His records] had that plain country sound that nobody had." Buddy Guy later said that Reed's voice was "thick like Mississippi mud, that sang over the funky rhythm, to where you had to reach for a drink or a woman."[48] When Buddy started to play with Big Papa Tilley and the Country Boys at a small club in Torras, Louisiana, on Sunday evenings, Phil was too young, but nevertheless, "Papa let me sit in too. And after Torras closed at 8, we all moved to the Rock House in Innis. They played Lightnin' Hopkins and Muddy Waters stuff. And the 'Big Papa Stomp,' and that's how I learned to play the boogie, cause it's a real blues boogie." It was at one of Big Papa's gigs that Phil Guy first saw Lightning Slim. "I had never seen Lightning Slim play an electric guitar, and he came in by himself and played it . . . 'cause I'd never heard a sound like that."[49] Sometime in 1955 Buddy Guy left Big Papa's band and moved to Baton Rouge as a member of other bands, sitting in with Lightnin' Slim, Tabby Thomas, and others. Phil, still just fifteen, took over Buddy's slot with Big Papa alongside other young-sters like Raful Neal and Leslie (Lazy Lester) Johnson. Neal mainly played songs by Little Walter and Jimmy Reed, not least because "that's all I could play." When Phil Guy also moved to Baton Rouge in 1957, he and Buddy made some demo recordings in WXOK radio studios for Diggie Doo, though nothing came of them at the time. One song, "The Way You Been Treatin' Me," emerged many years later on an album. Buddy moved to Chicago in the later part of 1957 and started a career with Junior Wells, Otis Rush, and others that led to one of the longest solo careers in the blues. Phil remained in Baton Rouge and made his first recordings for Peacock Records of Houston in 1958 as a member of Raful Neal's group.

Raful Neal was born in New Orleans but was raised by an uncle and aunt in farming country in Chamberlin, West Baton Rouge Parish, near Erwin-ville. Born on June 6, 1936, he grew up like James Moore on the west side of the river and was also self-taught on harmonica even though, he said, his relatives "laughed at his attempts." By the time he moved into Baton Rouge, he was fascinated with blues-harmonica playing. He was inspired particularly by Little Walter, who had moved north to Chicago and whose "Juke" was a number-one R&B seller in 1952. In the mid-1950s, Neal got to see Walter playing at the Temple Roof Club: "We would go to the Temple on North Boulevard and catch all the stars. White kids would sit on their cars outside and listen. Little Walter was my favorite. I saw him one night, and the DJ asked me and my band to come up and do a number. I was a little scared so I said, 'I don't have any harmonicas.' Little Walter said, 'That's no problem, I got seven right here.' So we played—and we rocked 'em, too. It was me and Buddy and Phillip Guy. We thought we was baaad. But we weren't as bad as Little Walter. I think we got him mad, 'cause he came back up and got his chromatic harp—I had never seen one of those—and blew us off the stage. I was nineteen at the time."[50]

Neal has said that his first band was the Clouds, a trio with Buddy Guy on guitar and drummer Murdock Stewart, who also played regularly with Big Papa Tilley.[51] Lazy Lester played guitar with this group sometimes at venues including the White Eagle in Baton Rouge and the Paradise Lounge at 116 North Twenty-Fifth Street in Port Allen. After Buddy Guy moved to Chicago, the Clouds continued with Phil Guy and others joining in. In 1958 they were on Peacock Records of Houston with "Sunny Side of Love" and "Crying Heart," issued in Raful's name. Little came of Raful's disc, though, and both he and Phil Guy remained part of the Baton Rouge scene. Guy remembered how they would play clubs like the Carousel for white patrons and then move across the bridge to the black clubs of Port Allen afterwards, where the laws were less strictly enforced: "You know there wasn't mixing [of the races] at that time. . . . we would go across the bridge because the ferry had closed, to the Blue Light where Tabby [Thomas] and Raful [Neal] would be, or the White Eagle. Everybody there know you and you stay there all night. . . . You couldn't do it in Baton Rouge because the clubs always closed up over there at 1 o'clock. . . . Back then I grew up under Lightnin' Slim, Slim Harpo, and Big Papa, Schoolboy Cleve, Boogie Jake. Those were the main guys then and there, and of course, Silas Hogan and all those [older] guys."[52]

Raful Neal said he had known about Slim Harpo for some time but had not met him until one day in the late 1950s. "The first time I saw him was at a club in Gonzales. We were on our way back from a show in New Orleans and we just stopped when we saw the sign, could hardly get through the door. We became good friends."[53] Later on, Neal said, Harpo would lend him his 1956 Buick to take his band to gigs, and Harpo advised him about playing white gigs at frat parties. Harpo was instrumental in getting Neal gigs at the CYO. An ad in the *Advocate* of January 4, 1963, read: "Rayford [*sic*] Neal and the Clouds, a new Baton Rouge band, will present its first program at the CYO Center Friday. Miss Ann, a vocalist, will be an added attraction." The ad noted that Neal was known for his impersonations of Jimmy Reed, who apparently remained a CYO favorite. Neal went on to acquire regular spots at the white Carousel Club in Port Allen and the Bentley Hotel in Alexandria, along with a residency at the Streamline in Port Allen on Saturday nights. "In those days, the blacks didn't have no money, so I played for them for little or no money and then play for the whites to pay my bills. We played regularly at the Club Carousel across the river for three years. That's where I made my connections to play for the whites."[54]

Another harmonica player who arrived on the Baton Rouge scene in 1957 as a potential rival to Harpo was Moses Smith, a man with an imposingly strong voice who was, therefore, immediately dubbed "Whispering" Smith by J. D. Miller when he started to make records for Excello in the 1960s. Smith was born on January 25, 1932, in Union Church, some twenty miles west of

Brookhaven, Mississippi, and learned to play harmonica in his mid-teens from his brother-in-law. He was given a harp as a present at age fourteen and took to studying the records of John Lee Hooker and Muddy Waters, among other Mississippi stylists. After his sister moved to Baton Rouge in 1957, Moses followed her there. He quickly found work at a service station, where one day he met Lightnin' Slim and started to turn up to play at local bars and clubs. He joined Lightnin's regular group of players in 1958, at that time including "Kingfish," Lazy Lester's brother, on bass and Kenneth Sample on drums. Smith remembered that Lightnin' Slim worked for a time as a porter at Southern University and would give informal concerts for the students there in addition to making the bars at night. Smith continued with Slim's band off and on until 1966, though he also worked with his own group between 1960 and 1964.

By the time Moses Smith arrived in town, another harp player of note was about to leave. This was Leslie Johnson, Lazy Lester, born on June 20, 1933, at Torras in Pointe Coupee Parish. He explained in his engaging conversational style, "You got a sign that says you just entered [Torras] and there ain't enough room to put up a sign that says you just leavin'."[55] Leslie was the fourth of nine children whose father worked in a lumberyard. He moved to Scotlandville at the age of three and has spoken about listening to blues records owned by his mother and her boyfriend and also to country-music radio such as WSM's *Grand Ole Opry*. He has said that he learned to play harmonica as a teenager listening to the discs of Little Walter and Jimmy Reed, but he also said, "Nobody taught me nothing. I just caught the sound of it and figured I could do it, and I did. . . . My brother Robert had a guitar and Gable [Gabriel Perrodin] used to come out and play the guitar and we would sit down and listen to him."[56]

At some point, Leslie inherited his brother's guitar and started to turn up at blues gigs and jams. These included the White Eagle Club in Port Allen, where he fell in with harmonica player Raful Neal. Lester told interviewer Scott Bock, "I met Slim Harpo long before [I met] Lightnin' Slim. He used to play in a little club called the Magic Bar down on Mulatto Bend. He was very talented. He was a great guy." There is no trace of the Magic Bar today, though there was a Magic Theater in Port Allen and Wishadell's Dream Club not far from Mulatto Bend. More likely, though, Johnson saw James Moore jamming at Johnny Magicci's club out in the country from Torras, which musicians recall as a little blues place run by an Italian man and frequented by Lightnin'

Slim and Poppa Tilley, among others. In school in the late 1940s, Leslie had formed a band with a guitarist friend, John Jackson, along with Donald Bates on drums, Jack King on trombone, and Sammy Brown on trumpet, and they played local parties and gigs for several years. Lester worked at a grocery store in Baton Rouge and lived in Scotlandville when he joined the Rhythm Rockers with Eddie Hudson as vocalist, Sonny Martin on piano, and probably John Jackson too. These musicians all grew up with rock 'n' roll as well as the blues and, in Leslie's case, country music. When he started making records, he was capable of making as bluesy a harp sound as anyone could want, but his rhythm and his vocals were nearer rock 'n' roll.

By the time Leslie Johnson started to make records with Jay Miller, he had left Scotlandville and was living in Rayne, on the other side of Crowley from Baton Rouge. John Jackson had gone there to work for a construction company, and Lester followed him, working in Rayne and trying to sit in with bands wherever he could. It was back in Baton Rouge that he first saw Lightnin' Slim play a gig, and after Slim had performed, Lester says he sat in with the band while Lightnin' "was occupied with the women." Next day he met Lightnin' on a bus back to Rayne and decided to tag along with Slim to Jay Miller's studio, when he learned Lightnin' was due to record that day. He hoped to persuade Miller to record him too. Instead, Miller was preoccupied with finding the harmonica player he had lined up for Slim's session, and it was only after much driving around that Lester mustered the courage to tell Miller he was sure he could fill in at the session behind Slim. Miller was impressed with Leslie's playing, and when he found he could turn his hand to guitar and drums too, he started to use him both as a lead artist and as a session man. Leslie was a laid-back character and was happy to fit in with Miller's plans. Because of his slow-talking approach to life, Miller renamed him "Lazy Lester" for the label of his first record, "I'm Gonna Leave You Baby" backed with "Lester's Stomp," in 1957. Leslie was happy with that; he has often agreed that "I ain't never been in too much of a hurry." He became part of Miller's studio setup, working with blues, Cajun, and rock 'n' roll bands, and Miller became a kind of mentor to him, and a friend as far as any middle-aged white man with a head for business and a black youngster who was already known for his drinking and unreliability could be. According to Miller, "I put Leslie in the studio . . . and when I turned on the equipment and signaled him to begin, I was surprised by what I heard. It was so much more than I had expected. I was immediately convinced this was an artist of great potential." According to Lester, "I became the highest-rated, most underpaid guy. That's educational."[57]

Meanwhile, Cornelius Green was making a name for himself as "Lonesome Sundown" on Excello Records. Green was born twenty-five miles southeast of Baton Rouge in Donaldsonville on December 12, 1928, and said he was self-taught on the piano before he moved to New Orleans in 1948 and started to learn guitar. He worked as a porter at the New Southport club, and as a laborer and driver, returning to Donaldsonville in 1950. By 1952, he said, "I could play guitar pretty good by then,"[58] and he moved again, this time to Beaumont and Port Arthur, Texas, in 1953. There he joined the hot zydeco band of Clifton Chenier and recorded with him for the Specialty label before settling in Opelousas in 1955, marrying, and forming his own small band. He stayed there for many years but was not unknown in the clubs of Baton Rouge, sharing band members with artists based there. He made a trip to meet Jay Miller and commenced recording for Excello in a range of bluesy styles. Miller coined his new name, and Sundown coined some signature guitar moves that started with his first disc, "Lost without Love." He had no large hits, but Miller liked his versatility. Sundown's wife was a religious woman who didn't enjoy his musical life, prompting Miller to write Sundown a song, "My Home Is a Prison," a song that Harpo would record too. John Broven called it "a striking example of Miller's talent as a songwriter." Sundown once confirmed: "Jay Miller wrote the song at the session. He would get an idea from an incident and begin writing. At that time my wife didn't like me in the music business and she called the studio [to find] me. Mr. Miller detected my agony and displeasure and began writing. That's the way a song is written."[59]

Matthew Jacobs, the second cousin of Little Walter and the man who played the "sting" on Harpo's "I'm a King Bee," was a newcomer to the Baton Rouge scene, arriving there in 1955. He was born in Marksville, some ninety miles northwest of Baton Rouge, on August 2, 1927, and had learned to play piano and guitar and to perform at parties and clubs by the early 1950s. He credits a local man named Ernest Barron for teaching him guitar and recording artist Lightnin' Hopkins for inspiring him. According to his Army registration card of 1945, he "works by the day—fixes roads everywhere." At some point he played in a band with harp player Carlton Jacobs, brother of Little Walter and by all accounts nearly as good at both playing and drinking. At another point, he moved briefly to Chicago with Walter but did not like the life there. When he arrived in Baton Rouge, he found the mid-1950s blues scene to his liking: "Buddy Guy was in a club across the street and I was in a club on this side and people would just go from one club to the other. We'd both have a full house. . . . There was a lot of clubs—lot of clubs."[60] Soon, Jake teamed up with drummer Joe Hudson, first as a duo, and then with a full band known as the Rocking Dukes. Cleve White was briefly a member of the group at the same time as Jacobs. Lazy Lester was also in the Hudson band at one time. It was apparently a favorite band of Diggie Doo, who recorded them for radio broadcasts over WXOK. It was thus that on February 15, 1955, they could be billed as "Joe Hudson and his radio-recording Rocking Dukes dance band" when they appeared at a "Big Dance" for the Capitol Athletic Club at 3812 Scenic Highway. Their featured vocalist was billed as "Papa Lou." The Rocking Dukes appeared every Tuesday at the Capitol Club through 1955 and by August 5 had added to their entourage: "Rock 'n' roll Tonight—to the music of Joe Hudson and the Rocking Dukes, and featuring Little Theresa, Queen of the blues and jive."

In 1956 the Hudson band moved to the Bantam Club in Prairieville, where they played every Saturday night, the *Advocate* carrying a large picture ad for "Joe Hudson and his recording Rocking Dukes (black)" on January 28. The night before, the band had played a big benefit show in aid of polio victims at the Temple Roof Gardens, sponsored by Diggie Doo, and on August 25 the *News Leader* carried a picture of Hudson along with news that "Joe Hudson and his Rocking Dukes will play a gala Labor Day dance atop the Temple Roof. Presently his seven piece band is on a tour of Louisiana, Alabama, and Florida. The band features Ray Charles Jr. on piano and Little Guitar Slim on rock 'n' roll guitar." Perhaps it was Matthew Jacobs masquerading as Guitar Slim's little brother, but if so he soon became better known as "Boogie Jake" because his lead guitar work drove the Rocking Dukes along so well. In 1957 he recorded a session for Jay Miller with a new vocalist, Lester Robertson, and in 1959 he rerecorded his song "Early Morning Blues" as the debut release by Minit Records in New Orleans. It was a local hit and was subsequently leased to Chess Records in Chicago. Jake formed a band to tour across the South for a couple of years after this, but in 1961 he moved to Berkeley, California, and dropped out of music for many years.

Another migrant to Baton Rouge was pianist Robert Milburn from Houston. Born on December 31, 1935, he learned to play from his brother Amos, who was eight years older and who scored several R&B hits in the late 1940s and early 1950s, including the number-one best sellers "Chicken Shack Boogie," "Bewildered," "Roomin' House Boogie," and "Bad Bad Whiskey." By 1951 Robert was playing gigs in Texas too, and he sat in with Little Richard and the Tempo Toppers that year. It was a busy year. He met his wife, Irene, while on tour through Baton Rouge, and by the year's end he had moved to the Red Stick permanently. He formed a band billed variously as his Orchestra, his Box of Rhythm, or his Skylarks until he settled on the Blue Notes. In February 1955 he was advertised at the Carousel Club with his Blue Notes and featuring torch singer Lois Butler. His regular black venues were the White Eagle Club and Buddy Stewart's club in Port Allen, but he moved around the local area, being advertised at the Bantam Club in February 1957, the Club Carousel in November 1958, the big March of Dimes charity show in February 1959 (where he "captured the show" with his "versatile" R&B band and his singer Lester Robertson), the American Legion in July 1959, and the Moonlight Inn through the early 1960s.

Not a bluesman as such, but one of the leading players on the Baton Rouge black music scene in Harpo's era and beyond was Buddy Stewart, a schooled musician who normally played saxophone, and who was as accomplished at playing the nightclub blues as he was other, more formal kinds of music. Born in Iberville Parish a few miles south of Baton Rouge in April 1927, Junius Stewart was known as "Buddy" by the time he started pursuing music as a career in the 1940s, interrupted only by two years in the Army, starting in 1950. He became better known in the 1960s as a booking agent and record-store owner, but his early career was spent playing in the Claiborne Williams band, whose musicians all read music and worked mainly at "society" venues. Williams was a violinist, originally from Ascension Parish near New Orleans, who was based in Donaldsonville as a teacher of all musical instruments and who had led the St. Joseph Brass Band and a separate dance band for many decades before Buddy Stewart joined in the 1940s. Williams's orchestra worked on the riverboats taking passengers to towns up and down the Mississippi as well at club venues before taking a regular spot at the Bantam Club in Prairieville through the late 1940s into the early 1950s.

Williams died in 1952, but Buddy Stewart and others continued with a band in his name into the 1960s. Around December 1956, when the Williams band switched to Club Louisiane, R&B had taken over Prairieville in the form of Dave Bartholomew at Cal's and the Hawketts, the Nite Owls, and Bobby Charles at the Bantam. Dave Bartholomew had played with the Williams band years earlier, saying, "The Claiborne Williams band was considered a society band. They played for nothing but whites. We were all around Baton Rouge, New Iberia, Lafayette, Opelousas, Lake Charles and into Texas. The band was very popular and I was making nice money with them, especially considering the times."[61] A little further down the road, Bobby Mitchell and Sugar Boy were regulars at the Town and Country in Donaldsonville. In the wider Red Stick area, a range of other music was being advertised through 1957, including R&B veteran from New Orleans Smiley Lewis, LSU student Dick Holler, another white rocker Jimmy Clanton, the Jokers rock 'n' roll band, and Robert Milburn.

At some point in the mid-1950s, Buddy Stewart started his own band, playing jazz and popular songs as well as R&B. Starting in September 1956, newspaper ads appeared for Buddy Steward's [sic] band at the Carousel Club, and by October the ads were making clear that "Buddy Stewart and Orch (colored band)" were playing "every Friday, Saturday and Sunday—Club Carousel." The band shared the Carousel stage with Cy Holley and his Dukes of Blues. On New Year's Eve 1956, the State-Times gave revelers their options: the Carousel had Cy Holley and Buddy Stewart and his Rock 'n' Roll Boys, probably an offshoot of his big band, while elsewhere the Pedigree Lounge on Highway 190 had Joe Pinetop's Houserockers featuring Marion Thomas, "Blues Queen of the South." The News Leader of August 25, 1956, carried a picture of said Marion Thomas with several other local girls lined up outside the Temple for a show starring Little Richard. The same month, there were big ads in the News Leader for two R&B shows on the same night, August 13; Fats Domino was at the Temple Roof, and Shirley and Lee were at the Purple Circle auditorium. The paper said this would be a test of whether black Baton Rouge could support two dances on the same night, and was happy to report later that they had both played to packed houses. On a more local level, Buddy Stewart's band supported many rock 'n' roll shows as well as R&B, particularly at the Rhythm Club, which opened at 1362 East Boulevard in July 1959. Stewart's orchestra played the Rhythm Club the following month behind Carol Fran, whose Excello disc "Emmitt Lee" was a big regional R&B favorite, the first of many shows there billed under the heading "Buddy Stewart Presents."

The "Joe Pinetop" who had been advertised with the Houserockers that August by the Pedigree Lounge most likely was another Baton Rouge R&B musician, Ernest Joseph Thomas, known to all as "Tabby" Thomas. Ads for the Pedigree through 1957 made it clear that the house band there was pianist

"Singing Tabby Thomas" and his orchestra. Thomas appeared under at least two other names in 1956 and 1957, reflecting his ubiquitous nature and his unsettled style.

Thomas was born on January 5, 1929, in Baton Rouge and said his first musical experiences were in the church choir. He also listened to his mother's wind-up Victrola and her blues records by Peetie Wheatstraw and Son House.[62] At McKinley High School, he was a football star but also won the school's talent show as a jokester. When he was out drinking in clubs as a teenager, he heard blues shouter Big Joe Turner and promptly decided to become a singer. He said that when he was growing up, North Boulevard was packed with couples going to and from downtown clubs. The biggest venue, the Temple Roof Gardens, had Count Basie and all the top jazz and R&B artists: "I used to go and see all of them over there, every big band there was. Baton Rouge was a Monday night town. On a weekend [the bands] would make good money [in New Orleans or Houston,] but on a Monday they would come at a cheaper price."[63]

Thomas's family apparently encouraged him to study theology at Leland University after high school, but this did not last. Then in 1947 his girlfriend became pregnant way before Thomas was ready to settle down, and he moved to Detroit to stay with his Aunt Laura and to listen to the likes of John Lee Hooker playing the blues on Hastings Street. While there, he decided to respond to an Air Force recruitment poster and soon found himself posted to San Antonio, Texas, then Guam, and eventually Riverside, California. After his service, he moved to San Francisco, working at Wrigley's Shoe Store and living on his own for the first time. He continued with his singing too, as the diverse R&B influences of Roy Brown, Charles Brown, Lloyd Price, and Little Walter took hold. He later said, "When I saw Roy Brown and that band play, I knew exactly what I wanted to do for the rest of my life."[64] Then, one night in 1950, his friends put him up to audition for a talent show. Aged twenty-one, he entered a contest at the Ellis Theater sponsored by KSAN radio and said he won the top prize over both Jamesetta Hawkins, better known later as Etta James, and Johnny Mathis. Tabby was working in the shoe store when someone told him about a nearby recording studio and record company run by John Dolphin, Hollywood Records. He has described wandering in on his lunch hour and recording four songs the next lunchtime for a straight $150 fee. His first disc, "Midnight Is Calling," appeared on the Hollywood label as by "Tabby with Que Martin," the studio leader. By this time Tabby had started to play piano and to learn the saxophone. He undertook some radio promotion of his record and played some small promotional shows in California. He was also enjoying the lifestyle: the money, the girls, and the beachfront existence. He later told his son Chris that "he and his buddies would get together for beach parties. They'd sing, drink wine, and flirt with girls, having an all-around fun time."[65]

Then, suddenly, in the summer of 1952 Tabby Thomas told John Dolphin he was going back to Louisiana immediately. He said, "I was running wild out there. I was smoking marijuana and getting loaded. . . . a friend told me, 'if you don't go home you're going back home in a box.'"[66] From California, Thomas initially went to New Orleans to try to make it in the nightclubs there, such as the Dew Drop Inn at 2836 LaSalle Street. This did not last, however, and by 1953 he was back in Baton Rouge. He took a day job with the US Post Office and continued attending North Boulevard when people like Louis Jordan, Johnny Ace, or Ray Charles were in town. He has described how "B. B. King would have a line out there at 6 o' clock [for a 9 o'clock show]." He also revived his own singing career after he ran into Big Mama Thornton touring through Baton Rouge on the back of her R&B hit "Hound Dog" and said he played some shows with her. He seems to have signed on as a musician with bandleader Buddy Stewart too, and sometime in 1953 they both decided to try to get onto records. They drove up to Jackson, Mississippi, but were turned down by Trumpet Records and Champion Records before meeting Jimmie Ammons of Delta Records. It was a small operation—"this man had a studio in his kitchen, and we recorded [there]"—but it did put Tabby's name on disc again with the R&B songs "Thinking Blues" and "Church Members Ball." Delta also issued "Wheeling and Dealing" by Buddy Stewart and his band.

Realizing that little was going to come of his two discs so far, in 1954 Tabby Thomas decided to approach Jay Miller in Crowley. He visited Miller one Sunday and saw one disc issued on Miller's Feature label. He was backed on record by Bob Johnson's Orchestra, in reality a group of musicians put together for the purpose by Robert Clyde Johnson, who had been a teacher and the band director of McKinley High School since 1946. Johnson, who was eight years older than Tabby, had a degree in music from Southern University—where the university's marching band was known as "the human jukebox"—and had been in the US Navy Band. He continued to run a group known as the Bob Johnson Combo for many decades and remained a teacher until 1994. Tabby Thomas married in 1955 and took a day job delivering mail, and apparently decided not to continue pursuing Jay Miller for further record releases. It was four years before he would be back in Miller's studio, and on Excello.

It was less than a year, though, before Tabby Thomas started to play local gigs again, and an ad on March 9, 1956, for the Club Wagon Wheel read: "Dance, first appearance, Tabby Thomas and his Swingsters." A month later he was advertised as: "Tabby Thomas, a local singer, and his 9 piece orchestra [who] will play for the Junior Miss club at Ethyl Recreation Center." Then he moved to the Pedigree Lounge as "recording star, 'singing Tabby Thomas' and his orchestra." On August 18, the *News Leader* carried a photo of Tabby's band and a story calling Tabby a "young impresario on the way up. . . . Thomas is prominent in local R&B circles and negotiating to play some shows in Michigan. Thomas, 26, has all the makings of being another Roy Brown. . . . Presently, he is gigging around the area for local niteries, both white and colored. He is married to Joselyn Marie Johnson with one child." On April 12 the next year, Tabby was featured on a "Big R&B and Rock & Roll Show" along with an array of vocal groups and singers at the Miss Rhythm and Blues contest.

Tabby continued playing the Pedigree Lounge and other Baton Rouge venues through most of 1957 before the *Morning Advocate* of September 6 revealed the truth behind his quick flight from California five years before: "Baton Rouge postman is arrested for California authorities: A local negro postman, wanted since 1952 by San Francisco authorities on a rape charge, was arrested here yesterday morning. Ernest J. 'Tabby' Thomas, 27, of 915 Myrtle Street is booked as a fugitive from justice pending arrival of Californian officers. He was indicted March 6, 1952, on a rape count and is now wanted on a parole violation." The next day, the paper reported further: "Police received a wire from Sheriff Carberry of San Francisco saying the superior court would not authorize bringing Thomas back to California because of a technicality. The Sheriff appreciated the cooperation of Baton Rouge police." Tabby returned to the free world and to the Baton Rouge clubs under something of a cloud.

Slim Harpo had a different kind of cloud hanging over him through 1958, a hiatus in his fledgling recording career caused partly by Jay Miller's remodeling of his recording studio and his preoccupation with rock 'n' roll sessions and partly by Harpo's own reluctance to go along with the industry custom of allowing the owners of a recording enterprise a share of songwriting credits and income. Nevertheless, despite their differences about money, in May 1959

Miller and Harpo did agree it would be mutually beneficial to go back into the studio.

RECORDINGS, MAY 1959

By the time of this session, Guitar Gable's group had left J. D. Miller's fold following a disagreement over a song. Gable and his singer "King Karl" Jolivette had recorded bluesy ballads such as "Life Problem" and "Irene" for Miller, and then they recorded "This Should Go on Forever," a song written by Karl that was to become one of the anthems of swamp-pop music. However, Miller delayed sending their original recording of the song to Excello, considering it not very good, and it did not appear on disc until after Miller had recorded it again by Cajun country singer Rod Bernard as a custom session for the competing local label, Jin, run by Floyd Soileau in Ville Platte. Soileau owned Floyd's Record Shop, a major retail, wholesale, and juke sales outlet for all kinds of Louisiana music. Bernard's disc was leased to Argo Records, the subsidiary of Chess in Chicago, and became a top-20 pop hit in the spring of 1959. Miller was able to keep the publishing for his Jamil company, whereas he would have lost it to Excellorec Music if he had made Gable's version of the song available to Excello. Gable and Karl quit Miller at that point, thinking theirs should have been issued and become the hit version. Miller did not agree. He said the song had been only half-written until he completed it and, as a stakeholder in its success, he thought Bernard's recording stood a better chance in the white pop market.

In the absence of Gable's musicians, it seems that Miller allowed Harpo to bring in a number of Baton Rouge–based players who had been helping him form his own group for local gigs. According to Lazy Lester, "After the first sessions, Slim's next ones was made with Boe Melvin on guitar and Wilbert Byrd on drums,"[67] although, aurally, Leroy Washington is on this session too. Born in September 1940, Melvin, whose full name was Melvin Boe Hill, was a young but talented multi-instrumentalist from Jackson in East Feliciana Parish, some thirty miles north of Baton Rouge. He played bass on records with Boogie Jake and later formed the Nighthawks band with younger members of his own family. Wilbert Byrd was born in rural west Baton Rouge in 1936 and was from a family prominent in the entertainment and hospitality businesses. It is likely that the bass player was Thomas Lee Kinchen, known for some reason as "TJ," a twenty-two-year-old from Denham Springs just to the east of Baton Rouge, who often played with Byrd and whose relatives, Simmie and Jesse, would later play with Harpo.

The session led to Harpo's third single release, "You'll Be Sorry One Day" and "One More Day," along with two then-unissued songs, "Late Last Night" and "Cigarettes." Despite Harpo and Miller's standoff of recent months, both of the issued songs were written by, or at least credited to, "J. West." There is a slightly different approach to the guitar parts on this session, with more lead playing in place of the slowly buzzing bass, and a more up-tempo, almost rocking, style throughout. It's a little more Chicago than Louisiana, a little more Leroy Washington than anyone else. Lyrically, "You'll Be Sorry One Day" is another chapter in the emerging saga of a man being ignored and mistreated by his woman, but Slim concludes "that's alright" because she'll regret it one day. In fact, in "One More Day," he's received a letter from his baby who's on her way back home. This time, he's got the upper hand, and he concludes she's been gone too long. These two songs appeared as Excello 2162 in August, and Excello took out a small feature ad for the disc in *Billboard* for four weeks straight. Despite this, the disc apparently received less attention from wholesalers and the public than Excello had hoped. In truth, many of Slim's early Excello singles took the standard blues format with lyrics adapted from well-known couplets, relying more on the sad mood created by the musicians and the lyrics than on the true originality of the song. Songs like "Wondering and Worryin'" and "One More Day" simply lacked the arresting line or two that had so elevated the King Bee song.

In "Late Last Night," unissued at the time, Slim reverts to worrying about being treated wrong, and he sings with some conviction above a slowly rocking beat. There are excellent guitar and harp parts, and the drummer's accents add considerable interest. There is a similar band sound on "Cigarettes," where Harpo moans about people always bumming a smoke from him and gives examples of how and why. The only surviving take of the song contains a verse where the original rhyme for "buddy, what do you need?"—probably "I got to have some weed"—is covered up by a badly done splice inserting the non-rhyming word "cigarette." It may have been a heartfelt song, although Slim was often seen in promotional pictures with a cigarette. According to Lovell Moore, Slim "was very moderate regarding smoking and drinking. He was a true family man, kind and loving." On "Cigarettes," the determined bass guitar and drums are augmented by minimal lead guitar notes, giving almost a proto-rockabilly feel underscored by the lack of harmonica. The song was probably Harpo's own, but interestingly Jay Miller had used smoking as a theme in a song he wrote with country singer Lefty Frizzell, "Cigarettes, Beer and Mileage." Both Miller and Frizzell would have remembered western swing singer Tex Williams's huge 1947 hit, "Smoke! Smoke! Smoke! (That Cigarette)." The chances are that Harpo would have remembered it too, having grown up with country music and other popular local forms as well as blues. William Gambler confirmed his stepfather's range of interests: "Slim liked more than the blues. A lot of his songs are more than that. He listened to what was popular at the time, and whatever it was he liked, he tried to play. All kinds of music."[68]

On August 29, 1959, Slim's mother, Pearline Moore, died. The *Times-Picayune* listed her among the deaths at Charity Hospital in New Orleans, aged sixty-eight. William Gambler remembered that time but "couldn't really say how it affected him, other than these things people take in different ways. It didn't alter him, nothing changed in his lifestyle."[69] So, as close as he had been to his mother, Slim was soon back on the road and Jay Miller was still finding him bookings; surviving letters confirming a booking in Birmingham, Alabama, required Harpo to play two shows on November 23, one to a black audience and one to a white crowd.[70]

THE KING BEES

It is not known precisely when Harpo formed his own road band, but there are ads for Slim Harpo and his King Bees dating from 1958. The cast of band members changed down the years, and had already done so at least twice by the end of 1959, when the group of men who played gigs with him started to settle down. The players were nearly always young men from the local area. The most prominent were James Johnson, born on the Alma sugarcane plantation in August 1939 near Erwinville in Pointe Coupee Parish, just northwest of Port Allen; Rudolph Richard, born in Church Point near Opelousas, Louisiana, in September 1937; Sammy Brown, born in Baton Rouge in January 1943; and one slightly older man, Willie Walter Parker, known as "Pro," born in Gurley, Louisiana, a little north of Baton Rouge, in 1933.

Lead guitarist Rudy Richard remembered the day he joined up after working in the fields at his father's farm. "Daddy had a big farm, and I was picking cotton," Richard recalled to local journalist John Wirt. "Slim showed up in a Buick. Who was this guy in this Buick? It was some kind of metallic purple

with an ivory top. He had a hat on I'll never forget. Walked up to us and
spoke to my daddy about needing a guitar player. My daddy looked at me,
and I looked at him. Man, I was raring to play!"[71] Richard told more of this
tale to others:

> Lonesome Sundown recommended me to him. I was in Opelousas picking cotton
> and this Buick car calls by. Slim had a nice car, some kind of ivory color. . . . So
> this guy gets out of the car and said Sundown had told him I was ready to play.
> I had to really do some talking to persuade my parents to get away. But I had an
> uncle named the same as me, and he told my daddy, "Let that man go. He wants
> to play and he can play pretty good." I thank my Uncle Rudolph for that. Said I
> might never get that kind of opportunity again so he said, "Go ahead." . . . Slim
> was already popular then. He already had a guitar player, James Johnson, but I
> believe he just wanted another guitar player. . . . Next thing I know is I'm on my
> way to Baton Rouge to play with Slim Harpo. I was sure excited. I bought a brand
> new Telecaster guitar.[72]

Richard told interviewer Frank Scott that when he first joined them, Harpo's
band was James Johnson; Willie Parker; Roosevelt Gauthier, who also sang;
and drummer A. J. Edwards. That changed about the time Richard arrived,
and he told Steve Coleridge: "Back then Slim had Johnson and me on guitars,
'Pro' on sax, Sammy K. Brown on drums. We were called the King Bees. This
was the band that he used for live gigs, not always in the studio."

It should be noted that Harpo had some competition for the use of his
band name, the King Bees. In 1957 an R&B vocal group called the King Bees
appeared on Lloyd Price's label KRC Records out of New Orleans with "Can't
You Understand," and the name was later used by groups on Volt Records
out of Memphis and Noble Records. It is unclear whether the vocal group
decided on their name after taking a fancy to the title of Slim's first disc.

Rudy Richard was in his early twenties when he joined Harpo. The son
of Valentine and Josephine Richard, he did not have a strong musical background, but in many ways he had a typical bluesman's story: "I made my
first guitar from wood . . . with baling wire stretched across. . . . I don't know
how I figured it out, but I wanted to play so bad." He was in Church Point
then and took some lessons from a man who played accordion and guitar.
He got himself a real guitar, and then he met Cornelius Green (Lonesome
Sundown): "That man could play real well. He taught me so much, in fact, I
got to the point where I could play all his licks." Talking to Steve Coleridge,
Richard said, "In 1954 I had the chance to join Good Rockin Bob's band in

Opelousas. This was at the Moonlight Inn. I was with him for three or four months on and off, then I joined Sundown at Monday night jam sessions at the Blues Paradise Club. Slim and Sundown were good friends, that's how I got with Slim." To start with, Richard traveled from Opelousas to play with Harpo on weekends, but this soon became too complicated and Rudy actually moved in with James and Lovell at their house. "We started getting a bunch of jobs," he told John Wirt, "so I started staying with him for a good while. His wife was just like a mother to me." Lovell Moore said, thirty years after Richard moved in, "Rudy lived here for quite some time after we brought him from Opelousas. Then he rented a small little white house just across the street. He's been there since."[73] Slim's keenness to keep Richard close to him is understandable. As John Broven put it, "Richard's wonderfully fluid, tasteful, almost jazzy guitar work adds so much to Harpo's recordings. Classic laidback Louisiana, with time to spare and not a note wasted."[74]

James Johnson played a crucial role in Harpo's band, sometimes taking the lead but normally anchoring the music with that buzzing bass guitar sound that so characterized Slim's music. The son of sharecroppers in Pointe Coupee Parish, Johnson told the *Advocate* years later that he bought his first guitar from a pawnshop on Main Street in Baton Rouge when he was about fifteen years old. He was inspired by a show at his high-school auditorium by the up-and-coming Texan bluesman Albert Collins with his Rhythm Rockers. "I worked and got money to buy school clothes and stuff," Johnson said. "I bought some school clothes, but I bought that guitar, too. Man, [my mother] whupped me, but it didn't do no good. I kept banging on my guitar."[75] He learned a little about his acoustic guitar from older neighbors, and he learned to read music from his high-school teacher, "but what I wanted to learn was blues, and she was playing classical stuff." Starting as a largely self-taught bluesman, Johnson played with "Big Papa" Tilley around his local area before joining Slim Harpo and his King Bees. "Big Papa got religion," he explained, "but he knew I had helped him out so he hooked me up with Slim Harpo. Slim said, 'Well, I could use a guitar player. Do he know anything?' After I ran a few licks, Slim said, 'it sound pretty good.' So I start playing bass with him then."[76] Johnson had not met Harpo before Big Papa took him along to audition: "I'd been knowing *about* Slim since I was a kid, knew who he was. But when he made 'King Bee' I didn't even know him then because I was with Big Papa. Another who played with Big Papa and me was T. J. Kinchen from Denham Springs. He played guitar and bass, and then he left to play with Slim Harpo, before I did. Also, Boe Melvin played with Slim before me. Then Boe got his own band, and he'd come and try to get me to go to Chicago and all these places, but I wouldn't go."[77]

Harpo's saxophone player, Willie Parker, had been crippled with polio as a child and still used crutches to get around and to balance himself while he played. Parker was listed in the city directory as a student the year before he joined Harpo but by 1960 was listed as an "entertainer." He lived with his parents at 1758 Napoleon Street just south of downtown. James Johnson said, "He was ten or twelve years older than me and had been a college student. He was already called 'Pro' when I knew him, probably for professor or something like that. He was tight with Sammy Brown. They both lived across town and were more prosperous than we were. I was still in Erwinville then. I lost touch with them after we stopped playing together." Other early members of the King Bees road band included trumpeter Otis Johnson—no relation to James Johnson, who remembered, "Otis also played saxophone, guitar, or bass and was a great musician"—and a man named Ernest who is seen holding Slim's guitar in an impromptu early 1960s photograph along with Rudy Richard, James Johnson, Willie Parker, Otis Johnson, and one of Slim's first drummers, A. J. "Flip" Edwards.

To many of the younger players who joined Harpo's band or were hired to fill in on occasion, Slim must have seemed a daunting figure at first. For one thing, he was very tall, and could tower over people, and for another there was the long scar from his right ear across his cheek that hinted at a tough past. But the main thing was, as Phil Guy said, "He was one of the seriousest guys about the music thing. A lot of times a lot of guys would quit him because he was so serious about it. When there was a gig to be done you had to be there on time and you had to be doing it. . . . I mean this guy was really something else; that shows you can't judge a book by the cover. He was incredible. He started traveling around before anybody else, was doing all these gigs, sometimes he'd take his band, sometimes he'd go by himself. Yeah, I liked Slim Harpo."[78]

Some of the shows Harpo and his King Bees played in 1959 can be tracked through local newspaper ads. They were still regularly at the Acadian Club and sometimes at the CYO. There were regular mentions of him in the *Advocate*'s "Teen Age Party Line" column and in the society pages as the supplier of music for white events such as debutante balls, teen hops, and special parties. Then, in September and October, there was a big run of ads for Harpo's regular gig at the Glass Hat on North Boulevard. Lynn Ourso, a musician with the Playboys band, said: "I got to see Slim and Rudy play together for several years in the late '50s and '60s, mostly at The Glass Hat and often at LSU fraternity parties on game days. When the Playboys would be on break from our LSU frat gigs, John Fred and I would usually find the King Bees close by. Slim's rockin' blues sound was spectacular and the crowd of dancers loved them. Rudy was truly a special blues guitarist with his beautiful blues riffs and cool rhythms. Back then I only saw him on electric guitar making his Crowley brand of R&B. He was usually sitting, playing his blond Fender next to the sax man who could not stand because he had leg braces—but their musical energy was undeniable. We were in blues heaven."[79]

On September 25, 1959, the *State-Times* entertainment section advertised "Slim Harpo and his King Bees, nightly, Glass Hat, 2342 North Blvd. Reservations taken." The big movie that night was *South Pacific,* and other live shows included the Claiborne Williams band at Tony's Restaurant and Lounge on North Foster Drive, Buddy Stewart at Club Carousel, and Joe Jones at Cal's Club. The smaller, very local, black clubs were rarely advertised, but on October 15, 1959, the *State-Times* located the John Tilley blues band at the East Feliciana Agricultural Fair in Clinton. The fair lasted three days and featured livestock shows, famous Tennessee walking horses, the Clinton High School band, a football game, and a dance. The ads advised that "Saturday will be Negro day, and the show will close that night with a dance with music by Big Papa."

Harpo's Excello recording compatriots only ever rated one ad in the *Advocate.* This came on December 18, 1959: "A double barrel blues attraction is slated at the Catholic Youth Organization Center, 2245 Florida Street tomorrow night from 8 to midnight. Featured recording artists will be 'Lightning Slim' whose hit record was 'The Rooster Blues' and Lazy Lester of 'Late Late in the Evening' Fame. Both are from Texas." This mistake about their origins underlines that neither artist had any kind of profile outside the localized clubs of the black communities across the Baton Rouge area. Lynn Ourso recalls seeing Lightnin' Slim playing with Harpo at the Glass Hat around 1960 but confirms that Lightnin' had little of the following among the white student crowd that Harpo enjoyed.

Despite his growing popularity among the white crowd, Harpo still took a backseat at the CYO to white rock 'n' rollers and to black artists from outside the area. Jimmy Reed had debuted in Baton Rouge in July 1958, and a large picture ad alerted fans that he was back at the CYO Center on January 9,

1959, "by popular demand." By March, John Fred rated a full article on his pop success with "Shirley" and his recent appearance on the Alan Freed TV show in New York.

RECORDINGS, NOVEMBER–DECEMBER 1959

Harpo returned to the studio in November or December 1959, following the shows he played in Birmingham. It is likely, by all accounts, that the late 1959 session, or sessions, featured Slim's road band for the first time, augmented again, variously, by Boe Melvin on guitar and Sonny Martin on piano. Martin had been the pianist in the teenage Rhythm Rockers with Lazy Lester and singer Eddie Hudson. James Johnson confirmed: "The first recordings I can remember making with Slim was the time when we made the 'Blues Hangover.'" He added, "I did that on guitar, tuned the E string down to G natural. That was me and Pro, and the drummer was Sammy K. Brown, he was tight with Pro. Wilbert Byrd was the drummer with Slim before Sammy, before I was there. He got killed in a car wreck [in Port Allen in 1969]. Sammy was four years younger than me, and I was young then." Johnson doesn't remember a pianist, though, saying, "We never did have no keyboard player on any session I was at. But J. D. Miller overdubbed a lot of things after we had finished. That was his way."[80]

The product from the session(s) was dated December 12, either when Miller sent the tape to Excello or, more likely, when it was received in Nashville. That winter, Miller and Harpo worked together on many songs with the aim of breaking through to a wider market. "Bobby Sox Baby" was clearly an attempt at a popular, rock 'n' roll–styled song with its incessant beat, swooping piano, and rockabilly guitar. Perhaps it was inspired by Harpo's new exposure to white college audiences at places like the CYO. Maybe it was a little outdated in its lyrics or too primitively played, or maybe Miller decided to hold it back for a session with a white rock 'n' roll singer, but either way it was not chosen as a Harpo single. Instead, Miller went back to the blues and to the buzzing bee theme. "Buzz Me Babe" and "Late Last Night" appeared on Excello 2171 in February 1960. "Buzz Me Babe" was another song about Slim's stinging prowess as a king bee but it opens with a variation—his baby is buzzing him, on the telephone. Musically, it is like its predecessor but taken with a little more "attack," which James Johnson attributed to the presence of Boe Melvin, and still with the slammed-down drumbeat favored by Baton Rouge players in the wake of Lightning Slim's first discs. The rumbling bass guitar parts are augmented very noticeably here by percussion effects made on a box or something like Jay Miller's famous saddle. *Billboard* found it "a fine waxing featuring a solid beat and bright work on the mouth organ. The chanter sings it with spirit. Strong wax." The flip side, "Late Last Night," was the song tried out at a fast pace in the previous session, now reappearing as a low-down blues with a basic blues structure but a stronger lyrical impact than many:

I walked all night, baby, out in the cold and rain
I walked all night, baby, out in the cold and rain
Well when I found my baby, was makin' love to some other man
Oh but she hurt me so bad.

The song was supported by an atmospheric harp solo and rock-solid drumming of the type favored by Lightnin' Slim. Strangely, though, the pianist has an intricate and incongruously fast piano solo going on in the background. *Billboard* was encouraging about its overall sales potential—"Slim Harpo tells about the way he is being treated by his baby on this listenable blues item. Good wax for the field." In any event, it kept Harpo's name current, but it was not the chart hit everyone hoped for.

Unissued from the session—most likely aggregated over a number of dates—were six other songs. There is another fast version of "Late Last Night" with riffing saxes and ringing lead guitar solos, almost rock 'n' roll, that surprisingly remained unissued at the time. In the same vein was a rocking version of "That Ain't Your Business," the song recorded at Slim's earliest sessions, now complete with Chuck Berry beat and a wailing harp solo. Next, Slim revisits the reflective "Things Gonna Change," recorded at an earlier session. This is taken at a faster pace, and there is a fine guitar solo from Rudy Richard that complements Slim's mood perfectly. Slim's howling harp introduces the bluesy "What's Going On," a song he would record again on Imperial as "What's Going On Baby." Then came the song James Johnson remembered as "Blues Hang-over," although here it is in its earliest form under the title "Talking Blues." The band would return to it on another session. Two further songs were made at or around this time with added piano, apparently by Katie Webster. "You Ain't Never Had to Cry" was a slower, impressive version of a song also recorded later as "Don't Start Cryin' Now" while "That's Alright" was a different version of the song earlier recorded as "You'll Be Sorry One Day."

THE SOCIAL WHIRL

Through 1960, Harpo and his band continued to keep busy locally, and sometimes more widely afield. Nevertheless, he was continually in competition with R&B, rock 'n' roll, and dance bands for the local dollar and was barely making a living some nights. On February 12, 1960, he was at the Acadian Club in competition with pioneering New Orleans R&B pianist Professor Longhair at the CYO Center, and with Baby Cross's Combo featuring vocalist Sonny Martin and pianist Robert Milburn at Joe's Club, one mile west of the Mississippi bridge. On March 11, he and the King Bees were at the Glass Hat, in opposition to "Smiling Lewis," recording star Smiley Lewis, and Buddy Stewart at Cal's Club. March 17 was a major night in the white calendar: "Dance to Star Slim Harpo: the largest crowd of the year is expected at the Acadian Club Saturday night when 'Slim Harpo' and his band will play for the club dance."[81] For the next three weeks he was at the Acadian again, in competition with the Bantam Club, in Prairieville, which boasted Sugar Boy followed by Buster Brown and Buddy Stewart's Top Notchers. Then, on April 9, he was very close to home at the Bellemont Hotel, which hosted the local students' Delta Zeta sorority "man of the year" show.

A report the next day described how "ancient Greece formed the setting for the dance which was held Saturday evening in the Caribbean Room of the Bellemont. Slim Harpo and his band furnished music for the occasion as guests and sorority members danced amid a scene depicting the ruins of a Grecian city."[82] At that time, the Bellemont was the plushest venue in town and the place of choice for social events for those who could afford it. Thirteen days later, the *Advocate* described a "busy weekend for teenagers" with various shows, including Rocking Dave Allen from Houston, Johnny Fairchild from Mobile, Buck Rogers and his Jets of Baton Rouge, and, intriguingly, "the sophomore Junior Miss will present 'Somewhere over the Rainbow' with Slim Harpo and his King Bees in the Bellemont's Continental Room Friday night." By now, Slim and his band of young musicians were probably becoming used to being part of the white social scene, if only as the hired musical help to a themed high-school prom. Slim was becoming accustomed to tailoring his act to rock 'n' roll and dance functions, and he was already playing fewer pure blues venues than when he had started as a professional.

On the first weekend of May, Slim was at the CYO again, billed in a large boxed ad in the *Morning Advocate:* "King of Blues to be at CYO: the 'blues king of the south,' Slim Harpo, is slated to appear at the CYO Saturday." In a small article about Slim on the society and entertainment pages of the *State-Times,* which were otherwise full of stories and photos of white teens, students, party organizers, and white rockers like Jack Scott, it was clear that he was in increasing demand: "Slim Harpo, known as the 'blues king of the South,' will be featured with his orchestra at two dances scheduled for this weekend by two teen-aged groups. . . . Harpo, one of the most popular recording artists here, is known for his recording of 'I'm a King Bee.' The dances are at Montel's Catholic Youth Organization Center Friday and the Acadian Club Saturday night."[83] It is clear that Harpo and his band were developing a very good live act which kept him in demand even though his recent records had not made the impact of "I'm a King Bee."

With Slim's developing local fame came some local downsides. Four years after he had reported the theft of eight harmonicas to the police, he was again reporting the loss of musical instruments of significant value. On or about May 20, 1960, James came home to find that some instruments belonging to him had been stolen, and it was some little time before they were recovered. Eight months later, on January 14, 1961, the *Morning Advocate* reported cases heard in the District Court the day before: "Erwin Lee Edwards was sentenced to serve 5 years in the penitentiary for theft. The case involved the theft of musical instruments valued at $1369, the property of James Moore." Edwards was noted in the court records as a thirty-four-year-old colored male who had other cases of theft and forgery to answer. It is notable that there was no recognition by the white-focused newspaper that James Moore had any kind of blues fame or name as Slim Harpo.

RECORDINGS, SUMMER 1960

Some six months after their last recordings, around June 1960, the band of Richard, Johnson, Parker, and Brown was back in the studio, probably with Sonny Martin again on piano and possibly with Boe Melvin on bass. The session produced Harpo's fifth single, "Blues Hang-over" and "What a Dream," released on Excello 2184 in September 1960. It was something of a departure from Slim's previous discs and has been a real favorite among collectors of blues records for many years. "Blues Hang-over" was a further version of "Talking Blues," introduced at a walking pace by Slim's harp solo and underpinned throughout by a gently moaning sax part. It was possibly written at the end of a long night, surveying the scene of empty bottles. Slim talks ruefully about events he can't quite comprehend:

Lord, I wonder what done happened
Ain't nobody here but me
All these empty bottles on the table here
I know I didn't drink all this by myself
I must have a blues hangover
What's this, my check?
And I don't have change for a grasshopper, and that's two crickets.

And it's not just Slim with a hangover; he says he's going off "on the stem now, with James, Rudolph and Tomcat," confirming the presence of some of his road band as musicians on the session. Although being on the stem could be taken as something like on a drunk or on the razzle, in fact local folks recall the stem as being East Boulevard, where several of the black nightclubs were located. Harpo rarely took drinking as his theme, and he is remembered as being at the dry end of the spectrum as far as bluesmen are concerned, but that's not to say he never partook. In another verse Slim alludes to having his favorite food, jelly cake, made for Christmas, apparently referring to his real favorite and at the same time delivering the double meaning more associated with blues lyrics. We are told, sadly, that Santa ate it all before Slim had a chance. Ray Moore confirmed, "My aunt Lillie made a great jelly cake, my uncle James loved jelly cake. You can hear him talk about it in one of his songs." Lovell confirmed she made them, too, "and Slim took them on the road."[84] "What a Dream" opens in a doomy mood, but Rudy Richard's active lead guitar fills add interest as Slim develops another lyric casting himself as the outsider trying to win back his woman's love—"I need your lovin' baby, I don't have no earthly friends." He confides it's like a dream to be in his baby's arms, but he wakes up to find she's gone, asking: "What can I do, what can I do to overcome? / To make up for my mistakes baby, undo the wrong things I've done."

The other songs apparently made at this time included "Yeah Yeah Baby," a fast-paced directive to Slim's girl to come on home. It features one of his fastest harp solos, inspiring British singer Paul Jones to write: "Harpo was very much his own man on the instrument, despite the detectable influences [Little Walter and Jimmy Reed]. His work on the chromatic harp . . . such as 'Yeah Yeah Baby' is lovely and often original."[85] Then there were two versions of "Dream Girl," an atmospheric blues about a vision of loveliness who used to let Slim buzz around her hive but now drives around in a long black limousine and won't let him be her "chauffeur." Drivers, riders, and chauffeurs were well known in blues lyrics, though not often in the same song as the bee allegory. Possibly Slim was recognizing the fairly recent revival by Memphis Minnie on Checker Records of her older hit "Me and My Chauffeur."

At the June session, Slim also recorded "Don't Start Cryin' Now," a rocking tune pushed hard by the drummer and bass guitar leading into an eloquent guitar solo from the Chuck Berry school of rock 'n' roll supported by sax and harp riffs. The recording would be pulled as a B side for release some months later. There is a surviving alternative version with piano and less rocking drive. Also recorded was an instrumental that started life with no title and was issued as such in 1976 on the British label Flyright. It would be remade as "Moody Blues" at Harpo's next session. The unissued version has a far better chromatic harp solo, but the guitar playing is less sophisticated.

Rudy Richard talked to Jeff Hannusch about sessions like this: "Most sessions were pretty easy. Usually we had an idea about what we were going to do before we went into the studio. J. D. Miller was alright—he had some good ideas when we recorded. Slim normally just sang and played harmonica on his records. He might have played guitar on one or two songs [later], but Slim wasn't really much of a guitar player."[86]

Records like "Buzz Me Babe" and "Blues Hang-over" may have just about held their own in the marketplace, but the truth was that, after the initial flurry of success, Slim Harpo's disc sales were not increasing. Apart from the vagaries of the record business, where luck played a strong hand, the reasons had to do with the amount and type of promotion the discs received. The fact was that Nashboro-Excello was a relatively small company, "family-run" by Ernie Young and his secretary Dorothy Keaton from ramshackle buildings in downtown Nashville, where managerial offices, shipping rooms, and recording facilities were all housed together. There were just a handful of employees headed by first Ted Adams and later Shannon Williams, who spent as much time in the shipping room as they did as heads of sales or promotion. Everything was controlled by Young, whose sales method of choice was to expose all his releases on his sponsored disc-jockey shows over radio WLAC, then to promote the popular ones again and again, and to include the other Excello discs that didn't do so well in his "special offer" sales packs. Even in the case of Slim Harpo, whose track record and potential everyone accepted, Shannon

Williams recalled, "There would come a time where if [Ernie] didn't feel like the orders warranted it, he might not press any more, because a pressing plant wouldn't set up just to do a very small quantity."[87] Ernie would simply move out the stock he had and then turn his attention to the next batch of releases. It was a business model that served him well for many years.

THE BEACH BLUES

While Harpo continued to develop a local white following, and the world generally was taking up the more shaking music of R&B and rock 'n' roll, Slim's contemporary blues musicians remained almost completely below the radar. Slim remained with his established audience at the Acadian Club. On June 10, 1960, "Slim Harpo and His Orchestra" were scheduled there, opposite Sugar Boy at the CYO. Two weekends later, there was an ad for several dances, one by Harpo at the Acadian and another by his sometime guitarist. At the CYO, "a special feature will be the rock 'n' roll band 'Boogie Jake' Jacobs and his House Rockers who are famous for 'Early In The Morning.' . . . The House Rockers are well known in this area and are popular recording artists."[88] Boogie Jake had both of the first two singles on the Minit label owned by Joe Banashak in New Orleans, although the credit on the second disc was to Matthew Jacobs because some disc jockeys had found the "Boogie Jake" credit on the first disc offensive. Sax player "Skinny" August Dean said: "I started out with Boogie Jake. . . . in the band we had Boe Melvin, Sammy Thornton, a guy called Joe on organ and two dancers. We used to play Annie Mae's on Louise Street."

Dean also talked about playing with Lightnin' Slim and said that he learned sax "from a guy with no legs [sic], named Pro. I met him when I played with the Nighthawks. I was playing with the band when he came on stage and burned my ass off! I asked him how I could play like he did and he asked me how much time I got! He didn't want to teach me but I persuaded him— started off a gallon of wine a class. . . . Blues is the greatest feeling—that's what Pro taught me. You can't teach it to somebody, they have to teach themselves."[89] After being in the service and living in Canada for twenty years, Dean returned to play blues in Baton Rouge in the 1990s with Larry Garner. Back in 1961 and 1962, Boe Melvin and the Nighthawks were managed by Shirley "Cadillac" Jackson, who Tabby Thomas described in the *News Leader* as "the former blues shouter and owner of Club 33. She has found the golden touch—money keeps pouring in and Club 33 is the showplace of the city with a live broadcast every Saturday afternoon."[90]

In mid-July, Harpo started at a new venue, Thunderbird Beach, a recently developed leisure beach and amusement park near Denham Springs. The Beach had opened a year earlier, sometime around July 13, 1959, when an ad was placed in *Billboard* magazine for a park manager. The following season, Harpo was booked to appear there some Saturdays and almost every Sunday afternoon, and this lasted for a couple of years between spring and fall. While he was there on July 16, 1960, the other music available in the area included Dave Bartholomew at Cal's Club, Sugar Boy at the Town and Country in Donaldsonville, Irma Thomas and Robert Parker at the Bantam Club, Dale Houston at Joe's Club "across the river" in Port Allen, and rock 'n' roll with Eddie Cash at Paul's Lounge. Another new venue presented itself when the *State-Times* of November 24, 1960, reported: "A holiday dance featuring five local bands is scheduled tomorrow night (Friday) at the Ogden Inn, teenage gathering spot, 3021 Government St. All young people in the area are invited to attend and cast their ballot to help decide the Inn's choice of 'Number One colored band in Baton Rouge.' Competing for band honors will be Slim Harpo, Joe Valentine, The Twisters, Lester Robertson, and the Emanons. Cold drinks and potato chips, no blue jeans. $1 admission." The paper did not go on to record who won this segregated honor, but likely it was Harpo because, it was reported on December 23, "the annual formal high schools Xmas dance at the Baton Rouge Country Club will feature the music of Slim Harpo and his band."

THE RISE OF SWAMP-POP

While Slim Harpo, Lightnin' Slim, Schoolboy Cleve, and others were recording what became known as swamp-blues for Jay Miller, we have seen that Baton Rouge was also home to R&B groups and to bands, both black and white, playing the newfangled rock 'n' roll that threatened to become the music of choice for younger people and to make well-paid bookings more difficult to come by for dance bands and for smaller blues groups. Gradually the rhythm bands and the rockers developed an amalgam of musics, later known as swamp-pop, that was popular right across Louisiana, and which centered, in Baton Rouge, very much on the CYO dance club and the promotional and recording activities of Sam Montalbano and his record label, Montel.

S. J. "Sam" Montalbano was from an entrepreneurial local family of Italian origin whose businesses were in real estate and fruit and vegetable sales. Carl Montalbano disapproved of his nineteen-year-old son's decision to go into promoting music and records after he left Catholic High School because he had no background knowledge, but, Carl said, "he told me music was in his blood." Sam was born in Baton Rouge in February 1937 and by the mid '50s was heavily interested in the new sounds of R&B and rock 'n' roll. His schoolmate was a singer, Jimmy Clanton, and in 1957 Sam started to put on Friday-night dances at his school under the banner of the CYO and the Montel-Sinac Dance Club. Sam had become known as "Montel" because his football coach at Catholic High found his real name too long to be yelled out when Sam did something wrong at practice. Then Jimmy Clanton got himself onto Ace Records in Jackson, Mississippi, and started playing shows further afield. Montel became his road manager, looking after finances and bookings for two years, and when Clanton's second disc, "Just a Dream," became a number-four national pop hit in August 1958, this became a worthwhile occupation. Montel was still running the weekly teen dances at the CYO, though, bringing in national stars like Fats Domino, Ray Charles, and Frankie Ford, along with some local discoveries. The first of these was another schoolmate, two years his junior, another local football star, John Fred Gourrier. John Fred and some friends formed a band called the Playboys in 1957—named for Hugh Hefner's new magazine rather than Bob Wills's old western-swing band—and started playing rock 'n' roll at the CYO and other local venues. Then Montel came across two local black R&B singers—Lester Robertson, who had been in Joe Hudson's group, and former gospel singer Lee Tillman—and started to book them at the CYO also.

Early in 1958, Montalbano decided to set up a record company to promote his artists. The first on Montel Records was by Gwenn Douglas, followed by "My Girl across Town" by Lester Robertson and the Upsetters and "Shirley" by John Fred and the Playboys. Robertson's disc became a top seller in Louisiana. An *Advocate* ad on October 17, 1958, confirmed Robertson would be at the CYO Friday night dance, "held every week after the football game." It was to be the "first appearance in three months of this popular recording artist who just completed a three month tour of the Southern states with his band the Upsetters with his popular hit record on Montel, My Girl Cross Town and Take It On Home To Grama." Then, John Fred's record became a small national hit, making number 82 on the *Billboard* popular charts at the start of 1959. By then, Montel had high hopes for an R&B group from New Orleans who had settled in Baton Rouge and who were the most popular of all at dance venues around town, black and white. They were James "Sugar Boy" Crawford and his Cane Cutters, who were not in fact cutters of cane like Slim Harpo and many of the down-home blues players.

Crawford was born on October 12, 1934, in New Orleans. A trombonist and pianist, he had formed a band called the Sha-Weez, named after a Creole phrase used by carnival Indians, "Chapaka Shawee." He was popular on the radio show of "Dr Daddy-O," and soon the Sha-Weez were recording for Aladdin in 1952, produced by New Orleans bandleader Dave Bartholomew. In 1954 Crawford adapted and recorded a carnival song, "Jock-a-Mo," picked up by Leonard Chess, who invented the new name for the group, the Cane Cutters. The song became a big hit in Louisiana and came back at Mardi Gras year after year before being reworked as "Iko Iko" by the Dixie Cups and becoming a big hit all over again in 1965. Promoter Frank Painia, owner of the Dew Drop Inn in New Orleans, booked Sugar Boy into cities across Texas, Louisiana, and Alabama, including black clubs around Baton Rouge. By 1955 he had become a favorite at the Carousel, a white nightclub in Baton Rouge, and many of his band members—including Billy Tate, Edgar "Big Boy" Myles, and David Lastie—had relocated there. Then he was booked by Montel and found he had an entrée into the white college circuit. On June 13, 1958, the *Advocate* carried a big ad for "Sugar Boy and Canecutters featuring Big Boy Myles at CYO Center's Montel-Sinac Dance Club." Elsewhere the same night, Dave Bartholomew's band was at Cal's Club with singer Tommy Ridgely.

Two months later, Sugar Boy was at the CYO again, an ad of August 5 proclaiming, "CYO Center tonight—air conditioned for your dancing comfort, Sugar Boy and his Cane Cutters." On September 18, the CYO ad read: "Teenagers will dance to the rock 'n' roll and rhythm 'n' blues music of one of the most popular vocalists and bands ever to appear in Baton Rouge, tomorrow night. James 'Sugarboy' Crawford and his recording band also features two recording artists, Bill Tate and Big Boy Myles." For some reason, perhaps its Catholic Irish connotations, Sugar Boy's version of the slow ballad "Danny Boy" became a hugely requested song in Baton Rouge, and Sam Montel recorded it as the third disc on Montel Records at the end of 1958. Sugar Boy continued to play gigs in Baton Rouge until his career was curtailed in 1963 when he suffered a severe attack by police. He said he was driving to a job in

Monroe when the police stopped him for being drunk and speeding: "They hit me with a pistol and I was in hospital and paralyzed for a year. . . . After I had an operation, the first time I saw a piano I knew what it was but I didn't remember how to play it. It was in '63 when everybody was upset because of the freedom marches. . . . I just got caught on the bad end of a deal." Crawford came back to music after a few years but remained a low-key presence on the local scene only.[91]

Over in Crowley, while Sam Montel was tapping into Baton Rouge's newer, younger talent, Jay Miller was also drawing into his studio a number of new singers and bands from all over Louisiana and East Texas. The pattern he had established with both hillbilly and blues, that of recording music locally with the aim of attracting a bigger record label as a partner, would be continued into the rock 'n' roll era when he formed Rocko, Zynn, and other labels and further diversified his recordings. He confirmed, "My intention was to release the records and hope the songs and records would be picked up by the major companies." Into the late 1950s and through the 1960s, Miller was continually trying out new artists, label names, styles, and sounds. He worked hard to improve his studio sound, and in 1958 he tried to build a new, better studio in the Constantin Building, 986 North Parkerson, but was unsuccessful. After struggling with a new and expensive but dysfunctional echo chamber and other sound problems through that year, he instead decided to attach a new recording studio to the house he had moved to in 1951, two miles north of his downtown businesses at the junction of Highway 13 and Highway 10. He started recording there in 1959, and artists who made sessions at that studio such as Johnnie Allan and Warren Storm agree that he moved most of his recording activity there around 1960. Despite varying degrees of success in licensing his music to other labels and despite changing studios several times, Miller was nevertheless successful in creating records that had a distinctive Louisiana sound. Partly, this was because he was comfortable with blues, Cajun, and country styles and also happy—and rather brave given the highly segregated society of the time—to use a mixture of these musicians in his session bands. He was very comfortable working with all races and styles, mixing them into what record collectors and eventually the record business came to call swamp-pop in the wake of such Miller productions as Warren Storm's 1958 Hot 100 hit, "The Prisoner's Song."

Swamp-pop was largely made by young singers and musicians from Louisiana and East Texas who had their roots in Cajun music, zydeco, or New

Orleans R&B but whose sights were set on making rock 'n' roll sounds aimed at the Hot 100 rather than the country or R&B charts. As well as Jay Miller in Crowley and Sam Montel in Baton Rouge, other record men who recorded swamp-pop styles were Floyd Soileau in Ville Platte, Louisiana, who had the Jin label and, like Miller, leased songs to major record labels; Johnny Vincent Imbragulio, who had Ace Records in Jackson, Mississippi; and Eddie Shuler in Lake Charles, Louisiana. Montel and Vincent tended toward the teen-ballad end of the market while Miller, Soileau, and Shuler recorded a wider range of music, all with the lazy swing of the swamps. Early swamp-pop hits included Jimmy Clanton's "Just a Dream," Joe Barry's "I'm a Fool to Care," Rod Bernard's "This Should Go on Forever," Cookie and the Cupcakes' "Mathilda," and Phil Phillips's "Sea of Love."

Ultimately, Jimmy Reed's "Honest I Do" was as much the template for swamp-pop records as anything else was, helping to explain his popularity among the white college crowds and the tendency to attribute his influence to the likes of Slim Harpo. Even Lightnin' Slim, whose music was virtually a definition of the blues, would be persuaded to enter the fray with swamp rockers like "Hello Mary Lee," from 1961, retaining the blues harp sound but using Miller's top session players to make a relentless rhythm and fluidly rocking guitar and piano solos. Lightnin' followed with "If You Need Me" in 1963, still with blues harp but otherwise with a fully fledged swamp-pop beat and part-narrated teenage-love lyrics. The difference was that Lightnin's deep country voice, so fitting for the blues, sounded flat and heavy for the pop market. Rather better was "You Know You're So Fine," also from 1963, a mid-paced, Cajun-influenced swinging rocker.

By the time Jay Miller got around to trying out Lightnin' as a swamp-pop singer, though, he already knew who the master was at taking the swamp-blues into more lyrical territory. It was Slim Harpo.

Former slave cabins below the levee near Mulatto Bend (Courtesy West Baton Rouge Historical Association)

One-stop store for gas, goods, and great music, west Baton Rouge
(Courtesy A. E. Woolley Photographs and Papers, Mss. 4650, Louisiana and Lower
Mississippi Valley Collections, LSU Libraries, Baton Rouge, La.)

Slim Harpo's birth certificate, as Isiah Moore (Courtesy William Gambler)

Early morning ferry, Port Allen to Baton Rouge, 1950s (Courtesy A. E. Woolley Photographs and Papers, Mss. 4650, Louisiana and Lower Mississippi Valley Collections, LSU Libraries, Baton Rouge, La.)

Baton Rouge, looking southeast toward New Orleans, 1952 (Courtesy A. E. Woolley Photographs and Papers, Mss. 4650, Louisiana and Lower Mississippi Valley Collections, LSU Libraries, Baton Rouge, La.)

Looking east from Mulatto Bend to Baton Rouge across the Huey P. Long Bridge
(Courtesy West Baton Rouge Historical Association)

A bustling Third Street, Baton Rouge, 1953 (Courtesy A. E. Woolley Photographs and Papers, Mss. 4650, Louisiana and Lower Mississippi Valley Collections, LSU Libraries, Baton Rouge, La.)

Policing the bus strike, North Boulevard, Baton Rouge, 1953 (Courtesy A. E. Woolley Photographs and Papers, Mss. 4650, Louisiana and Lower Mississippi Valley Collections, LSU Libraries, Baton Rouge, La.)

EXCELLO Records

Excellorec Music BMI

Rhythm-Blues Time-fade (a)

NASHBORO RECORD CO., 177-3RD AVENUE, N., NASHVILLE, TENNESSEE

I'M A KING BEE
(J. Moore)
SLIM HARPO
45-2113

'King of Blues' To Be at CYO

The "Blues King of the South," "Slim" Harpo, is slated to appear at the Catholic Youth Organization center on Florida St. tomorrow night for the regular dance for teen-agers. The dance is slated from 8 p.m. to midnight and is attended by teen-agers from Baton Rouge and surrounding towns.

"Slim" Harpo has recorded many records in his career, among them "I'm a King Bee."

The dances at the air-conditioned CYO center are presented by the Montel-Sinac Dance Club and sponsored by the Baton Rouge CYO. "Slim" Harpo is currently one of the most popular artists on the Baton Rouge scene.

The dances are well-chaperoned, and no one wearing blue jeans will be allowed to enter.

Above: An original 45 rpm pressing of Harpo's first disc (Author's collection)

Left: Announcement from the "Teen Age Party Line" page of the *State-Times,* May 5, 1960, of an upcoming CYO dance featuring Harpo (Author's collection)

Butch Cage (*left*) and Willie B. Thomas, 1959 (LP cover, Folk-Lyric Records)

Robert Pete Williams, 1960s (Courtesy Arts Council of
Greater Baton Rouge)

Otis Hicks, aka Lightnin' Slim, 1958 (Courtesy John Broven Collection at the Library of Congress and Ace Records)

Leslie Johnson, aka Lazy Lester, late 1950s (Courtesy John Broven Collection at the Library of Congress and Ace Records)

Slim Harpo dressed for the big city, on tour in the Northeast, 1961
(Author's collection)

4. RAININ' IN MY HEART

A Trip to Chicago | Recordings, November 1960 | Success at Last | Recordings for Imperial, June 1961 | A Night in Mobile | All-American Bandstands

A TRIP TO CHICAGO

The record release that would really count for Harpo, "Rainin' in My Heart," came after his next session, in November 1960. But first, Miller had made some bookings at Chicago clubs for Harpo and others of his blues artists, including Lightnin' Slim, Lonesome Sundown, Lazy Lester, and Carol Fran from Opelousas, once described as the "best gal" of Lightnin' and Sundown.[1] Miller kept some notes indicating that Harpo was booked there on November 17 and 18 via Bill Hill's Colt Agency for $450.

One of Miller's main recollections later was how he was perplexed and annoyed to hear that his artists had mainly played other people's hits for the Illinois crowds rather than promoting their own recordings. This was particularly galling to Miller because, as he said, "I bought a brand-new Volkswagen bus to send them all to Chicago in. It was the first in the state of Louisiana. I remember going down to the docks at New Orleans when it was being unloaded."[2] For the musicians, the excursion was not a success either if Lightnin' Slim's recording "Trip to Chicago" can be believed. Lightnin' describes how he's "so tired and so glad to be home from one of the most miserable trips I ever took. It took us three days and three nights to get there—'cause we did have a little trouble. Blowouts, flats, brake lock, and some of everything. Good thing we was in one of those little buses—there was nine of us." They took turns driving, including "old Slim Harpo. He said he never drove a 'little' bus before. He broke down on the middle of a mountain—and that's when we had to start to pushing—seems like we pushed most way from Kentucky to Louisiana." In an alternative take of the song, they pushed all the way from Kentucky to Illinois too. Apparently the nine people who went included Carol Fran's brother and bass player James Johnson from Harpo's band.

For Slim Harpo's part, he was glad of the money in Chicago because mainly he was still playing locally at his regular gigs and at rural places like Holmes Juke Joint in Clinton, Louisiana. Larry Garner, a bluesman of a later generation, who learned in part from James Johnson and Rudy Richard, talked about growing up in Clinton as a guitar enthusiast. He had an uncle who taught him blues songs, and he listened with his cousins to disc jockey "John R" on WLAC from Nashville. Also, "down the dirt road about a mile through the woods, they had a juke joint. And on Friday and Saturday nights back then, wasn't no, 'hey we shut down at 2 o'clock'—they played almost 'til the sun come up, and I could hear this coming through the woods all night long . . . Holmes Juke Joint . . . Silas Hogan, Guitar Kelley, people like that, Slim Harpo and guys like that."[3] Guitarist James Johnson recalls playing at such venues when he had a day job to go to next day and might receive very little money for a long night's playing. On the other hand, William Gambler was clear about the problem, remembering the years when Harpo was still casting around for his next big record:

> After "King Bee" then there did come a change in his life. He formed a band. He was in more demand, played more gigs. But it still wasn't a big living. He didn't pay the band a lot because he wasn't making anything! Sometimes the musicians were paid well at a white club, but most times when they'd go out to play at an ordinary little club around here they'd make about $60 a night—between them! He always paid them what he could afford. He had to set up a small trucking business. . . . this was after he had formed a band and made some success with music. He would go out and book his own gigs for himself, but also we all were involved. From the age of 15 or 16 [1957/58], I would drive him and the band to gigs in the local area. I could go into a club back then, no problem. [When he started] he had just a little band. He'd play little local clubs and I'd be on the door, or my mother would, and it would be maybe 25c or 35c per person, and there'd be maybe a hundred people in there. That's places like Lee's, the Green Parrot, Club 36, Wishadell's, everyday places. Until desegregation came, he just accepted that's how it was. What else could he do? When he did get bookings at white clubs, he would charge maybe up to one dollar admission at the white places, where the students would go. Locally in Baton Rouge that was the Acadian Club, the Glass

Hat, the Cotton Club, Blue Bull, the Jazz Room; none of these venues exist today. "Rainin in My Heart" was very popular for whites—we'd call that a country song really—and after that is when more people would approach him, you know, to play places for whites.[4]

To a young Rudy Richard, it was all new and exciting whatever the pay or the venues, and his abiding memory of his early days with Harpo was that they were busy ones. He said, "We had a job Mondays, Tuesdays, Wednesdays, Thursdays, Fridays, Saturdays and Sundays. I was rollin'."[5] He told about playing in Chicago with the band the first time, peeking out from behind a long curtain on the stage. "The people, oh Lord, it looked like a bunch of wasps. I'm going, 'Oh Rudolph, look what you got to face.' I was a country boy. I wasn't used to all that. But I did pretty good."[6] He also said he was responsible for the band adopting a sharper dress sense, something for which Harpo soon became known. Richard noticed what the slick Chicago bands and vocal groups wore on stage and talked to Slim. "I would say, 'Man, you have to tighten that because we're going on a big band stand, and you dress kind of shaggy,' I wouldn't tell him exactly like that because I didn't want to make him mad and get rid of me, and he would say, 'Yeah, Rudolph, you right. Those guys are dressed to kill.'"[7]

Rudy probably did well to want to avoid making Slim mad. William Gambler witnessed several eruptions of what he calls Harpo's "controlled temper." To William, "he really was a nice person, he was. But he had a temper, and it would come out every so often. If he was provoked in a certain way he'd go round knocking holes in the walls. Punching them, you know." Apparently, Slim could get mad at the drop of a hat over not much that William could understand. "We knew there were things not to do, you know, back at home." It was the same with his band members, where there were always areas of contention just below the surface. "With his musicians, see, he would get mad when they'd play too fast or play louder than he was singing. That was a no-no with him. And he would tell them straight, for sure. It was necessary for them to know. He wanted it his way and he was older than most of them. You can't have but one leader. That was his way."[8] Philip Guy recalled the day he first met Harpo, saying, "Slim was a big guy. If you didn't know him you'd always take him wrong because he looked mean, and he was very serious about his music."[9]

On the other hand, there is always a camaraderie and shared experience within a band, things only they know about each other—until those things start to come out. Lovell may not have enjoyed some of the stories she heard about trips to far-flung places like Chicago and even to nearer towns along the regional roads. She started to travel with Slim on his out-of-town trips after those first few shows, confirming, "I didn't travel too much around home with James [but] I went with him to Opelousas, New Orleans . . . and if it was out of state I traveled with him." It probably didn't harm her cause to be on hand when the female fans started coming around. She recalled: "After he started recording, the first time he went out of town it was to Chicago. There was quite a few of them went. After that, whether I felt like it or not, I went with him, to see to that." She soon realized how unusual her situation was. "It must have been a long time, about two years, before anybody would believe I was his wife. They didn't want to believe it, they could not believe it. All the time he toured, not one [other] artist on tour had his wife with him."[10]

By all accounts, although she was not in fact, legally, his wife, Lovell played an increasing part in Slim's musical life once he started to be known and to tour more widely. She acted as his unofficial minder, promoter, and song-partner, encouraging him to make the most of his talents and of his laid-back personality. Her son recalls, "My mother started going on his tours to help him along. She was a companion, but also he needed some help." The implication is that Harpo was not just in the sights of good-time women but, because of his nature and limited formal education, he was something of a target for people who might tempt him with ways of relieving him of his money. Harpo was not good with paperwork and contracts, certainly, and it seems that Lovell took care of those things as well as the physical writing of his songs. She once described how she wrote a lot of his songs with him. "He'd just tell me what to write, we'd trade ideas. . . . most of the songs were written while we were traveling. I kept several legal pads with me and he would think of something, I would think of something and when we got home or to a hotel we would put it all together and he would get his harmonica and guitar, that's the way he did it, and he did not read music." One of Harpo's drummers, Jesse Kinchen, described Lovell's role: "She was his backbone. She took care of all the business and wrote down all the stuff and took care of the money for him." The road life was alien to her, but she saw it as important that she was there, even though, as she said, "All I could think about was to get back to church so I could sing in the choir, the Elm Grove Baptist church on 38th Street. I love church. Slim went with me too. I gave him an ultimatum: 'I follow you, I help you, you have to go to church with me' . . . and he did it."[11]

According to Jesse Kinchen, Slim walked the line only up to a point: "Slim would take a little drink—a small glass, nothing like any musicians I knew. But he had this girl named Clara, and messed with her for I guess around five years because Ms. Lovell was the type that just sit down, didn't drink, smoke, nothing. She had already heard people talking, you know, but she loved Slim so much, she just ignored that." William Gambler had a good relationship with his stepfather, whom he called James or Cuz, never Slim, and as an occasional driver and helper with the band, he was well aware of the extent and the limits of Slim's vices, saying, "James used to like playing cards. He'd gamble a little, but he wasn't a drinker." There was something else, though, underlining Lovell's decision to go on the road with the band. William confirmed, "He used to run a few ladies. Like all musicians, the opportunity came to them I guess and it wasn't too many could turn it down. My mother knew, but she didn't say. He used to talk to *me* about that though. He had one in particular; she was there for quite some time." By the end of the 1960s, Clara was working at Wilson's Restaurant, later known as Rose and Thomas's Café and Bar, at 1320 North Boulevard opposite the Temple building. William remembered that "she worked at one or two other places too," and it was clear that Harpo had met her after hours through his music.[12] Jesse Kinchen described how James was in the habit of going to eat after a gig, "and Wilson was open all night." After out-of-town tours, Slim would agree that Lovell should go get her hair done while he took care of whatever pressing visits he had to make back in town.[13]

Despite his outside relationships, Slim was keen on telling people about the part played in his career and his life by Lovell. Toward the end of the 1960s, he told interviewers in New York, apparently genuinely as well as by way of explanation of her unusually constant appearance at his side, "We have a real good relationship. I just like to have her with me. I only leave her when I have to, you know. Only left her three or four times in the last nine or ten years. Just about everything I've done, she's had something to do with it."[14]

His stepson recalls that in general Slim was a good person to be around. He would give the young William jobs to do, keeping the house painted and the yard clean, and William in return was "an obedient child," at least by his own reckoning. Slim tried to pass on his abilities as a mechanic and a musician, but William did not like getting his hands dirty in engines and he found he had no musical ability either. Whether it was drums or guitar, even harp, "nothing worked." He did like to drive Slim's cars, though, when he became older, "but I had a problem with cars, getting in wrecks." William told Slim he thought he was jinxed, but Slim retorted, "No, you're careless." Nevertheless, William would drive Slim to gigs, drop off posters or placards at clubs, collect money at the door. "He knew that whatever money I got would still be there. He paid me just like I was in the band." The two got on well, and William remembers the many times "we'd play cards or we'd sit and talk and he'd tell me anything, you know. He didn't hide anything. Sometimes we'd go out to a club and it would be getting late to where I had to go to school next day but he'd be in a card game. He used to play poker for money. But he wasn't foolish about it. Some of the people would gamble the house or the car or whatever, but Slim didn't do that. He'd figure that if he could make anything up to $200 then that was a good night's work, you know, and it was more than he'd make playing music in the 1950s and more than he could get working construction."[15]

RECORDINGS, NOVEMBER 1960

Around November 1960, Harpo and Miller engaged in a session or, more likely, sessions that produced at least eight songs. Three would appear the next year on his first LP, one would be pulled out of its box later as a single, and three others would remain unissued for many years. But to Miller, there was one other song that really stood out, the swamp-pop ballad "Rainin' in My Heart."

It was another song ostensibly about love problems, but although the song was simple, its wording and construction were a class above many other reflective, bluesy songs. As well, the ballad had an unusual energy generated by the drummer, who plays a busy rhythm rather than a solid beat. This keeps the song moving despite the laid-back nature of the vocal, harmonica, and guitar chords. It was a marriage of low-down blues and Louisiana pop with Slim's harp almost taking on the quality of a zydeco squeezebox or Cajun accordion. There was a plaintive spoken plea midway, an Ink Spots–like recitation that was quite unusual for the time albeit that Elvis Presley was high on the charts with the recitation-laden song "Are You Lonesome Tonight?" at the time of this session. As one commentator said, "One of the features that makes 'Raining' so striking and attention-grabbing is the contrast between that whispery, conspiratorial singing and the mellifluous speaking voice in the recitation. It's actually quite startling."[16]

"Rainin' in My Heart" was a song that Miller said he had to work on for some time over a number of recording dates. Only three versions have survived on tape, and it is possible that the earliest of these was made as far back as the December 1959 "Buzz Me Babe" session. That version was pulled for inclusion in Slim's second LP in 1966 and reappeared in 1979 on a single issued on Jay Miller's short-lived Blues Unlimited label. A second version, probably made at this November 1960 session, remained unissued until surfacing years later in Europe on an Ace Records CD. The best version, recorded at this session, was the one Miller had been striving for. It was issued as a single right away, and would change Slim Harpo's fortunes even though Miller was still not satisfied with the production. Miller said, "I recorded it at three different sessions. And I really didn't get what I wanted, frankly speaking. I felt we had gotten all I could out of it so I sent it to Ernie Young with a letter apologizing. I thought it was a good song but that was the best we could do. And it turned out it wasn't too bad, because it sold a lot of records."[17]

The musicians on this session were largely Slim's road band, according to James Johnson, who played bass on the session. In that case the drummer would have been Sammy K. Brown, even though singer/drummer Warren Storm told interviewer Becky Owens he was "definitely on 'Rainin' in My Heart' and others" and Lazy Lester told Gene Tomko he was certain the drummer on the session was Joe Percell from Baton Rouge. Twenty-year-old Percell had been born in New Orleans but was living in Baton Rouge with his mother and grandparents at the time. He later moved to Detroit.

The unissued songs from this November session included "My Home Is a Prison," a strong blues performance by Slim and the band that later appeared on Harpo's first LP. It might have been a single, but Excello had already issued it by Lonesome Sundown, one of Miller's very best blues artists. It's an unforgettable title with some equally memorable lines about why the singer shot his baby. Lazy Lester recalled playing harmonica on one song by Harpo, and it could be this one because the harp and vocal overlap. Equally, Harpo may have played harmonica before overdubbing his vocal; Miller told John Broven that they did just that on another track from the session, "Lover's Confession." Two instrumentals were made at the session. "Moody Blues" built up slowly with guitar and drums anchoring an extended sax solo that gave way to an excellent extended harp solo, while "Snoopin' Around" starts as a harp workout and continues that way until a fluid guitar solo takes over. Someone, probably Lazy Lester, adds a clip-clop percussion effect to enhance interest. The other three songs show the range of material Harpo and Miller were trying out. "Wild about My Baby" was quite simply rock 'n' roll, with crashing drums, excitable guitar solos, and a swooping piano part throughout. It remained unissued until Jay Miller used it as the B side of the alternative version of "Rainin' in My Heart" on his Blues Unlimited label nearly twenty years later. "That's Alright Baby" was another breakneck-speed delivery of an "I'm leaving you" lyric that employs some memorable if not original lines—"you been bragging 'bout your woman / Take a look at mine." Fine guitar and harp solos and a kicking drumbeat complete the track. In contrast, the deliberate beat of "Lover's Confession" allows Slim to deliver some simple, heartfelt messages to his loved one—"Long as I live / My love will be true / I'm so proud of you." Hopefully it was directed to or written by Lovell, or Slim was in trouble that day. Finally, "Please Don't Turn Me Down" is a reflective harp workout with a great overall feel interspersed by two unremarkable blues verses. It would be pulled out for release as a single three years later.

SUCCESS AT LAST

Jay Miller's chosen best cut of "Rainin' in My Heart" was issued as Excello 2194 in January 1961, backed with "Don't Start Cryin' Now" from the June session. Excello took out an ad in *Billboard* in mid-month stating that "Rainin' in My Heart" and Lightnin' Slim's latest, "I Just Don't Know," were "2 to watch," and the label followed up on March 20 with an ad saying of "Rainin'" that there were "10,000 sold in New Orleans and [it's] heading up the charts." The other trade paper, *Cash Box,* found "Don't Start Cryin' Now" to be a song where the "tempo moves up to jet speed and Harpo follows the combo on a rafter-shaking journey," whereas "Rainin'" was a "slow moaning, earthy blues. . . . he takes the song for a tuneful ride. A real weeper . . . has the goods to deliver." Delivery was only gradual, though, and despite Excello's continued *Billboard* ads—on April 3 it was "breaking for a hit"—it was not until May 22 that the disc finally made it to number 20 on the national R&B chart. It stayed on that chart for many weeks but peaked only at number 17 at the end of July. However, on May 29 it surprisingly entered the popular music Hot 100 at number 87, went to number 69 after three weeks, then dropped out of the Hot 100 before climbing again slowly but steadily until it reached number 34 on July 17. Back in Slim's hometown, white rock 'n' roll singer John Fred was greatly impressed. "To me, 'Rainin' in My Heart' was just so real, so soulful. You had to like Slim Harpo."[18]

Yet, on July 2 the *Sunday Advocate* published a truly weird review of the record as if they didn't know it had been selling well for months: "'Rainin'' features a lonely harmonica opening and a plaintive vocal . . . real rock-a-billy music right out of the hills. It is so corny and hicky that it can't miss hitting." On Wednesday, July 5, 1961, Slim Harpo was a featured guest on the national pop-music TV show *American Bandstand,* fronted by host Dick Clark. James Johnson remembers the band was not required for that show: "He was on *American Bandstand* by himself. He pantomimed to the record. I saw him do it, on TV." Slim's neighbor Arlene Batiste agreed. "I remember when Slim was on *Bandstand,* I saw that right here on the TV. That was a big event then. He sang 'Rainin' in My Heart.' I just loved his music." Unfortunately there appears to be no surviving still photography or footage of Harpo's appearance on the show. A strange clash of memories surrounds the screening of the show, too. In some contrast to the memories of Johnson, Batiste, and others, William Gambler's main memory of the event was this. "It *would* have been a big event, all except for one thing . . . they didn't show that edition of *American Bandstand* in Baton Rouge. It came on every Saturday, but when he was on they didn't put it on the local channel. We all sat there around the TV to watch, and it didn't come on. They screened something else." Gambler's belief is that, although the show apparently aired in New Orleans and Lafayette, the powers at the local TV station pulled Slim's show because they did not want a black singer exposed to the white teenage audience. If it did happen that way, it was a local decision aimed at Slim because, as Gambler recalls, "a lot of black kids watched *Bandstand.* It was one of the few places they could normally see black, R&B, performers on TV."[19]

By the end of May, white rock and ballad singer Dorsey Burnette had recorded a cover version of Slim's song and seen it on the market by early June. He had just joined the Dot record label whose head, Randy Wood, knew a hit when he heard it. *Billboard* reported that Wood had signed Burnette in the morning, recorded him in the afternoon, air-mailed acetate dubs to key disc jockeys nationwide over a weekend, and started shipping his discs midweek. The record may have taken some sales from Slim, but it was a rather labored vocal supported by a full orchestra and strings and without any of the magic of Harpo's version. The success of Slim's original of "Rainin'" led Excello to issue an LP that fall, *Slim Harpo Sings "Raining in My Heart . . . ,"* Excello

8003, collecting together some of his singles. Note that the LP title added a "g" to "Rainin." Ernie Young had started Excello's LP series earlier in the year with Lightnin' Slim, and Harpo's was Excello's fourth and possibly best-selling LP to date though the label never was much geared to the album market.

At last, Harpo and Miller had found the song that took Harpo's career to another level. He was now selling not just to the R&B market but to devotees of the swamp-pop sound and to ballad fans. British singer Paul Jones went so far as to say "Rainin' in My Heart" "was a country record, albeit by a black singer."[20] "Rainin'" was the first of Harpo's discs to be issued abroad, appearing on Pye International Records in England twice, first in 1961 and again in 1963 at the time of the British boom in R&B bands. Rolling Stones guitarist Keith Richards was as taken with "Don't Start Cryin' Now" as he was with the hit side, so much so that nearly fifty years later he was still talking about the disc, somewhat fancifully: "You can almost smell the swamp coming off of this thing. Incredibly wry lyrics and I love the delivery. It's almost sleazy. At the same time, there is such a strength, quite a variety of rhythms and hints of Cajun stuff involved. This was done down in the swamps and it smells like it, sounds like it, feels like it."[21] In contrast, bass-guitar man James Johnson was more down to earth about it all. Looking back, years later, he said, "We didn't know which band or which song was going to make it, but Slim hit at the right time. They had better musicians out there than us. We just an old blues band, and we got lucky, really."[22]

At home, Slim was already selling to white record buyers and appearing more and more often for northern audiences and at colleges. William Gambler remembers making two long driving trips with his parents, to Kansas City, Missouri, and through Ohio working with a house band. He also drove on trips to Auburn, Alabama, where the band was James Johnson and Willie Parker. "They played all the university venues in the South at that time, when he had 'Rainin' in My Heart' as a popular record. He was one of the first to do that, particularly LSU, Ole Miss and Auburn, Alabama. Also he had started to use Percy Stovall in New Orleans as a booking agent." Stovall was a very important mover and shaker in the music world of New Orleans, and William Gambler feels that it was Stovall who organized Slim's appearance on *American Bandstand*. "He got onto *Bandstand* through an agent he had somewhere, Percy Stovall. Then later he had Dick Alen in New York. But neither one of them got him a whole lot of work."[23]

A young Excello employee at the time, Shannon Williams, said, "I know for a fact that 'Rainin' in My Heart' did sell over half-a-million copies" in its first few months of release.[24] But with the success of the song came more arguments. There had already been a standoff over royalties in 1958, when Harpo would not record, and now the tension between Miller and Harpo intensified. It was partly about speed of payments, but it was also about who was owed what in the first place. Not least, it was about who wrote "Rainin' in My Heart." Jay Miller's deal with Excello was that when they issued any recording he had provided to them, he received in return a percentage of each record sold, from which he had to cover his costs and pay the artists and musicians for their time. The deal allowed Ernie Young's Excellorec Music to publish all the new songs Miller submitted that were released on Excello and for Excellorec to take the standard publisher's half of the publishing royalty per disc sold. The writer(s) of a song, whether they were a performer like Harpo, someone else, or Miller himself, received the other half of the publishing income. This meant that Miller made more money on recordings where he was also solely or partly the songwriter.

So, the origin of the song was important to all parties, and there are at least two very different accounts. Slim Harpo described how he came up with the song, telling one of his booking agents, Dick Alen, "I was supposed to play a show one day and it started to rain. Well I got there and they told me the show had been cancelled because of the rain. So I called my wife to tell her. 'It's rainin,' I said, 'and it's rainin in my heart.' Afterwards I realized what I had said and I started hummin' on it. When I got home I sat down and wrote it."[25] He was more specific in another interview, saying, "I played in Oxford, Mississippi for two days, Friday and Saturday, and the weather was bad. My wife wasn't with me, so I called home and she said, 'How's it there?' and I said it's OK 'but it's raining—and it's raining in my heart because I want to see you,' you know. So when I got home, we wrote that song." Lovell Moore was equally precise in her own, but differing, memory that Slim was in Lawtell on that rainy day: "'Rainin' in My Heart' came about when Slim was due to play Richard's club on a Friday night and it was raining hard. The cover charge was one dollar and it was raining so hard nobody came out. We wrote the song at 3 a.m. in the morning back at home."[26] Just possibly the phrase about rain resonated with Slim because he had some memory of a 1950 R&B hit by Peppermint Harris titled "Raining in My Heart," spelled with a "g," an entirely different song. It is likely, too, that he was aware of the country ballad of the same title by Felice and Boudleaux Bryant that Buddy Holly took into the pop charts in 1959.

The title and the content of the song have been matters of dispute down the years, both with other musicians and with Jay Miller. In contrast to Slim's version, musician Jimmy Dotson told interviewer Gene Tomko that he came up with the title for the song while sitting with Slim and others having breakfast one morning before a session in Crowley. Jay Miller always insisted that he wrote part of the song, but not the title. He told Dave Booth: "Slim gave me the idea, the name, he'd been working on. He said, 'Mr. Miller, I just can't come up with the song.' He said, 'I know you can,' because he knew I wrote so many of those other songs."[27] So Miller completed the song, later telling Steve Coleridge: "I gave him [Slim] 25%, and the thing was he wanted to buy a car, so he sold me back the 25%. You hear all kinds of stories about that; he wrote it, I stole it, or I bought it. Fact is, I [only] bought the 25% I'd given him for the title of the song, that's all. At the time Slim didn't know it was going to be a big song, you understand."[28]

It's worth dwelling on the lyrics of the song because of the disputes about it. There are only two verses, the first one repeated at the end, and a spoken verse.

Rainin' in my heart
Since we been apart
I know I was wrong
Baby please come home

You got me cryin'
'Bout to lose my mind
Don't let me cry in vain
Try my love just once again

Spoken:
Honey, I need your love
Darlin', you know why
If you would, come back home
There'll be no need for me to cry.

Are these the lines of a bluesman or a country songsmith, or a mixture of the two? Either way, the magic is not actually in the words themselves but the combination of the Cajunly harp playing, the swirling, swampy tune, and the perfect melding of music and lyrics.

Lovell Moore confirmed years after Slim's death that she received a quarter of the royalties from the song, which would have been correct as it represented half the songwriting royalty. Total royalties due went half to Excellorec Music as the publisher and half to the songwriters. Lovell also agreed about the importance of cars to Slim, perhaps accepting that he was capable of making the kind of deal with Miller that Jay described. Apart from Slim's general interest in engines and machines, he and his wife and band needed good transport to their live shows out of the local area. Lovell said, "We traveled in a Buick at first, then we bought a station wagon and then after that we had two or three Cadillacs."[29] William Gambler recalls Slim had an ivory-colored 1953 Buick until he bought a tan 1959 Cadillac. Tabby Thomas, writing in the *News Leader* in January 1962, noted, "The word is out that if you ain't got a Cadillac, you just ain't in style. Diggie Doo, Slim Harpo, Curtis Taylor, Sam Bengal, all the local bigtimers are joining the Cadillac club." The month earlier he described how "Slim 'Raining in My Heart' Harpo is riding around in a crazy Cadillac, playing one nighters around Louisiana."

When "Rainin' in My Heart" was first issued on disc, it was credited jointly to James Moore and Jerry West (J. D. Miller's blues-writing name), and it is still registered that way with BMI today. It is one of the 498 songs of which Jay Miller/Jerry West is registered as composer or part-composer. That's a lot of songs, more perhaps than a busy entrepreneur might have time to write, but in interviews Miller always seemed to be very clear about distinguishing the songs he wrote from scratch, songs that were *really* his own work, from the many other songs he helped his artists to write, to improve, or to polish for release. Talking about his own songs like "It Wasn't God Who Made Honky Tonk Angels," "Me without You," and "Cry Cry Darling," he said in a radio interview with Dave Booth, "I must have written about twenty-five songs." He included "Rainin' in My Heart" in that category. As for the majority of his copyrights, as John Broven wrote, Miller was "a sensitive songwriter in the blues, country and rock 'n' roll idioms. Accordingly he had the priceless ability of being able to knock into shape the most amateurish of songs, for which he demanded his share of the writer credits, like any good song doctor would."[30] Miller was an established songwriter, unlike many other bosses of independent recording companies who put themselves down as songwriters without ever writing a word or a note—the Taubs, Lings, Joseas, and the rest of the names that appeared on the labels of most Modern and RPM discs, and some Chess records, to name just a few. Whatever else he did, it was almost certainly Jay Miller who decided that "Rainin'" should be spelled without a "g" on the record label and in copyright documentation, distinguishing it from the hit songs of Harris and Holly and ensuring payments reached the right place.

For Lovell, who had an emotional stake in Slim's songs and was the self-appointed custodian of Harpo's interests, it was tough to see him with a hit song for which he didn't get all the monetary rewards: "When James started with Jay Miller he didn't know a lot about the music business—and of course nobody tells you, you have to learn the hard way. The man really wasn't straight. . . . I don't know what he told James, what he said to him at the recording session—I didn't go with him—but I remember telling James 'please, don't give Miller Rainin' in My Heart,' because Miller had asked for it. But I knew he'd done it anyway; he's just like that, you know. It hurt me really because I tried to prevent it."[31] Lovell had been in the habit of going along to recording sessions whenever she could to help look after Harpo's interests, in the same way she attended shows when Slim went out on the road. But by now she had lost that option. She explained, "J. D. Miller told me I was not welcome to come back to the studio. There had been arguments about song royalties."[32]

RECORDINGS FOR IMPERIAL, JUNE 1961

It was worse than that in Miller's eyes. Slim and Lovell were fussing about song credits and trying to get out of Slim's recording contract just at the point when he and they were starting to see some real return for all the effort they had put in. Miller was visiting music contacts in California—including Randy Wood, who had offered him a production role with Dot Records—when he received a call from Ernie Young, saying he had heard that Slim Harpo had cut a session in New Orleans for Lew Chudd's Los Angeles–based Imperial label. Miller happened to be in a position to go over to see Chudd in Hollywood. "And I told him, 'I understand you recorded one of my artists that I have under contract.' He said, 'Yes, he wanted to record for us . . . he's union and you're not.' [I said] 'Well, when he signed up with me he didn't even know what a union was, and I'm quite sure that [union rules] won't supersede our legal rights.'"[33] Miller told Chudd that he would sue him and put Imperial out of business. He was bluffing, but when he got back, he called Ernie Young's lawyer in Nashville, Jordan Stokes. "He says, 'send me a copy of your contract' [and then] he called me back and said 'don't worry about it' and he wrote a letter for me to Lew Chudd." The upshot was, as Lovell conceded, "After we went to Imperial to record in New Orleans, we never heard anything [more] about that . . . we never had any correspondence out of them or nothing like that. After the contract was broken—apparently he was still under contract with Jay Miller—he went back and made some more records."[34]

It would be another two years, however, before Miller and Harpo could come to an agreement about that next session for Excello. While they were arguing the terms under which Harpo would recommence recording, Miller said, "We put his contract in suspension—meaning, that whatever time he didn't record for me after I asked him to come into the studio would be added to the contract period."[35] Miller wrote to Harpo by registered letter to explain this. William Gambler remembers that it was always an issue of contention between Miller and the Moores. "My father never signed another contract with Miller," Gambler said. "But Miller had a return receipt that was supposed to be from the post office. It had some signature that nobody could recognize. Miller said my sister, who was maybe 12 years old, signed for the contract. This is what he used to keep my father from recording."[36]

It is unclear who made the approach that led to Harpo's renegade Imperial session, but it was not unusual for an artist with a sudden hit to be made offers by other established independent record companies and even by major ones. Imperial was based on the West Coast, but their main R&B star, Fats Domino, recorded in New Orleans under the direction of bandleader Dave Bartholomew. It may have been Bartholomew who approached Harpo, but just as likely it was the New Orleans club owner and booking agent Percy Stovall, keen to see Harpo on a bigger label than Excello so that he could book him into bigger venues. Either way, Jay Miller was in no doubt that "someone with Imperial Records went to see him and painted him beautiful pictures. They went to New Orleans and cut some sides, while I was in L.A."[37]

Dave Bartholomew was involved in a production capacity with many Imperial artists. He was born on December 24, 1940, in Edgard, Louisiana, some forty-five miles southeast of Baton Rouge on the west bank of the Mississippi. The family moved to New Orleans in the 1930s, where Bartholomew was taught music by Peter Davis, who had once taught Louis Armstrong. He started to play trumpet with brass bands, joining Toots Johnson's band from Baton Rouge and then Claiborne Williams's band in Donaldsonville. He was in the Army during the Second World War and on return formed his own band in New Orleans. He was widely known to have the best band in town, and he also backed many touring singers, appeared on radio, and started working as a session band at Cosimo Matassa's pioneering recording studio. DeLuxe Records recorded him behind many star artists and also issued discs under his own name, including the minor R&B hit "Country Boy" in 1949. Imperial Records' boss, Lew Chudd, stayed in California day-to-day and so persuaded Bartholomew to start producing and scouting new artists for Imperial, including Smiley Lewis, Fats Domino, and Lloyd Price. When these artists started having major R&B and rock 'n' roll hits in the 1950s, Bartholomew pruned down his own band's schedule and performed mainly in his local area. He was a regular weekend fixture at Cal's Club and the Bantam Club in Prairieville.

Slim Harpo's Imperial session was held on June 27, 1961, at Cosimo Matassa's Governor Nicholls Street studio. Matassa taped most of Imperial's southern recordings. As far as is known, and can be heard, the musicians were Harpo's usual road band. James Johnson confirmed: "Yes, we did go to New Orleans to make records there. That was me and Rudolph, Pro, and Sammy. But I never did hear about those songs again."[38]

The key song at the session was intended to be "Still Rainin' in My Heart," seen as a follow-up to Slim's current hit. It was taken slightly faster and with rather more prominent sax riffs and guitar figures augmenting Slim's familiar story. The other three songs recorded were "Something inside Me," a spirited yet conversational vocal performance of a lyric about uncontrollable feelings that still left room for extended workouts from harp and lead guitar; "A Man Is Crying," a Chicago-style rhythm behind a sensitive blues lyric which Slim had earlier recorded as "What's Going On"; and "Tonite I'm Lonely," a slightly contrived attempt at a pop song—"I sit in my classroom / Writing your name," and so forth. All in all, this was a tuneful and well-recorded session, cut rather "cleaner" and less muddy than Miller's preferred sound, but lacking something in comparison nevertheless. The tapes of all four songs remained in their boxes until years after the legal dust had settled.[39]

A NIGHT IN MOBILE

Three days after the ill-fated New Orleans session, Harpo played a show on a Friday night for a high-school crowd at the National Guard Armory in Mobile, Alabama. Amazingly—because he did not then know that the Imperial deal would come to naught—he allowed the show to be recorded by two music enthusiasts, David Kearns and Joe Drago. In a different world, the tape might have ended in the hands of a small record company somewhere and led to another round of legal wrangling. As it happened, Kearns just wanted the tape for posterity, but when he rediscovered it many years later, he arranged for it to be issued by AVI, by then the owners of Excello. Even then it was a near thing. He had sent the tape to Excello, but "two or three years went by and I didn't hear anything, and then one night I got a call from Rob Santos," Kearns said. Santos was the A&R man running AVI for owner Harry Anger. "[Santos] had found the tapes in the top drawer of a desk. They were in an envelope with my name and number on it, so he called and said, 'What's this all about?'"[40] It remains a fascinating, incredibly valuable, almost matchless, record of a top-rate blues musician at work at the height of his powers. Louisiana music expert John Broven points out, "It's the only extant contemporary swamp-blues live recording that I know of and, even better, it coincides with his first big hit. His wonderful recording band was so *tight* on stage. OK, it was an impromptu recording but still incredible."[41]

David Kearns's accounts of his encounters with Harpo and the shows he personally witnessed back in that time help to flesh out our picture of Slim Harpo. Kearns said:

I think it was 1960 during my junior year in high school that Slim Harpo and the King Bees began playing for dances here in Mobile. Most of these Friday or Saturday night affairs were held at the Sage Avenue Armory and were sponsored by one or more of the high school fraternities or sororities that flourished during that era. Slim and the band may have played six or eight of these dances during my junior and senior years. Of course, I can remember Slim because he was the star of the show. He was tall and lanky but carried himself well. He was always well dressed in a conservative business suit, starched white shirt and a tie and perhaps looked more like he was dressed for Sunday morning church than for playing the blues. Off stage he was soft spoken and articulate with a definite Southern accent. I would classify him as urban and not at all country in his speech and mannerisms. He was very approachable and during intermission he would spend a few minutes taking requests and talking with us even though I'm sure he would have preferred to be resting up for the next set. At the end of the evening, when probably he just wanted to get back to Baton Rouge, he would linger a few more minutes talking about the music, answering our questions and graciously accepting our praise before heading off into the night.[42]

Although it was still just a few years since James Moore first started playing harmonica for local, largely black, gatherings and events, as "Slim Harpo" he was already used to playing to white crowds and was apparently happy to be doing so, at least financially, and he kept the same band together for some years. David Kearns remembered Slim's band too: "I remember Rudolph Richard because his thick glasses and slightly bucked teeth reminded me of Peter Lorre in the old Mr. Moto movies. He was also, along with James Johnson, a heck of a guitar player. I know James Johnson was there but I have no clear recollection of him. Willie Parker was memorable because, due to a disability, he played the saxophone while balancing himself on crutches. The drummer was probably Sammy K. Brown but I really have no clear recollection of him either. I think James and Rudolph alternated the bass parts. There was also a singer who spelled Slim and covered tunes that were popular at that time. I think that was the lineup for all the shows I saw during 1960 and 1961."[43]

Turning to the show that was recorded at the Armory, Kearns confirms that this was taped by himself and his friend Joe Drago. They had no experience of recording, but Drago happened to have access to a Heathkit recording machine and a Shure microphone. It was a show in two sets, both played on Friday June 30, 1961. Kearns believes "the performance we recorded was typical of all the shows that I saw back then as far as the material performed. The cover tunes from both Slim and the band were mostly recognizable and there was a heavy emphasis on danceable numbers. After all, these were dances, not concerts they were playing for."[44]

The show had been booked through Percy Stovall, the New Orleans nightclub owner and promoter, after Kearns's friend John Thompson had seen Harpo and the King Bees play a show at LSU in Baton Rouge. Harpo was a favorite performer at dances held regularly at other places like the old Cawthorne Hotel, the Elks Lodge, and the Skyline Country Club. "The other bands had been slicker, usually with saxophones as the lead instrument," Kearns recalled. "But Slim Harpo just blew us away. With the blazing guitars and his harmonica, it was a totally different type of music than what we were used to."[45]

The several hundred white teenagers sweltering in the June heat in the large Armory building were in party mood at the end of the school year, and Harpo's small combo was warming up the crowd with a set of familiar R&B instrumentals. Then, as David Kearns describes it, Harpo, carrying a fishing tackle box, walked through the open door and over to a position behind the bandstand. [He] set the tackle box on a chair. He opened the box and sifted through the harmonicas packed inside. He selected several and put them in his coat pockets. . . . From behind the bandstand [he] "whooped" into a microphone. Using his voice as an instrument, he "hooted" along with the music. As the King Bees kicked off the next number, their version of the Mar-Keys brand new hit "Last Night," [he] picked up one of his harmonicas and began to blow into the microphone. The amplified sound of the blues harp gave the music a new dimension. . . . Slim Harpo was about to take the stage. . . . Slim tapped out the beat with his foot, his harp kicked off an uptempo blues, and the King Bees joined in, their sound becoming more intense and focused on the blues.[46]

It was thirty-six years before a CD of part of this concert was issued. Only in 2015 was there a boxed set of Harpo's music that included all those parts of the two recorded sets that are of sufficient sound quality, together with both introductions and some of the instrumental music that gives an indication of what the band sounded like without their leader. It included also two examples of vocals, one taken by a member of the band, possibly James Johnson, and another featuring the warm-up singer, known as "Tomcat." James Johnson said: "I remember that show; that was recorded. It was me and Rudolph, Sammy and Pro, and Tomcat. He was another singer Slim carried to shows to open, and then he'd make announcements and bring Slim on. Tomcat came after Roosevelt Gauthier who first did that for Slim, and a guy named Willie did it too."[47] This is one of the very few live recordings to capture a successful blues band at the height of its popularity, let alone a swamp-blues band.[48]

The first few warm-up instrumentals by the band, based on R&B hits of the day, were not recorded well enough to be issued, but most of the problems were ironed out in time for the band's "star time" theme. When Slim was introduced to the crowd, he launched into a relatively fast version of "Hold Me Tenderly," the B side of a recent Bobby Bland hit, and followed with the old tune "L'il Liza Jane," which had been popularized recently by New Orleans stylists Smiley Lewis and Huey Smith. Then came Slim's current hit, "Rainin' in My Heart," which has not been issued due to poor sound quality, and his first hit, "I'm a King Bee," which suffers at the start from a tape-reel change. This was followed by "I Got Love if You Want It" and the instrumental now known as "Buzzin'" that he had yet to record. In fact, the tune was a version of the Junior Wells instrumental "Cha Cha Cha in Blue" that came out on Chief

Records late in 1957, was reissued on Profile Records in 1959, and appeared on Chief again in 1961. Slim called it by that title at his shows until it was recorded later as "Buzzin'." Then he went into four R&B songs associated with Jimmy Reed, Lee Dorsey, and Little Walter, two of which were fairly recently on the charts and one, "Big Boss Man," had only just broken into the charts the month before. Then he threw in the New Orleans favorite, "When the Saints Go Marchin' In," and Ray Charles's "I Got a Woman," neither having been issued due to sound problems and the microphone wire being dislodged by an enthusiastic fan. Then came versions of songs by Bobby Bland and John Lee Hooker. The first set of the evening was completed with a long version of Slim's "Moody Blues" and an extended version of Lazy Lester's recent recording of a Jay Miller song, "Sugar Coated Love." The tape ran out just as Slim was completing this song and taking his break. "Sugar Coated Love" was in the same vein as Jimmy Reed's "You Got Me Dizzy" and was about as close as Slim ever got to the Reed sound.

Slim later told how his favorite artists were the blues heavyweights Muddy Waters, B. B. King, and Howlin' Wolf, but these live recordings demonstrate the wider range of bluesmen, soul singers, and southern sounds that occupied Slim in mid-1961. They also demonstrate that he was up to date with current and even breaking hits as well as influential older blues songs. Whether the set played by Slim and his band would have been exactly the same were they playing for a black audience in a local club is not known.

During the break between Slim's shows, the second singer joined the band for songs made popular by the likes of Larry Birdsong, Ernie K-Doe, Lonesome Sundown, and Ray Charles, and another member of the band sang one tune. These recordings were rather average in their performance, but two of the songs—the Cookie and the Cupcakes hit "Mathilda" and the Elmore James tune "Talk to Me Baby"—have been issued as an indication of what happened that night, as has the band's version of the breaking Mar-Keys hit, "Last Night." Then it was the "star time" theme again, and Slim reappeared for a short valedictory set where "I'm a King Bee" was followed by a Little Walter song, "I Don't Play," and a second version of "I Got Love if You Want It." Second versions of "Li'l Liza Jane" and "When the Saints Go Marchin' In" appear to have been crowd requests and generated much audience chanting before Slim signed off with his current hit, "Rainin' in My Heart."

Guitarist Rudy Richard said later, "[On shows] we played all his hit songs . . . but I used to hate waiting to play that sting on that 'King Bee.' I always thought I was going to miss it. I never did, though." These live record-ings show the range of Richard's playing and the styles of other members of Harpo's band. They were indeed a tight unit. Writing later, interviewer Steve Coleridge thought "Rudy Richard's guitar playing is not the straightforward Mississippi, Lightnin' Hopkins style often associated with Louisiana, but is an amalgam of Louisiana and east Texas, with ninth and augmented chords."[49] Richard himself credits his learning years with Lonesome Sundown as being important: "I started going by his house and, man, he really started putting something on my mind then. He didn't want me to play dirty licks. Keep it clean, you know? And Sundown taught me not to play too loud. If you play too loud, people are going to tolerate it for awhile, but the next thing you know you're going to be playing by yourself. But that never happened to me. And whatever you play, try to do it correct. I hate to see a guy just playing notes. It's all right to play lead, but always have your chords to carry. Like when a guy's singing, always bring him some chords. You got to play chords behind the guy. And when you do solo, drop a little chord in there some-where. I've got a habit of doing it. It's gotten to be a natural thing."[50]

ALL-AMERICAN BANDSTANDS

Slim's TV appearance on *American Bandstand* came just a few days after the Armory show, and in fact it was trailed to the Mobile crowd when Slim was introduced. Tellingly, he was described to the white teen crowd there as "a rock 'n' roller." Less than a month later, he was still in high demand. He topped the bill over Jan and Dean, the Vibrations, Jerry Fuller, Rod Bernard, and other acts at the "Show of Stars" held at the Corpus Christi Coliseum on July 22 in association with the "Miss High School of Texas" contest.

During the period Slim was away from the recording studio in the wake of the standoff over songwriting, he took more and more bookings at white colleges on the strength of his pop-chart hit. Harpo was among many blues singers who played regularly for the Delta Kappa Epsilon fraternity—the Dekes—at the University of Mississippi in Oxford. Lovell told Steve Coleridge, "During the boycott we were working a lot at colleges in Alabama and at 'Ole Miss'—this was before it was integrated. All the white kids were real nice to us, to me, and there were no problems at the universities themselves." But this was not the case out on the road, and one incident in particular stuck in her memory:

The worst problem we had was in Hattiesburg or some little place in Mississippi on the way back from Oxford. Three guys started following us on the road on motorcycles, forced us off the road as a matter of fact. When Slim got a chance he speeded up and we made it to a service station thinking we might get some help there. But the guys followed us there. James got out and he showed them his musician's union card and said we'd just played a dance at Ole Miss. This one guy took the card and his knife . . . and just shredded it. Said the only good nigger is a dead one, stuff like that, you know. So, somebody had called the police and then we were told to follow the police car and the guys are behind us. After we had gone about three miles, down through some trees—I was so scared—we came upon a big house. James got out and went in as they asked and he told me, "If anything happens to me, you just take off." But where? I didn't know where I was. Well, he went inside for a long time and finally he came to the door with one of the motorcycle guys and I heard him say, "All right, sir," and then he got in the car and said "let's go," and we took off. Finally I asked him what had happened. He said it was a judge's house, and the guys had said we forced them off the highway—whoever it was, they made James pay them some money. I never want to experience that again.[51]

Apparently this was not an uncommon experience for black musicians in parts of the South at that time. Down in New Orleans, Huey "Piano" Smith recounted to his biographer John Wirt how he had to learn to leave towns after a show by a back route to avoid falling prey to police stopping him for a minor violation and relieving him of his night's pay. In 1963, Sugar Boy Crawford's major head injury occurred in similar circumstances, and bluesman Raful Neal also remembered the conditions within which they played white venues. "We played all over the Southeast, LSU fraternities, clubs in Memphis, Jackson, Montgomery, all around. And we were at Oxford at 'Ole Miss' when Kennedy sent the National Guard in 1963. We was afraid when we saw those soldiers with those rifles, but we had signed a contract, so we played. The show went off real nice."[52]

The early 1960s were times of political uncertainty, with an increasing drive behind those who worked to achieve racial equality, including desegregation of schools and public amenities in the South. Baton Rouge was by no means at the forefront of social and political action, but like most southern cities, it had those who backed reform and those who opposed it. It also retained the institutionalized racism Hubert Humphrey had so vividly described after his sojourn there twenty years earlier and which songwriter Randy Newman criticized and satirized in the decade after Slim Harpo's death.[53]

On February 1, 1960, four black college students sat down at a whites-only Woolworth's lunch counter in Greensboro, North Carolina, and set the scene for an important phase of the civil rights movement. Students in other cities followed suit, and on March 28 some people at Southern University staged a similar sit-down at the Kress store in Baton Rouge, and were promptly arrested. On March 30, about two thousand students from Southern rallied at the university, at the Kress store, and at the bus station. When the action quietened down, their leaders were expelled.

Nevertheless, as David Kearns reports:

> I never heard Slim say anything that could be construed as social or political commentary during that period. I think Slim was a businessman who recognized that most of his audiences were made up of white kids of high school and college age who might not look at the world we lived in in the same way that he saw and experienced it. It would not have been prudent to alienate any of his fan base by trying to educate them about the travails of a black man in the segregated South. Slim was breaking down social barriers in his own way. He was relating to us with his music. He may have gone back to his family and friends in Baton Rouge and voiced his feelings about what was going on, but I think he recognized that his role when playing for a white audience was to entertain, and he always did a wonderful job of that.[54]

Most of Slim Harpo's major shows for white fans in 1961 were also in the South, some very locally. On March 19, 1961, he was in New Orleans to play the "Big Show of 1961" at the Municipal Auditorium, where WNOE radio announcers brought on a strong R&B cast including Johnny Adams, Eddie Bo, Jimmy Jones, the Five Satins, Bobby Mitchell, Lee Dorsey, Chris Kenner, Clarence Henry, Earl King, Smiley Lewis, Benny Spellman, and the Tommy Ridgely band.[55] Three days before he was at the LSU campus, where the Phi Chapter of Sigma Nu held its annual "beatnick" party: "Music was supplied by Slim Harpo and his King Bees. Dr. and Mrs. Rees served as chaperones."[56] Soon, Harpo was in New Orleans again taking top billing over Lightnin' Slim in a double-threat stage show on May 25 at the High Hat Club on Orleans Street, and that month he also recommenced regular shows at Thunderbird Beach, where the publicity read, "Bring the family, stay all day—featuring record star Slim Harpo singing 'Rainin' in My Heart' at 2 pm. No extra charge." The following week Slim's appearance there came as part of the "Fun in the Sun" dance. On June 3, the Thunderbird—"the best beach in close reach," twelve miles northeast of Baton Rouge—had a Saturday dance with Lester

Robertson and Sunday afternoon dancing to "recording star Slim Harpo." On the same weekend, Cal's Club had Buddy Stewart, and the Ogden Inn on Government Street was advertising a high-school dance every Friday night, kicked off by Boogie Jake. On June 9 the ad in the *Advocate* for the Ogden Inn said: "You've got to hear Boogie Jake tonight, folks. He rocked the house Tuesday." The same paper advertised other events that weekend when Harpo was at the Acadian and the Thunderbird. "Harmonica Smith," Moses Smith, was at the Thunderbird too; Dave Bartholomew was at Cal's; Jessie Hill at the Bantam Club. In some contrast, there was a big ad for Margot Fonteyn and the Royal Ballet at the Varsity Theater.[57]

In June 1961 came the launch of a new music venue to compete with Montel's CYO shows. Joe Messina, who had also booked the CYO Center, was now using Cedarcrest Hall, on Aubin Lane off Airline Highway, twice a week for teenage dances. Messina was described in the *Advocate* as "formerly with the Dixie Kats that included Jimmy Clanton and Dick Holler. . . . Initiating the series will be top recording star, Slim Harpo whose 'Rainin' in My Heart' is a favorite with local teens." The ad confirmed that, during the summer, other stars would be Chris Kenner, Sugar Boy, Frogman Henry, Eddie Bo, Jimmy Reed, and John Lee Hooker. "Messina estimates 200,000 teenagers have been entertained in the last four years by shows he has put on featuring Harpo, Fats Domino, Larry Williams and others."[58] The white teenagers turned out, too, for local white rock 'n' roll groups such as that of Dick Holler. Holler was from Indiana but studied at LSU and appeared on the teen TV show *Hit or Miss*. In May 1956 Holler formed the Rockets band with Jimmy Clanton to play at the Carousel Club, and the following year both boys were recording for Ace Records of Jackson, Mississippi. Later in the 1960s, Holler wrote two novelty pop songs that became top-10 hits, "Snoopy vs. the Red Baron" and "Abraham, Martin, and John."

Local ads in July 1961 reassured fans, "Harpo [is] still at the Acadian, Saturday nights," but the reality was that he was starting to pick up more work away from home. On August 19 the *New York Amsterdam News* noted the impending first appearance of Harpo at the home of black R&B and rock 'n' roll: "R&B Revue will reopen Apollo Friday—After two weeks of furious renovating and redecoration, the Apollo Theater will reopen with a very exciting R&B revue. The cast reads like a list of the most popular recording artists of the last few months—Dee Clark, Ernie K-Doe, Clarence Henry, Phil Upchurch, Slim Harpo, Carla Thomas, and others." On August 21, Harpo was featured in a block ad for the "Recording All Stars" show at the Regal in Chicago, "a new brilliant stage revue featuring an outstanding array of today's hottest stars, with Sam Cooke, the Drifters, Carla Thomas, Ernie K-Doe and Red Saunders orchestra providing the backings." Suddenly, Slim was on the northern package-show circuit as a solo act working with other bands. Ads in the New York and Chicago press found him sharing the entertainment pages with the likes of Odetta, Sammy Davis, the Drifters, and Frank Sinatra. To confirm the new order, the *Sunday Advocate* of August 27, 1961, was explaining that "the Moonlite Inn, French Settlement, brings you Slim Harpo's Band—The King Bees"—the band, note, not their boss.

When he returned from the North, on September 22 and 23 the *State-Times* carried large picture ads for Harpo: "The Texan Lounge presents In Person, direct from American Bandstand—Slim Harpo and his entire band. Friday and Saturday nights, Highway 190, Port Allen." The local boy had finally done good in the eyes of the white press.

No ads for Harpo and his band ever identified the players, and although most witnesses concur that Rudy, James, and Pro were the core of the King Bees, it is clear that the group expanded, contracted, and changed as the job and financial circumstances dictated. Often Pro's sax playing would be augmented by a trumpet player, Otis Johnson, born in New Orleans but reared in Baton Rouge. Johnson remembers:

I began playing piano and took lessons in music. I studied it all, and in 1957 I started playing in the Capitol Junior High School Band. I just met Slim Harpo one day somewhere and we started talking about playing and then I came into his band playing trumpet. That was in 1961, up until I went into the Army in 1963, and then I'd play when I was home on leave. Slim always treated me right but I just played and did what I was told. As far as I know, he was a nice person, always seemed to have a joke to tell. He was funny. In those days there were steady gigs at Wishadell's Dream Club on Thursday nights, Jesse's club at Clinton on a Friday or Sammy Talbot's in East Feliciana, then on Saturday it would be anywhere in or out from Baton Rouge, and Sunday was the Streamline at Port Allen. Slim had Rudy, James, Pro, and A. J. Edwards. He was the drummer when I joined and still was after I left, although Sammy K. Brown made a few gigs with Slim sometimes. A. J. was from West Baton Rouge like Slim and he also sang good, though Slim carried another singer too, Willie something, who did a lot of Bobby Bland stuff. After the Army I played bass guitar with Slim for a while when James Johnson played lead after Rudy left.[59]

5. BUZZIN', SCRATCHIN', HIP SHAKIN', BREAD MAKIN'

THE CONTRACT BLUES

Harpo and his band gigged locally and undertook regional tours for two years before stepping back into Jay Miller's studio in 1963. In the absence of a properly planned follow-up to his big hit, Miller had had to settle for Harpo's first LP, issued in 1961, containing several of his singles and some other tracks taken from earlier sessions. Curiously, Miller and Excello did not issue any singles drawn from past sessions, as would have been standard practice, but this may have been linked to the legal situation that at once encouraged and discouraged both parties to settle their dispute.

In taking on Miller, Excello, and established music-industry practice, Harpo was one of the few blues artists of his era who took a stand against "the man." In not settling his dispute he was potentially losing money and momentum, as Ernie Young pointed out when he wrote on February 2, 1962, to Donn Fileti, a college student–radio man in Virginia who had inquired about Harpo having, he understood, recorded for Imperial Records. The label may have been making noises to the trade about a forthcoming Harpo disc. Young replied, forcefully: "Regarding Slim Harpo, he is under sub-contract to us. A man in Louisiana holds the original contract on him. The contract this man holds on Harpo is perfectly good, it has been checked by my attorney and he reports to me that the contract is good. We heard today that there is a new record out by him, thus far we have not heard anything about it. Slim Harpo had not amounted to any too much before 'Rainin' in My Heart' came out. This is the tune that made him and prosperity got the best of him. Evidently he does not want to record for the man who holds his contract, and by not doing so it hurts him and also myself. Naturally court proceedings will be taken by the manufacturer and the man he is contracted to."

In any event, there was no single issued by Imperial Records, and Harpo remained inactive with Excello. In an uncorroborated account, Tabby Thomas once said that Ernie Young called him one day looking for Harpo. "He told me, said, 'Tell James Moore I got eleven hundred dollars up here for him, for some royalties . . . and tell him I'm gonna send it to him as soon as he go in the studio and cut something.'"[1] Quite apart from the unlikely use of a go-between, although Ernie Young was as concerned as anyone that there was no sign of any new Harpo recordings to follow up his hit, he was not likely to have forced a solution between his main record producer and his hit-maker. Shannon Williams said, "Ernie wouldn't cross Miller like that because it would mean that he would probably never get another piece of product from Miller. He never crossed him. He looked at Harpo as Miller's artist; I don't think Ernie Young wanted to get involved with those kind of people and artists. I doubt if he could have made records like Miller did."[2] Although Young had "produced" his own sessions of Nashville-based gospel and R&B since the early 1950s, Ernie's method involved little more than letting the tape roll. He knew that he would not have been able to extract what Miller could from Slim Harpo or anyone else, let alone re-create Miller's swamp-blues sound.

In 1962, when Young was despairing of Harpo, Excello accepted for release some Jay Miller recordings by a younger Baton Rouge harp player, Jimmy Anderson, originally from Mississippi. Their logic in looking for a replacement artist in Harpo's style was sound, but the reason they recorded and released Anderson playing "I'm a King Bee" is hard to fathom other than that Excellorec Music owned the publishing. That was taking going back to square one to the extreme. Miller also recorded Silas Hogan for Excello at this time, along with Whispering Smith and Tabby Thomas, thus adding other Baton Rouge artists to the contenders for the blue space created by Harpo's absence from the studio. Miller certainly took the view at the time that Slim was not irreplaceable—though he would turn out to be wrong.

As for Slim, who believed he was in the right in his stance about royalties, his resolve may have been strengthened by his enduring popularity and ability to book live shows. In addition, though he barely knew it yet, his music was being taken notice of abroad. In England, where "Rainin' in My Heart" had been issued as a single, fledgling white R&B bands were playing "King Bee," and there was a wave of blues-appreciation magazines fueling interest in the blues and in Slim Harpo. The very first edition of the would-be influential *Blues Unlimited* reported in April 1963 on Miller and his artists, saying Harpo "has made several worthwhile discs . . . good examples of modern down-home blues . . . [but] unfortunately . . . Jay has been unable to get him to the studios since. A pity, for Harpo has a unique voice and plays good harmonica."[3]

According to neighbors of the Moore family back in west Baton Rouge, Slim Harpo let neither success nor arguments with record companies affect him. Connie Dents was the eleven-year-old daughter of Slim's neighbor from school days, Menty Dents, the year Slim hit with "Rainin' in My Heart." She described how "Slim was in his twenties when I was born and he lived over in Baton Rouge, but I knew his three sisters who lived at the Bend, and every Sunday he'd come to the Bend and visit with his sisters. Me and all the kids would be there and he'd sit and play music for us. Slim always had time for you. He was a very loving person and I never heard anyone say anything bad about Slim."[4] Arlene Batiste was a teenager in Mulatto Bend at that time: "I used to see Slim all the time around here. Because his sisters stayed here side by side, and he'd go to see all the kin. James got on well with his sisters. They all was nice people, and Doris went to my church at St. John. And Charlie Reed, 'Son' Reed, my neighbor 'cross the street, was some kind of kin to Slim through his wife. Son did well, had a good business, owned some trucks and Slim drove for him, worked with him, all the time I was growing up."[5]

Fortunately Slim was a careful driver and didn't get into the papers like Son Reed. On August 3, 1962, among the fifty-six people in court that month was "Charlie Reed Sr. of Route 2 Port Allen charged with reckless driving and three counts of driving while intoxicated." It was as well Slim was more careful because, as Connie Dents described, he ferried all his young friends and relatives around: "After he had his big hit record, he got a red Cadillac that he'd ride up in. It was something we'd look forward to every Sunday when he was in town; he'd come home and sing to us and play the harmonica and ride us all in that car."[6]

MORE BATON ROUGE BLUESMEN

Whether Slim was riding high on the charts or riding local kids around the block, he always seemed available to help other musicians and to put in a good word for them with J. D. Miller if they wanted to get on records themselves.

Jimmy Anderson, the singing harp player who recorded his version of "King Bee" for Miller, said "my manager took me to Crowley after Slim fixed it up."[7] This was in the latter part of 1961, and at the very time when Harpo and Miller were arguing about Harpo's own contract. Anderson said that he and Silas Hogan drove over to Crowley to see Miller at Harpo's insistence.[8] Possibly Harpo was still harboring the notion of changing record labels and was trying to provide his own successors to Excello. Anderson was not originally from the Baton Rouge area. He was born on November 21, 1934, in Natchez, Mississippi, the only child in a sharecropping family. He started playing harmonica at the age of eight, borrowing one from a friend, and soon he was listening to the blues shows from the influential Memphis radio station WDIA. He enjoyed the recordings of Muddy Waters, Howlin' Wolf, Little Walter, and Jimmy Reed, and at some point in the mid-1950s he moved away from home to be nearer better jobs and better musical venues. He came to Baton Rouge and worked for soft-drink companies Royal Crown and Wright Root Beer, and tried to play music wherever he could. He was living on North Thirty-Fifth Street, not far from Harpo, when, he said, "I met Slim way back when I used to walk around with an acoustic guitar and a harp on a rack and I played the bass part of Jimmy Reed numbers on the guitar and blew the harp. Everybody in Baton Rouge called me 'Little Jimmy Reed' so that's how I started. Slim was working as a bricklayer and I was walking by his house."[9]

Around 1959, Anderson started meeting up in the evenings with some musicians Harpo had recommended. They soon decided to form a band comprising Anderson on harmonica and vocals; Eugene Dozier on guitar; Andrew "Guitar" Taylor on second guitar, the man who had been on Harpo's first recording session; and Oscar Hogan on drums. Oscar was Silas Hogan's nephew, and Anderson explained: "I would go to Silas' house and we'd rehearse the band. We got a few little gigs around Baton Rouge and different places."[10] He also said, "I would go by Slim Harpo's house and we would jive a bit on harmonica and stuff like that. Anywhere Slim Harpo would have a gig there was no admission [fee] for us. He would let us come up and do some numbers. Lightnin' Slim would do the same thing, Silas Hogan would let me sit in. It was like that then."[11] Anderson and the band, by then known as the Joy Jumpers, played Miss Cain's in Baton Rouge; some clubs in Scotlandville; the Sticks in Jackson, Louisiana; Big Joe's Lounge in St. Francisville; and the State Line Club near the Mississippi border. "Our show was nothing but the blues, Jimmy Reed that was my favorite, B. B. King, Silas Hogan stuff. Oscar would do Fats Domino, all on guitar, and Guitar Taylor would sing some blues and I would sing some blues."[12]

Anderson and the Joy Jumpers' first record, "I Wanna Boogie," appeared on Jay Miller's Zynn label in early 1962 and saw some exposure when leased to the larger Dot label in California. The same year, Anderson was switched to Excello when Miller had the notion that Ernie Young would prefer to release a record by someone a little like Harpo if he couldn't get anything new by Harpo himself. The first was "Naggin'," a catchy rocking blues with a mush-mouthed vocal and screeching harp of the Jimmy Reed variety, and then, Anderson confirmed, "It was J. D. Miller's idea to record 'I'm a King Bee.'" In all, Anderson saw three discs on Excello, and his "Goin' Crazy over TV" was an out-of-the-ordinary lyric about how everything else suffered when television took hold, but there is no indication they sold very well. In Anderson's telling, he quit recording in 1964 because Miller kept all the money, but in reality there may have been little due.

Anderson and the band did continue to play gigs, but then, Anderson said, "Eugene Dozier got into trouble. That was when I picked up playing the lead guitar. . . . Then Guitar Taylor's wife stabbed him to death," and that was the end of the Joy Jumpers. On April 5, 1968, the *State-Times* reported that one of four Negroes indicted for murder that week was "Mary Agnes Rheams, 24, of 1410 Boyd Street, for murder in the fatal stabbing of Andrew Taylor, 42, of the same address, March 17." Taylor bled to death after being stabbed in the thigh. A police report on March 18 said, "Taylor and the Rheams woman had been arguing loudly prior to the fatal stabbing." They were also concerned that "the Baton Rouge Police building had been in an uproar" while Rheams was being fingerprinted after the arrest. Taylor's daughter, Monroe Elizabeth Williams, had appeared and "pulled a .22 caliber gun from her purse and started for the door leading to the fingerprint room" before being overpowered.

Jimmy Anderson had by then taken to playing as a duo with a drummer known as Zack the Cat, and changed his style to that of B. B. King. In 1969 he returned to Natchez because "the police were after me for alimony and kept putting me in jail." He worked as a guard on a casino riverboat and pursued his music as disc jockey "Soul Man Lee" on WMIS and WNAT radio, also having a show on country station WZZB in Centreville, Mississippi. Although he had not played music since 1969, he was persuaded to go abroad to London and Holland in 1993 to sing his blues. He said then that he had had to relearn all his records from a tape.

Silas Hogan had first met Jay Miller when he backed Jimmy Dotson on recordings for Miller's Zynn and Rocko labels. Hogan then recorded three songs for Reynaud Records, Lloyd Reynaud's label, in Opelousas in 1961, which remained unreleased for many years, before returning to Crowley with Jimmy Anderson to record for Miller. Hogan made eight singles on Excello between 1962 and 1966, making an important contribution to the overall picture of swamp-blues music, although there was little to distinguish Hogan's style either vocally or musically. He was now in his fifties, and although he knew local musicians of an earlier generation and was capable of playing some fine blues, on his discs the spirits of John Lee Hooker, Jimmy Reed, and Lightnin' Slim were never far away. Highlights included the rollicking "I'm Gonna Quit You Baby," the Latin beat and spoken exchanges on "Just Give Me a Chance," and the brooding mood of "I'm in Love with You Baby." His "Airport Blues" was an engaging update to the theme of the bluesman waiting for his baby to come back, and the heartfelt "Out and Down Blues" was memorable too, not least for its slightly Harpo-ish style. On titles like "So Long," the sound of Slim Harpo is present, too. On the debit side, "So Glad" was nondescript funky soul, "Lonesome La La" was in Buster Brown's R&B groove, and "You're Too Late" was a mannered Jimmy Reed impersonation. Hogan's discs appear not to have sold in huge quantities, and he later told a visiting musician, "Man, the only thing that I got out of them records was publicity."[13]

Hogan's recordings often featured the harmonica playing of Sylvester Buckley or Moses Smith. Smith played on later sessions by Lightnin' Slim too, and he also saw four singles on Excello in his own right as "Whispering" Smith, explaining: "I have a real loud voice. That's why Miller gave me that name. He wanted to surprise people."[14] The discs came out in 1963 and 1964 and started with a deliberate and despairing "Mean Woman Blues," not the rock 'n' roll song. Although none of his discs were particular hits, Smith always said that Miller looked after him well. From 1962, Smith led his own occasional band with Sammy K. Brown on drums when available and Ernest Ambrose on bass. Smith played for a while on both the college circuit and the round of black clubs, briefly joining Harpo at the Thunderbird beachside venue.

Henry Clement was never a harp player nor a bluesman, but he did play harmonica on one of Lightning Slim's early discs on Feature. He was a multi-instrumentalist, a twenty-year-old from the French section of Crowley who moved to Baton Rouge to study at Southern University. He stayed in town for four years, running student bands named the Drops of Joy and the Trojans and backing his sister Bernadine's doo-wop vocal group, the Gaynotes. Clement recorded for Miller's Zynn label in 1958 as Little Clem & the Drew Drops (actually the Gaynotes), playing all the instruments on "Plea of Love." By the time he made his fourth disc for Miller, issued in 1960 and 1961 on the Spot label as "Trojan Walla" and on his Zynn label as "Trojan's Walla," he had an instrumental that was well received in clubs but sold little. Clement moved to the West Coast and continued to perform a second-line, Mardi Gras type of show well into the current century.

Tabby Thomas, who had been one of the first players from Red Stick to seek out J. D. Miller, returned to Miller's new studio around 1959. He had only been active in music on a local basis for the first few years after his marriage in 1955, but he spent some of that time perfecting his piano playing and his saxophone technique. Thomas had a good voice that he had already adapted to suit a range of ballad and R&B styles, from the nightclub mood of "Thinking Blues," when on Delta, to the raucous jump blues of "Mmm I Don't Care," while on Feature. Now, he and Miller came up with a new R&B style for two discs on Rocko and Zynn, one backed by the swamp-pop ballad "Tomorrow (I'll Be Gone)," before his take on New Orleans R&B, "Hoodo Party," became a big local dance hit on Excello in 1961, followed by his version of the dance craze "Popeye Train." Never an innovator, Tabby continued to record for Miller until 1965, by which time Miller dropped him and other bluesmen, feeling the local blues scene was dying in the face of soul music. To some extent this change was chronicled by Tabby himself, who contributed a news column headed "Blues and Jazz" to the *News Leader* during 1961 and 1962. In December 1961, Tabby was promoting the Nighthawks band and their new R&B disc on Montel, their former leader Boogie Jake having moved to California to be a preacher. He noted Slim Harpo was currently playing one-nighters around Louisiana and that Lester Robertson had been called up by Uncle Sam.

The next month, Thomas was featuring blind saxophonist J. B. Tagnor, mainstay of the Joe Houston R&B band, and campaigning with the zeal of a convert for a new auditorium for the growing black community to help curb juvenile delinquency. He also reported the results of a local poll to find the best male vocalist of 1961—Bobby Bland came in first, with New Orleans acts Ernie K-Doe and Chris Kenner at five and six, trailed by "this city's own Slim Harpo chosen number 11." He noted, too, that Ray Meaders, formerly Diggie Doo, had moved away and "at present is deejaying in Memphis, Tennessee," where he helped break the first hits by Carla and Rufus Thomas. In February 1962, at home, "rock and roll singer Papa Lou, formerly singer with the George Williams band, is getting ready for a recording session" on a new contribution to the craze for Popeye dance tunes. The Nighthawks, Bobby Powell, and Joe Tex came in for Tabby's further support while he also proffered some of the "latest musicians' hip talk" around town: "hey sweet, buzz the stud, my ax in hock; I got a gig, I gotta dig, I need this bread to gas my head." Tabby also mentioned his own disc, "Hoodo Party," released by Excello the week ending February 17 and played on WLAC that night.

Lazy Lester was recording all through this time, continuing to work with Miller as session man and leader. In all, he would have fifteen singles on Excello between 1957 and 1967. Lester was a wonderful harp player, a good guitarist, and a fine songwriter, with his own songs geared at the younger teenage market rather than the blues jukeboxes. His records took their influences from rock 'n' roll and country as much as from pure blues, and "I'm a Lover Not a Fighter" and "Sugar Coated Love" were fascinating discs that deserved to be hits. "Take Me in Your Arms" was pure swamp-pop, but Lester's deepish voice was perhaps not memorable enough for the teen crowd. In a blues vein, "Go Ahead" and "Late in the Evening" were among his best sides. He remembers Miller favorably: "He was a real fine guy. He wrote a lot of the songs, and me and Miller used to make the songs together because he played a nice guitar. . . . I made some good records with him and I got good royalties, but I goofed up so much I had to give it right back. He was mostly for himself, I knew that, but he did everything he could for me. Everything he did right, I did the opposite."[15] Lester's goofing mainly consisted of being drunk a lot. As Miller said, "I tell you I liked Lester, but he just wouldn't leave that booze alone. He'd drink anything, anytime, any place."[16] This drinking tended to attract the attention of the authorities, although Lester rationalized this: "Miller, there was people who didn't like him, and anytime they see me out there they would grab me and put me in jail and it would be $17.50. They would do it just to aggravate him."[17]

On one occasion Miller was indeed aggravated with Lester, and his response demonstrated both his paternalistic view of his players and his deeply rooted white southern approach to solving local problems pragmatically. He said, "Lester got drunk and broke into my store one night while I was very sick with the flu. Later, I found out what Lester had done and that he was not in the city jail but had already been sent to Angola. I was furious because I liked Lester and had been taking care of him, got him work, loaned him money, and so on. So, I called the judge, who was a friend of mine, and gave him heck because I'd not been notified of Lester's sentencing. I wanted him back in my custody, and said, 'How in the world do you expect Lester is going to repay me if you have him locked up in prison?' He was quickly returned to my care."[18] This was possible because the system at the State Penitentiary in Angola was one where the inmates were often sent to work for community benefit. This extended to "loaning" workers to businesses and farmers in a form of indenture.

All this time, Lightnin' Slim was still plying his trade in the smaller black clubs and taking larger white venues whenever Miller could find them. In 1959 his Excello recording of "Rooster Blues" had become a number 23 R&B chart hit, but this never quite led onwards and upwards and, for his part, Lightnin' never cared to alter his down-home style. "Rooster Blues" was a rocking blues that recycled some memorable older blues lines, including those about the little red rooster visiting the little red hen with the imperative of "rocking with you tonight." Miller had Lightnin' leave out the couplets that rhymed with "luck," but nevertheless it was a song and a performance that would be imitated for years by southern musicians, black and white, on account of its risqué lyric and its driving beat. Drummer Jimmy Dotson said: "He was a nut for the backbeat, and he wanted you to slam that backbeat in . . . whoom . . . and the drummer in most cases tonight wouldn't be the one he used last night."[19] When he was in Baton Rouge, Lightnin' would play the local black clubs, including those in Mulatto Bend and Port Allen. Arlene Batiste saw him at the Streamline and the White Eagle as a young teenager, but she didn't get to go to recording sessions like her sister, Barbara [Carter]: "She used to go riding with them, Lightnin' and Harpo, up in Crowley when they'd record there. Went to the sessions, she was a year older than me. She got to go because my mom, Annie Collins, and Lightnin' Slim were very close at that time and he treated us like his children. Now that's a different Collins family than Dan Collins who Lillie Moore married, but see, we so close in this community, we treated each other like family."[20]

Jimmy Dotson filled in behind Lightnin' and Harpo occasionally. He was born in Baton Rouge but moved away until the mid-1950s, when he started gigging with various bands until he fell in with Silas Hogan's group. He remembered, "We had a following, we played from club to club. I played drums for Lightnin' Slim for a while and with Slim [Harpo] it fluctuated, I was a kind of utility musician. If they needed a drummer I'd go play drums, if they needed a bass player, a guitar. . . . I couldn't play any too good on any of them but I could fit in. But they had a tremendous following, Lightnin' Slim and Slim Harpo. They would go from club to club, sometimes we would play Sunday afternoon somewhere back over north Baton Rouge in the park area from two o'clock to six and the place would be full of people. OK, then we would go across the river and they'd just line up in cars and follow us across the river [to Port Allen]."[21] Lightnin' Slim was not often in Baton Rouge for long, though. He would stay in Crowley or Rayne and play gigs at the Silver Slipper in Arnaudville, the Four Leaf Clover in Church Point, and the Hide-A-Way Lounge in Rayne, using a number of musicians, including Lazy Lester and Jimmy Dotson, venturing also into New Orleans or eastern Texas. The oft-told story is that he drew the line at going into Mississippi when Jay Miller booked him a university gig there, saying, "but Mr. Jay, over there you'se got to call a white mule Mister." By all accounts, Lightnin's concern for his safety and liberty was continual. William Gambler remembers that, even when Lightnin' was based in Baton Rouge, as he often was, "he was in jail a lot."

When not on the road or in some kind of trouble, Lightnin' was known for his large and ever-changing number of wives and girlfriends. As he sang in "Lightnin's Troubles," a fast blues where he exhorted the guitar to boogie awhile, "Well I'm sometimes up Babe / You know's I'm sometimes down / Sometime I'm here / Sometime I'm out of town." Then he offered his female listeners the prospect that "sometimes I'm all alone." When he sang "Just a Lonely Stranger," the break in his voice made him sound almost impossibly forlorn. Woman troubles no doubt contributed in equal measure to Lightnin's celebratory and doom-laden songs. An early 1960s summarizer of his recordings, Mike Leadbitter, felt that Lightnin' had "a perfect voice for the blues; deep, vibrant, and often very moving." His guitar work was noted for its stark simplicity and his lyrics for the way "superstition, lust, bad luck, hope, and rough humor are well represented. The songs are often leant charm by a murderous use of the English language and leading comments from his accompanists. Always the mood was low-down." Jay Miller continued to record Lightnin' regularly because he saw him as "a real blues man," explaining this concept to writer Paul Oliver in the early 1960s: "I'll listen to anyone that will come to my studio. . . . If you see an ole country boy, that's your blues man; not your other guy that knows his music on a higher level—because he's not a blues man no more. . . . If they don't *feel* the material they're singin'—that's it. People can distinguish whether they're authentic or not or whether it's just a synthetic singer and that's all. . . . Now Lightning Slim, of course, as far as knowledge of music I would say he knows less about knowledge of music than anyone else that I record, but for all that he's one of my best sellers for the simple reason that, what he does, he does feelin' it. . . . Slim seems to give out more of something real."[22]

More than anyone else's, Lightnin' Slim's discs embodied the nature and purpose of jukebox music, each one separate yet each reliable for its down-home feel, for sentiments its target audience in the black community could recognize, and for danceability, slow or fast. Lightnin' was the first of many. All in all, Miller recorded over a dozen blues artists from Baton Rouge or the rural parts of Louisiana and gained a reputation for being able to capture the blues of that swampy region. One writer felt that, in the music of Harpo, Lightnin' Slim, and the others, "It is almost possible to feel the sticky heat of Louisiana and the call of the bull-frogs. This was the blues, gravelly, primitive, and poignant."[23]

LOUISIANA FOLK BLUES

In a parallel universe to that inhabited by Excello Records and its commercial approach, three of the older-style Baton Rouge musicians also found themselves on record by the early 1960s as purveyors of folk song to the growing academic community of folk-blues enthusiasts.

Just before Robert Pete Williams was sent to the penitentiary for life, a professor of English at Louisiana State University, Dr. Harry Oster, applied for a folklore research grant for the summer of 1955. Oster, from Massachusetts, was in his twenties and had only an interest in Yiddish folk songs as background, but he soon started to find people in Louisiana to sing him traditional French ballads and Cajun songs and others who introduced him to the world of African American song. He started to travel to the penitentiary at Angola to search for traditional work songs. There he and a jazz collector colleague, Richard Allen,[24] discovered Robert Pete Williams in 1958. Allen recalled that most of the black prisoners who could play music were interested in songs that were current, offering to sing Oster R&B songs when Oster was looking for some ancient handed-down song from slavery days, but Williams was different. Allen referred to the time in the 1930s when an earlier folklorist, John Lomax, had discovered a folk-blues singer there and had him released, taking him onto the national and international stage. "They had all heard of Lead Belly. Everybody in Angola knew that he had gotten a governor's pardon for his music. So they were all naturally anxious to record for us."[25] When it came Robert Pete's turn, Oster and Allen found he had some songs and narratives that were very personal to him and that described his experiences in life. When Oster asked him if he knew a song about prison life, Williams said he didn't, but that he would make one up. The result was "Prisoner's Talking Blues" of which Williams said later, understatedly, "It's a sad blues. I wasn't happy in Angola." Another song recorded the same day explained: "Some folk got six months, some got a solid year / But me and my buddy, we got lifetime here."[26] Fiddler player Butch Cage spoke on the same theme, telling Paul Oliver that, at some unspecified date, he "went to the pen, you know, and I was on the penitensha and I had to serve my time out. Well some had six months and some had a solid year. . . . that's what they sing 'cause that's a prisoner song."[27]

Oster and some friends had formed the Louisiana Folklore Society in 1956 and started issuing LP records on the society's own label, starting with *A Sampler of Louisiana Folk Songs* in 1957. By 1959 Oster had recorded Robert Pete Williams and two other inmates in Angola singing their own songs for an LP of *Angola Prisoners' Blues*. That year, Oster formed his own low-key record label, Folk-Lyric, recorded Williams again, and issued an entire LP of his songs, *Those Prison Blues*, one of the songs being "Pardon Denied Again," in which Williams describes the failure of his third request to be pardoned. Oster had somehow been persuaded of Williams's innocence of the crime for which the judge had gone out of his way to reinforce the jury's decision, saying, "the man was certainly guilty," and in October 1958 *Time* magazine carried a feature on Williams written by Oster. Gradually, Oster helped Williams build a case for parole, and he was allowed out in December 1959. He had served just three and a half years of his life sentence. The proviso was that he work on a farm locally and remain in his area for another five years.

On parole, Williams introduced Oster to his musician friends in the Baton Rouge area, principally Butch Cage and Willie B. Thomas. Between 1960 and 1962, Oster recorded a number of them singing at Cage's home in Zachary, and the result was the important Folk-Lyric LP *Country Negro Jam Sessions,* described by writer Peter Guralnick as "a rowdy footstomping collection of field recordings made in perfect innocence . . . [that best captures] the raucous, joyful atmosphere of the backwoods country blues."[28] As well as fiddler Cage and guitarist Thomas, there were performances by Clarence Edwards and his brother Cornelius, Sally Dotson, Hilary Blunt, and Robert Brown, known as "Smoky Babe." In Oster's eyes, "In the back country of the deep South the roots of negro folk music are still alive and vibrant." In his LP notes he paints a picture of a lonely guitarist on his porch being joined by his friends until a jam session ensues, attracting so many people to dance that the walls of the little shack start to bulge. Oster describes Cage as "a mellow old man with an infectiously gay smile whose wickedly syncopated fiddle music is a rare survival" of an older fiddle-playing tradition and who holds the fiddle down on his chest and saws sideways. Willie B. Thomas is described as a forty-nine-year-old janitor and preacher who "unlike most religious negroes sees no harm in singing sinful songs, secular songs such as the blues. . . . Clad usually in a big black hat and a grimly ministerial black suit he throws every fibre of his meagre 4 foot ten inches into his singing and guitar flailing." The folksy appeal of Thomas's recorded tale "Who Broke the Lock," in which he explains the old-time habit of hiding the booze in the hen house, is undeniable. To Oster, Clarence Edwards was a good-looking young man "currently work- ing in a junk yard during the week and playing as part of a trio, two guitars and drums, on weekends at dances." Edwards was one of the best of the local blues singers, contributing to Oster versions of songs such as "Smokestack Lightning," made popular at the time by Howlin' Wolf and Muddy Waters. Smoky Babe—Robert Brown—was "a migrant worker from Itta Bena, age 35, currently working odd jobs in Scotlandville." Brown had migrated to Scot- landville from Mississippi by way of steel mills in Alabama, the nightclubs of New Orleans, and the river barges of Baton Rouge. It was in Scotlandville at Field's grocery that Lazy Lester met Smoky Babe and fell in with him on a subsequent recording session for Harry Oster. "He was just a little street guitar player, hung around the drinking tree on Bradley Road where everybody would come, drink wine, play guitar, play harmonica, sing. Unless we played on Bradley Road at Field's grocery or something like that, that's about the onliest club he would come to, when we was in walking distance from him."[29] Lester was given the name "Henry Thomas" in case J. D. Miller ever came to hear he had played harmonica on Oster's session. Together, the recordings by these men and their friends capture superbly a mixture of old blues and interpretations of newer blues, folk songs, and religious songs. On the blues items, the sound of Cage's fiddle elevates the performances with its nuances of folk, hillbilly, and blues phrases. Willie Thomas displays an enthusiastic guitar style and no little vocal ability, and Smoky Babe was a really fine guitarist and singer. Sally Dotson contributed an engaging "Your Dice Won't Pass" at a Smoky Babe session recorded at the home of Robert Pete Williams's sister. She recorded again in 1966 for an expert blues researcher, David Evans, along with her brothers, Lee and Robert Jenkins, and Isaiah Chattman, a neighbor of Robert Pete Williams who recorded with Silas Hogan in the early 1960s.

As soon as he started to record his folk bluesmen, Oster was keen to expose them to a wider audience, and so it was that Butch Cage and Willie B. Thomas were thrust, probably blinking and amazed, into the spotlight at national folk-blues festivals. On June 25, 1960, the local paper reported how they got on a plane with Oster to play at the annual and prestigious music festival in Newport, Rhode Island. They were described as "Cage, 66, an old time fiddler from Zachary, and Willie Thomas, 25 [quite some typo], from Scotlandville, guitarist and singer of spirituals and currently employed by the City-Parish." The spotlight was to have fallen on paroled convict Robert Pete Williams, but this had to wait a few years because, as the *Advocate* reported on June 9, Williams had been deprived of the Newport trip: "A parole officer recommended that the ex-convict be denied a request to leave Louisiana." Oster had tried to appeal, "but state Governor Jimmie Davis said, 'I am not in the habit of overruling parole officers.'" This was despite the success Governor Davis had had in his former life as a country singer with a markedly bluesy tinge, famous for recording and writing songs like "Tomcat and Pussy Blues," "Penitentiary Blues," and "Easy Rider Blues" before making "You Are My Sunshine" into a popular standard and one of the state songs of Louisiana. The newspaper noted that Robert Pete Williams had tended livestock near Denham Springs for seventy-five dollars per month through his servitude parole granted in December 1959, whereby he would work on the farm of Rudolph Estley, former penitentiary governor.

Soon after making his Folk-Lyric sessions in Louisiana, Harry Oster moved away to other states to continue his folkloric work, but he did relate his work in Baton Rouge in his 1969 book *Living Country Blues,* more widely published in 1975. His was invaluable work, although he had no background as a blues collector and therefore tended to accept that the blues songs he recorded were far more original than they actually were.[30] There is no record of Oster ever encountering Slim Harpo on his trips to uncover the folk music of the area. By the time Oster started recording the blues in 1958, Harpo was already a recorded artist and would probably have been considered too modern for Oster's purposes. Had the two met a few years earlier, though, it would have been fascinating to know what Harpo might have provided. Perhaps some folksy train-whistle blues picked up from the Grand Ole Opry from the black harmonica player DeFord Bailey, or some version of a story ballad channeled through Lead Belly, perhaps an original blues song based on a recent Lightnin' Hopkins, Muddy Waters, or Little Walter opus, perhaps some rockabilly about suede shoes, but also, just possibly, a stunningly unusual reworking of the now-unknowable local styles of the likes of the legendary Meddy brothers or Henry Gaines and other long-lost black musicians.

RECORDINGS, SEPTEMBER 1963

The suspension of Slim Harpo's recording contract was maintained by Ernie Young and Jay Miller through 1962, and the impasse was not broken until late summer 1963 when Miller and Harpo negotiated a new contract. Miller said, "Slim called me and said he was ready to shake hands and start anew. He said, 'Let's make another contract and start over again.'"[31] William Gambler remembers it as a more pragmatic move: "I guess he felt he needed to make some money. I didn't think it was right . . . but during that time there wasn't a thing that you could really do. You couldn't go get a lawyer to go against Miller. This is the way it was."[32] It was still something of a reverse for Miller, a businessman who, one visitor observed, "has to avenge the smallest slight or the fact that someone has 'put one over on him.' Law suits are always being planned or pending."[33] The reality of the situation was that it had been a very unusual and courageous move by James and Lovell to hold out for what they thought was their due, but Miller had invested in Harpo's success, too, and it was a good move for all parties when the matter was resolved.

The new contract apparently provided for all future songs written by Harpo to be credited solely to James Moore so he would now receive half the mechanical royalties, with Young's Excellorec Music taking the other half. This was double the income Harpo would have had previously in situations where a song was credited to both Moore and J. West. He did also receive public-performance royalties from BMI. By not seeking any composer credit, Miller (West) was losing money but unlocking the potential to make more discs and to increase his income through the percentage per disc paid to him by Excello.

In September 1963, Harpo rejoined Miller in the Crowley studio to record the much-delayed new single. He was apparently not accompanied by his own band, for Miller had assembled a new group of Cajun and country-rock session musicians over the last few years. Drummer Warren Schexnider, who recorded for Miller as "Warren Storm," said the session band was typically himself, bassists Bobby McBride and Rufus Thibodeaux, and guitarist Al Foreman, along with blues pianist Katie Webster and R&B tenor sax man Lionel Prevost from Clifton Chenier's zydeco band, appearing on Miller's books as Lionel Torrence. According to Storm, "We'd be on call day and night to back up practically everybody Miller brought in—Carol Fran, Lonesome Sundown, Lazy Lester, and Slim Harpo."[34] However, in the case of Harpo's comeback session, Jay Miller told interviewers that the session players were Al Foreman, Rufus Thibodeaux, and drummer Austin Broussard plus sax players Boo Boo Guidry, Harry Simoneaux, Peter Gunter, or Bobby Fran. The session produced five songs of which "I Love the Life I'm Living" and "Buzzin'" were chosen for release as Excello 2239 in October 1963. Excello took an ad in *Billboard* on October 26 for "I Love the Life I'm Living," saying, "Not since 'Rainin' in My Heart' has Slim Harpo had one like this." Of course, close readers of the magazine would have known he hadn't had one at all. "I Love the Life I'm Living" was the clue to the session and to the chosen Cajun and swamp-pop musicians. It was Miller's vision of how Harpo could develop his crossover appeal through a country-sounding song and instrumentation. It opens compellingly with Slim's harp and the saxes melding together to play the swinging, mid-paced swamp-pop tune in unison before Slim starts to admit that all those pleading songs he has recorded have had an effect. It's no longer raining in his heart. In this sequel, now he's got his girl, he loves life. His line "There's no one else like you" was a far more commercial con-clusion to be pitched to the wider record-buying public, in Miller's eyes, than a typical blues. Although disc jockeys such as "John R" in Nashville seemed to agree by playing the record often, sales were good but not great, and the disc peaked at number 134 in the "looking ahead" section of *Cash Box* that predicted discs likely to get into the top 100.

The B side of the disc, "Buzzin'," an instrumental tune with a sprightly Latin rhythm and swirling harp solos, was titled as a not-too-subtle reminder of Harpo's original theme, and the composition was credited to Harpo and West despite the new contract. An alternative take also survives, with a less complete guitar solo. The tune had earlier been played at Harpo's live session in the Armory in Mobile when the announcer gave away its real title, "Cha Cha Cha in Blue." The tune was first issued by Junior Wells, and it is not clear what its real origins are, but it is unlikely that it was composed by Harpo as claimed on the label of the Excello disc. As writer and musician Hank Davis observed, "There were several times, and 'Buzzin'" is one of them, where a real skilled musician came in to do fills. Often Slim's band was doing backporch picking. The new guy isn't a pure blues guy; he's sticking with the changes but he's a lot more skilled than the band, a real picker smart enough to lay back and just add bits of color in the spaces."[35]

Also from this session were "My Little Queen Bee (Got a Brand New King)," another not-so-subtle reminder of Harpo's past glories, that was pulled out as a single, Excello 2246, in April 1964, probably in some desperation on Miller's part, good as it was in its own right. A surviving alternative take has a different guitar line behind the vocals. Then, too, there was "Harpo's Blues," a slightly misleading title for a classy R&B item with a well-arranged horn section and fast-flowing guitar solos. In the song Harpo celebrates his newfound freedom from the girl who treats him in evil ways. It was also pulled as a single, Excello 2265, in the fall of 1964, coupled with a B side, the slow brooding blues "Please Don't Turn Me Down," drawn from a three-year-old session. The final track was "Little Sally Walker," unissued at the time, a mix of nursery rhyme, pop dance tune, and soulful riffing that was rather unfinished. Perhaps a more polished version would have been made if the song had been available for Excellorec to copyright. Syl Johnson had written and recorded the song on Federal in 1961, and Rufus Thomas recorded it for Stax in the year after Slim's version appeared.

THAT'S LIFE

For much of the late 1950s and early 1960s, James Moore must have been uncertain how his career in music was going to develop. There were periods of success interspersed with times when bookings were difficult to get, and there was the segregated nature of the music venues to consider. Locally, he would still play at clubs for white patrons across east and west Baton Rouge, particularly the Glass Hat on North Boulevard in the east part of the city, as well as the black clubs in west Baton Rouge where he had first started. He found the white clubs and his forays out to white college campuses across the South more rewarding, both financially and, often, in terms of encouragement. William Gambler helped drive his stepfather to gigs but reflects that the African American audiences of the day were not enough to support a bluesman's life: "They would listen to it and dance to it, but as far as going out and supporting the black blues men, they didn't really do it. We struggled for a long time with the music because he wasn't making a whole lot of money. He was making more than he was making on the construction job, more than a dollar an hour. I'm real proud of him, but when I was growing up, I was saying to myself, 'I wish he could go get him a job like everybody else.' Of course, I didn't tell him that!"[36]

What James Moore did do was to continue with his trucking business, starting with one and eventually having three vehicles to transport anything from farm goods to construction materials and scrap. William said: "Charlie Reed in Mulatto Bend, that was Slim's cousin, Charlie ran some trucks, and he may have helped Slim with his. But Slim didn't have any partners in that. Slim had two trucks of his own, a big one and a bobtail, flat bed. He would pay people to drive for him. When he was away this other guy would drive."[37] Two years after his big hit record, Slim was still essentially a part-time professional musician.

Nevertheless, by 1963, the Moore house on Thirty-Sixth Street was rebuilt and enlarged. On February 18, 1963, the *State-Times* listed the building permits granted the week before, including "James Moore, 906 N 36 street, brick ven [*sic*] residence, Peerless Homebuilders, contractor, $7000." At the house in 1990, Lovell remembered, "I've lived here since 1948. It was a frame house, wooden house, first. Then James had this one built, the brick house, in '63. It was after he started with the truck business, hauling scrap iron, and that's why we've got two driveways. He used this for the car and the other one for the truck. We'd go as far as Bogalusa loading up scrap iron, he'd get paid by the load."[38] It would not have been easy to miss the twin-business Harpo house in those days, not least because, as musician Jesse Kinchen described: "Slim had a trailer, and on that trailer was 'Slim Harpo' all in yellow and on the back of it he had 'I'm a King Bee' and it had a bee on it, and the bee got a crown on its head."[39]

What Harpo thought about his place in the world as a solid citizen and new home builder is unclear. Even William Gambler doesn't know: "I really couldn't say about his politics. He didn't really get involved. I did register to vote in 1960 when I was 18 and he didn't stop me. But before then they had the citizenship test and it was kinda hard for him to take that. And anyway, he wasn't making enough money. He made his money from the white organizations that booked him to play, and then he didn't want to get involved in politics."[40] The building of the new house even contributed to gaps in our knowledge of Slim's earlier life, as William recalls, because "while the work was being done we had to move everything into just one room, and a lot of things were thrown out at that time."

Through 1962, Harpo had maintained his weekly slots at the Acadian Club. On March 3, he was playing at their annual Mardi Gras Ball from 8:00 p.m. to midnight. It was not recorded whether the crowning of the king and queen of the ball took place to the strains of "I'm a King Bee." Among other venues Slim played that year were several college fraternity houses. On May 5, the Kappa Sigma frat house was the scene of their annual South Sea Island spring party. According to local news reports, "During the afternoon the crowd ate 450 pounds of boiled crayfish. Slim Harpo and his band provided the music for the afternoon party, while the bands of Lonesome Sundown and Lazy Lester entertained in the evening." Although this was a dream swamp-blues lineup, the report was on the society pages and mostly went into minute detail about the table decorations and which young lady prepared what, with little appreciation of the musicians or their art. Three weeks later, though, the paper had a large boxed story: "Dance to Star, Harpo Cats: Slim Harpo and his harmonica cats will perform tomorrow night at the CYO, admission $1. Raining In My Heart, a Harpo record, has sold almost a million copies." The next week, the ad for the CYO Center again recognized Harpo's status: "May 25, Slim Harpo and his band—big hit record Rainin' in My Heart—$1 admission."

At the end of October, the *Advocate* advised music fans: "An overflow crowd is expected for tonight's sixth annual battle of the bands at the CYO Center, 2245 Florida . . . Tickets at Sammy's Record Shop North and Third, Adele's, and CYO." The report a week later confirmed:

> More than 1200 teen-agers packed the Catholic Youth Organization Center on Halloween night October 31 to witness the 1962 Battle of the Bands . . . with a high spirited football atmosphere, four of the most popular bands in the Baton

Rouge area competed against each other. Slim Harpo did a rendition, Raining In My Heart, which proved popular as did the fabulous Little Pony singing All These Things. Benny Spellman of New Orleans also sang his two hit records Fortune Teller and Lipstick Traces plus a tune he participated with, Mother In Law. As the votes were counted there was a deadlock between the Night Hawks and Lee Tillman singing with the Buddy Stewart orchestra. Dance chairman S. J. Montalbano asked for an applausive [sic] vote, which indicated Lee Tillman the winner.

Interestingly, Lee Tillman had just signed up with Montalbano's record label, and so had the Nighthawks led by Boe Melvin, who had just recorded a version of "Boogie Chillen," previewed at the CYO on October 12.[41] But when did democracy play a part in the blues? Despite not becoming band-contest winner that year, Harpo retained his spots at the Acadian and all his regular event-day gigs such as the Baton Rouge Country Club's formal Xmas Dance on December 23. The same pattern of white clubs, formal society dances, and college gigs supported by local appearances in black clubs would be repeated by Harpo right through 1963.

This was a time when those who played in Harpo's band became acutely aware of his increasingly professional attitude to gigs, caring little for those who would be drunk or late. In this approach, Harpo was taking a leaf from the book of one of his influences, Howlin' Wolf, the 1950s R&B hit-maker who was also an older man who often employed much younger bandsmen and wanted them to deliver his style of music and his professionalism. Memphis bluesman Amos Patten has recalled Wolf's style in managing his younger and wilder musicians: "You either do it like the Wolf said do it, or you had trouble. He was a straightforward type of guy. Wolf wasn't no rowdy type of guy." Another bluesman, Little Arthur Duncan, agreed that "Wolf was business all the way, and when he played someplace he always carried himself so he could be booked back there."[42] Return business gained through a good reputation as a man as well as an artist was one of the key things Harpo was looking for, too.

MORE SWAMP-POP

Through 1963, Sam Montel was continuing his pattern of show promotion and record producing, with weekly CYO dance events and one eye open to new musical talent. He had expanded his Montel Records catalog and formed another label, Michelle, with his brother Mickey. Using studios in Lafayette (La Louisianne) and New Orleans (Cosimo), Montel continued recording his CYO discoveries Dale Houston, John Fred's Playboys, Lester Robertson, and others, and, as we have seen, brought in soulful R&B singer Lee Tillman to the label as well as Slim Harpo's sometime guitarist, Boe Melvin, and his Nighthawks, who also backed singer Miss Ann. On November 17, 1963, there was a full-page *Advocate* story on the Montel brothers. Sam told the paper he credited Mickey with "a sixth sense of what songs and singers will work out." Apparently one of these senses was that Sam's established white pop-ballad singer Dale Houston would sound good together with another local singer, Grace Broussard, sister of popular Cajun singer Van Broussard. The result was a number-one national pop hit for Dale and Grace's "I'm Leaving It Up to You" on Montel Records. It had been launched on Michelle and transferred to Montel after the duo went on a tour across Texas to Las Vegas, ending with an appearance on national television on the Dick Clark show.

"I'm Leaving It Up to You" was in many ways the quintessential swamp-pop record. Its swirling, swaying rhythm provided a constant backing for the stop-start reading of the lyrics, which asked the fundamental question, "Now do you want my love / Or are we through." Dale and Grace would have remembered clearly where they were when President Kennedy was shot; they were in Dallas for a big Show of Stars, where they would sing the number-one song in the nation, and had just waved to the passing entourage. As with so many popular hits of the time, Dale and Grace were white, but the song had black origins, in this case having been recorded by R&B singers Don and Dewey six years earlier. The Montel record was the culmination of several years of hits by young Louisianians, both black and white, often of Cajun or Creole origin, usually brought up on hillbilly or R&B and always capable of producing emotional lyrics above a laconic, swampy beat. There were faster songs, too, from Bobby Charles's 1955 hit "Later Alligator," a song picked up by Bill Haley during the first flush of white rock 'n' roll, to Johnnie Allan's Cajun-influenced version of Chuck Berry's "Promised Land" in the early 1970s. Usually the songs with the lilting melodies were the hits, though. In the first flush of swamp hits in the late 1950s, Jimmy Clanton, Phil Phillips, Rod Bernard, Joe Barry, and Cookie and the Cupcakes had made the charts. Now, in the 1960s, there were further pop hits for Cookie and his R&B group with "Got You on My Mind," Barbara Lynn with the bluesy "You'll Lose a Good Thing," and country and pop hits for former Jay Miller artists Rusty and Doug Kershaw and Jimmy Newman. Right in the middle of this mix was, of course, Slim Harpo's "Rainin' in My Heart."

J. D. Miller was one of the first and the most industrious of the producers of swamp-pop, just as he had been with the Louisiana blues that became known as swamp-blues and before that with postwar Cajun and local hillbilly music. As well as his 1958 hit with Warren Storm's "Prisoner's Song," Miller recorded some classic minor hits for Excello, including Carol Fran's "Emmitt Lee," Tabby Thomas's "Hoodo Party," Guitar Gable's "Congo Mombo," and the original of "This Should Go on Forever," as well as records on his own Rocket, Rocko, and Zynn labels by Rocket Morgan, Joe Carl, Al Ferrier, and many others who contributed their own takes on localized rocking and rolling styles.

For his production deal with Excello, though, Miller mainly stuck to blues-based music and R&B. In 1963, Harpo's records were rubbing shoulders in the Excello catalog with Lightnin' Slim, Lazy Lester, Silas Hogan, Whispering Smith, and Lonesome Sundown as well as a number of Nashville-based artists recorded by Ernie Young himself.

RECORDINGS, JANUARY 1964

The second of Harpo's post-dispute sessions was held in January 1964, and this time his own band was back in the studio with him along with August Ranson, James Johnson's brother-in-law, on bass. The country experiment was gone, and the focus was on R&B, though it was a rather loose focus, ranging from John Lee Hooker's "Boogie Chillun" and Fats Domino's "Blueberry Hill"—neither of which was an Excellorec copyright and neither of which was issued at the time—to two new songs that were chosen for release. "Boogie Chillun" was taken at a faster than usual pace with attention-grabbing guitar riffs and solos and an unusual percussion sound, while "Blueberry Hill" followed the Domino style very carefully but less convincingly. The new songs were "I Need Money (Keep Your Alibis)," issued as Excello 2246 in April 1964, and "What's Goin' On Baby," issued later on Excello 2261 around October 1964. "Alibis" was introduced by Slim's now trademark plaintive harp playing and quickly developed into a rocking, rhythmic tune in the mode of "Got My Mojo Working." The title was repeated insistently, as was the catchy riff, and there are memorable guitar solos—in all, Ray Charles meets Muddy Waters in the form of Slim Harpo. "What's Goin' On Baby" was a contender, too, having been recorded earlier for Miller and then for Imperial as "A Man Is Crying." It's a promising slow blues about how Slim can't get through to his baby on the phone, but he resorts to age-old blues lines about what might be going on—"must be a two legged mule kickin' in your daddy's stall"—before the song fades out.

The year 1964 had started unpromisingly for Harpo. On January 2, the *Morning Advocate* reported a local truck accident: "A nine-year old Negro boy, Raymond Clark of 1114 North Acadian Thruway, was treated at the hospital after he walked into a trailer being pulled by an auto in the 3400 block of Zion Street shortly after 6 pm. The auto was driven by 39 year old James Moore of 906 North 36 Street and was headed west on Zion Street when the boy walked into the side of the trailer, police said." This report preceded a reduced number of ads for Harpo's performances through the year, possibly indicating a reduction in his attraction for local white audiences who were starting to succumb to the Detroit sound, to Merseybeat, and to American rock bands recycling the British sounds. On February 6, Harpo and his King Bees were featured at a teenage dance at St. Gerard Gym, and two days later they were at the annual Acadian Club Mardi Gras day.

RECORDINGS, JUNE 1964

It took until a new session in June 1964 for Harpo and his usual band members to record for Miller the song Slim had probably seen as his next hit if the Imperial deal had gone through, "Still Rainin' in My Heart." Perhaps Miller did not think a rearrangement of the artist's own hit song was necessarily a winning move, or perhaps it took Harpo three years to admit that he had written and even recorded a sequel. Whatever the reason for the delay, the song was now rerecorded and issued on Excello 2253 in June 1964, but as the B side behind another song from the session, "We're Two of a Kind." This was a rather catchy song that Miller felt had sales potential with its spirited yet bluesy guitar and harp solos and its unusual, almost-spoken message—the girl needs to stick with the singer because they're so similar in how they treat one another: "You say I'm wrong / I know I'm right," and so on. A shorter alternative take was recorded too. A third song from this period was "Sittin' Here Wondering (Wondering Blues)," a guitar-led track that appeared as Excello 2261 around October 1964. It was a slice of Chicago blues that drew lyrically and musically from some of Slim's influences, including Muddy Waters, with some B. B. King mixed in. Slim talks through the lyric while Rudy Richard takes impressive and extended guitar solos. The session was concluded with a song that remained unissued at the time, "I'm Waiting on You Baby." It was almost a contender, with a lazy-paced yet effective double-tracked vocal and a bluesy harp solo wailing above a Latinesque rhythm, but like many Harpo recordings from this period it lacked real star quality. Possibly the continued tensions between Harpo and Miller didn't help the creative process, and certainly Miller was still trying to achieve the sound he wanted to get out of the studio at his home.

Harpo's 1964 releases appear to have received little interest within the music press, and this would continue into the New Year, though it was not just Slim who slipped under the radar. Excello got little attention from the trade press and virtually none through 1965 when the pages of *Billboard* were full of pictures of Merseybeat groups. Few blues or R&B records at all made the pages that had hitherto carried numerous reviews. The emerging sounds of Detroit soul and of southern studios like Stax did get attention, but increasingly in the context of soul replacing R&B and becoming mainstream music. *Billboard* did not publish an R&B chart at all in the period December 1963 to January 1965. The blues of Slim Harpo or anyone else was not the sound of the times. As Slim went into the winter of 1964, he was still running his haulage business, personally driving trucks full of sugarcane along Airline Highway from the fields to the refineries in Baton Rouge docks. He was still playing local venues regularly and still making periodic forays further afield, playing increasingly to college audiences. James Johnson remembers how the college dates, usually on Saturdays, were followed by Sunday shows back home: "Me and Rudy used to be so mad. Slim would leave one and two o'clock in the morning to make it to the gig the next night. And we had to get out of bed, man, and hit the road. That took a toll on me."[43] Rudy Richard agreed, telling the *Advocate*, "that man was a hard worker. [But] it was something about his style of playing that just would tickle everybody. And he blowed so hard. Like, your amplifier speaker—it would vibrate. That man had that much wind to blow."[44] In this, it seems that Harpo was akin to Little Walter Jacobs, who was renowned for his controlled power.

Three years after the tape recordings he made of Slim in Mobile, David Kearns was responsible for booking acts for his fraternity gatherings:

> I didn't see Slim and the King Bees again until the fall of 1964 when I came across them playing at the Thomas Jefferson Hotel in Birmingham, Alabama for a private party after a football game. I think the band lineup was pretty much the same on

the front line with Slim, James, and Rudolph. He gave me his business card and said to call him if I could get him a gig. I was responsible for booking acts to play for my fraternity at Auburn University, so I called him soon after and Slim answered the phone. After talking for a minute, he put his wife Lovell on the phone to go over the details and soon after I received a contract in the mail. Mrs. Moore was very capable of doing all the paperwork for him. She would send a neatly typed Union contract to sign and return along with a $100 deposit, the balance to be paid in cash the night of the performance. Slim considered me his agent at Auburn and insisted I take $50 per booking. After collecting the balance due, Slim would give me a typed check made out to me for my $50 commission. I can definitely say that Mrs. Moore took care of the business details for Slim but I think Slim was always in charge. He was probably a pretty smart guy. I remember he was articulate, personable, and seemed quite at ease when dealing with young white kids. He was usually pretty businesslike the few times I talked with him on the phone. One thing I do remember is how thrilled I was when someone knocked on my door at the fraternity house and told me I had a person-to-person call from Slim Harpo. That was the night he asked me to find them a place to stay. I felt pretty important.[45]

Harpo was notably missing from local gigs during the spring and summer until August 7 when the *Advocate* took an ad for "Slim Harpo at The New Riviera, one mile west of river bridge." Then on December 14 he was on the society page of the *State-Times* again: "The Alpha Omicron Pi Sorority annual formal Xmas ball was held on December 12 in the ballroom of the Jack Tar Capitol House where Slim Harpo and his orchestra furnished music for dancing around a silver Christmas tree decorated with red ornaments. The highlight of the evening was a presentation to the president of the sorority." From this account, Harpo may have been cherished as a local music-maker, but he was still part of the wallpaper in many respects.

MY GENERATION

By the end of 1964, local ads for Harpo had really thinned out, partly because he was looking further afield but also because local entrepreneurs like Sam Montel were increasingly promoting visits by northern pop and R&B acts, followed within a few years by British Invasion groups like the Who and Herman's Hermits along with new-wave black musicians like Jimi Hendrix. The Beatles had performed in nearby New Orleans as early as September 1964.

Although a second big hit had so far eluded him, Harpo would soon begin to feel some benefit from the new generation of bands starting to record his songs. Earlier in 1964, the Rolling Stones had included "I'm a King Bee" on their first LP, exposing Harpo's style to a young European and worldwide audience James could have hardly imagined. In October 1964, they appeared on the *Ed Sullivan Show* on national television during their first tour of the United States, and their LP sales rocketed, treating a new young stateside audience to the Harpo style along with the bluesy sounds they took from Jimmy Reed and others. Their bass player, Bill Wyman, said years later, "I have always enjoyed Slim Harpo's records. He should have got much more attention. We recorded 'I'm a King Bee' at IBC studios in London in the spring of 1964. Mick [Jagger] really got hold of the song, making it very clear what he was singing about. . . . We even named our 1965 live EP 'Got Live if You Want It,'" in homage to Slim's first disc.[46]

Around this time, Harpo was playing some shows with John Fred, who with his Playboys band was very popular on the southern college circuit in the 1960s. John Fred Gourrier had already had some success with the New Orleans R&B of "Shirley" for the Montel label in 1959 but more significantly would have his own number-one hit in 1967 with "Judy in Disguise (with Glasses)" for Stan Lewis's Paula label of Shreveport. John Fred once described the impact of the Rolling Stones on Harpo: "I ran into Slim in the lobby [of the bank]. He said, 'John Fred, have you ever heard of the Rolling Stones?' I said, 'Yeah Slim, they're from England. They're one of the most popular bands over there and over here too. They were on the Ed Sullivan Show last week.' Slim said, 'You think this is any good?' Then he showed me a BMI royalty check for $25,000 that was for 'I'm a King Bee.' I said, 'Yeah Slim, that sure looks pretty good to me.'"[47] It's a wonderful story, although John Fred had earlier told this different version: "Slim came to me, he said, 'John Fred, John Fred, guess what happened, the Rolling Stones recorded one of my songs! I said 'Who in the hell are the Rolling Stones?' He said, 'Well, they said they're gonna be big.'"[48] Either way, the drift of the story was that Harpo, whose career had been shaped in a white-dominated business, was beginning to have some cards of his own to play.

For the moment, though, Slim was still living in a world that put him and his fellow blues musicians at a disadvantage, as John Fred also described: "[Those guys] were kinda trapped in the South, they were born just at the wrong time. They didn't have much influence locally, that's the amazing thing," compared to the music of the Beatles or the Rolling Stones. John Fred continued, "Slim Harpo was a very good friend of mine. . . . I played gigs with

them. I was closer to the black people than the white in those days. . . . We'd
drive down to New Orleans, and we had to go eat in the back. It used to make
me really mad. . . . I didn't really understand it. But if you said anything about
it you got a knock at the side of the head. You just ate back there and that was
it. He didn't question it, I used to question it. It didn't make any difference to
him. Slim could roll with the flow, you know what I mean? I loved him. He
was great in person. . . . Slim could have been big. . . . Slim Harpo's generation
was awful rough on the black man, you got to remember that."[49]

A local college musician, Lynn Ourso, recorded with and later managed
John Fred, recorded with Slim, and went on to found the Louisiana Music
Commission. He also remembers those hometown gigs:

> I met Slim while I was still in high school and I've always been a fan. I first became
> aware of Slim through his recordings played on WXOK radio in Baton Rouge
> and WLAC radio in Nashville and I first met him at the Glass Hat club in the late
> '50s, a club where he played a regular gig on Wednesdays or Thursdays as best I
> recall. I was a regular at his Glass Hat gigs, after my football practice. Lightnin'
> Slim or Lazy Lester would sit in there sometimes too. I spent a lot of time at the
> Glass Hat, soaking up the absolute best real live blues that I've ever heard. Then I
> had a band playing frat parties on the LSU campus; when my band would break
> I'd see Slim playing down the street. He was truly one of the greatest blues harp
> players of the era. Slim Harpo was an imposing, handsome figure, maybe 6'6" tall,
> always immaculately dressed, usually wearing an expensive looking suit, polished
> shoes and a white shirt and tie. And I should emphasize he was a kind and true
> gentleman. One sweet memory I will never forget was that I wanted to play blues
> harmonica so at a Glass Hat gig I asked Slim one night how to know what key the
> harmonica should be in when I buy one. He kindly explained, in his gentlemanly
> way, that "if you are going to play in the key of E, you need to buy an A harp." And
> he added that I should buy only Hohner harps, which he said I could find at the
> local City Pawn Shop. Later, Slim would come by the bank where I worked and I
> would cash his writer's royalty checks.[50]

RECORDINGS, JANUARY 1965

In January 1965, Harpo and Miller held the next of their now regular twice-
yearly recording sessions in Crowley, again with the road band augmented by
an added organ part from Katie Webster and percussion effects probably by
Lazy Lester. Katie Webster was likely thinking of Harpo's mid-1960s sessions
when she said, "Slim Harpo and I never really got to meet too much. . . . all

of the work that I did I always dubbed it onto his records. . . . [But] when you go into J. D. Miller's studio you have to cut perfect records. You cannot make not one mistake, [Miller] seems to have microphones in his ears."[51] The lead song at this time was "Midnight Blues," a fine example of swamp-pop that merged the blues with a country story-song, but that only appeared as a B side on Excello 2278 over a year later in 1966. It had a fascinating clip-clop percussion enhancing the basic rhythm and a melody that anticipated later zydeco hits such as "My Toot Toot." Another B side was recorded also, "Loving You (The Way I Do)," eventually issued on Excello 2282 in 1967. This was a reflective song about how hard Slim is taking his girl's latest misdemeanors. There's a fine guitar solo along with understated organ riffs. A third song from this session remained unissued at the time, but "You'll Never Find a Love (As True as Mine)" was an effective swamp-pop ballad sung tenderly by Slim. It lacked perhaps a little hook or memorable instrumental part that would have elevated it.

DESEGREGATION BLUES

Around the time that Harpo would have been receiving his first Rolling Stones publishing money in 1965, Australian blues fan Rick Milne arrived at Jay Miller's electrical and music store in Crowley only to find that Miller was out of town. The store assistant contacted Miller in Lake Charles, so Milne "decided to wait. The shop is in poor repair generally, wood floor, lots of musical instruments for sale on one side and a great stack of Excello and other records on the other side." While waiting, Milne talked to the twenty-three-year-old assistant who told him she looked after the place most of the time and that the shop was at that stage more a hobby of Miller's. He worked mainly on a housing project and had only a small amount of time to spend on music. "I talked to the girl about the recording artists. She said 'they're all dirty, greasy drunks etc,' all said matter of factly without the slightest malice. Crowley is a very segregated city." When Miller arrived, he explained that all recording was now done at his $20,000 home studio. "He said he didn't plan to record new blues artists as the market is not increasing and new artists would mean less sales for the established ones. Lightnin' Slim was his 'most popular and consistent' while Lazy Lester was 'an incurable alcoholic' and Lonesome Sundown 'found religion.' Slim Harpo was not Jay's favorite singer."[52]

Miller was a man of his time and place, though. In segregated Crowley, he genuinely saw himself as a friend to the blues artists, but he operated his music business in a paternalistic manner where the word of the boss man counted. His friendships with blues artists such as Lazy Lester, who regularly assisted in his studios, did not stop him releasing a series of right-wing political and racist country records on a label called Reb Rebel when trade became slow in the late 1960s. The white performers, particularly Pee Wee Trahan, had sometimes been involved in blues recording sessions for Miller and, like him, apparently just saw the records as "business" within the prevailing culture. Miller later said he regretted the racist nature of some of the recordings, credited to artists named Johnny Rebel, James Crow, and Son of Mississippi, but felt vindicated in a business sense when one Rebel disc by Happy Fats LeBlanc, giving political advice to "Dear Mr. President," started receiving awards for sales of over 100,000 copies in 1966. Fortunately, it appears that the more indefensible discs such as "NAACP Jig-a-boo Gemini" and "Nigger Hatin' Me" did not sell that sort of volume, though they were largely under-the-counter sales and unlikely to figure on any sales chart.

Desegregation moved slowly in Louisiana. As the *New York Amsterdam News* noted on February 27, 1965, in a report from Baton Rouge, "Louisiana Tech and Northwestern College [in Ruston and Natchitoches], the last two all-white colleges in the state, were ordered to desegregate immediately by a Federal District Judge." The Louisiana State Board of Education conceded that Negroes had been rejected because of their race. The year before, in Baton Rouge, Maxine Crump, the young girl from Maringouin, had become the first black undergraduate to attend Louisiana State University as a resident on campus. LSU had previously admitted a few black graduate students under court order, but in 1964 Maxine was one of the first to realize that while she had always expected to attend Southern University, she now had the option to go to LSU: "I thought, So what? I've been a minority all my life! It was nothing. I didn't see where it was going to be anything hard about it for me. . . . I had been treated black all my life. I had been treated less than. If I could get a good education out of it, that's all that mattered to me. I didn't care about the fact they weren't going to like me. I decided I'd like them. I never disliked white people, no matter what they did. I didn't see where they had done anything for me to dislike. I just saw them making ignorant decisions."[53] It's difficult to be sure whether Slim Harpo would have put it quite that way, but many of his actions indicate that he might not have been so far apart in his thinking. He may even have known Maxine's father, Emmanuel Crump, who had a nightclub, Prospects, in Maringouin until it closed in 1959 because of declining interest in the blues and increased competition from music shows on television.

Many clubs survived, though, and an issue that went across all races was that of Sunday opening and the proliferation of "social clubs" formed for that purpose. On July 7, 1965, the *Advocate* devoted two pages to the practice of the Green Parrot Bar running a "social club" in order to evade the Sunday closing laws and to make a slick buck. The Green Parrot, owned by Albert Christenberry at 100 North Thirty-Fourth Street, was one of Harpo's very local black venues. The story also featured Gat's Bar and Lounge of 1360 East Boulevard, owned by Charlie Gatlin, another Harpo stronghold.

RECORDINGS, OCTOBER 1965

In the summer of 1965, Jay Miller had told visiting fan Rick Milne that Slim Harpo was in a rut and "must have exhausted versions of 'King Bee' and 'Rainin' in My Heart.'" Tabby Thomas observed the matter from a different angle, describing how Harpo felt that he was not making enough from his records or his local gigs, saying, "and that kills you; when you're ready to record, you don't have the feeling for what you're doing. Slim Harpo, he had got like that."[54] That may have been so, but Miller's second Harpo session of 1965, made in October, was the one that recaptured Slim's mojo. It delivered both sides of a single that would hit number one on the national R&B chart through the spring of 1966. Perhaps Slim was inspired by the interest shown in his songs by British beat groups. He once said of the Rolling Stones' recordings of his songs, "It meant a record was re-born, you know. It was good for me and for the record, you know."[55] He also offered the information that "those songs helped me out and inspired me to do something a little different called 'Scratch My Back.'"[56]

The A side of Slim's "different" disc was a deceptively simple blues riff with a mostly spoken vocal describing how to do the chicken-scratch dance to an insistent "itchy" rhythm. Submitted to Excello as "The Scratch," and issued around December 1965 as "Baby Scratch My Back" on Excello 2273, it was by no means the first blues disc to be based on a pecking chicken rhythm—and Rufus Thomas had had a song called "Chicken Scratch" out on Stax only that fall—but it would prove to be the most successful. Slim once explained the song's origins: "I wrote those words with my wife, because I'd often get an itchy back. I'd have a bath and after it I'd say 'I'm still itching,' and I'd ask her to scratch my back for me. So this kept on and one day she said we ought to write a song about this. And I wrote the melody and she wrote the words."[57]

As is often the case with a popular song, other people remember the story, or parts of it, differently. Singer John Fred said, "I was there when he wrote 'Baby Scratch My Back,' he wrote that at the back of Tommy's Record Shop" in Baton Rouge.[58] In contrast, James Johnson said that the song was worked out as they went along at the recording session: "I started doing that Scratch lick one night, just started it right there, and the others came in and we finally put it all together, ran it down and that was it."[59] In other versions, Johnson said he started the riff at a show one night and the others joined in. Johnson remembered that his brother-in-law August Ranson played the bass, and "the only time I ever saw Lazy Lester play on a session was on Scratch My Back." Certainly, Jay Miller's trademark extra percussion sounds abound on this disc. Drummer Jockey Etienne told Becky Owens: "I remember playing drums on 'Scratch My Back.' . . . Lester played skull heads on that song—when you hear a 'knock, knock, knock' sound, that's Lester on skulls."[60] Rudy Richard had left Slim at this point, and some of the musicians recall Boe Melvin playing second guitar. Notwithstanding the popularity of the earlier chicken riffs in Memphis and elsewhere, and indeed the already famous scratchy guitar of Jimmy Nolen on James Brown's hit recordings, James Johnson confessed to the *Advocate* in 2006 about the chicken scratch: "I started that mess. So many people do it now." He remembered that J. D. Miller always said that he could have made it sound better, "but original is original. You can't beat original."[61] In 1969 Harpo himself told Jim Delehant that the song "was an attempt at rock and roll for me, but I'd much rather do the blues."

Lazy Lester agreed that he was the extra percussionist here. However, he almost missed the session because he was sent for a few months in 1965 to the state penitentiary at Angola, known locally as "the Pon de Rosa," and about which Lester recorded "Pondarosa Stomp" the following year. Jay Miller told Dave Booth: "I thought so much of all those artists, and Lester was darned near a member of the family. He and my father were so close, they were fishing buddies. But Lester was a bad boy, too," thinking of Lester's drinking and those regular scrapes with the law.

The flip side of "Baby Scratch My Back" was "I'm Gonna Miss You (Like the Devil)," an atmospheric blues describing the latest scenario between

Slim and his two-timing girl. A third song from the session was not issued at the time, but "I Don't Want No One (To Take Me Away from You)" was nevertheless a fine, moody ballad with James Johnson again taking the lead guitar part.

Through January 1966, "Baby Scratch My Back" appeared in *Billboard* as a "Top Seller" across all markets in New Orleans. By January 22, it was also on the "Top Seller" lists in Baltimore and Miami, entered the national R&B chart at 38, and was "Bubbling Under" the pop Hot 100. By March it had climbed to 28 pop while sitting firmly at the top of the R&B chart. It peaked at 16 pop on March 26 but remained on the charts into May. By then, Mississippi-based bluesman Frank Frost was on the market with a similar groove titled "My Back Scratcher," and his Jewel Records disc was on the R&B charts by August. Also in August, Slim's was listed as the second-best-selling single of the year to date, behind Sam and Dave's "Hold On, I'm Comin'." Excello's continuing sponsorship of late-night record shows on Nashville's powerful station WLAC was important: "In those days WLAC could break a good R&B record," Excello vice-president Shannon Williams told John Broven. "'Baby Scratch My Back' was a new Excello release and got play every night. Then other DJs around the country picked it up. The record stood on its own merit and was a hit." Tabby Thomas spoke about the impact of the disc on Harpo's life: "I was on my way home one day, and Slim had a flat tire. He had an old brown Cadillac—'I'm trying to fix this tire.' I said well, Slim, I just heard your record, man, that tune is taking off. You better check man, and call the office and see. He said, 'I'm gon' do that, man, I'm gonna call.' And the next three weeks I saw him, he had a new Cadillac."[62] But apart from his interest in cars, Tabby said, "he was just a nice guy. He didn't let the music go to his head." Slim's other contemporaries agreed. Rudy Richard said, "I remember Slim calling me up and saying, 'Rudolph it seems like everywhere I go when I turn on the radio all I hear is 'Scratch My Back.' It didn't go to his head, though; Slim was still a good old country boy."[63]

THE SCRATCH EFFECT

In the emerging soul era, when Motown and Stax were dominating black music from Detroit and Memphis, Slim Harpo's hit was a throwback to an earlier, rawer era of blues. But it turned out that one of the hottest R&B and soul artists of the day was impressed by "Baby Scratch My Back." James Brown invited Harpo to tour with him for some five weeks in the spring of 1966. In his autobiography, Brown, who had been abroad on tour, said, "The first thing we did when we got back together was plan a concert at Madison Square Garden for March 20, 1966. It was hard to put together. People didn't think I could draw well in such a big place by myself, so to quiet 'em down I added Len Barry, Lou Christie, Slim Harpo, the Shangri-Las and the Soul Brothers to the bill. By the time it was publicized most of the tickets had already been sold."[64] Brown was not keen to admit that Harpo's recent number-one R&B hit and Christie's pop hit "Lightning Strikes" might have had something to do with the sales. On March 28, Harpo found himself at the Houston Coliseum with Brown, and within weeks he had played in New York again at the Apollo. The *New York Amsterdam News* previewed forthcoming events in the black music calendar that spring and noted on March 20 that on April 5 there would be a repeat version of the major show at Madison Square Garden: "James Brown all star revue with Slim Harpo, the Shangri-Las, and others."

Some nightclub owners were as impressed as James Brown with Slim's new hit, and went to unusual lengths to secure Slim's services. Up in Gary, Indiana, bluesman Lester "Big Daddy" Kinsey said, "I was about the only harmonica player around that could play 'Scratch My Back' and they actually billed me as Slim Harpo! We played Waterloo, Iowa; we got into town about two in the afternoon, and I see posters all over town with my picture, you know, 'Slim Harpo.' . . . They said, 'now, Big Daddy, you stay back in the dressing room . . . until we bring you on, and come out blowin.' . . . When I come out I set the place on fire. Nobody ever questioned it [but] I guess people wondered. Some of 'em did say, 'Mr. Harpo, you put on a little weight!'"[65]

Back home, his new song gave Slim's local gigs renewed impetus. A large ad in the *Advocate* on February 11, 1966, proclaimed proudly: "Golden Slipper presents recording artist Slim Harpo singing his latest hit number Scratch My Back and others. 7 pm stag or drag." Harpo's drawing power continued in the North, too, and by March 19 the *Chicago Defender* was advertising the forthcoming "1966 'Big Show of Stars' opening at the Regal Theater on April 1 with the Temptations, Junior Walker, Sam and Dave, Slim Harpo, and the Red Saunders orch." Harpo was still making his way back from the North when the May 28 edition of the *Norfolk Journal* in Virginia reported on "Stars slated to shine at Auditorium: Local rhythm and blues fans will greet a galaxy of entertainers in The Biggest Show Of Stars 1966 on June 4 at Norfolk Auditorium. Included in the one night concert will be stars such as the Marvelettes, Percy Sledge, Robert Parker, Slim Harpo, backed by the Joe Tex Big Beat Orchestra." On the day of the show, the Norfolk paper chose to go with a full-length picture of Harpo to advertise the event, the caption explaining that Stevie Wonder and Solomon Burke would now also be on the bill. By June 24, Harpo had made it back south to New Orleans, where the *Times-Picayune* trailed his two shows in one day at the Carver Theater: "Slim Harpo, on stage in person—today only." Also performing were the Royals, and between the two performances there would be an on-screen "TNT" show featuring Ike and Tina Turner, Ray Charles, and Bo Diddley.

Lovell remembered well the long drives to the North and back, describing for example, how "we played a club in South Carolina and we left at three in the morning and we had to be in Madison Square Garden in New York at three that afternoon. . . . We got stopped by the cops a coupla times—the first one that stopped us went to school at LSU and James had played at their fraternity and he let us go, and he just told us, 'OK Slim, take it easy.'" She also recalled that the Apollo and Madison Square gigs were played with the house bands, "because Rudy and the boys weren't on every engagement with us."[66] In the case of this trip north, though, she had forgotten that, although Rudy was no longer with the band, James Johnson did in fact make the first 1966 trip to Madison Square Garden, a show he remembers as his most unusual. "Believe it or not, it was just me and Slim and the orchestra," he said. "I was worried about how we was going to sound." In the event, Johnson's biggest problem was not James Brown's orchestra but the logistics of carrying his Vox amp through the New York streets. "I said, 'Man, Slim, you big time now. Why you ain't got no valet?' [He said] 'Aw, you can do it. Come on, let's go.' And he's gone with his little harmonica case and I'm fussing with this amp and a guitar." Johnson remembers rehearsing with Slim and the orchestra in the afternoon at the Garden. "You know, Slim had his music wrote out. He handed them the music. They played the hell out of it. We did a good show with the orchestra, but I'm just glad we came on before James Brown. First time I had played with an orchestra. Last time, too."[67] Speaking later of his trips to the big city, Harpo said, "New York City was fantastic. I'm just a country boy but I like to see the rest of the world."[68]

Early in 1966, a New York–based writer and editor of *Hit Parader* and other music magazines, Jim Delehant, had started searching for information about Harpo, a man with a big hit record but little available promotional material. In May, he telephoned Ernie Young because "anyone who has tried to get information on Excello artists knows that you might as well go and look on the back of a tomato soup can." Young gave him Jay Miller's number but said, "He ain't worth a ding dong damn when it comes to photos of his boys." Failing to make contact with Miller, Delehant called Harpo's house to find he had left to tour with James Brown just two minutes earlier. As Delehant recalled,

> A week later, I found Slim in a front row seat [at Madison Square Garden] digging James Brown's turn onstage. "Let's go back," he said, "and I'll introduce you to Mrs. Moore. She goes wherever I go." Mrs. Moore said, "I don't know which of us has more fun." Slim and Mrs. Moore travel the country in style in a 1966 Cadillac. "We take turns at the wheel," said Mrs. Moore, "and when we get hungry Slim runs into a store for some canned spam, sharp cheese and potato chips." Mrs. Moore said at home Slim fixes things and tinkers with a trucking business with a couple of friends. He listens to James Brown, B. B. King, Big Joe Williams, the Impressions. She likes the Dixie Hummingbirds and spirituals. She says, "My man did a little bit of everything before he became a singer, but he finally found out what he wants to do most." Slim said, "Ever since I was a little kid, I played harmonica. I got three sisters and they're all married now. My nephews and nieces dig their show-biz uncle."[69]

It's notable that in this interview Slim introduces the subject of marriage through references to "Mrs. Moore" and to his sisters' marital status. No doubt it was on his mind because James and Lovell had been married on April 30, 1966, at the Municipal Building, Manhattan, when he hit New York for his shows there. William Gambler remembers, "It was the Madison Square Garden trip. My mother had been with him to other places, Chicago and such places, but this one was her first to New York and when they came back they told me they was married then." It's not clear whether this was a fairly impromptu event or long-planned. Maybe it was Slim wanting to make a statement to Lovell, or maybe it was a mutual desire for a low-key event away from family and friends. Either way, Slim told Delehant that "the kids worry more about us on road than we do about them keeping the house up, but they're very happy that their mom and pop are able to see the country." Interestingly, Slim also told Delehant that he was thirty-six years old, losing six years for publicity purposes in time-honored show-biz tradition.

One of Slim's nephews, Ray Moore, confirmed that Harpo's return from his travels was always eagerly awaited, along with the mementos of his shows.

Uncle James would always bring us photos from his promotions. I was very proud of him, and wanted to be just like him. I look like him in his younger pictures, I was tall just like him. I recall seeing him on *American Bandstand*. Every time he record a new song, I would stay up late and tune into the Nashville radio station and hear his new release, the signal from Nashville was only strong at night. He would always give me some of his older harps to play with. I was never any good at playing the harp. He would always let me play his guitar both at his house and at my house and I would play so long that my thumb would be sore. He would always play and sing for me at home when I ask him. One of the biggest time in my life was when they got my uncle to play on campus at my high school during a daytime program. That day I was the big man on campus, I even got to drive his Cadillac for the first time around the campus. I have seen my uncle play at the local clubs in Mulatto Bend and he have also taken me on the road to a few local clubs in New Roads and other surround places. At one time I collected the money at the door during one of his gigs. I did not get to go to some of the big trips like The Apollo, or Nashville but I recall after his local gigs that I went on, we would take all of the guys in the band home and then park the trailer on the street beside one of the band member house. I recall him having his trailer built; it was the size of today's 5×8 U-Haul. It was painted yellow and had his name on both sides of the trailer with all of his hit songs on it.[70]

When researcher Rick Milne finally managed to talk to Harpo in 1966, he found that Slim was "quite unaffected by success" and happy to talk about other local musicians. He said that Lonesome Sundown was "one of my best friends," that Silas Hogan "plays his own harp and is one of my favorites," and that Lightnin' Slim "would do much better if he had an agent."[71] David Kearns encountered Harpo again in the spring of 1966, this time at WBAM radio in Montgomery on their *Shower of Stars* show. Slim contacted Kearns in Auburn, Alabama. Kearns remembered:

He asked me if I could find them a place to stay because they wanted to come on Friday to be rested for the WBAM show on Saturday. When I was unable to locate a motel or hotel for them, with my fraternity brothers' approval, I called Slim back and offered to let them stay in the fraternity house attic. It was a finished attic with beds and mattresses. I think at that point he asked if they could rehearse in our party room on Friday night. The rehearsal turned into a party attended by several hundred people. Our cooks made sure the band was well fed before they left for Montgomery on Saturday morning. I'm sure Slim was happy because the band's travel expenses were significantly reduced for the weekend. A dollar went a lot further back then but with the traveling expenses the band incurred to get to Auburn, a lot further from Baton Rouge than Mobile, none of them, including Slim, were getting rich. I remember that unlike many of the bands I dealt with back then, Ms. Lovell always sent a standard musician's union contract to sign and return. I'm pretty sure when Slim and the band first started coming to Mobile the booking fee was $250 and Percy Stovall got a portion of that. Slim's fee may have gone up to $300 by the time the live recordings were made in 1961. Then when I was booking Slim at Auburn he was charging $400 and giving me $50 that I gave back to the fraternity, so he was grossing $350.00. I told him he didn't have to do that, but he insisted.[72]

By the mid-1960s, Slim was starting to think about diversifying his music and his approach to it. James Brown had shown him the soul route, but he wasn't sure that was really for him. He was a bluesman at heart, and he saw some bluesmen becoming popular nationally with college audiences and at music festivals. He resolved to improve his guitar playing. Kearns remembers: "After one of the gigs at Auburn, Slim and several of the band members were joking around with each other while packing up after the show. He told them he was going to learn to play the guitar so that he could leave them at home and keep all the money for himself like John Lee Hooker. They all laughed, and one of them said something like he had heard Slim try to play guitar so he wouldn't be worrying about that for awhile. Slim told me he was learning guitar because he wanted to do a solo blues album like John Lee Hooker, who was making money on folk blues festivals."[73]

Over in Dallas, Lightnin' Hopkins was also being courted to make gigs and albums for the new audience for folk blues, influencing a new generation of white musicians. According to writer Jeff Hannusch, Harpo did play some shows as a solo act and has cited those he played for the coffeehouse clubs at the Louisiana State University campus using a Gibson ES-335, a very popular semi-hollow-body electric guitar that may be seen in some of Harpo's publicity photographs, and a harp rack. Slim's businesslike approach to his music did not always go down well with his band members, and this may account in part for the large number of people who played with him both before and after the heyday of his classic road band of Rudy, James, Sammy, and Pro. James Johnson liked Slim and stuck with him for eight years, but he never fully figured him out: "Slim was kinda odd to get along with. Everything had to go his way, or not at all. That's how it was. He was a good guy—but he didn't always treat us right, we thought. Sometimes he'd play with the whole band, sometimes he'd go out with a half band, sometimes by himself. One day he wanted to just pay us union scale. And we didn't really know how big he was, back then. He was a friend, sure, but he was older than we were and he tried to act like we were kids, you know. Everybody called him 'Chief' then. 'Baby Scratch My Back' changed things for him, but it changed nothing for us. He didn't pay us no more money."[74]

James Johnson particularly disliked traveling in discomfort, where often the band was cramped up in an old van bought from Jay Miller while Slim traveled ahead in his own car. He remembered one time when Slim persuaded him to go on tour across to Florida. "I quit my job to go with him. He said he'd pay me $150 [per show]. We hadn't even got to Denham Springs when he changed it to $100, and when we got to Fort Lauderdale he said he was only gonna pay me $50. It was rough."[75]

RECORDINGS, FEBRUARY 1966

With the lessons of the unfortunate aftermaths of "King Bee" and "Rainin'" well and truly learned, Harpo and Miller returned to the studio promptly within four months, in February 1966, determined to find a proper follow-on disc to "Baby Scratch My Back." Miller already had chosen a B side in "Midnight Blues" from the previous session, and now he recorded three songs, choosing the fast-paced, hypnotic shoeshine beat of "Shake Your Hips" as the A side. It was another dance-instruction song—"everybody doin' it, from the grown ups down"—but listeners would need a lot more energy to do this dance than the "Scratch" as Slim and the band got into their groove. There was an understated guitar solo, a riffing sax, and percussion embellishments by Lazy Lester. Katie Webster provided a rhythmic enhancement on organ. Slim goes through some standard instructions about what parts of the body to shake and when. Then, suddenly, he's there, in his own song—"Well I met a little girl / In a country town / She said 'what do you know / There's Slim Harpo.'" Next thing he's down there on the floor following his own instructions. "Shake Your Hips," Excello 2278, was issued in June 1966 and immediately chosen in *Billboard* as a Spotlight pop hit, described as "two blues based sides. Dance-teaching tune is backed by a solid blues weeper with harmonica backing." On July 2, it was noted as a Breakout Single in Pittsburgh.

Despite this, the single failed to make any of the charts other than number 116 on the *Billboard* Bubbling Under chart on July 23. The two other sides from the session, unissued at the time, were "Baby You Got What I Want," a fairly limited lyric but a fascinating combination of entrancing zydeco rhythms and beats, and "Your Love for Me Is Gone," a gospel-influenced song with swirling organ and animated vocals that also contains a fine bluesy guitar solo. It seems that "Shake Your Hips" was a more influential disc than its chart position indicated, and it sold widely over a long period. Kirk Beasley, a budding Nashville musician and songwriter in the office of Combine Music, recalls when the boss, Bob Beckham, came out of his office holding a piece of paper aloft: "We heard a yell and he appeared with a huge smile. We all knew the Rolling Stones had released 'Shake Your Hips' on their Exile on Main Street LP but Beckham had just found out Combine owned the publishing rights to that song. He had the first royalty payment in his hand. A celebration was quickly forthcoming."[76]

On the back of Slim's live shows, his LP sales increased and the label issued his second album, *Baby Scratch My Back,* Excello LP 8005, in the fall of 1966. That October, some music reviewers in newspapers welcomed the LP as "twelve new sides."[77] In truth, it was a repackaging of six singles, give or take an alternative version or title here and there. *Billboard* gave it a Pop Spotlight review on October 1, saying: "Leading with 'Shake Your Hips' Harpo combines blues harmonica, a soft voice and a driving electric guitar for a pulsating, rocking package. Based on his hit 'Baby Scratch My Back' Harpo should crash the charts hard and fast." Excello even took the unusual step of advertising the LP in *Billboard* later that month—"Going strong. The smash LP follow up to the top ten single." It didn't quite pan out that way, but the LP remained long-term in the Excello catalog nonetheless. Meantime, "Baby Scratch My Back" had been logged by *Billboard* as the third-best-selling R&B single of 1966 and number 86 in all pop sales.

This was all in spite of Ernie Young's self-help business operation at Excello. Shannon Williams said: "Oh, I remember when Slim Harpo hit big with 'Baby Scratch My Back.' It was just madness, you know, Mr. Young and [secretary] Dorothy Keaton trying to handle this hit, just the two of them. He finally would get to where he would allow the pressing plant to direct-ship, this was something that was far into his thinking, though, he thought everything should come to his back door and we should ship it away. But when Harpo's 'Baby Scratch My Back' got so big he discovered he couldn't do that—the majority of it would be shipped from the plant—but he tried."[78] Young was concerned about the pressing plants making extra copies to be shipped out of their back doors, a practice that was far from unknown when Ernie had started out in 1950 and that persisted into the 1960s and beyond.

Despite Slim's success with "Baby Scratch My Back" and "Shake Your Hips," his income as a professional musician was still far less than might be imagined today. William Gambler had left Baton Rouge to join the Air Force in 1962, returning home in 1966 to find that Harpo was as much if not more than ever involved in running his small haulage-and-scrap-iron business. He witnessed this firsthand for a couple of years until he moved to his own house in Baker around 1968. He said, "Slim continued with running his trucks even after he had big records, because it was a necessity. He had to do that. Slim was never really popular during his time like people think today. Even after he had 'Scratch My Back,' selling scrap iron was still his main source of income, I'd say."[79]

Back in Slim's home patch, neighbor Arlene Batiste recalls that Slim still played at the Streamline Club in Mulatto Bend in the mid-1960s:

> That was where Slim Harpo played most every Sunday night when I was 18 or 19. I'd see him there, and another time it would be Lightnin' Slim or Buddy Stewart with his nephew Chuck Mitchell, or Harry Johnson, a saxophone player who had a man called "Chewing Gum" singing. Mr. Gordon Wells was the owner, and Mrs. Wells and I would help them out in the kitchen, but when Slim Harpo came on I'd go out there and start to dancing at the front. Slim would be up there on stage and would have James Johnson with him playing bass and Rudy Richard playing guitar. But then it changed, and Philip Guy was playing the guitar then. Slim was mainly blowing that harp and singing, and his leg would be going, you know, ooh they were some times, yes indeed. I went to a lot of clubs, loved music. Streamline was a big old club, with a barroom part and a dance floor and eating tables and living quarters in the back. But the oldest club here in Mulatto Bend was called Joby's, belonged to two brothers called Milton, not musicians. But they had music, Slim would go there. It had a gambling shack on the side. We'd go there, we'd go to Wishadell's over the river in Scotland, to the White Eagle and Blue Bull in Port Allen, all those.[80]

Batiste remembers, "Slim was a very nice person, you could always hold a conversation with him, and Ms. Lovell, she was a nice lady, very nice. She used to come out to the clubs with him sometime. I loved his music. But I don't think the black accepted him as well as the white—because he used to play at a lot of different white places. You have to go where the money is at, I guess."[81]

William Gambler also remembered Slim at these clubs: "In Mulatto Bend there were two black clubs. There was Joby's, that was the first, it stayed small, and right nearby was the Streamline and that grew big. Slim played in those. Then there were four or five white clubs right off the bridge on the west side, all half a mile apart. The Candlelight and the others." But Gambler disagreed about the day-to-day staple element of Slim's music work. "Well, day to day Slim played mostly black clubs, always, every week. But they were local, didn't advertise, people knew about them. Wishadell's, Streamline, White Eagle, all those. He played white places when he could because of the money there, but it never was day to day."[82]

RECORDINGS, SEPTEMBER 1966

Whether his star was on the rise or not, Harpo's revised recording contract was about to run out when he got together with Jay Miller in a Crowley studio for the last time in September 1966. He recorded three songs, with a slightly different group of King Bees.

By now, Harpo's road group had started to change, with new members joining either temporarily or for longer hauls. James Johnson remained the most constant, but other guitarists, bass players, and drummers came and went. The drum seat had apparently been passed to Roosevelt Sample, known variously as "Kenneth" or "Sam," sometime after 1963. Sample was in the Army from May 1957 to May 1963 and, strangely, he is named by discographers as the drummer on some sessions by Lightnin' Slim and others right through his service years. Just possibly his home leave coincided with Lightnin's sessions, but he is not known to have recorded with Slim Harpo.

Sample was born in August 1934 in Baton Rouge, where his father, Roosevelt senior, was the janitor at Woodlawn High School. Sample said he had first worked with Lightnin' Slim, then Buddy Guy, and was with Slim Harpo for five years before working with Raful Neal in the 1970s.[83] He worked in construction as well as music. Between music gigs he found himself no stranger to controversy, the most high-profile event being reported in the *Advocate* of March 15, 1968: "East Baton Rouge grand jury clears two men: One no-true bill was returned in the case of Roosevelt Sample, 33 year old negro of 3835 Tuscarora had been booked for murder in the shooting death of David Lucas, negro. Police said Sample was sitting in his car outside a small bar, Williams Café on the levee just south of the new I-10 bridge when Lucas came up and said he needed some money. Lucas pulled a knife. Sample told police he got a .22 caliber revolver from between the seats of the car and fired into the ground. When Lucas kept coming Sample fired again hitting Lucas in the chest."

Returning to his construction work and occasional music gigs, Sample was in the papers again ten years later. On June 10, 1978, Roosevelt Sample, aged forty-four, was listed as one of several drivers of concrete-delivery trucks arrested for selling six thousand dollars' worth of concrete directly from their trucks to Gilbert's Funeral Home without the concrete company's knowledge. Sample had long since been replaced in Harpo's road band by several drummers, most notably Jesse Kinchen, whose relatives T. J. Kinchen and Arthur "Guitar" Kelley, had often played at local clubs with Harpo. Philip Guy played guitar with Harpo for a time, and at some point Otis Johnson rejoined the band on the road as well.

Harpo's September 1966 session was played, according to the memories of local musicians, with bass player August Ranson and drummer Jesse Kinchen. James Johnson was on guitar, backed up either by Boe Melvin or by Slim himself. Rudy Richard, who had little to say for Slim as a guitarist, was in and out of the band at this point, becoming unreliable. Richard admitted he did take a little something before facing the bigger and bigger audiences he was seeing: "I wasn't really no big drinker, but to build your nerves, I said, 'Look at the people in here. I got to do something,' I was a whiskey head then. Big Boe Melvin came in and I think he made a record with Slim then."[84]

This time the signature song was another Harpo original, "I'm Your Bread Maker, Baby," which appeared as Excello 2282 in November. It was announced by Slim hollering "bread maker baby" like a street seller with his wares. He followed with a wailing harp before the band launched into an almost funky clip-clop rhythm. After a number of dance-instruction discs, this was a rhythm for other late-night activities. The flip side of the record was the excellent blues "Loving You (The Way I Do)," which Miller exhumed from tapes made eighteen months earlier. He presumably was not satisfied with the two unissued songs from this last session. They were "I Gotta Stop Loving You," a perfectly good blues ballad with Slim's trademark fade-out harp solo, and "Stop Working Blues," a memorable stop-time blues about a woman taking money to give to another man—"the more I work/Seem like to me the less I have"—with an extended guitar solo. The title of the song would prove pertinent to the Harpo-Miller relationship.

Considering the success of "Baby Scratch My Back," there seemed no reason why "Bread Maker" too should not have been a hit, and *Billboard* chose it as an R&B top-10 Spotlight release on November 26, even saying, "This wild, wailing number is a topper for 'Baby Scratch My Back' and should meet with fast sales impact. Much pop potential as well." The disc was a "Breakout Single" in Milwaukee in December and in January 1967 was listed as "Bubbling Under" the pop 100, but this was a false dawn and the disc failed to chart.

THE END OF AN ERA

To make things worse for Jay Miller, he suddenly realized that his investment in developing Harpo's recording career was at an end. In July 1966, Ernie Young, who had started out in the music business in the 1940s while in his forties, was planning to retire. He arranged to sell Excello and its parent company, Nashboro, to the Crescent Amusement Company, who asked Shannon Williams, one of Young's former employees at his retail and wholesale business, Ernie's Record Mart, to run the record label. In the period when Young was moving toward retirement, but at the same time trying to handle the distribution of "Baby Scratch My Back," Slim and Lovell Moore were still harboring the feeling that Slim could do better than to work through a personal contract with Jay Miller, who in turn had his own deals with the record label. Lovell said: "With Miller, when he paid, he just gave James a check. He didn't know if he was getting paid for his music or what. He never saw an itemized sheet, to see what was being sold, and this was the way it was . . . [so] I just bided my time and just before his contract was up I wrote to Jay Miller and told him that James didn't care to record for him anymore. I sent it by registered letter. Of course he tried to deny it, but he could not. After that contract, we went to Nashville and talked to some people . . . Ernie, whatever, and we had contracts. To me it was just the right thing to do because J. D. Miller was sending the records he made to Ernie [anyway]."[85]

Ernie Young passed the Harpo issue on to his successors when he finally retired in October 1966. Speaking for Nashboro, Shannon Williams confirmed: "Slim Harpo's contract with Miller expired, and Harpo vowed that he would not sign with Miller again. Harpo didn't want nothing to do with

[Jay] and insisted that he would never cut another song for Miller. . . . It was a matter of money, royalties. In order to not let Harpo escape, Nashboro-Excello made an offer which he accepted. Miller claimed that we had stolen his artist from him. That was the last straw [for him]."[86]

Jay Miller didn't make any more recordings for Excello, even though his overall deal to produce blues recordings for them apparently still had three years to run. Miller felt betrayed by Excello and by Harpo, but he also recognized that he had made an error when drawing up his second contract with Harpo in 1963: "That's where I made my big mistake. I made another contract for two years and I misdated the option [for one year not two]. . . . it was on a technicality that [Excello] got him out from under me."[87] At the time of the "Bread Maker" session, Miller had thought he had a further year's option on Harpo, but he didn't.

Shannon Williams and the Crescent Company interpreted the production contract between Young and Miller to mean Excello owned all the tapes Miller had sent them. When they signed Slim Harpo directly to Excello, Miller demanded all his master tapes back, by Harpo and by other artists. Excello refused, and a twenty-year legal case ensued, which Miller did not win. Williams remembered that, initially, he still wanted to work with Miller on other artists: "We tried to work with him all the same, 'Let's continue the relationship you've always had,' but Miller was pissed about Harpo signing directly with Excello that he just never did get over that. He looked at that as underhanded. And we tried to say, 'But he would have gone and recorded for somebody else because he had no intentions of recording with you.' But it still didn't make Miller feel any different; I don't know that we ever got a thing from him after that."[88]

Apart from all this, Jay Miller had a construction business to run and was better known in his home area as housing director for the city of Crowley and a member of the city health committee in the 1960s. In 1967, blues researcher Mike Leadbitter visited Miller in Crowley, calling at his new shop and studio, "Modern Music—Zynn Records," located since 1965 at 411–413 North Parkerson, where he sold cameras and musical instruments. His store and studio were being run by his sons Bill and Mike and by Cajun musician Rufus Thibodeaux. There was a new half-finished studio being built a few doors away above a beauty parlor owned by Miller's wife in the Ford Building at 425 North Parkerson. Leadbitter described Miller as "a big man in Crowley. . . . His financial interests are wide and varied. . . . His nature is shrewd and aggressive, giving you the feeling that he has literally torn his way to the top of Crowley society. . . . to his friends he is extremely generous. His hospitality is lavish and he loves to entertain."[89]

At the time of such visits from foreign blues aficionados, Miller said that the well of blues talent had dried up. Some of the old-timers were still playing, but Miller said the up-and-coming black musicians in America had little interest in recording blues of the type he knew and loved. Miller later described how "the blues had gone out altogether, you couldn't get black kids to do any blues. . . . I know that by virtue of my own experience. Now [1990] there is a resurgence of interest in the blues, but not the old gutbucket blues. . . . I like those downhome blues, it's more authentic."[90]

Over a period of nine years—mostly creative, sometimes flourishing, sometimes turbulent years—Harpo's talent and Miller's recording abilities had combined in Miller's small but well-crafted Crowley studios to produce a sound and a style that at once encapsulated the blues tradition and took the swampy sounds of Louisiana to new levels and heights of success. However, the repeated failure to follow one big hit with another meant that both Harpo and Excello were left feeling that a new start and a new sound were in order. Accordingly, the new regime at Excello scheduled the first post-Miller session for somewhere they felt was musically hot—Memphis, Tennessee.

J. D. Miller (*right*) at a recording session with Lonesome Sundown
(Courtesy John Broven)

SLIM HARPO
AND HIS KING BEES

AREA Code 504

FOR BOOKING - DIAL DI. 3-9611
OR WRITE JAMES MOORE OR LOVELL MOORE
906 N. 36TH ST.
BATON ROUGE, LA.

"MUSIC FOR ALL OCCASIONS"

Slim's calling card, early 1960s, apparently ready to play anything
(Courtesy David Kearns and Bear Family Records)

HIGH HAT
CLUB ★ ★ ★
New Orleans, La.
PROUDLY PRESENTS

FRIDAY MAY 25, 1961

★ # SLIM HARPO

LIGHTNIN
HOO DOO BLUES

I'M A KING BEE
RAININ IN MY HEART

★

SLIM
ORLEANS N. VILLERE

9:00 SHOW & DANCE 9:00
P.M. ROUZAN P.M.

The Baton Rouge blues come to New Orleans. Note the picture of Lightnin' Slim has been reversed in error on the poster. (Courtesy Bear Family Records)

THE TEXAN LOUNGE

Presents in Person Direct
from American Bandstand

"SLIM HARPO"

& His Entire Band
Friday & Saturday Nights
Hwy. 190, Port Allen

Harpo finally gains some hometown recognition, 1961
(Author's collection)

One of the various lineups of the King Bees (*standing:* A. J. Edwards,
James Johnson, unidentified, Willie Parker; *front:* Otis Johnson, Rudy
Richard). Richard identified the standing guitarist as a relative of
Harpo named Ernest. (Courtesy Otis Johnson)

Harpo's first LP, complete with misspelled title (Author's collection)

Jimmy Anderson's Joy Jumpers, 1962. *From left:* Eugene Dozier, Oscar Hogan, Jimmy Anderson, Guitar Taylor. Taylor played on Harpo's King Bee session. (Courtesy John Broven and Ace Records)

Slim Harpo and Rudy Richard, looking sharp, mid-1960s (Courtesy William Gambler)

80--412

STATE OF LOUISIANA
PARISH OF EAST BATON ROUGE } *Official Certificate*
BE IT KNOWN, That by virtue of a License from the Clerk of the District Court in and for said Parish of East Baton Rouge, dated _____ Sept 10 __19-43, I have celebrated the Rites of Matrimony between _____ James Moore _____ and _____ Verna mae murrell _____ parties named in said License, on this _10_ day of _____ Sept _____, 1943, in said Parish in presence of three lawful witnesses.
In testimony whereof, witness the signatures of the said parties, three witnesses and my official signature, made on the date named herein.

WITNESSES: PARTIES AND OFFICER:

Returned and Filed _____
September 13 19__
Deputy Clerk.

A 122080
THE CITY OF NEW YORK
OFFICE OF THE CITY CLERK
MARRIAGE LICENSE BUREAU—BOROUGH OF MANHATTAN

Marriage Register
No. 8175-1966

Certificate of Marriage Registration

This Is To Certify That _James Moore_
residing at _906 North 36th St. Baton Rouge LA_ born _February 11,1924_
at _Lobdell LA_ and _Lovell Jones_
residing at _906 North 36th St. Baton Rouge LA_ born _May 5,1924_
at _Dorseyville LA_

Were Married

on _____ April 30,1966 _____ at _____ Manhattan NY _____
as shown by the duly registered license and certificate of marriage of said persons on file in this office.

Dated at the Municipal Building, Manhattan

June 7 '196 7

VOID IF ALTERED OR SEAL NOT IMPRESSED

City Clerk of the City of New York

RF 446A - 97½M Sets - 701312 (65)

James Moore's marriage certificates, 1943 (*top*) and 1966 (Author's collection and courtesy William Gambler)

James and Lovell Moore, 1960s (Courtesy William Gambler)

Slim Harpo in action at a Nashville publicity shoot, late 1960s (Courtesy Bear Family Records)

An enthusiastic trade ad from Excello Records (Author's collection and courtesy Bill Millar)

Silas Hogan in the 1960s (Courtesy Ace Records and Rob Santos/AVI)

Slim Harpo in repose at the Nashville publicity shoot, late 1960s
(Courtesy Bear Family Records)

Harpo playing the basement blues in Nashville, late 1960s
(Courtesy Bear Family Records)

James and Lovell Moore after a show, late 1960s, with
unidentified friend (Courtesy William Gambler)

James and Lovell Moore, late 1960s (Courtesy William Gambler)

Historical marker at Mulatto Bend (Courtesy Gene Tomko)

The author (*left*) with Harpo's nephew Otis Kelly and Harpo's stepson
William Gambler (*right*) outside the Moore property at Mulatto Bend
(Courtesy Jennifer Hawkins)

(Courtesy Bear Family Records)

6. THE MUSIC'S HOT

TIP ON IN

In February 1967, the Crescent Company underwent an adjustment to their ownership and managerial arrangements. By May, Bud Howell had joined Nashboro-Excello as president, and he and Shannon Williams moved the company to the former Woodland Theater building at 1011 Woodland Street, a mile east of downtown Nashville. Ernie Young's downtown premises and studio had been sold, and so a new recording venue was required. The Crescent Company proceeded to remodel part of their theater building into the Woodland Sound Studio, although it would not be operational until the following year. In April 1968, *Record World* reported Woodland had been "opened in January by [Excello] General Manager Bud Howell, and . . . its electronic features are the most modern that can be found." Woodland was operated for Crescent by engineers Glenn Snoddy, who had worked in Nashville's very earliest studios; Lee Hazen; and Jim Pugh. At first, the studio was exclusively for Nashboro-Excello artists, but soon the engineers built a wider reputation even though the studio was many blocks removed from the Music Row center of the country-music business. By 1969 a second studio had been added, and the enterprise was sold to Snoddy and his colleagues with Nashboro-Excello merely renting studio time there.

Back in the spring of 1967, though, Excello had to seek a different place in which to make their first post-Miller recordings with Slim Harpo. They went for a change of musicians, too. James Johnson said: "I didn't make any sessions with Slim after he left J. D. Miller. He made the next ones in Tennessee with the Bar Kays."[1] In fact, Excello settled not on the Stax studio and the Bar Kays but on the Royal Studio at 1320 South Lauderdale Avenue in Memphis. Owned by Hi Records, the studio had a track record of chart success through Bill Black's Combo, Gene Simmons, and Ace Cannon, and an R&B roster led by Willie Mitchell and Don Hines. Hi's studio was run by one of the founders of the company, Ray Harris, a former rockabilly singer on Sun Records, and the house band was led by Willie Mitchell, who had a stake in the label and organized personal appearances by its R&B artists. At the end of 1966 and the start of 1967, he took an "All Star Rhythm and Blues Show" around Memphis and the mid-South, featuring Hi artists Don Bryant and Venise Stark along with Booker T and the MGs from Stax—and Excello's Slim Harpo. An ad for their December 30, 1966, gig in El Dorado, Arkansas, shows Slim with third billing behind Booker T and Willie Mitchell.

Shannon Williams remembered the conundrum about how and where to record Slim. They were used to dealing with Nashville-based artists. "Well, of course, after we signed Slim the question was, 'What are we going to do with him now?' So it was a case where we felt like we should take him to a better. . . . Nashville just is not a blues location and the players are not here, let's take him somewhere that we think maybe he can turn out a hit. It just happened that the Royal recording studio which was Hi Records in Memphis, Tennessee, was the place because of their track record at the time. We got in touch with this guy named Ray Harris [at Hi], he set the whole thing up, said he could get the pickers and Willie Mitchell and these guys that played there. It was like a house band, I guess. And they loved to do it."[2]

Harris and Mitchell's studio band comprised the Hodges brothers— Charles, Mabon, and Leroy—on organ, guitar, and bass, along with drummer Howard Grimes. However, Grimes told one interviewer that he never recorded with Harpo, and in contrast Jesse Kinchen has spoken about making the trip from Baton Rouge with Slim to record.[3]

Although Shannon Williams produced many gospel sessions for Nashboro-Excello and gospel was his favorite music, he was keen to use other producers drawn from the musicians and songwriters in the black community in Nashville. First came Robert Holmes, followed by singer Freddie North. Bob Holmes was from Greenville, Mississippi, and grew up in Memphis with Baptist church music before working with jazz musicians.

He moved to Nashville to go to Tennessee State University, studied classical music, and became a teacher and part-time session pianist with country singers like Marty Robbins and Jimmy Dean. But, he said, "the situation for black music in Nashville was bad. The musicians' union really discouraged you from joining."[4] Holmes worked with producers Bill Justis and Bill Beasley making sound-alike budget records for Beasley's budget-priced Spar and Hit labels. Pioneering Nashville R&B musician and producer Ted Jarrett found the artists while Holmes did the arrangements. Jarrett said, "Bob Holmes was the finest arranger I ever knew. He was the musical director for the television show 'Night Train' in 1964 and we became good friends."[5] Bob Holmes recorded and produced for Ted Jarrett's labels in Nashville before and after a short period with Nashboro-Excello. Holmes himself made some pop-soul records on Jarrett's Ref-O-Ree label in 1969 after he left Nashboro-Excello. At Nashboro, Holmes worked on some gospel sessions, Nashboro's bread-and-butter music, and with R&B vocal groups like the Avons, but he was keener to work with Slim Harpo because of his demonstrated crossover capabilities.

Kirk Beasley was at the warehouse of his father's Spar Records on Nashville's Charlotte Avenue one day when Ted Jarrett and Bob Holmes dropped by with Slim Harpo. As Beasley recalled, "The Charlotte Avenue location was just down the street from the New Era Club where a number of major black artists performed back in those days. Ted was always bringing artists around to either meet my dad or show them the business operation. The folks who worked there were big music fans and they appreciated when artists would visit. I think Ted remarked that Slim Harpo had been a truck driver, which played well with the warehouse staff. Like a lot of artists he was fairly humble when not on stage and not in their own milieu. I think I asked if he was 'Mississippi Slim,' a man my dad had recorded years before, which set off a lot of laughter at my expense."[6]

When records from Harpo's Memphis session came out, the labels credited Bob Holmes as producer but, Shannon Williams explained, the session was really produced by Ray Harris: "Bob Holmes was very short-lived with Nashboro. Of course he was Nashboro's first black employee because we felt like we needed that presence. He was in on a few sessions . . . but he wasn't interested in gospel at all. . . . he brought to the label groups such as the Avons and the Hightones, and two or three local Nashville R&B groups. His interest was that kind of group. He was the respectable black front to the company, a very good jazz musician in his own right, good jazz pianist. He was with me at the Slim Harpo Memphis session but honestly neither one of us did a lot of work on that."[7]

For Harpo, too, the switch from Jay Miller's studio to those chosen by Excello was not easy. It was one thing to finally make the break from J. D. Miller's personal contract, but that meant Harpo also had to confront the question about where he wanted his music to go. All along, he had demonstrated the ability to craft a blues song that was out of the ordinary or at least to have the ideas or the titles for songs others could finish, and he always had an idea of the style the backing musicians should play, but to date Miller had controlled the overall sound and product that came from their sessions. Whether Slim had brought in his own musicians or used Miller's men at a session, the music they made had ultimately always been what Miller thought would work. Now, Harpo had the possibility to start with a blank sheet and produce his own sound. But it was also possible that he would have to let Nashboro-Excello appoint session men and producers and just do what they wanted. The evidence during the next three years would show that a little of both scenarios came to pass. Most of the songs Harpo would record in the post-Miller years were his own, although this became less so over time, and there nearly always remained the Harpo trademarks—the harp solo, the harp fade at the end, the insinuating vocal style, maybe a little less "nasal" than ten years before, and the overall "swamp" effect attributable not least to the laid-back, persistent, repeating rhythms. Nevertheless, it was also very noticeable that Excello would record Slim much "cleaner" than Miller had and with different lead guitarists whose solos owed much less to the Louisiana style than to B. B. King or the Chicago styles that were becoming the blues norm. The result in the second phase of Harpo's recording career would be the retention of his individuality but the wrapping of his talent in a succession of styles that reflected the struggle he and other artists and labels had in the 1960s to keep the blues current, changing in his case subtly and sometimes not so subtly from swamp riffs to R&B riffs, to soul riffs and country riffs.

RECORDINGS, APRIL 1967

As far as can be told, Harpo's first post-Crowley recording session for Excello took place in Memphis around April 1967. It only produced four tracks, of which "Tip on In" became a single in Parts 1 and 2, vocal and instrumental. Credited to Robert Lee Holmes and Slim Harpo as writers, "Tip on In" was based on a well-known slang saying that may have earlier inspired the hit jukebox instrumental of 1945, "Tippin' In," by Erskine Hawkins. When in his lyric Slim suggests going into a club down the street, he calls it the Tippin Inn. Rather than a new style for Harpo, it was pretty much in the vein established by the last few Miller sessions, with Slim in conversational vocal mood and the band playing a repeated riff to create what writer Colin Escott has described as "one of the most elegant grooves in all R&B."[8] Part 2 of the disc is basically an instrumental riff with harp solos, but it concludes with an invitation to Slim's girl to come to a fish fry; just "tip on in." Strangely, the songwriting contract for the session, signed by James Moore and Excello's Dorothy Keaton on April 10, 1967, lists the song's title as "Crazy Clothes Blues," which sort of fits. Slim was paid one hundred dollars for the songs at the session and would get 50 percent of the publishing royalties. Shannon Williams again:

> So we'd all go down to Memphis to do this, and it turned out very well, there were no problems at all. Everything went real smooth. Of course, the material was things Harpo had already worked on and his wife actually helped him write most of that stuff. Although her name may not be on these records she wrote a lot of these songs. Harpo loved it. He felt this was such a switch, he was very up on this whole thing. Recalling the record, I think the Hi session men got down with him. Willie Mitchell didn't have much to do with the session, it was mostly directed by this fellow Harris. We were just sort of bystanders, second players, we might have had a suggestion or two but very little. As I recall it, it don't seem like Harris was too much on for Harpo's harmonica but that of course is a trademark, we insisted on it as I recall, "you must play this thing." . . . and I recall the difficulty in mic-ing as to where Harpo could both do his guitar and his harp and sing. He played guitar on all of the [later] records, [but] it was sort of ordinary.[9]

Harpo had been able to play adequate guitar for many years, but he had recently taken to playing some electric lead, and he had also worked some shows as a solo. Lovell said of his later years, "He would never finish an engagement until he had played his guitar."[10] It is likely that Slim plays the dry scratch that keeps time while Teenie Hodges plays lead, and in that case Slim must have overdubbed his harp solo. By this point, of course, Rudy Richard had left Harpo's group, not least because the decision to record increasingly with session men had not been to his liking. Memphis drummer Howard Grimes has recalled playing with Harpo on live shows early in 1967, including the WDIA-promoted live show the Starlite Revue, with a Memphis band led by Ben Branch or Fred Ford.

Released in May 1967 as Excello 2285, "Tip on In" was a *Billboard* "Spotlight Pick" as a future R&B hit. It sold steadily to the scratch-my-back crowd, and an Excello ad in *Billboard* on June 10 claimed, "Tip on In—R&B sound at its best from the hitmakers—over 12,000 sold in Chicago first two weeks." From there, the disc entered the national R&B chart at 41 on July 8 but soon peaked at number 37 at the end of July. On August 12 it was reported bubbling under the Hot 100, but by September no pop hit had materialized.

The three other songs included in the April contract and apparently recorded at the Memphis session were "Hey Little Lee," "I'm Gonna Keep What I've Got," and "I've Got to Be with You Tonight." The latter two were issued as Excello 2289 in October 1967. "I'm Gonna Keep What I've Got" starts with the trademark Harpo swampy harmonica notes before the band gets into another dance groove. The harp appears again bringing in "I've Got to Be with You Tonight" before Slim launches into his lyric about seizing the moment. There are pleasant lead-guitar and harp solos, but overall this single was more about the groove than anything else. It did not resonate with reviewers on release, made only number 124 in *Cash Box,* and disappeared rather more quickly than the folks at Excello must have hoped. "Hey Little Lee" was held over as an album track. It has another funky bass-guitar-and-drums groove, and the poker-faced vocal delivery and upbeat guitar solo belie the subject matter— either Little Lee gets back together with her man or "the hearse gonna give you your last ride." This may have seemed an exciting and exotic notion to the new generation of young rock fans buying Harpo's albums, but it was a very real scenario some years earlier in some black clubs of Baton Rouge.

In the latter part of 1967, Harpo seems to have spent more time at home, playing more local gigs than he had for a couple of years. Sometimes he teamed up with two rising stars of the R&B/soul world who had made Baton Rouge their base, Joe Tex and Bobby Powell. Joe Tex had started out as a Little Richard imitator but then had R&B chart success with "Hold What You've Got" in 1965, followed by another dozen top-10 hits. Bobby Powell was a blind gospel singer who turned to R&B in the 1960s and made a number 12 R&B hit late in 1965 with "C. C. Rider," recorded and issued by Baton Rouge R&B musician and club owner Lionel Whitfield on his Whit label. All three local hit-makers gave up their time on June 22 that year to play a benefit for the Blundon Orphanage, the *Baton Rouge News Leader* reporting Harpo would be there with "Joe Tex, the little man with the big voice, and Bobby Powell, also Buddy Stewart with singer Chuck Mitchell." Tex, really

Joseph Arrington, was from Baytown, Texas, but a favorite in Baton Rouge. For Christmas 1967, the *New York Amsterdam Times* reported: "Recording Star Joe Tex a real Santa in Dixie: Tex personally presented 1172 gifts to local youngsters having contacted local Head Start organization about what he can do for needy youngsters. He bought 1172 pairs of shoes, shirts, assorted goods and gave 2000 youngsters a party at the new YMCA gymnasium. Music for the occasion was furnished by local musicians, Sammy Thornton, William Byrd, Tabby Thomas, Charles Amar and others."[11]

In the new year, it was Harpo taking back the local limelight, working with Sam and Dave and Syl Johnson at the Lakeshore Auditorium on the first Saturday of 1968. The *News Leader* report on January 28 said, "One of the scene stealers was Baton Rouge's own Slim Harpo. The guy is a 'must' in the entertaining business. Did I hear somebody say they wanted to scratch his back? He's got a wife."

RECORDINGS, LATE 1967

It was probably toward the end of the year before Harpo recorded again. Shannon Williams couldn't be sure. He said: "I recorded 'Tip on In' [but the later sessions] I don't recall at all. . . . I was busy by that time with my gospel [sessions] and building the label to an extent that I had no time for that. Of course Bud Howell never went into a studio in his life, unless it was to party, some cocktail party." Probably Robert Holmes was again the nominal producer of Harpo's second post-Miller session. Although it is possible that Harpo and Holmes traveled for a second time to the Royal Studio in Memphis, and although Excello's remodeled Woodland Studio was barely finished, it appears that the session that produced "Te-Ni-Nee-Ni-Nu" and "Mailbox Blues," released as Excello 2294 at the start of 1968, was the first Harpo made in Nashville.

By now, Harpo had lost both Rudy Richard and James Johnson from his touring group and was becoming more and more used to playing with other bands and with session musicians. Guitarist Phil Guy had been around Harpo since his days with Big Papa and Raful Neal as a teenager, and he had joined Harpo's group after Rudy Richard's departure from the Harpo fold around 1966. Richard recalled, "I stopped playing for a couple of years and later I came back. I got into a little conflict. I really stopped, and then I thought, 'Man, what are you doing? It took a long time to learn, so why stop?' So I got right back to it."[12] It seems that Rudy carried on playing some local shows with Harpo but did not figure on tours or recording sessions. There has been some uncertainty about the guitarist on this session, created by Guy himself. In one interview he said, "I recorded with Slim. . . . I did 'Te-Ni-Nee-Ni-Nu' with him. . . . I was going to do the 'Scratch' but I didn't get on that session."[13] However, in another interview some years later he explained that he had recorded "Tee-Ni-Nee-Ni-Nu" on his own account years after he briefly worked with Harpo, and said, "I never did record with Slim Harpo, but I played on a show with him. I never did go on the road with him."[14] It seems, instead, that one guitarist on the session was a teenage player from Montgomery, Alabama, making one of his first sessions, Sheffield Walker.

Walker's recollections were that he had arrived in Nashville to go to college in 1966 and switched from trumpet to guitar after becoming inspired, diversely, by the playing of B. B. King and Chet Atkins, and he started playing with local R&B groups on weekends. He said he was playing in the Jimmy Church band all over Tennessee, and with a group led by bass player Billy Cox, with whom he started doing studio work: "And they told us to go to the Excello Records one day. . . . Billy Cox was the one who got all that together. . . . and Slim Harpo came up and I played on that album with him. I never had met Slim Harpo before that. I was seventeen or eighteen years old and had never paid too much attention to the people there, except Slim Harpo, and he was just an old man to me at the time, just playing the blues. I feel so bad for that now but that is how youngsters were." Walker felt that his first Harpo session took place over two days. "We had two guitars, a drummer, and a bass player. . . . The other guitar player was a guy named Frank Smith and he was going to school at Fisk University, and the drummer, all I knew him by was Dino and he had played with so many other guys. We all got together and did this stuff. Slim Harpo would say and hum what he wanted, and we would play it. . . . We had no preparation for it, we just went in the studio and made it up as we went, and if you have good musicians you can do that."[15]

They did have good musicians, of course, despite the earlier hesitancy of Shannon Williams to use black musicians in Nashville. The city had known a vibrant blues and R&B scene since the 1930s, and places like the New Era Club were regular venues for residencies by the likes of Fats Domino, Little Richard, Etta James, and now, Slim Harpo. Local black musician and entrepreneur Ted Jarrett had been arranging and producing for Excello and other labels for fifteen years, encouraging singers like Larry Birdsong and Gene Allison and bands like the Imperials and the King Casuals that featured, at times, guitarists Jimi Hendrix and Johnny Jones and bass player Billy Cox. Both Cox and Hendrix had backed Slim Harpo on one-off shows and small tours in recent years.[16]

"Te-Ni-Nee-Ni-Nu" was at once Slim's latest dance groove and a further statement of the swampy sound of Louisiana, evoking the feeling that conjurers were around and it was a steamy night in New Orleans. Tabby Thomas once said, "Me and Slim wrote that," and that Excello cut him out of the songwriting credits, but Lovell Moore said the song was written in part by her. She recalled: "I never expected to be writing songs. It was comical. I'd write something and he'd sing a line. That 'Te-Ni-Nee,' that sounded like nothing when I wrote it down. I don't even know what it means really. But it worked."[17] It's just possible that it had something to do with Teenie Hodges's name, or that Harpo remembered the title of a top-40 instrumental from 1958 by Dickey Doo and the Don'ts, "Nee Nee Na Na Na Na Nu Nu." Rudy Richard attested to Harpo's songwriting abilities, saying, "He could start writing a song and if he'd get to where he couldn't write any more words, he'd say, 'Rudolph, I'm going to take me a nap.' And when he woke up he had the rest of the words. It's true, man."[18]

"Mailbox Blues" was Slim's version of the age-old lyric about the longed-for letter that doesn't arrive among the bills. As is usual in the blues, and indeed country and popular music, the missing letter is from his woman and it brings bad news. The title line may have started out with Sleepy John Estes's 1940 recording of "Mailman Blues," but for the most part the lyrics are new, and part-credited to a young black disc jockey, Reginald Stuart, on WSIX. Born in Nashville, Stuart later worked as a journalist on Nashville newspapers and TV stations before joining the *New York Times* as a business reporter. The tune and the rhythm are taken from the then-recent blues hit of Albert King, "Crosscut Saw," a song Sheffield Walker said had inspired him to make the guitar his main instrument. Albert King had copied it from a disc by the Binghampton Blues Boys from Memphis, who first revived the song from an original recorded by Tommy McClennan in 1941. The lyrics are just as memorable in the hands of Slim's band. An unissued song, probably from this session, was "Stick Your Chest Out Baby," an unusual lyric about a woman who seems to have been put down by another woman. Singing hoarsely to a soul beat, Slim describes how she's fine-looking but can look even better, responding to a list of body features counted off by another voice, perhaps a member of the band. Rejected at the time, it was issued on an album the year after Slim's death.

When Excello 2294 appeared in February 1968, the label took a large ad in *Billboard* trumpeting a change of direction—"Excello turns on the soul sound"—and pushing "Te-Ni-Nee-Ni-Nu" as a hit. The song's title, they explained in *Billboard* on February 24, "in record talk—means a smash hit." The record entered the R&B chart at 48 at the end of March and stayed for several weeks, peaking at number 36 on April 27 when Excello again took a big ad: "Excello soul is Sound-Sational." This *Billboard* ad featured photos of Slim along with the Kelly brothers, Roger Hatcher, and Kip Anderson. The label's new ownership was making a big effort to raise Excello's profile and diversify its product. They even issued a "live" LP of speeches by Martin Luther King, *Remaining Awake (through a great revolution)*, which gained good reviews as "Excello's tribute to his memory." Locally in Baton Rouge, the *News Leader* of March 24 carried a photo of Harpo and a caption exhorting folks to listen to "Te-Ni-Nee-Ni-Nu" on WXOK. A month later, the paper reported proudly that "Slim Harpo, currently on a cross country tour, has two albums in the best seller category in national polls."[19]

As memorable as "Te-Ni-Nee-Ni-Nu" was, later that year Harpo confessed to an interviewer, "The company was expecting a lot of that record, and also 'Tip on In' before it. They didn't do exactly what was expected. But anyway, we are still trying."[20]

RECORDINGS, SUMMER 1968

By the summer of 1968, Excello's new studio was in full swing and Bob Holmes produced a Harpo session there that yielded at least three tracks to be included in a new LP later in the year. The musicians' union files have not survived from that period, but it is likely the recordings again involved a Billy Cox group along the lines Sheffield Walker has described. "My Baby She's Got It" was about a "soul sister who don't ever wanta stop," another variation on the earlier Harpo song "You Got What I Need." Next up, "I'm So Sorry" was in the B. B. King mood, complete with expansive guitar solos, a song about how a man was doing all right until he fell in love. "I've Been a Good Thing for You" was another brooding ballad, about how Slim's given his woman everything, until now, when she appears not to be the "innocent saint" people thought. There's a smoothly evocative guitar solo and Slim's signature harp fade-out. For some reason, none of these tracks was considered for release as a single.

Hot on the heels of that summer session came another, in a new location. As Excello cast around for the ideal combination of studio and musicians to work with the rejuvenated Slim Harpo, the decision was made to try their luck at Rick Hall's increasingly successful Fame Recording Studios in Muscle Shoals, Alabama. A session in late summer was produced by saxophonist Aaron Varnell, who had joined Rick Hall at the Fame Studio in the early 1960s and recorded on sessions by Clarence Carter, Bowlegs Miller, and others for the Fame label and for its big client, Atlantic Records. Varnell was on singles by the Fame Gang, the label's session men. He had strong Nashville connections, though. He had recently been in the Nashville group the King Casuals, originally formed by bass player Billy Cox and guitarist Jimi Hendrix in 1962 but now fronted by guitarist Johnny Jones. Varnell also produced records on the Sound Stage 7 label, the subsidiary of Monument, for owners Fred Foster and John Richbourg. William Gambler remembers Slim traveling to Muscle Shoals to make these recordings, but apart from Varnell and Billy Cox, the only identified musicians on Harpo's session are Jimmy Johnson on guitar and Roger Hawkins on drums, with unknown bass, keyboards, and horn players.

The Fame session produced Harpo's next single. The song planned as the A side was "Mohair Sam," written by hot Nashville songwriter Dallas Frazier. It had been a number 21 hit on pop's Hot 100 for Charlie Rich at the end of 1965, but someone saw that in Slim's hands the song could have a new lease on life. Slim had been taken on by an influential New York managerial agent, Dick Alen, based at 200 West Fifty-Seventh Street, on the strength of his tour with James Brown in 1966. Formerly a promoter of major R&B singers with Shaw Artists and Universal Attractions, Alen had also been road manager for jazz players such as Woody Herman, and he had been involved in sending artists to Europe as well as bringing the Rolling Stones to the United States. He had Chuck Berry and Aretha Franklin on his books and had recently taken on Charlie Rich on the strength of "Mohair Sam" and booked him into New York's premier black venue, the Apollo. Rich was as laid-back as Slim and, coming from different directions, each man was capable of as perfect a marriage of blues and blue-eyed country soul as the other. Slim sang the song about the fast-talking, slow-walking, good-looking man in an engaging manner over an impressive rhythm set up by the Fame musicians and horn arrangements that enhanced the song well. The flip side of the record was "I Just Can't Leave You," a well-recorded if standard blues with spotless guitar solos. Excello 2301 was released in the fall and first picked for success in September by a disc jockey in South Carolina before becoming a predicted top-20 disc in the review spotlight section of *Billboard* on October 12, 1968. After five weeks just outside the *Cash Box* top 100, though, "Mohair Sam" peaked in mid-October at number 113.

The October 12 edition of *Billboard* contained a reflection piece on the seventeen-year history of Nashboro-Excello, during most of which it had been run conservatively by Ernie Young with just a handful of employees and a strong focus on mail-order sales. Now, two years on, Shannon Williams and Bud Howell saw the possibility of greater development. They told *Billboard* their Woodland base and new studio were "designed with the purpose of capturing the Nashville Sound and also providing a home base for the spiritual and R&B field in the city." Also, the company "leans to independent producers and has had excellent results." *Billboard* concluded, rather obviously: "Success is measured in many ways but one of the most accurate of the yardsticks is financial gain. In the first 6 months of this last fiscal year, Nashboro realized an increase of 100% in dollar sales."

Meantime, Slim Harpo was maintaining his road work and contemplating the best way to effect his own increase in dollar sales. He remained essentially a bluesman, but both locally and nationally he found himself working with bands who played a funkier style of R&B or soul. His nephew, Ray Moore, confirmed that Slim and the blues were not always the head of the bill. "I recall him opening up the show for Al Green in Baton Rouge when 'Backup Train' came out."[21] Both Harpo and Excello were under some degree of pressure to find a way to maintain his sales in a changing market. To the *News Leader,* he was now a part of the new scene. In September he was at the reopening of Jacksons Private Club at 1320 North Acadian Highway, Baton Rouge, along with Boe Melvin, Johnny Adams, Buddy Stewart's Top Notchers, and Chuck Mitchell. On October 9, he was "the popular rhythm and blues artist" who would headline the big benefit show at Independence Hall for Blundon Orphanage. At the end of that month, the *Leader*'s "On the Avenue" page, which worked hard to promote the black music scene in town, pointed out that the club scene included not only Harpo but Katie Webster—"Queen of the Blues"—and her Uptight Combo along with James

Carr, "Top recording star" from Memphis, at the Golden Slipper, formerly the Blue Bull, at 2500 North Boulevard. All this was in the context of renewed interest in black music locally. There was a major ad for James Brown's hit "Say It Loud I'm Black and I'm Proud," selling at forty-nine cents at the Fifth Ave Shoppes at both Third Avenue and 8842 Scotland Avenue.[22] In the new year, Harpo was reported "on hand to do his bit" at a late-January benefit show for Roy Stewart, longtime drummer with Buddy Stewart's Top Notchers, who had injured his legs in an auto accident. Harpo was there along with Johnny Adams, Ernie K-Doe, Bobby Powell, Irma Thomas, Tabby Thomas, Raful Neal, Chuck Mitchell, and "Baton Rouge's former queen of soul, Gerri Jackson."

SCENE IN THE ROCK SOCIETY

Based on the success of "Tip on In" and "Te-Ni-Nee-Ni-Nu," Excello issued their third Harpo album in the late summer of 1968. Also titled *Tip on In*, Excello LP 8008 contained the title track and Slim's latest two singles along with several sides recorded earlier that year by Bob Holmes at Excello's Woodland studios. One of Holmes's roles was to help take the Nashboro-Excello company forward with the times, and he said in his LP sleeve notes that Harpo, who plays the "wildest harmonica in the business," and whose music has been acknowledged by the Rolling Stones and modern rock musicians, was now "a legend in his own time. . . . Slim Harpo is a member of that 'rock society' who has maintained an earthy sound but kept up with that ever-changing beat." As if to illustrate his point, the LP was chosen as a Massachusetts disc jockey's programming pick on December 21, 1968—in the "Progressive Rock" section of *Billboard*. This change in style did not sit well with everyone. *Blues Unlimited* had been the first specialist magazine to support Harpo, but now their reviewer lamented the loss of the Miller sound. "The new Harpo sings straight and relies on jerky rhythms. Does he now play lead? Whoever it is is so much like B. B. King or Albert King it irritates. I like 'Tip on In' but on this album the same formula is applied until it palls."[23]

However, by now, Harpo was starting to gain some prestigious gigs on the East and West Coasts as well as the regional bookings he and his wife continued to make, as Lovell confirmed: "Sometimes they would come to us, and we had an agent in New York and he would book jobs for us, other jobs we would go out and find them. We would buy posters, have them printed and put them in various places and when they would get ready for him to play they would call us. Almost every day of the week when he had the hit records, and even when he didn't have an engagement, he would pick up his guitar and play."[24]

Dick Alen Management marketed Slim as being both authentic and of the moment. Its promo sheets were full of phrases like "one of the most exciting blues artists around, Slim is a master of the harmonica," and [Slim says] "to play the blues, you have to live a hard life; any good songwriter writes from his personal experience." This tone was picked up by northern reviewers in November and December 1968 when Alen booked Harpo into entrepreneur Steve Paul's club, the Scene, 301 West Forty-Sixth Street, whose ads for the shows got across a clear message: "Uninhibited dancing and listening encouraged."

The ad for the Scene on December 6 proclaimed: "The Blues-Rock Event of the Year! American Underground Debut of Slim Harpo." In small print were added the words "with Lightning Slim." In fact, Harpo had made his debut at the Scene in November. Writing in the New York Times, Mike Jahn reviewed the show where Slim was backed just by Lightnin' Slim and drummer Jesse Kinchen, saying: "He is not a showman like B. B. King and he is nowhere near as flashy as Albert King. His band is smaller than most blues groups. . . . Slim Harpo does nothing to attract a rock audience. All he does is play the blues—authentic, country blues—and invite people to come hear it, if they want to. The band deals in authenticity—not fireworks."[25]

Blues fan and budding writer Peter Guralnick also witnessed a show at the Scene, remembering that Harpo's records were getting a lot of radio play in Boston at the time. Guralnick went along with Harpo's earlier records in his mind, too, "but seeing Harpo on stage was an education. There was much more breadth of talent there than I had expected. I was impressed by his versatility and it was a memorable set that stayed with me. Harpo and Lightnin' were on stage together all the time but Harpo served as Lightnin's musical director as well as his own. Lightnin' had his guitar but Slim played all the guitar for both of them. Harpo's was a wonderful set, far more interesting and diverse than Lightnin' Slim's who stuck unwaveringly to the familiar sound of his records. Harpo seemed very much at ease on stage. You felt that he was creating something that was taking place that night, on that stage, and it really drew in the audience." Guralnick had two other surprises as well. "Slim sang in his natural voice. It was pretty notable, though I guess not entirely unexpected."

Also, "As I recall, Slim didn't play any harp at all." Finally, when Harpo was finished and a very noisy Canadian blues band came on stage, "I went to the men's room, and there were Slim Harpo and Lightnin' Slim, also trying to escape, and we talked a little bit. It was a big thrill for me to get to talk to them both for a while, though once again it was Harpo who took the lead."[26]

While he was at the Scene, Slim Harpo gave an interview to rock photographer and writer Sue Cassidy Clark, who preserved his words on tape. Speaking in a warm, conversational, but precise voice, with an infectious little laugh at key moments, Slim exhibited the clarity of diction of the practiced bandleader who wanted to get on in the world. He also had vestiges of an apparently natural tendency to speak with a blocked nose, bringing into question how far his singing voice was ever really changed back in 1957. Harpo made it clear that "this is the first time I've played blues, I mean *all* blues, to a white group of people. I was surprised they really accepted me. See, [normally] we was kinda versatile. We'd play some blues, some rock 'n' roll, some different types of music. If you played colleges you had to be versatile, you know. Especially at the college gigs the kids like rock 'n' roll stuff. But this time at The Scene they asked me to play just blues, so I got Lightnin' Slim too because I figured that would be the best. We all are from Louisiana—we wanted to get that down-home sound. I just do it commonly."[27]

Harpo also went some way to explaining the diverse reviews and testimonies from those who witnessed his shows in New York, saying, "At the Scene I'm doing two shows a night, with Lightnin' Slim. We wanted to be sure that we got all our music heard, you know, so we agreed that one show I'd sing more and the next show the other man would sing more, and sometimes I'd play harmonica and other times guitar, and we'd do it like that."[28] Although Harpo had long since eclipsed what little fame Lightnin' Slim had outside his local area, he always seems to have recognized a debt to his friend and to have been unselfish in his actions around Otis Hicks.

Though Lightnin's music and his persona were more rudimentary than Harpo's, as Peter Guralnick noted, he did speak a little to the blues fans who caught his unheralded shows in New York:

The blues has been a real good thing ever since I got into it. All the places I've ever been, they still love the blues. I still play the same way as when I started. And I love the blues. I'll never leave it. I've been out of the business for close to six years and I just got back a couple of months ago. My old friend Slim Harpo called me up and asked me if I'd like to be in his band. He talked me into coming back. [We] teamed up years ago in Baton Rouge. We'd just play for friends at a birthday party or wedding or something like that. We never really made any money at it. We had a lot of fun. Slim and I worked in the fields a lot down there but I always had to have another job besides my music. I'm really happy working with Slim Harpo now and I'm gonna stay with it as long as it lasts. The more we play, the better we get and there's just three of us. When we get all our songs together, we're gonna be hard to beat.[29]

Despite the gregarious reality of Harpo's nature witnessed by Guralnick, in his few interviews in New York, Harpo reinforced the image of the novice backwoodsman emerging blinking into the bright lights of a new world. He spoke to veteran reporter Bob Austin of *Record World* (and formerly of *Cash Box*) in December, when he was reported to be in his third of four weeks at the Scene, having originally been booked just for one week: "My first night I felt kinda shaky. I didn't have any idea how my kind of music would take in New York. I always thought this was mostly a jazz town. But after my first set, I almost felt like I was home. . . . By the time we're ready to leave this town, a lot of people are gonna know we've been here."[30] Slim had been to New York before, of course, but the difference now was that he was playing for white audiences rather than as part of a show with James Brown. Fred Kirby reported in *Billboard* on December 7 that Harpo had "scored impressively" at the Scene with a strong assist from Lightnin' Slim. In the show he saw, in contrast to the one Guralnick witnessed, Harpo had backed Slim on harmonica before switching to guitar for his own set of "down home blues" such as Toussaint McCall's "Nothing Takes the Place of You" and "rhythm numbers" such as "Te-Ni-Nee-Ni-Nu." Slim came to the conclusion, he told Austin, "judging from the applause, I notice that I get a bigger reaction for a slow blues number than I get for a fast song." Harpo also talked to Austin about his pleasure when rock artists recorded his songs; apart from the royalties, he thought, "that must mean they're pretty good. I write most of my songs with my wife Lovell. If I get a melody, she'll come up with the words."[31] Lovell Moore recalled the touring days: "We wrote songs while we were traveling—songs like 'Te Ni Nee Nu,' 'Mailbox Blues,' 'Scratch My Back.' We also did 'I'm a Bread Maker,' all that stuff, we did just about all of them while we were traveling."[32]

One of Slim's shows at the Scene was caught by folklorist Pete Lowry, who sent his review to *Blues Unlimited*:

Louisiana in New York: In a rather surprise move Steve Paul, owner of The Scene, now closed by New York Liquor Authority, booked Slim Harpo into his club. The surprise was that it was not as a single using pick up backing, but with Lightnin' Slim and drummer Little Jesse Kinchen—nothing else! . . . The evening turned out to be all I'd hoped it to be, with Lightnin' doing nearly half of each set. . . . here was the best of him: tough, straight-forward guitar, and Harpo very much into things on just harp. . . . and then Slim Harpo strapped on his guitar and came to the mike. "Shake Your Hips" and "Rainin' in My Heart" preceded a Jimmy Reed medley. . . . Second set . . . Harpo came on much better with "Who's Gonna Be Your Sweet Man," "Hi Heel Sneakers," "Tell Me Baby," "King Bee"—expected and requested—ending with "Big Boss Man." . . . This was an interesting group—hard to believe there were only three men playing—that projected an incredible sound together. . . . Harpo is vastly underrated both as a singer and harmonica player . . . a very fine harp man, adequate on guitar, and quite good playing both at once. He tends to concentrate on harp then, letting the guitar play a time-keeping role. It is probably his using a rack that has got him labelled as another Reed copy. . . . from hearing him elsewhere with Jimmy Cotton, he puts Cotton to shame, that should give readers a frame of reference.[33]

James Cotton was one of the premier harp players from Memphis, relocated to Chicago, and a veteran of Sun Records as well as the Howlin' Wolf and Muddy Waters bands.

At the end of Harpo's time at the Scene, club owner Steve Paul wrote to Dick Alen, Slim's agent, in a letter dated Christmas Day, 1968, saying: "It is not often that The Scene's desire to present good music by the best players is so happily completed. Slim Harpo is a happy exception. As you know, while we present many different types of music, blues seems to be our favorite. In the case of Slim Harpo the underground, the establishment press and the public have shared our opinion. It is because of this that Slim Harpo is now playing his fourth engagement at The Scene in a two-month period. We could think of no better person than Slim to have brought back for our special year-end blues show."

Harpo's drummer for the Scene engagement was Jesse Kinchen from Denham Springs, near Baton Rouge. The New York gigs were his first with Harpo, although he says he had played on recording sessions going back to "Bread Maker." He explained:

I started playing with my uncle "Guitar Kelley," who had played with Slim Harpo too before me. We called him "Butter," that was his name, and I played with my uncle, and with Silas Hogan for a while. Then I met Harpo through being at the barbershop. If a man wants to find out what's going on he goes to the barbershop, where all the talking's going on. I went to the barbershop with my cousin Simmie, and Slim Harpo was there, and my cousins knew Harpo, had played with him. Slim, he never was a guy who'd talk too much—he was a guy who had his own style—but I guess my relatives was down there telling Slim about me, saying, "We got a cousin who can play some drums, you know." I'd won a talent contest and all. And so another day I was with a girl on Louisiana Avenue and there's a knock at the door—it's Slim Harpo, in his blue and white Cadillac, looking for a drummer to go to play at the Apollo and the Scene and the [Nassau] Coliseum in Long Island. I said, "I'll go." We rehearsed at Slim's sister's house after me and Slim and his wife drove up to Pontiac in a Cadillac. I was about seventeen, going on eighteen. My parents were worried—how's he going to eat, and all—but Slim said "I'll pay him and treat him fair." When I came back I had mohair suits and patent shoes and everything.[34]

Lightnin' Slim had relocated to Pontiac, Michigan, from Louisiana in the mid-1960s, following a wreck in Jay Miller's favorite Volkswagen bus. Later, in 1971, Lazy Lester visited Pontiac, and in 1975 he too moved up there with Slim's sister. He said, "Slim's sister, Matilda, she married this guy Willie Murray, he was from Montgomery, Alabama, and they moved up to Pontiac, Michigan. At one time Lightnin' Slim moved up there, and he lived in Slim's sister's house. So in 1971 I went to visit Lightnin' there and decided I would move up there too. Murray, he'd came back south. She had a huge house up there. I had my own living quarters in the house."[35] Lester and Jay Miller had called it quits around 1966, although Lester had already moved for a time to Monroe in northern Louisiana where, he said, he worked as a lumberjack and then a driver and furniture mover. Around 1969, he moved to Chicago for a very brief stint, where he continued similar work for Capitol Furniture Company, making only occasional musical gigs with Buddy Guy or Junior Wells before returning home. He moved his base to Pontiac, he said, in July 1975 because "Miss Tillie asked me up. She wanted someone from back home to be close at hand . . . since her husband . . . had passed away." In Pontiac he worked at an auto parts plant and was largely retired from music, though he played occasionally with Eddie Burns, Chicago Pete, or Bobo Jenkins, venturing into Ontario, Canada, as well. Eventually, he restarted his career and moved to Paradise near Sacramento, California, with a new partner, a Finnish fan named Pike Kakonsen.

On the strength of Slim Harpo's New York shows, followed by well-received appearances in Boston, Excello issued another LP, *The Best of Slim Harpo*, Excello 8010, in January 1969, mixing Crowley recordings with newer ones. The LP sleeve carried notes by a New York disc jockey, Jack Walker of WLIB, underlining the impact Slim had made with his shows in the Northeast. Walker's notes concluded that, although the LP came to the market in "revolutionary times," the blues was to be loved as a constant, and Slim Harpo *was* the blues. Excello took a large ad in *Billboard* on February 15, pointing out that Slim's album was "True Authenticity in Delta Blues" and "Pure Blues at its very best." The album cover showed two people in close-up—Slim, playing the guitar, and an admiring female looking on. Fittingly, perhaps, the lady was Lovell Moore and not a model. At the same time, Excello reissued Slim's first LP—saying it was "still pounding out sales"—now with a new pop-art cover design aimed at the psychedelic-rock crowd.

Following the trend for "rediscovered" blues artists to play folk-music festivals a few years earlier, by the mid-1960s a number of major blues artists had appeared on the same bills as rock groups, not least Lightnin' Hopkins, John Lee Hooker, B. B. King, and the two giants of Chess Records in Chicago, Howlin' Wolf and Muddy Waters. All started to be approached about recording with white musicians in the hope of widening their sales, and Chess, in particular, put effort into albums like *Electric Mud* in 1968 only to have Muddy make less than complimentary comments about the wah-wah sounds. Wolf was equally scathing in later years. Muddy Waters did acknowledge the effect of foreign interest in his blues, telling a New York college audience, "I had to come to you behind the Rolling Stones and the Beatles. I had to go to England to get here!" B. B. King agreed, telling another New York crowd he had been coming to their city for twenty years, "and no-one in the press heard of me, but things are looking up now." Slim Harpo, who was in the midst of some significant changes in his recorded sound, remained largely silent on the subject apart from one interview at the end of 1968, when he was asked about the success of B. B. King and Albert King on the northern and college circuits. He replied, self-deprecatingly, "Oh yeah, but those guys are really good," indicating that he still saw himself as a backwoodsman. "I think my style was a little bit different. I'm a country boy and I've had a life in poverty. Life wasn't all peaches and cream with me, you know. . . . and I like to think my music is singing about some things I've actually lived."[36]

He seemed to feel that the more popular blues players like B. B. King had changed their styles over the years. "They came from the country like me. I think B. B. [re]developed his style afterwards. These guys *had* that down-home feeling, but they changed it. But I wouldn't ever do that. I won't ever change the way I play. In my style of blues, I would [always] do it commonly." When asked about playing for northern audiences and even potentially for people abroad, he said, "I always thought the blues was just for people out in the country, you know. In big cities, people have so much else to listen to. So, I was surprised at how well our music was accepted. I'm hoping I will go to England and Europe and those places. I think it will be educational for me."[37]

With his increasing exposure to rock venues on the coasts, and to music journalists, Slim found himself for the first time being asked to explain his harmonica style and to deal with naïve questions about whether he was influenced by players the writers had heard of, the likes of Sonny Terry or Walter Horton, and why he had been seen using a handkerchief to muffle his harp sound. He explained, patiently, to Sue Cassidy Clark in 1968: "I've been playing a little bit better than twenty years now. I can play in E, A, or B natural and I get different sounds. I use a handkerchief to half-cover the harp and it gives the effect of a horn, you know. And I can get other sound effects. It depends on how you hold it, you know. Or I can use a rack to get a regular sound. I never did try to play 'like' anyone else—but if I play a song 'by' someone else then I try to play it as near as I possibly can, on their song, whether it's Elmore James or James Brown. But I have my own style. I just try to be Slim Harpo."[38]

RECORDINGS, EARLY 1969

On his return from New York and Boston, Harpo and Excello realized that "Mohair Sam" was not going to become the size of hit to match all their ex-pectations and requirements. Soon there was a recording session at Woodland in Nashville resulting in another single, Excello 2305, which coupled "That's Why I Love You"—where Slim recounts how his baby's been good to him, for once, and provides his trademark harp solos—with the contrastingly soft, soulful, swampy ballad "Just for You." Despite his interviews about never changing his style, this took Slim well away from the blues form—a song about the love light burning in his heart and his eyes full of tears as he thinks "we've been together so many years." It could have been a significant stylistic development in Slim's career, had it sold, though he probably saw it as a continuation from the balladry of swamp-pop and in his mind was still within the spectrum of what he called the blues played "commonly." However, when the single was released in the spring of 1969, it received surprisingly little attention or sales.

It is probable that Slim also recorded other songs at this session, notably "Mutual Friend," a sparse blues reflecting on the good times with a woman who has now left. It has an extended contemporary guitar solo by a player who has not been identified. Lovell Moore remembered going to the Nashville sessions and how the songs she and Slim had written were translated onto tape: "I would write a song, he would get out his guitar and play it. Then he would go in the studio and play it just with harmonica and guitar, to let the session musicians hear how he wanted it to be played, you know. And the studio musicians would play—they caught on right away. It really wasn't hard to record like that."[39]

"THE HARP"

As the year 1969 unfolded, it proved to be one of Harpo's busiest, giving him ever-wider-ranging experiences on both the East and West Coasts as well as in the recording studio. It wasn't long before Slim was back in front of the New York crowds, playing gigs at the Fillmore East and Electric Circus rock venues as well as smaller university gigs, including Hunter College that February. Slim's New York agent went into overdrive, the booking information from Universal Attractions playing to a market very different from Slim's down-home blues following: "Blues is happening in today's complex society. . . . 'The Harp' likes to entertain people, and feels that being in the profession is an education in itself. Slim enjoys playing on stage and grooving for all types of cats. . . . Slim the person is a beautiful cat who blows his mind over trucks and trailers. To experience the beautiful cat's life expressed in blues form catch 'The Harp' when he does his thing on the underground circuit."[40]

On February 28, Harpo played two nights at New York's Fillmore East with British bands Ten Years After and John Mayall's Bluesbreakers. For *Billboard,* Fred Kirby reported that these bands followed "Slim Harpo, a top notch Louisiana bluesman who, appearing with a new backup group, The Weight, reached into his bag of top Excello numbers to come up with the rocking 'Te-Ni-Nee-Ni-Nu' and the country blues 'Rainin' in My Heart.' Also his hits 'King Bee' and 'Baby Scratch My Back.'"[41] The band described as the

SLIM HARPO

Weight remains mysterious but perhaps included a keyboard man because Slim's publicity of the time, in an attempt to modernize his image, said that he liked to play "with two guitarists and an organist." The group known as "The Band" who backed Bob Dylan had just that lineup and had recently released a song called "The Weight." While it is unlikely that writer Kirby confused the song with the group, stranger things have happened. Those were "heavy" times. In any case, one fan was not impressed by the coupling, recalling: "I saw him live at the Fillmore East, third on the bill under John Mayall's Bluesbreakers and Ten Years After. I sensed that Slim was struggling under the weight of the stiff, heavy-handed white rock band recruited to back him for this engagement—but he was still Slim Harpo, after all."[42]

Although the apparent attempts to create a new nickname for Slim, "the Harp," did not stick, Harpo spent June 12 to 17 playing again at the reopened "happening" New York club, the Scene, where once again "uninhibited" drinking, dancing, and listening were advertised as the order of the day. On his first night, Harpo supported Alice Cooper, but for the rest of the week he was the headliner. Universal Attractions was at pains to point out that "the Harp" had appeared with greats like James Brown, Joe Tex, Wilson Pickett, Solomon Burke, Stevie Wonder, and Percy Sledge and that now "his entry into the underground sector of musical entertainment is a new facet in a long and hard career." Even so, while he was at his highest profile, Slim was still peddling the line of his agent, telling Jim Delehant for a June 1969 feature in *Hit Parader*, "I'm just a country boy, but I like to see the rest of the world."

It was probably during his early 1969 stay in New York that Harpo somehow became involved in a demo recording session at the Brill Building, the home of northern pop songwriting, demo studios, and assorted publishing and record companies. A young white guitarist and songwriter, Tony Forte, from Newark, New Jersey, had studied blues guitar and written a song about a train journey that he titled, for some reason, "Big Black Car." Five years later he formed a band with Steve Simmels and others called the Hounds and recorded a folky, bluesy, rocky version of his song. But, incredibly, as he explained it:

> I was working with a producer [Jimmy Levine], making demos at the Brill Building in New York. I was like just out of school, kicking around, running from building to building, you know. The first thing I really did, professionally, was work with Slim Harpo. He was there when I was and this great blues singer Slim Harpo

wound up recording my song. Slim recorded that song in the same studio after learning it from me. He copied my phrasing almost note for note, it was crazy. My friend said, "If I did nothing else but have a song recorded by Slim Harpo, I would be like totally happy," and, yeah. Listen to that guy's harp, it's so powerful. Slim was great, what a great guy, oh man, huge hands, big man. The back up guys were the then pit band from the Broadway production of *Hair*.[43]

Harpo's scratchy demo, in which he is supported by guitar, bass, drums, and, unusually for him, piano, has appeared on the Internet for some years but has not been commercially available.

From his early 1969 gigs in New York, Slim flew to California, where he played the Whisky a Go Go in Hollywood from March 5 to 9. From March 27 to 29, he was playing a Sunset Boulevard club, Thee Experience, with Alice Cooper. Lovell Moore remembered those trips: "We both drove to shows and engagements. I would do most of the driving at night while he slept and he would take the wheel during the day. The band played with us as far as New York and California. . . . the band drove the cars with the equipment, but to them places like New York, we flew."[44]

While Slim flew from New York to the West Coast that March, Jesse Kinchen remembered driving out to California for the March gigs with his guitarist cousin Simmie Kinchen and Otis Johnson, formerly Slim's trumpet player, who now came in on bass and guitar. "Slim took the plane because they wanted him some place first, before the Whiskey a Go Go gigs. Slim gave us an envelope each with $50 for the journey. Otis drove for 24 hours, to Tucson in Arizona—and by then we had no money and needed two new tires at $40 a tire. So Otis called Slim and they wired some money. We played one gig in Tucson, just to make money to get out of there."[45] Otis Johnson also has clear memories of that trip but disagreed about the funding:

When Slim had gigs in California in 1969 he asked me to go along to play bass. The band was me, Simmie Kinchen on guitar and Jesse Kinchen on drums. Slim gave us $10 each and a Mobil credit card for gas and we drove Slim's car out there pulling his trailer with all the instruments. We left early Saturday and didn't arrive until late Monday. It was some journey. When we got there we played gigs at the Whisky a Go Go and other places and Slim paid us $35 a night. After a while out there, it got to where there was nothing to do all day and I came back home on the bus. The others stayed, and a guy from Baton Rouge, Lloyd Palmer, who was already out there, joined them on bass. He played guitar and bass and later used the name King Lloyd.[46]

Simmie Kinchen was the leader of a band working around Baton Rouge as Simmie and the Uptighters, both on their own account and as a backing group for incoming artists such as Katie Webster. They apparently shared some gigs with Boe Melvin's Nighthawks and possibly traded membership, too. An ad in the *News Leader* captured them on June 30, 1968: "At the Golden Slipper on North Boulevard, Simmie and his Uptighters Weds, Nighthawks Thurs, the Bar Kay band Saturday evening." There was a hit group in Memphis called the Bar Kays, but this Bar Kay band played Baton Rouge's New Colonial Inn every Thursday so they may have been a different, local group. Perhaps this is why James Johnson remembered that Slim Harpo "recorded with the Bar Kay band" rather than the Mar-Keys after he left the King Bees.

Harpo's California shows were at the fringe of the rock music world, either opening for big-name white bands or headlining above up-and-coming white acts. *Los Angeles Times* writer Pete Johnson caught him at the Whisky a Go Go on March 7, 1969, heading a show with hard-rock quintet the Illinois Speed Press. He noted that Harpo "is not a major contemporary blues figure—not on a par with Muddy Waters, Howlin' Wolf, Jimmy Reed or B. B. King—but represents a distinctive blues sound." Johnson erroneously thought that sound emanated from Nashville, but he described the show well enough: "A trio—guitar, bass, and drums backs Slim Harpo [who] like many blues singers takes a while to warm up, but once he gets going the results are effective." Starting with an instrumental jam and some standard blues vocals, Johnson found, "as the evening wore on Harpo's voice developed a graininess which supplied the emotional depth missing earlier. His singing is not as rough and powerful as many other blues artists but he has a distinctive high nasal style. The best numbers of his opening night set consisted of a revamped 'Long Distance Blues' and Lightnin' Slim's 'Rooster Blues.'" This set seems to owe as much if not more to the abilities and preferences of the backing band as to Slim himself, though the reviewer had already mentioned Harpo's hit songs and may have felt it unnecessary to describe them.

On Slim's return to Baton Rouge from California, the *News Leader* described how "Slim Harpo of 'Scratch My Back' fame breezed into town last week for a short visit between road engagements that are taking him from coast to coast. Slim and his group had just finished a tour of the Eastern seaboard where he drew wide acclaim as one of the true blues artists in the country today. Earlier this month, Slim and his band, who now include the swinging sound of Simmie and the Uptighters, carried their Southern brand of soul music into the niteries of sunny California and left a terrific impact on the west coast."[47] The Uptighters went back on the local club circuit, backing Katie Webster at the Five Crown Social Club. Concerning this later incarnation of the Harpo King Bees, William Gambler remembered, "Yes, Otis Johnson, he played with Slim at that time, and Simmie—he was a guitar player. He was one of the Kinchens too, like Jesse the drummer."[48] Jesse Kinchen remembered the local Baton Rouge gigs as well as a trip to Philadelphia and the trips to the East and West Coasts: "We went out there, and then we came back and did some local gigs here, the Cotton Club, the Carousel, that was with Percy Sledge, the Pink Elephant, the Five Crowns, the Casablanca, Byrd's Satellite Lounge, that was all with Simmie and Otis and a bass player, Frank. The Peppermint Club, Golden Slipper, Glass Hat, all those. We'd eat after the show at Rose and Thomas's Cafe, that used to be Wilson's. Slim would get gumbo, his favorite food was gumbo."[49]

RECORDINGS, MARCH 1969

At some point while he was in Los Angeles in March, Slim took time to soak up the sights and scenes. While walking on Sunset Boulevard and reflecting on his newfound fame with young, white audiences, he had the inspiration to write about what he saw. One result was "The Hippy Song," which, apparently, he recorded almost immediately. Lovell remembered: "He recorded that in California in between engagements at the Whiskey a Go Go club there. It was done in a rush."[50] This and other songs were logged as received by Excello on April 9, 1969, and when "The Hippy Song" was later issued on an album, it was clear that the sound of that song was different from most of his others. It was taken at a very fast "big boss man" pace that was aimed at the rock-music crowd; it provides a recognizable base for Harpo's philosophical lyric explaining "long hair don't make you bad." Slim takes two excellent harp solos and, overall, the song works. At this time, on the back of his forays into the wider world, it seems that Slim underwent a little change of personal appearance. Family photographs show that he had forsaken the dark-suit-and-tie look for something more casual and colorful, a little more hip if not exactly hippy. From the same session, "Dynamite" was a guitar-led piece of R&B boasting about what happens when Slim's baby lights his fuse, in some contrast to the hesitant, sensitive Harpo of many of his early blues lyrics. Both "Dynamite" and another song, "Jody Man," have the same sound, and it seems other songs were attempted, too, including a version of the emerging blues standard "Got My Mojo Working," on which the drummer stops playing after a minute and a half, perhaps due to a technical problem, and so the song has never been released. "Jody Man" was a very fine blues sung with some full-throated passion by Slim above a strong bass line and a ringing lead guitar. Slim provides a harp solo midway. This is essentially Chicago bar blues where the band pays homage to the likes of Muddy Waters, Jimmy Rogers, and Little Walter.

"Jody Man" was one of many R&B and soul songs about the legendary man who spread his loving around, the equivalent perhaps of country music's blueprint "cheating" songs, that gained prominence in the 1960s and 1970s. Often the man in the song would be named Jody Ryder or Joe "The Grinder," but it was not a new concept.[51] Its first widely accepted appearance came in the Army, where it was known as the "Jody Call" or the "Duckworth Chant" after 1944 when a black private, Willie Duckworth, got flagging troops to revive themselves and march better to the calls. It may well go way back to the era of work songs, and Buddy Stewart from Baton Rouge recalled it in Army use: "There were hundreds of Jody verses—I know because I called 'em—'Ain't no sense in going home, Jody's got you girl and gone.'"[52] Louis Armstrong released "Jodie Man" on Decca in 1945, and although Armstrong's song also had a particular wartime bias against draft dodgers and ne'er-do-wells, it may be his record about the two-timing man that Harpo remembered. Slim's own version appears to have inspired Johnnie Taylor's huge soul hit "Jody's Got Your Girl and Gone" on Stax in 1971.

It is likely that Harpo recorded these four songs, and others, with Simmie and Jesse Kinchen and perhaps Lloyd Palmer at the Audio Arts studio at 5607 Melrose Avenue, owned by former movie actress Madelon Baker and her husband, Jackson Correll. Audio Arts demo discs are among the effects inherited by Slim's family, including such apparently original songs as "I'm All Mixed Up," on the same theme as "The Hippy Song." Drummer Jesse Kinchen once described to Steve Coleridge how he played on a session with Harpo that produced about thirteen sides and for which he remembered being paid $350. He was uncertain where this was, but it was likely this extended Californian demo session from which a number of master tapes emerged.

RECORDINGS, APRIL 1969

When Harpo returned home from California in April 1969, he was soon needed again at the Woodland Sound studio in Nashville. This time his sound would be rather different under new producers Bob Wilson and Ben Keith, featuring white and black musicians brought up on roots music but working firmly in the here and now. Bob Wilson was a trained pianist from Detroit who grew up hanging around the Fortune Records studios and then at Motown before he was given a break by the local Golden World label. One of his instrumental recordings was placed on the B side of a top-30 hit on Ric-Tic by the San Remo Golden Strings in 1965, and Wilson found himself making a promotional tour as part of the San Remo Quartet. A series of visits to radio stations took him to Nashville where he visited disc jockey "John R" Richbourg, whose late-night WLAC shows he had listened to as a kid in Detroit. He was as amazed that Richbourg wasn't black as "John R" was at the boy's soul talent. "You're kind of like a white Ramsey Lewis," John R apparently told him, soon offering him a recording deal with Sound Stage 7 Records. Wilson recorded "In the Midnight Hour" and "After Hours" for Sound Stage 7 and then started session work for Shannon Williams at Woodland Studio on both gospel and blues sessions. He produced Willa Dorsey, the Kelly Brothers, and others—but he was keenest to work with Harpo. He felt that Excello had no real plan for Harpo, and "recording him in a more modern way was entirely my idea." Wilson had been on Bob Dylan's groundbreaking *Nashville Skyline* album, and "I was in a lot of college concerts and could see how much they all loved the blues. It really developed into a market, and Excello just wanted to sell records."[53]

When Shannon Williams agreed to try this new approach, Wilson brought in his friend Ben Keith as his coproducer. Keith was well established on the Nashville scene, having played steel guitar on Patsy Cline hits such as "I Fall to Pieces," and he later played with Neil Young and Willie Nelson, among many country and pop artists. For Harpo's tracks, Keith played a steel dobro guitar while Wilson was on piano and organ. The other musicians were the ones Wilson was working with at Sound Stage 7—Karl Himmel on drums, Mac Gayden on guitar, and Billy Cox on bass. Pee Wee Ellis, formerly with James Brown, and Norm Ray were on alto and baritone saxes. Karl Himmel's drums were in demand by artists as diverse as Bob Dylan, George Jones, and Charlie Daniels, while Billy Cox had played bass with J. J. Cale and others as well as his own King Casuals. Mac Gayden said of his young days in Nashville, "We all played soul music growing up. The black community here was stronger with young white musicians than the country community was. I grew up playing in black bands. . . . I used to play with Arthur Gunter when I was in high school."[54] Billy Cox remembered working with Hendrix and the latter's connection with Harpo. "Jimi's playing was always rooted in the blues. . . . he was basically a rhythm & blues player. That was his roots. His favorite players were Muddy Waters, Howlin' Wolf, Lightnin' Hopkins, Albert King, B. B. King and especially Slim Harpo. . . . He told me he played with Slim Harpo for a couple of dates."[55]

Wilson chose two unusual songs for Harpo to record as his next two singles. The first was a very different arrangement of Johnny Cash's hit "Folsom Prison Blues." It was a song that had hit twice already for Cash, and Wilson figured the time was right for a soulful version to underline Harpo's crossover potential. Slim's version is taken at a slow pace and produced within an inch of its life in contrast to Cash's minimalist approach (though "Crescent City Blues," the original of the song, which Cash took from dance-band leader Gordon Jenkins, was very much an arranged big-band song for a female torch singer). Slim's is a good version, nevertheless, managing just to keep the soulful horns, rock drumming, country steel, and Slim's harp from clashing. Notably, Slim sings about shooting a man in "Rio," rather than Cash's "Reno." Bob Wilson remembers that "Folsom" featured a guitar figure Gayden had come up with a few days earlier and that Cox played the eight-string bass he had used with Jimi Hendrix. He also remembers that the "session" actually took place in three parts: "I recorded the tracks on one date, put the horns on a couple weeks later, then Excello paid to bring Slim up to Nashville by Greyhound bus to work with me on overdubbing the vocals. He was only in town for three days as I recall, when we completed overdubbing his vocals, harmonica, and guitar, and he went back home to Louisiana." This layered, impersonal approach to recording was probably not what Harpo had in mind when he had first sought greater independence from Jay Miller but, according to Wilson, "we got along fine. I had been on the same show with him a couple of times in the past, so we had met before but did not really know each other. He was impressed with the tracks and arrangements and . . . of course, hoped for a big hit."[56]

"Folsom Prison Blues" was issued as Excello 2306. On June 7, 1969, *Bill-board* listed the record as a new release and a "Spotlight Pick" with a shot at the top 20. The flip side was "Mutual Friend." Wilson recalled, "They just pulled some old tracks they had in the can and used those for the B sides of my productions. We cut two more sides but they were not strong songs and not A side material."[57] It is not clear what these other sides were or whether they have survived.

The second A side to come from this unusual session was "I've Got My Finger on Your Trigger," a soul piece big on bass runs and Pee Wee Ellis's horn arrangements but light on the Harpo factor. The lascivious title is memorable, but the lyric doesn't quite live up to it and has to take second place to the band. "I've Got My Finger on Your Trigger" was issued around October 1969 as Excello 2309 with its flip side "The Price Is Too High," a good arrangement of a song written by Nashville's pioneer R&B artist, writer, and producer Ted Jarrett. In it, we are told mistakes come easy, temptation is enemy number one, but fortunately Ted and Slim don't have the price. It is likely that Jarrett produced this song around the same time as the Wilson/Keith tracks and that Pee Wee Ellis contributed horns to the arrangement in the same way he did with "Finger." The reception of the record was mixed. It did not make the *Billboard* charts, but *Cash Box* listed it at number 38 in their November 1 "Looking Ahead" chart. Bob Wilson claimed, "Slim did get some momentum from these two singles as they were played on WLAC and he got more air play than he had got in years. Also, *Rolling Stone* magazine reviewed the 'Folsom' single and said it was the best blues record of 1969, so I was pretty flattered at that."[58]

In the summer of 1969, Slim Harpo was on the road once more. During June 5–8 he was at the fourth Memphis Country Blues Festival with old-timers Bukka White and Furry Lewis as well as a selection of modern blues, R&B, and rock artists including Canned Heat, Albert King, Booker T and the MGs, and Rufus and Carla Thomas. By June 21 and 22, he was at the Toronto Pop Festival with Chuck Berry, the Byrds, Dr. John, and Blood Sweat and Tears. On July 26, he was in New York again at the Schaefer Music Festival, held in Central Park's Wollman Skating Rink, headlining with Sly and the Family Stone. Later that summer he was wanted again in California where, *Billboard* reported on August 9, Martin Otelsburg of Universal Attractions had set up Imperial Attractions in Los Angeles to book exclusively certain artists including Slim Harpo, Albert Collins, Bo Diddley, and Earl Hooker. By October 11 all these men were playing the Vancouver Blues Festival. This last tour was trailed back home in the *News Leader*, with a picture and story about the local man done good: "Slim Harpo—one of the nation's leading blues exponents, Baton Rouge's own. Slim is scheduled to be one of the guest artists at the Battle of the Bands at Rock's Golden Bull on September 16. He leaves later this month on a European tour arranged through Universal Attractions."[59] In fact, this was the tour of Canada and the North, with Europe still to come. Slim was certainly starting to get his paperwork in place to acquire a passport because on August 19, 1969, his half-sister Lillie had sworn a legal affidavit in Baton Rouge confirming "that James Moore is the identical person registered in the State of Louisiana as Isiah Moore . . . on February 11, 1924." Apparently he had managed to spend his whole life as James and Slim without ever needing to use or have his registered birth name changed. He was not the only one who had a surprise. In asking for her birth certificate, Lovell found that although she had been celebrating her birthday every May 5, she was apparently born on May 7.

By November 14, Slim was back at Hunter College in New York for the second time in a year, this time with Chuck Berry and Albert King. It was to be one of the last shows he ever gave.

RECORDINGS, DECEMBER 1969 AND JANUARY 1970

Perhaps because of Slim's increased profile, and perhaps because of the elongated time it took to make an album in the days of the "rock society," Excello allowed Harpo's next recordings to be made nearer to home and in a more relaxed atmosphere. On his return from New York, he worked on tracks for an album at the Deep South Recording Studio, located on Government Street in Baton Rouge. There were possibly two sessions, the first completed by December 6, 1969, when studio boss Sam Montalbano wrote to Excello, saying, "Enclosed is a 7 and a half inch demo mixdown copy of an 8 track session Slim Harpo did in our studio," and reminding Excello there were two earlier sessions by other artists still to be paid for. Montalbano first came across Harpo during his student days at Louisiana State University, when he booked Slim into the local CYO Center for weekend dance shows. Then he also met guitarist Lynn Ourso, born and raised in Baton Rouge, with whom he "partnered on various music projects." One of these was the Deep South Studio.

Ourso had started his first band, the Six Teens, when he was just that age in 1958 before playing bass and guitar and recording with John Fred and the Playboys from 1961 through his college days. When he finished at LSU in 1966, he joined Wayne Cochran and the C. C. Riders. After that he returned to Baton Rouge, formed a booking agency, and started managing John Fred and the Playboys, recalling, "We had a worldwide number 1 record ["Judy in Disguise"] at the end of '67 and early '68 that changed our lives forever." After touring heavily with the band and running his management-and-concerts agency, in 1969 Ourso developed the new recording facility in Baton Rouge with Sam Montel. As he recalled, "I was a major stockholder in Deep South Recording, Inc with Montalbano and others. Before that, Montel had a small mono studio in the same building, located in Sam's father's Fruit Exchange produce building, where our offices were also, on the River Road, about thirty yards behind the levee. I built and ran the new studio here until about '77."[60]

Ourso remembers clearly how he got to make a session with one of his idols, Slim Harpo:

One night when Sam Montalbano and I were hooking up the equipment in our new studio, Slim Harpo and his wife dropped in. Some players were hanging around and helping out. We had never even turned on the equipment before that night. Mrs. Moore was cordially introduced by Slim and I remember she wore a solid red dress. She sat in the control room in front of the board on a couch we had there. We talked about Slim's past records and J. D. Miller—he called him "Mr. Miller"—and then I believe it was Slim who asked about our going out in the studio and playing some while Sam was figuring out the board. I had a guitar and amp and someone had left some drums in the studio already set up. Chuck Mitchell, a local vocalist, sat down on the drums and I kind of recall songwriter Roy Hayes being there. Sam was behind the board; none of us really knew how it worked but somehow we got music up though the speakers and signals to the tape and we just played cover songs while experimenting with our new Scully 8-track and an Auditronics mixing board from Memphis. We were a rag-tag unrehearsed group of players and I don't recall them all—it was a shame we did not have my longtime group of "A team" players on the session; known as Cold Gritz, they were hired away by Jerry Wexler [of Atlantic Records] the week before. So, how we did it was Slim would call the songs and the key, and he would sing a bit of it while we warmed up—a little—and Slim would start the song, or count it off and away we would go with a one-inch tape rolling. It was just a few hours of jamming! Slim must have felt good about what we were doing because, before he and his wife left that night, we were outside the studio and Slim privately asked me about recording for us. He said he wanted to get a better royalty than the five cents he had been getting. Slim and I talked for a while but no more came of our discussion. This was a coincidental recording session—a wonderful coincidence—not planned. All the songs we did—five I think—were done in one night.[61]

Two of the songs that emerged from the evening of jamming were blues staples. "Boogie Chillun" had been recorded before by Harpo, and was a tune Ourso was used to playing with John Fred. This version is slower than Slim's earlier Miller-recorded version, not originally issued, and closer to John Lee Hooker's influential down-home blues version that became an R&B hit twenty years before. "Rock Me Baby" was based on older blues themes, too, notably Little Son Jackson's "Rockin' and Rollin'," but it had fairly recently been a hit for B. B. King. Slim's version is a solid blues with an understated but recurrent lead-guitar figure that leaves plenty of space for Slim's harp to take center stage and for him to do the lyric justice.

In all, the Baton Rouge session produced five titles that would all become album tracks the following year. Apart from "Baby Please Come Home," which was actually an updated and extended, and really very good, remake of "Rainin' in My Heart," perhaps the best and most commercial of the five was "The Music's Hot," with its hurrying drumbeat and engaging swing. It's a different sort of song for Harpo, too, essentially a rocking R&B version of a country story song, written by Roy Hayes, a local country singer who had a history of writing crossover music. His songs included "I'm Gonna Be a Wheel Someday," recorded first by Bobby Mitchell before becoming a number 17 pop hit for Fats Domino in 1959. Hayes recalls that, although he knew about Slim, they had never met until one day when they both happened to be at the Deep South Studio: "He asked me whether I had any songs; he wanted songs for an album he was working on. I did have some which I put on a tape for him to listen to. He listened, and said he'd like to record three songs. We went into the studio that same week and he made two of them right away."[62]

People had been writing songs about how newfangled rhythmic music miraculously made the old folks dance or raised the dead for as long as one rhythmic style had supplanted another. Dozens of poor rockabilly and R&B songs attest to this, but Roy Hayes's song "The Music's Hot" was a refreshingly good treatment of the theme. Slim's got one foot in the grave but, "I gave a great big shout / St. Peter, I cain't go tonight / They got a brand new rockin' sockin' record out." The answer to the question "where are you going" is "where the music's hot." Along with this song, Slim recorded Hayes's "You Can't Make It," a slow blues recounting all the reasons why a woman needs a man like Slim. The drumming and basic guitar riffs are minimalist, but the song is still more "arranged" than the blues jams like "Boogie Chillun" and may have had other guitar parts added afterwards. One critic found the "three note riff so effective with doubled harmonica, and it's one of his best latter day recordings. Whoever produced it, well, they were either brilliant or just lucky."[63] It raises the question of the extent to which Harpo played lead guitar on sessions. Lovell and others have attested to his increasing use of the guitar at shows in the days after Rudy Richard left, and Shannon Williams even said that Slim always played guitar at sessions, though not very well. Whether he developed his technique sufficiently to take lead solos on his records remains unknown due to the lack of written session data.

Not long after the session, as Roy Hayes told me, "Slim came to me and said that he'd made a demo recording of the third of my songs he was interested in, 'There's Nothing as Sweet as Making Up.' He said he had recorded it at a practice session at his house, and he left his tape with me to listen to. He had changed the song a little to put it into his style. He told me he thought it was going to be a bigger song than 'Rainin' in My Heart.' I said 'oh, sure,'—but I liked what he'd done with it. He'd made the hook sound really gospelly. So, three or four days later I called him at home to tell him what I thought . . . and I found out—he had died! I didn't know, I hadn't heard. All this happened within a few weeks of our first meeting."[64]

7. GOODBYE, SLIM HARPO

An Untimely Death | I Just Can't Leave You | Blues Hangover | They Knew the Blues | Harpo's Musicians | The Last of the Old-Time Record Men | All about the Music

AN UNTIMELY DEATH

It was reported in the *Baton Rouge Advocate* that "James Moore (Slim Harpo) died at the age of 45 at 2 a.m. [January 31, 1970] at Baton Rouge General Hospital. Was a resident of Baton Rouge and a native of West Baton Rouge Parish. Body will be at Hall's Mortuary, Port Allen . . . Services at 11 a.m. Saturday Feb. 7 to be conducted by Rev. L. E. Billoups pastor of St. John's Baptist Church at Mulatto Bend . . . and burial will be in the Mulatto Bend Cemetery. Survived by his wife, Mrs. Lovell Jones Moore . . . three sisters . . . a stepson and step-daughter . . . and a host of other relatives."

When James Moore was buried in Mulatto Bend, his plot was placed next to his mother and father and three members of his mother's family, Ike and Doshie Brown and Mack Brown, with spaces left for James's sisters and his brother-in-law Dan Collins.[1] After James's burial took place, his family had a headstone made saying he had died on January 30, rather than a day later as the newspaper had described. The difference probably reflects the early morning time of death given to reporters compared to Lovell's experience of his collapse late the previous evening. Either way, it's just another of many minor imponderables in the story of Slim Harpo. For the public record, the acting state health officer signed the death certificate showing death occurring at 10 a.m. on January 31. The certificate shows the immediate cause of death as "ruptured aneurysm, arch of aorta." This is not a "heart attack" as such, but a fatal breach in the main artery carrying blood out of the heart and through the chest area. The common causes of such ruptures include high blood pressure, smoking, and chest injuries, the latter two of which, at least, applied in James's case. Sudden severe chest pain is the most common symptom, along with a feeling that something in the chest is being torn. Again, this all apparently applied to James.

In the world of many blues and rock musicians, death at age forty-five might not be so unusual. But Slim Harpo was not the kind to live to excess, and his reported death from a "heart attack" took many by surprise. Ignoring the formal newspaper reports, some people came up with explanations of their own, and what caused James Moore's death at such a young age was the subject of conflicting gossip and rumor.

As befit an emerging member of the "rock society," a bluesman adopted by the wider music world, some rock-music newspapers chose to report that his death was drug-related. Slim had latterly been in the company of young white bands for whom a drug culture was part of life, as indeed it had been among blues and jazz performers for many decades—and cocaine use is one indicator for potential aortic rupture—but Harpo was known not to be a heavy drinker, let alone anything else, and his wife traveled regularly with him to his gigs. William Gambler is adamant: "Slim never did drugs."[2] Lazy Lester is unyielding in his view, too: "People talk crap about his death. Say he overdosed. He didn't do that. Say he had a heart attack. They don't know what they're talking about."[3]

Lester's view was that Slim "was injured under an automobile, putting in a new transmission. He'd bought an old Buick Century from J. D. Miller and some years later he was working on it. Something heavy fell on his chest, but he didn't go to hospital. Some time after that he would get pains and then they did take him to the hospital, and he died there."[4] Tabby Thomas said: "See what he did. . . . He called me on the phone, said, 'Man, I was picking up a motor.' He and another fellow, and the other fellow dropped his end, let all the weight fall on him see and bust one of the blood vessels in his chest, in his heart. . . . I said, 'take it easy, 'cause you don't never know what's happened.'"[5] Buddy Stewart told another version, about Slim's sugarcane haulage vehicles: "He used to work on his trucks and, I think on a Thursday, he was pulling an engine out of the truck and it fell on his chest. He was fine when I played cards with him on a Sunday night, but he was short of breath. The next day he was gone. . . . Slim had punctured his lung and that's how he died."[6] Raful Neal told a similar story about the truck engine: "He was kind of shaken up, but he was up and around the next day and looked fine when I went by his house. It was the day after I saw him that he passed. They said he had a heart attack but I think that truck engine crushed something."[7]

Some other musicians who knew Slim have tended instead toward the story that had him trying to end his long-standing relationship with Clara, the lady who worked at the late-night restaurant on North Boulevard. As is the nature of these things, the situation was becoming complicated, and both parties were "having trouble" over it until Slim decided to call a halt. In some versions of the story she accepted their breakup well; in others she put something unhealthy in his food, and in another she may have slipped something into the cough medicine Harpo regularly took to clear his throat and chest.

William Gambler's view is that Harpo's death was not quite so mysterious:

> He died of a heart attack, that's it. He had had one earlier, had had heart trouble but there was nothing said about it. He didn't know, or didn't seek medical attention. Some time before he died he had a problem with his chest. He went out to Denham Springs with one of his employees and they were picking up long pieces of iron and throwing it into a truck. I was there too. So, Slim picked up some iron ready to throw it and then he hollered, held his chest, said the iron hurt him, said it had jarred him in the chest. Thinking back, I believe he had a heart attack then and didn't know it. He wasn't a person that believed in going to the doctor. Black men didn't go to doctors. People say he was injured working on a truck engine, but that's not fact. During the time before he died he wasn't working on engines anymore. He used to, earlier.

It was up to a year later, Gambler said, when Slim had his fatal aortic attack: "My mother called me where I was living about six blocks away and said that he wasn't breathing. He was in the bed and he just reached over and hollered and [his body] hit her. That was it. I drove to the house and gave him CPR I'd learned in the service, but I knew he was dead. The fact is that Slim died in his bed at his home on 36th Street."[8] There was no ambulance service available to the family at that time, so Slim's body was taken to Baton Rouge General Hospital on Florida Street in a hearse from a local funeral home, and he was examined briefly in the emergency room there. By chance, one of Harpo's musicians was able to verify the story. Otis Johnson had taken a job as a driver at Gilbert's Funeral Home when he left the Army and was still there despite his foray out to California with Slim the year before. He confirmed, "The Home carried its own ambulances in those days. It was me who picked up

Slim's body from the Home and carried it to Baton Rouge General Hospital, me and an embalmer named Raymond Guidry."[9]

On February 8, 1970, the *News Leader*, as the black community weekly, carried an obituary and a photograph of Harpo on its front cover. Inside, their entertainment writer Andrew Lee Jones confirmed, "The sudden and untimely passing of Slim Harpo recently was a tremendous shock to this scribe as well as to many other of his friends and fans in the city and across the nation. Not too long ago Slim and I sat and talked about doing a special feature on him as one of the few 'down home' blues artists still in the entertainment business . . . [but] we never really got together again." Jones cited a European tour as the reason he and Slim didn't do the interview, seemingly unaware that the tour hadn't happened and in fact was not scheduled until later that year.

A month went by before the weekly magazine of the rock-music world, *Rolling Stone*, learned of Harpo's passing, but it carried a full story in March, probably because, they said, "he was working in a more commercial vein than most [country] bluesmen." The feature reported his death straight, summarized his career, and concluded: "Just when things were starting to look up for him . . . Slim Harpo was one of those little known bluesmen who found new doors opened for him by the English groups . . . and for Slim it meant new gigs in places he'd never dreamed of playing. [His songs] were marked by his sly, almost tongue in cheek vocal style, which made him seem like an easy-going guy, probably something of a character."[10]

I JUST CAN'T LEAVE YOU

To underline the distance music had come in Harpo's forty-five years of life, the *State-Times* music reviews on the days of Isiah Moore's birth and Slim Harpo's death seem from different worlds. Editions from 1924 featured largely classical and orchestral recordings while Paul Whiteman's Orchestra was "pleasant and melodious" on "Linger Awhile" and Ted Weems's "Somebody Stole My Gal" was praised as "a foxtrot full of snap and fire." The only live-music ad was for a dance at Port Allen Pavilion with music by Victor's Band, a Negro orchestra. In contrast, in 1970 the ads were for soul, country, and cabaret acts, though a recent R&B show by Bobby Bland was also being talked about in the *News Leader*.

On January 31, 1970, the *State-Times* front page was preoccupied not with

Harpo's demise but with President Nixon's speech about fiscal budgeting to keep the country out of recession and the threats of railroad unions to take the rail system on strike. Among the local news stories, some things probably remained depressingly familiar to James Moore's family: a dozen districts in Louisiana were still running segregated school systems and facing federal court orders to complete desegregation, and news of the black community remained heavily focused on church life or police and court reports. It was predicted that it would not be until the next national elections that registration to vote by eligible African Americans would reach over 60 percent. Elsewhere in the news, police were chasing "three negro men who sped away in a stolen car" after holding up a Scotlandville grocery store and two men who held up a nearby liquor store; "both bandits were negroes," police told the *Advocate*. The *News Leader* also led on schools but from the perspective that although desegregation couldn't now be stopped in the South, the mood of Congress was against civil rights. "The justice department asks for delays and the Supreme Court says there cannot be delays . . . ambivalent politics from the president. It can only embitter and dishearten black people." In the society pages of both black and white papers, the news of marriages, visits by notable citizens, and aspirational dances organized by teen girls continued as ever. The difference now was that an ad for a social event could no longer state, as so many had over the past ten or more years, that the crowd could enjoy "music supplied by Slim Harpo and his band."

At Excello, Bud Howell last spoke with Slim in the middle of January 1970, and he recalled: "He was really anxious to get going on the album; everything was fine with him. We were just talking about the new album and Europe; he was especially looking forward to going to Europe and was trying to get everything straight with his passport. . . . Slim was a fine gentleman. Always took his wife with him on tours, never gave anybody any trouble with drinking or not showing up for a show or anything like that."[11]

For musicians like Lynn Ourso, "We were working on an album and it was going to be great. But about a few weeks later Slim was gone, and I was devastated."[12] The album did come out, but probably not in the form it would have taken had Slim survived. It was issued in May 1970 as *Slim Harpo Knew the Blues,* Excello 8013, as part of a series of albums the Deep South studio made for Excello at that time. Ourso described how "Bud Howell and I met when he was down for a session we were doing for Excello and he noticed our master tape files. He glanced up on the top shelf and discovered the one inch master tape on Slim in my file cabinet; that became the *Slim Harpo Knew the Blues* LP."[13] The album contained eight recordings Slim had made in California and Baton Rouge in 1969 and two of his earlier hits, "I'm a King Bee" and "Baby, Scratch My Back." Strangely, "Rainin'" was not included under its original title, particularly since the sleeve notes by Al Jefferson of WHIN Baltimore made a point of saying "'Rainin' in My Heart' really vaulted him into prominence as a blues singer with universal appeal." The song was there, however, in extended form under the new title of "Baby Please Come Home." The original hit version of "Rainin' in My Heart" did reappear in March 1971 with an updated, overdubbed sound as one side of a valedictory or tribute single along with "Jody Man." Issued as Excello 2316, it failed to become the posthumous hit Excello must have hoped for, despite being picked by *Billboard* as a potential soul hit. The overdubbing and rerelease of the disc was triggered by a version of the song issued by Hank Williams Jr. in December 1970 that was in the country-music top 10 by March 1971.

Al Jefferson had concluded his *Knew the Blues* LP notes by saying that, while Slim was no longer among us, "the blues he leaves behind will continue with us always." In that, he was more prescient than he probably realized. Harpo's music has been current in record-company catalogs pretty much ever since.

As the 1970s opened, Slim Harpo and Excello had been looking forward to the completion of his new album in the expectation that his career was about to develop even further, and more widely. As Bud Howell said, arrangements were being made for Slim to tour in Europe in the spring of 1970 and for him to be recorded by a new label licensing his music in England. Harpo's discs had been issued in Europe ever since the Pye International label issued "Rainin' in My Heart" in England in 1961, after which he saw several releases on Stateside, including tracks on LPs drawn from various Excello artists, *Authentic R&B* in 1963 and *The Real R&B* and *A Long Drink of Blues* in 1964, the latter album shared between Harpo and Lightnin' Slim. *Authentic R&B* contained both sides of Slim's first-ever single and was particularly influential in Europe during the British R&B boom. The Harpo baton passed to President Records in 1967 and by 1970 had passed again to Blue Horizon, who issued his "Folsom Prison Blues" as a single in England. Mike Vernon was the force behind the deal. He remembers:

[We] got involved with Excello, then headed by Bud Howell, back in late 1968. . . .
we made a deal to license catalogue material from the extensive Excello group of
labels to be released on Blue Horizon via our CBS deal. Those releases featured
Lightnin' Slim and Lonesome Sundown as part of our Post-War Masters series.
Pleased with the way this series was being handled, Bud asked me if I would be
interested in working with Slim Harpo at some later date. As I recall, that was
to be toward the end of 1970. This was a really exciting prospect. Harpo was the
best-selling blues artist on Excello's roster so it was some accolade for me to be
asked to work with him. I had made it quite clear that it would be necessary to
come up with some "hot" new songs and Bud along with his A&R man Freddie
North agreed to that plan. Pete Wingfield and Duster Bennett had already written
songs for Slim to record for such a project, and that was confirmed as a "go."[14]

In the meantime, New York agent Dick Alen had set up a tour of England
and parts of Europe, including Scandinavia, for April and May 1970, and
musicians had been booked. When Mike Vernon took a phone call from
Bud Howell at Excello to tell him that Slim Harpo was dead, "the news came
as a shock. Bud himself seemed stone struck by the news. Besides being one
of the company's biggest selling acts, Slim was also a close friend of all those
working at Excello. He was liked wherever he went. . . . We shall never know
truly how sad a loss this has been."[15]

While he was alive, Harpo's releases and his career were managed as part
of a current scene and with an eye to the future. Once he was gone, the focus
changed, and the first of many compiled retrospectives of Harpo's music
appeared almost immediately, in 1971. In place of the planned Blue Horizon
recordings, Mike Vernon and pioneering blues researcher Mike Leadbitter
issued *Trigger Finger,* an LP that contained sixteen of Harpo's lesser-known
tracks from the Crowley and post-Crowley periods. Excello kept Harpo's LPs
in catalog and licensed some of his hits to ABC-Dunhill for their Goldies
series of single discs.

Lovell Moore said that after Slim died she was offered the possibility of
working with Excello and other Baton Rouge musicians. "Some guys in New
York wanted me to continue, you know, booking artists and stuff like that. It
would have been good if I was sure I'd be working with somebody I knew, but
for a woman to be traveling that much with a bunch of guys, and I had my
kids anyway. My grandson was born in December."[16] She later said, "What
meant more to me than [Slim's] music was him being a good husband and
father to my children. The only thing I regret is that he didn't live long enough

to enjoy the fruits of his labor."[17] Instead, her interest in music was limited to giving occasional interviews about Slim, to representing Slim by attending some latter-day music festivals—including accepting the 1995 national Blues Foundation award to Harpo in Los Angeles—and, of course, to managing his continuing income. This in itself was not straightforward.

William Gambler confirms that the songwriting and performance royalties due to Slim Harpo did eventually transfer to the family. "Yes, when he died they all went to my mother. But there were problems. She had to get a lawyer to get it. That was music sales." Problems lasted at least into the early 1990s when a Baton Rouge attorney, Harris Copenhaver, was still writing to the head of AVI, Raymond Harris, in California to seek up-to-date accounting of royalties from Excello recordings and to ensure Harpo's songs remained registered with BMI. In April 1991, Copenhaver had written to say that royalties to Lovell Moore were at least nine months overdue and, in September, Copenhaver urged the company "to bring the royalty data up to date since she is very much in need of these royalty payments at this time." He received some $3,500 in royalties for the six months ending in March 1991 and the promise of better accounting in the future. In January 1992, Copenhaver received $4,000 in royalties, but it is not clear that he fully understood how best to help Lovell in the face of the range of excuses offered by music-business professionals. His lack of knowledge is betrayed when he refers to Frances Preston of BMI, one of the first female music-business people in Nashville, as "Mr. Preston," and when he wonders how copies of a past judgment for J. D. Miller and against Nashboro-Excello in respect of songwriting royalties could affect Mrs. Moore. At least he did not have to chase BMI directly for songwriting money. Gambler says Lovell "didn't have no problem with BMI that I know of."[18]

The year 1976 saw the first of many LP albums (and later CDs) containing J. D. Miller's swamp-blues recordings aimed at the specialist collectors of blues and Louisiana music. They were issued by Flyright Records in England under the direction of researcher Bruce Bastin and included two albums by Harpo and later one CD. Having made contact with Jay Miller, Bastin took trips to Crowley from 1975 onwards to review, catalog, and reissue as much as he could of Miller's recordings. Miller's deal with Excello had been to produce finished master recordings for Excello to release, and consequently he had retained the rights and most of the session tapes containing alternative versions of songs or unreleased material. Bastin told *Blues Unlimited* magazine: "In 1975 and 1976 I went through Miller's tapes . . . systematically researching the tapes, and returned with some 200 tracks of unissued material for albums. [At] Jay Miller's shop on North Parkerson . . . imagine a wall of tape boxes 20 feet long and ten feet high plus odd cupboards full of tapes (often not in boxes and with no identification) and you have some idea of one end of the room adjoining the studio. . . . There was no index system, no speeds given . . . incorrect tapes in boxes . . . splices with sellotape . . . one box labelled 'Slim Harpo' yielded a white female vocal and piano." Bastin unearthed many gems from the Crowley studio and, listening to them as they appeared, concluded: "If the talent was Harpo's, it was Miller's skill which enabled it to emerge and be documented. . . . recordings didn't just happen, a number of factors had to come together. Just be thankful that it happened so often when Jay Miller was at the controls."[19]

Bastin also describes Miller's expansive nature and hospitality, inviting him to family gatherings and spending time identifying old tapes, including the ones where Miller played guitar himself if the musicians weren't doing what he wanted to hear. Bastin remembers Miller as a man who took charge and could handle most people and situations. "The only time I ever saw him defer to anyone was at his house when the phone rang. He answered, listened a second, then said 'Yes governor' and jumped up to attention. . . . It was Jimmie Davis—he hadn't been Governor of Louisiana for many years, but he sure still got Jay's attention."[20] By this time Miller had moved to a new home on Hoyt Avenue on the very edge of south Crowley. Bastin remembers his shock when he learned that Miller's father had used many of the unsold Fais Do Do and Feature label 78s as hardcore for Miller's new driveway and had given others away to a local fair to be used as shooting targets.

The Flyright reissues were well received, and by the arrival of the CD era, Excello, too, was keen to license its rarer songs and alternative versions to reissue companies. Outside the United States, Excello worked particularly with Ace Records in England, for whom John Broven transferred all the Excello master tapes to digital masters and compiled an impressive number of reissues, working hard to keep the name of Slim Harpo to the fore. Excello also worked with P-Vine in Japan. For the home market, Broven and others produced collector-oriented series on Excello, Hip-O, and other labels during the years when Excello became part of the AVI and then Universal groups. Finally, in 2015, Bear Family Records, based in Germany, issued the last word in Harpo recordings in a five-CD boxed set containing every recording Harpo made in his all-too-short career.

As well as the continued availability of Slim Harpo's music on discs, his legacy and his memory have been preserved by his friends and contemporaries who continued to play his songs, as have rock bands and new generations of musicians he influenced both at home and in countries Harpo probably never heard of. The earliest tribute to Harpo came from a man ten years his senior, Robert Pete Williams, a fellow sometime-dealer in scrap metal, whose single, "Goodbye Slim Harpo," was issued in 1971 on Parker Dinkins's Ahura Mazda label in New Orleans. In contrast to this small local release, the great and the good of white rock music continued to cover Harpo's signature tunes down the years, from the Grateful Dead to the Cramps and beyond. Another, and more literal, means of preserving Harpo's name and his music has been through the annual set of Slim Harpo Music Awards given in his name since 2003 as part of the continuing efforts by fans and promoters in Baton Rouge to keep the blues alive.

BLUES HANGOVER

The death of Slim Harpo was a big event among his contemporaries and the few bluesmen remaining from the generation above him. Talking to musicians in Louisiana in 1970, blues journalist Mike Leadbitter concluded, "It soon became clear that Slim Harpo was considered the 'Muddy Waters' of Baton Rouge and his recent death was widely mourned. It seems Harpo was responsible for introducing most of the Baton Rouge bluesmen to Jay Miller."[21] Unlike those blues players who had moved away to some degree of fame and fortune, like Buddy Guy in Chicago, the musicians remaining in town may not have had any real expectation or ambition to become successful recording and touring artists in the way Harpo had eventually managed to achieve. But they did still want to make music and, where possible, a decent living. Some had made records for specialist companies, but even they struggled to find their next gig unless they wanted to get on the soul train or change their style in some other radical way. Jay Miller, a champion of Baton Rouge blues, nevertheless admitted in April 1970 that he had recorded just one blues session in the past year, with Henry Gray, for his new Blues Unlimited label, named in honor of the British blues magazine edited by Mike Leadbitter and Simon Napier. The label would concentrate on "black" music, mainly zydeco with occasional swamp-blues releases. Many artists must have wondered what the future held for a bluesman from Baton Rouge in the emerging era of international rock music.

At the time of Harpo's death, the blues as such was decreasingly in evidence around Baton Rouge. A year or so before he died, Harpo was both accepting of this decline and trying to be upbeat about the future. He noted that many people living in his town were not local people like himself and didn't have his country tastes. He said "most of these people [have] moved out to Baton Rouge and New Orleans, and they listen to jazz or rock 'n' roll," adding defiantly, "but the blues artists are still real big there."[22] The fact was, though, that the pure blues scene, however defined, was confined to backroom get-togethers by the local players who had been there all along, the likes of Silas Hogan and Guitar Kelley. The wider entertainment scene for black people was focused on the clubs that once featured blues and R&B but now promoted soul music or blues at the soulful end of the spectrum. People like Boe Melvin were playing the clubs that catered to the black community, particularly Byrd's Satellite Lounge and the Jaguar, but found those people wanted to hear something a little more up to date than the blues of the Excello recording heyday of the 1950s and 1960s. The *News Leader* was full of ads for clubs that had gone a little more upmarket and modern. The "New" Glass Hat of J. H. Simms was promoted as the place "where the action is," advertising cocktails and college nights and ladies' nights, but not blues any longer. The message now was, "Come and join the Inn Crowd."[23] Freddie Gatlin had revitalized his lounge on Tern Street, advertising the plushness of "the fabulous Jaguar Room" rather than any music that might be heard there.

The regular newspaper column "On the Avenue," logging and reflecting entertainment goings-on in the black community, was urging local folks to go see soul men like Joe Simon at Rock's Golden Bull or the forthcoming James Brown Spectacular.[24] Among the old venues known to the bluesmen of Harpo's era, the White Eagle Club in Port Allen had "adopted a new policy promising a fun-filled and action-packed evening," while "a new atmosphere" had also been created at the popular Green Parrot on North Acadian, "one of the favorite gathering places for gaiety seekers." For white patrons, the clubs that once featured bluesmen and R&B artists of Slim Harpo's generation now gave employment to performers who delivered their message within a package of rock or folk-country-rock music.

The fortunes of black music in general were linked to the vagaries of city planning and development, and in turn to the progress of civil rights. In Slim Harpo's day, much of the downtown area was thriving and residents of all races had it as a focus for their daily lives. Some areas, in particular, were magnets for musicians and nightlifers alike. Back when the Temple Theater was built on North Boulevard in the 1920s, there were some forty merchants and businesses between Twelfth Street and Sixteenth Street. There were meat markets, grocers, a motor-car company, a furniture company, a dry cleaner, a hardware store, a jeweler, a tailor, a drugstore, a dry-goods store, a lumber company, a coffee company, and a funeral home.[25] Like Beale Street in Memphis, Deep Elem in Dallas, the Rampart Street area in New Orleans, or Harlem in New York, most cities had a focus for nightlife for the black community. In Baton Rouge, this area was once known as the Strip. Its music joints and thriving businesses served the crowds of people having a night out. In Harpo's time, some of this focus remained and was discovered by young whites, particularly students at LSU. Clubs like the Blue Bull, the Peppermint Club, and the new Glass Hat continued to do good business. The pioneering LSU student Maxine Crump, subsequently a broadcaster, a founding member of the Baton Rouge Blues Foundation, and a president of Dialogue on Race Louisiana, has recalled spending Saturday nights in the mid-1960s making her way "up and down the strip with groups of friends, hopping from bar to bar, dancing and swaying to the sound of local blues musicians."[26]

Gradually, during the late 1960s and the 1970s, this focus diminished, and at times it was only the visiting shows at the Temple by bluesmen of national substance such as B. B. King and Bobby Bland that kept the scene alive for the black community. By the 1970s the Baton Rouge Strip saw considerable structural and economic change, "urban renewal," and with it the dispersal of the African American community. In a decade when Beale Street, "the Main Street of Negro America," could be largely razed to the ground by the political and economic powers in Memphis, there was even less reason to protect black culture in Baton Rouge. Maxine Crump's view was clear: "Once desegregation came, blacks could go anywhere, so those clubs lost their clientele because they didn't have as many people on the weekends. Plus, the economy started changing. At the time, Baton Rouge was turning its attention to other things. I don't think the larger community saw that area as something to keep."[27] A majority of the white community had no vested interest in the Strip, and some black church leaders did not approve of the nightlife there. They together threatened to completely remove the blues from Baton Rouge. The Temple building survived the city planners, but this was despite events like the 1972 race riot that saw four people killed there.

In 1990, one visiting musician found North Boulevard "reduced to a state of almost total dereliction where Tabby's Blues Box, Protocol, and Rose & Thomas Café remain almost the only establishments open. Crack, combined with a high black unemployment rate, has sent crime figures soaring."[28] Between 1980 and 2004, Tabby Thomas maintained his Blues Box club on the Strip against all the odds. Silas Hogan, Henry Gray, and Jimmy Dotson would play there regularly, and Tabby was very much "in charge" of the musicians who came and went through his club despite their occasional rumblings of discontent. In his own somewhat limited performances, according to one observer, he turned the limitations of his music and his club into their qualities: "Tabby is a master of audience patter; 'When it's cold outside, it's cold in the Blues Box, when it's hot outside it's hot in the Blues Box, and when it rains outside . . . it floods in the Blues Box.'"[29] Tabby's son, Chris Thomas King, said, "It was more than just a club, but a cool, cultural thing to take [people] to Tabby's. Not just black and white people, but people of different classes, as well. It played a key role in helping this music shift to another generation to pick it up."[30] Before then, a new club, the Speakeasy, had opened opposite LSU and started bringing in senior statesmen of the blues and R&B such as Lightnin' Hopkins and Professor Longhair.

The year before Harpo's death came the publication of a book by Harry Oster about his recording exploits, including his work in Baton Rouge ten years before. He talked to the local press about the book, *Living Country Blues,* and about the state of the blues. Oster saw white interest in blues as "a romanticization by young persons of middle class backgrounds of what the older black performers stood for." He was concerned that talented young black people had stopped working within a blues style "because of their unpleasant associations with a degraded past," but he hoped that black people might come back to the music. He bemoaned the loss of improvisation in the blues. "The true blues singer thinks out loud in music. He makes personal comments as he goes along," even if he is only drawing from a repertoire of "standardized bricks which can be used to construct a variety of buildings."[31] He was thinking of Robert Pete Williams, not the electric blues of postwar Chicago, and certainly not the flashily dressed soul brothers of the emerging music scene.

Back in 1970, as Slim Harpo's final, posthumous LP, *Knew the Blues,* was being issued by Excello, a few record companies did remain interested in the way

Baton Rouge–area musicians of Harpo's generation arranged their bricks to make the swamp-blues sound. Chris Strachwitz, a German-born music fan living in California, started to make location recordings of bluesmen for his Arhoolie label in 1960, and ten years later he was reissuing Harry Oster's recordings, plus a whole unissued LP by Herman E. Johnson, and making recordings of his own in Baton Rouge. Strachwitz had been involved with folk-rockers Country Joe and the Fish and appreciated the West Coast hippie interest in the folk side of the blues and the international market among record collectors. He recorded an LP titled *Louisiana Blues* in Baton Rouge in 1970 featuring Henry Gray, Arthur Kelley, Silas Hogan, Whispering Smith, and Clarence Edwards.[32] At around the same time, Mike Vernon of Blue Horizon also saw the possibilities of recording Baton Rouge bluesmen for the enthusiastic new wave of white college fans of revival blues. Bud Howell had asked him whether he would be interested in producing music for Excello that would in turn be licensed to Blue Horizon, "recording Silas Hogan, Whispering Smith, Lazy Lester and the like, in a group situation. This appealed to me and we set the ball in motion. These were the Louisiana Swamp-blues sessions."[33]

Issued originally in England as a double-LP and later on Excello, these sessions were made in August 1970 at Lynn Ourso's Deep South Studio after a group of enthusiasts from Baton Rouge and New Orleans—Terry Pattison, James La Rocca, and Neal Paterson—had located Moses Smith, Silas Hogan, Arthur Kelley, Clarence Edwards, Henry Gray, and other musicians in and around Scotlandville. Without Lightnin' Slim and Lazy Lester, who could not be found at the time, the results, really, were patchy. Apart from Clarence Edwards, the vocal talents of the artists were all rather average, and their instrumental abilities were sometimes lost within rhythms and behind solos played by over-enthusiastic session musicians. The solo recordings by several of the players were something of an afterthought, but they stand up well and contain interesting song selections from a range of traditional blues sources. On the solo sides, the guitar virtuosity of Arthur Kelley and Silas Hogan is more apparent without the bass and drums and Moses Smith's harmonica playing continued to far outweigh his vocal prowess. Hogan contributed a version of "Honey Bee Blues," perhaps to evoke a Harpo connection, where his quest was to get stinging in order to reach the hidden honey. All in all, it was a pleasant-enough album, but there was probably more of the swamps in the song titles and on the cover artwork than in the grooves.

The interest in Baton Rouge and swamp-blues from other record labels led Excello to make whole new LPs in 1970 and 1971 with Lightnin' Slim, Silas Hogan, and Whispering Smith, followed in 1972 by the album *Live in Baton Rouge at the Speakeasy,* produced by Lynn Ourso and featuring once more Silas Hogan, Guitar Kelley, Moses Smith, and Clarence Edwards. It is rare for live recordings to be more effective than studio sessions, but this was an album on which the musicians could get into what was apparently a more usual and comfortable groove than on the studio sessions. Silas Hogan, particularly, benefited from the more casual atmosphere while contributing three songs, including "Greyhound Blues" and "Hoodo Blues."

Apart from Excello, there were few record labels interested in Baton Rouge bluesmen for the singles or LP markets during the later 1970s and 1980s. There were one-off singles and albums on Reynaud Records out of Opelousas and on Sunland Records based in Florida, which issued a *Louisiana Blues Anthology* featuring Raful Neal, Whispering Smith, Tabby Thomas, Robert Milburn, and Henry Gray.

THEY KNEW THE BLUES

The relative lack of commercial recordings of Baton Rouge blues after the first flush of interest in the early 1970s reflected the changes in the entertainment infrastructure of the city and the general mood of the civil rights era as it developed into soul power and black power. But the low profile of the old blues and the relative lack of new performers in the traditional styles did not mean that the local bluesmen were no longer playing. Many of them were out there somewhere one or two nights a week as they always had been, whether playing for themselves, for a small local gathering, or at some low-key club.

Robert Pete Williams was never really a professional musician nor had any ambition to be one. Because of his fortuitous discovery at Angola by Harry Oster, he found himself briefly on the folk-blues festival circuit, playing the Newport Folk Festival in 1964 after he gained his full parole and taking a country-wide tour in 1965. By 1966 he was even touring in Germany with the American Folk Blues Festival, but at no point did he develop any kind of an act or plan a career. Because of his wholly individual style of music, though, Williams was always destined to leave his mark. Apart from his ability to make up lyrics, "he'd do unusual things," said Richard Allen, who had been with Oster when Williams was auditioned there; "he'd be in three modes at once." When he later sang "Prisoner's Talking Blues" in the free world, said Allen, "I've never seen anybody look as sad as he did after he told his story. . . . They really believed him, believed he wasn't guilty."[34]

In 1964 Williams had been allowed to leave former prison governor Rudolph Estley's service during his parole, and he moved to Maringouin, about thirty miles west of Baton Rouge. He did a little farming, worked in a lumberyard, and then took up scrap-metal dealing again. Blues fans would occasionally turn up on his doorstep, and one such encounter in 1970 was skillfully described by Peter Guralnick in his 1971 book, *Feel like Going Home*. He characterized Williams as "a religious person, a sad, gentle man." He was living in tolerable conditions on an unpaved road neither as poor as some streets nor as affluent as others. He worked driving a scrap-iron truck and mostly turned down entreaties to go play the blues at local joints, saying, "I'm too old to fight. And some of the people don't know nothing else. They gets to drinking and right away they start pulling out knives." Williams retained his interest in music, though, and Guralnick listed some of the players he liked, including Lightnin' Hopkins and Slim Harpo, "all of whom he has met more as a fan than as a professional colleague since his release from prison." Williams had of course known James Moore in the days before he was imprisoned because other musicians have recalled both him and James Moore dealing in scrap iron before his incarceration.

In his later years, Williams did make some personal appearances and recordings, including a 1966 live LP in Berkeley, California, for Takoma Records and an LP made early in 1970 by Ahura Mazda Records of New Orleans. The latter included the song pulled as a single, "Goodbye Slim Harpo," which literally bemoaned in Williams's inimitable style the loss of a friend and the hope that they would be reunited somewhere. Lines like "Slim Harpo, he dead, in his grave / Goodbye Slim Harpo / Sleep on, sleep on, take your rest / Goodbye poor Slim / I'll see you again" were delivered emotionally and interspersed with some cutting slide notes. Williams recorded a number of other albums in the blues-revival years, each time displaying his own introspective approach. Guralnick again: "More than anyone else he shatters the conventions of the [blues] form and refuses to rely on any of the clichés, either of music or of lyric, which bluesman after bluesman will invoke. . . . [His blues] have a unique and personal vision." Musicologist David Evans had worked with Harry Oster in the early 1960s and noted, "Robert Pete, alone in the history of recorded blues, plays in minor keys extensively."[35] Evans also made some recordings in Baton Rouge: "I recorded a few guitarist friends of his but none of the others were in the same league with Robert Pete, who was a genius in my estimation."[36] In 1971 and 1972, after he had started to appear annually each spring at the New Orleans Jazz and Heritage Festival, Williams's style was captured in two films. On April 11, 1971, the *New Orleans Times-Picayune* picked up on the second of these festivals, saying: "Entertainment at the New Orleans Jazz and Heritage Festival in Beauregard Square: Blues artists who will perform are Roosevelt Sykes, Robert Pete Williams, Clancy Lewis, and Snooks Eaglin. The fair will open daily with a performance by Professor Longhair, described as a rhythm and blues great." The paper also described a jazz-soul set, street bands, Cajun singers, gospel singers, and samples of Louisiana cooking and crafts.

As the 1970s wore on, Williams continued collecting and selling scrap iron as he had always done, but he was in less and less good health and retired to a small house in Rosedale with his wife, Hattie Mae. Toward the end, he suffered from problems with his heart and the onset of cancer. He died on December 31, 1980, and was buried in Scotlandville. He rated a small obituary in the *Morning Advocate,* and in March, as the music-festival season approached, news of his passing was broken to the New Orleans festival crowd.

"Butch" Cage and Willie B. Thomas found intermittent fame on the college and folk circuits after their discovery by Harry Oster and their appearances at the Newport Folk Festivals in 1959 and 1960. They were recorded at these festivals and in their hometown and appeared too in a TV special, *Blues like Showers of Rain,* in 1970. Cage died in Zachary in September 1975, and Thomas died on November 23, 1977, at Lane Memorial Hospital, Zachary. With their passing, and that of Robert Pete Williams, much of the prehistory of Baton Rouge blues was lost forever, but some of the men from Slim Harpo's generation played on.

At the time of Harpo's death, Silas Hogan was still playing locally as a trio with Arthur Kelley and Gene Douzier, and sometimes with his son, Sammy Hogan, who could play bass, guitar, and drums and who took part in the Deep South sessions held in 1970 for the swamp-blues album. Silas Hogan had had his own share of life problems, not least the setback described in an *Advocate* report: the "death on Oct 21, 1967 of Lizzie Hogan, mother of Silas Hogan of Scotlandville and Jesse Hogan Jr. of Ohio who filed claim for $25,000 damages. She was struck by a car driven by Frankie Cunningham while attempting to cross Highway 10 two miles north of Baton Rouge city limit."[37] This would have resonated with James Moore, no doubt, and others who remembered his own father's death.

When local arts groups started to organize "heritage" shows of local music, Hogan was among those most often featured. On June 18, 1979, the *News Leader* carried a story with photographs of a performance at Clinton, and it was noted that among the local people, "500 turned out to appreciate their own." On the few occasions Hogan ventured outside Louisiana, the *News Leader* was there for his return, saying on July 26, 1984, there was due to be a "big blues extravaganza" at the Jaguar Lounge, 8211 Tern Street, Scotland-ville, on Silas's "return from the world fair." This was the Louisiana World Exposition that included "folklife exhibits." Blues fan and singer Julian Piper, from England, lived in Baton Rouge in 1987 and 1988 and provided some features for blues magazines, noting of Hogan that "people in Baton Rouge called him the Godfather, out of respect. The head of the Baton Rouge blues family, which is close-knit."[38] Hogan's own family included his wife and seven children. Piper characterized Hogan as a "tall man, always smiling, always had time for people." He noted that in those days Hogan really only played at Tabby Thomas's place, driving six miles to and from Scotlandville in an old red pickup with a battered windshield. He drank only orange juice because of his diabetes. Hogan continued playing for a few years after that and died on January 9, 1994. Tabby Thomas agreed Hogan was a father figure who never got angry and whose music was genuine: "There aren't many folks around that can play like Hogan anymore, the real blues. He didn't need all that wild fingering. He could hit one note and make you think of the apocalypse."[39]

When the *News Leader* covered Silas Hogan's gig at the Jaguar Lounge in 1984, it noted that the show would be given not only by Hogan but also by "Guitar Kelley, a living legend in the blues world." Kelley was, like Robert Pete and Hogan, a man little exposed to the outside world and who had never played for an audience beyond his own local people until he was recorded in 1970 by Arhoolie and Blue Horizon/Excello and by Excello for their live album. *Blues Unlimited* noted that year that Kelley's music could therefore "be taken as representing local tradition," though they did not examine whether this was an original tradition.[40] Through the 1970s, Kelley could normally be found teamed up with Hogan or other local players, staying true to his own musical preferences. By day, he worked as a laborer at Southern University for twenty-five years but at the same time found that outside interest in his music gave it a new audience. Kelley later said, "I do more pickin' in my blues thing. I fill in the pickin' while the other guitar player strums the chords. . . . Nobody plays the blues the way I do, no how, no way."[41] In fact, Kelley was not apparently playing anything at all original in his early days, and he was always a part-time musician who never went on to evolve his own style, so by the time he was interviewed in later years he was close to being correct that no one any longer played like him. He certainly did have a style that involved "more pickin'" than most. Into the 1980s, Kelley was still to be found playing at such venues as Aretha's Club across from his home on Abel Street in Baton Rouge and Richard's Club in Clinton on Saturday nights. He was sidelined by a stroke but continued to play. When he died on September 17, 2001, his passing was mourned by many, not least by Tabby Thomas, who gave him a venue for his music in later years. Thomas told the *Advocate,* "He was a stallion out there, get up and walk with the guitar. He was from that old school and he played his era. People loved it."[42]

Another man who "played his era" was Otis Hicks, Lightnin' Slim, the man who impressed Jay Miller so much more than most bluesmen. He had continued to record for Miller into the mid-1960s, but Miller was concerned that Lightnin's quality was not what it had been. He dated the decline to around 1963 when he said Lazy Lester became less reliable than ever. Miller always thought that when Lester missed a Lightnin' Slim session, the music suffered. Miller told visitors how Lightnin' had to be in a mood to make the blues and that he would pay Slim's wife or girlfriend of the moment to pick a fight with him before a session so he would turn up in a blue mood, and with a bluesy song. "The way I used to get Lightning to cut blues was this. Two or three days before I'd call him for a session, I'd give his woman twenty-five dollars to give him hell. . . . If she made a really good job of it, I'd give her the prettiest dress she'd ever seen on top of that."[43] For his part, Lightnin' was concerned about whether he, like Harpo, shouldn't perhaps have a better payment deal from Miller. Lightnin' had a different take from Miller on the decreasing success of his discs, saying, "He tried to put some changes in a lot of 'em. Some of 'em I went along with, some of 'em I didn't. He tried to put funny different changes. . . . I just couldn't agree to play with it."[44]

At one point Lightnin' stopped taking gigs Miller had organized out of Crowley. Then, in 1966, Lightnin' was involved in crashing Miller's favorite Volkswagen bus and "borrowing" a car from him. At that point Lightnin' was living in Baton Rouge again, on North Thirty-Eighth Street two blocks away from Harpo, where William Gambler recalls visiting him with Harpo.

According to drummer Roosevelt Sample, Lightnin' handed over his band to him, saying, "by morning I'll be gone." He went to visit relatives in Detroit and sent back word that he couldn't afford the fare home. Possibly he was concerned about his previous stay in the state penitentiary in Louisiana and preferred to be far away from the possibility of a return there. Jay Miller said he offered to help get Lightnin' back, but Lightnin' stayed away and soon moved to Pontiac, Michigan. There he lived in the house on Paddock Street belonging to Willie and Matilda Murray, and it was there to his sister's house that Harpo went at the end of 1968 to persuade Lightnin' to join him on his forthcoming gigs in New York.

After Lightnin' Slim played Harpo's shows at the Scene in 1969, there should have been a resurgence of interest in him, but instead he went back to his day job in Pontiac. It was there that promoter Fred Reif found him: "When I first re-discovered Lightnin' he was working in a small foundry in Pontiac and his hands were turning white. He took me there once. He soon quit as I was getting him more gigs. Lightnin' was living at the Murray house with Willie and Tillie, as they were called. He most likely rented a room in the house. I used to visit the Murray house a lot when Lightnin' had that room. When I used to go visit Lightnin', Miss Tillie was always very friendly to me and my friends. She was a big woman and she loved to cook. I remember one big dinner there that I was invited to. It was really the first time I had ever had 'soul' food."[45]

Reif managed to get Lightnin' back onto the blues circuit in the North, and soon Lightnin' was able to move into a house of his own with his girlfriend. By 1970, Excello had re-signed him and recorded an LP, *High and Low,* made at Quinvy Recording Studio in Sheffield, Alabama, and produced by Jerry "Swamp Dog" Williams with a larger band than Slim was used to. The LP carried an endorsement by B. B. King but was far from Slim's best work. Lightnin' started to go on tours in Europe in 1972 and 1973. There he was initially well received because of his unadulterated style, delivering precisely the music people had heard on his Feature and Excello singles. At London's 100 Club in February 1972, Slim played solo and with a band, reviewers finding his voice and guitar powers still strong and noting that he appeared to be enjoying himself. He came over as amiable and slow-talking. Reviewers wondered, though, as Jay Miller had when Lightnin' first played in Chicago, why he bothered with a string of Jimmy Reed songs when he had a rare opportunity to showcase his own talent as a songster.[46] In May that year he recorded in London for Mike Vernon, again with a band that was larger and more modern-sounding than his own laid-back style. John Broven recalls being at the studio behind the Marquee Club one Sunday afternoon when "Lightnin'" was implacable and spot-on at every take." Some later personal appearances were less well received, and people found it clear that time was taking its toll on Lightnin'. Otis Hicks, the man who opened the recording-studio door for Slim Harpo and other bluesmen from Baton Rouge to step through, died in Pontiac on July 27, 1974, of a stomach tumor. Thinking of the down-home blues, Jay Miller said, "Lightning to me was the greatest, not only of my artists, but all of them."[47]

Lazy Lester continued to record for Jay Miller until 1966, and his last Excello disc was issued that year. Lester also continued to work on and off with Lightnin' Slim, who in those days used an array of bandsmen including guitarist Joe Lasure from Opelousas; bass players Marion "Jap" Keys and "Kingfish," Lester's brother; and drummers Roosevelt Sample, William Byrd, and Sammy Drake, the latter from Crowley. They played school houses and black clubs all around Baton Rouge, across into Texas, and up into Mississippi. At some point Jay Miller finally decided the likeable and versatile young Lester was "an incurable alcoholic" and stopped using him. Visiting blues writer Mike Leadbitter found in Crowley in 1967 that "Miller was no longer interested in Lester who had borrowed a truck [with Lightnin' Slim] and crashed it. Miller says, 'They even put him in Angola and I bailed him out, but this time, "no." Lester still comes out to the studio and hangs around but he is only in his thirties and the entire situation is tragic.'"[48]

When Lightnin' Slim moved to Detroit in 1966, following the crashing of Jay Miller's vehicles, Lester stayed at home for a while, then tried out life in Chicago. In 1971 promoter Fred Reif persuaded Lester to go to Michigan to work with Lightnin' Slim, but it didn't work out for too long, and Lester returned to Baton Rouge again. After Lightnin' Slim died, Lester started to receive calls from Harpo's sister, who suggested she had room at her house and Lester could live and work from Pontiac, Michigan. In July 1975, Lester finally agreed, saying, "Miss Tillie kept bugging me to come up. She had been in touch with me for over a year . . . but when I got up here I turned sick and almost died. I stayed in the hospital four months."[49] Gradually Lester's drinking came under control, and his career was revived with the help of northern blues promoters who got Lester onto the festivals, college circuits, and international tours that had been unavailable to him at home. Reif remembers, "After Willie Murray died in 1974 or so, apparently Miss Tillie was getting lonely or something because she paid for Lester's trip back to Pontiac. Lester came up in 1975, I think it was. I really don't know the real relationship with her but he stayed with her until she passed away. When Lester was living there, that Pontiac neighborhood was a mess with lots of drugs and guns and crime. I only visited him a few times during that period."[50] Eventually, Lester found his way to California, where he reestablished his life as a touring musician, appearing at festivals wherever the blues was played. He even has his own Web site at the time of this writing and is one of the few surviving blues players from Slim Harpo's era.

Like Lester, Moses Smith also played harmonica with Lightnin' Slim through the 1960s, mixing and matching. In 1972 he toured in Europe with Slim and became a regular at the New Orleans jazz festivals. He was at several folk-blues festivals in the North and in Europe, being recorded live in Montreux, London, and Germany. One show with Lightnin' Slim captured him, "arms flailing, body weaving, and legs ducking; his performance was animation itself, a throwback to the country dance and juke joint workouts of yesteryear." In Baton Rouge, he made an LP for Excello/Blue Horizon at the Deep South Studio with Boe Melvin on guitar, produced by Lionel Whitfield. Smith also played with Tabby Thomas's Mighty House Rockers in the 1970s and in the 1980s recorded briefly with them for Sunland Records of Florida. He died in Baton Rouge on April 28, 1984.

Buddy Stewart, like Tabby Thomas, became one of the linchpins of the local music scene in Baton Rouge after Slim Harpo died. Through the late 1950s and the 1960s he maintained his band, the Top Notchers, playing residencies at white venues just as he had done through the 1950s as a member of Claiborne Williams's dance band. The Top Notchers played black clubs, too, and his guitarist, Harvey Lexing, described how they played with Harpo out on the west side at the Streamline on Highway 190, and worked gigs with Silas Hogan. They also supported all the top visiting R&B names like Jackie Wilson, Clyde McPhatter, and Johnny Taylor, who traveled without a band. Lexing said, "We was all freelance. All the musicians had to know everybody's stuff, like Slim Harpo, Lazy Lester, Lightnin' Slim." Otis Johnson confirmed, "After Slim Harpo, I played with Buddy Stewart's Top Notchers in the '60s and '70s. Stewart played at all kinds of balls and school proms as well as nightclubs. He had a busy band."[51]

Buddy Stewart also ran Top Notch Attractions from Nebraska Street in

Baton Rouge, where he worked as a kind of agent for many local artists—including Bobby Powell, Silas Hogan, Lightnin' Slim, Jimmy Anderson, and Tabby Thomas. He also represented Jackie Wilson at one stage and organized the local schedules for New Orleans stars such as Irma Thomas and Johnny Adams. His band occasionally appeared on records behind one of his several lead singers, and he may have been the owner of the Budix label, on which his nephew, singer Chuck Mitchell, recorded "Your Precious Love" sometime in the late 1960s. The song was credited to Buddy Stewart and Charles Dixon, which leads by some logic to Budix. In the 1970s Stewart opened a record store on North Acadian Boulevard, a spacious place that soon became a stop-over for record collectors on their way to Crowley, Lake Charles, and Ville Platte. Stewart dabbled in other ventures, including electrical repairs and a nightclub, the Playboy. He died in September 1997, aged seventy, following a heart attack.

Guitarist Philip Guy stayed in Baton Rouge through the 1960s, playing some gigs with Slim Harpo when Rudy Richard left the band in mid-decade. Before Harpo, he had worked with Robert Milburn's band and afterwards with several other groups. He said the local blues players would gather at meeting points like the Rockhouse in Innis or the Club Sixteen in Baton Rouge, and "all used to hook up."[52] In 1969, Guy moved to Chicago and embarked on quite an eclectic and successful career playing in the Buddy Guy band in the North, in Europe, and even in Africa. Phil Guy died on August 20, 2008, leaving his brother Buddy as the last of the Harpo-era bluesmen from the Baton Rouge area still playing successfully, albeit in a style much updated and divergent from what he learned at the feet of men like Big Papa and Slim Harpo.

Never much associated with Baton Rouge itself, Cornelius Green—Lonesome Sundown—often played in clubs there and maintained a good friendship with Slim Harpo. He was a big part of the swamp-blues scene in the eyes of Jay Miller, who liked Green's ability as a guitarist and singer and also his adaptability. Failing to make hits with discs like "Lonesome Lonely Blues" and "Hoo Doo Woman Blues," Miller made several attempts to add saxophone parts that were aimed more at the R&B and pop markets, but with no chart success. Nevertheless, Sundown continued to record for Excello until 1965, when he gave up music for construction work, joined the Apostolic Faith Fellowship, and became a minister of that church in 1966. He had been disillusioned with music and the lack of opportunities to play and to record, but he made a comeback LP in 1977 for Joliet Records, *Been Gone Too Long*, and, encouraged by label owner Bruce Bromberg, he played some shows in New Orleans and in Europe. In 1980, Green moved to Baton Rouge, and he had moved to Gonzales by 1994 when he had a stroke. He died there on April 23, 1995.

Although he never became part of the commercial recording scene, Herman E. Johnson was recorded in Baton Rouge in 1960 and 1961 by Harry Oster, who found his songs "Depression Blues" and "Leavin' Blues" particularly powerful and original. Johnson's depression was not the post–Wall Street crash but his current-day (1961) inability to find a decent job. Johnson had a deep yet expressive voice and a real command of the acoustic and electric guitars he played both with and without slide. Johnson was working as a janitor at Southern University when Oster met him, having recently been fired from the Esso refinery where he had worked for fifteen years. He had retired from his last job by 1972 when Oster's recordings were issued on an LP by Arhoolie. He died in February 1975 in Zachary, his very worthy contribution to maintaining blues traditions in Baton Rouge largely unrecognized.

Clarence Edwards also recorded for Oster, in 1959 and 1960, and saw three of his songs issued on the LP *Country Negro Jam Sessions,* issued by Folk-Lyric in 1961. Other songs from Oster's tapes were issued by Arhoolie in 1993. His voice was made for the blues, and his style reached far back to the dawn of blues records but also to more recent blues hits such as Mercy Dee's "One Room Country Shack" and Howlin' Wolf's "Smokestack Lightning." Following his recovery from the shooting incident in 1953, Edwards continued to work by day at Thomas Scrap Metal, a company formed in 1954 at 2939 Scenic Highway. At night, he occasionally played music with local musicians, including Slim Harpo and Silas Hogan. Through the 1960s, Edwards maintained a band, the Bluebird Kings, and worked every Saturday night for over ten years at a club in Calhoun near the Mississippi state line. Around 1970 he joined a group called the Cats, organized by his neighbor Henry Gray, who had recently returned to Baton Rouge after many years in the North. The Cats appeared at the New Orleans Jazz Festival annually until 1977, when Edwards left. Eventually gigs became hard to find, and Edwards concluded his blues style was out of date, saying: "People don't want to pay for that kind of music these days. I just got tired of losing sleep."[53] He had contributed arguably the best of the music on the Blue Horizon/Excello swamp-blues albums of 1970 but gained little recognition. Around 1990 he met visiting musician Steve Coleridge, who found him "a grey-haired serious looking man in his 50s," living in Scotlandville, then "an area with its good and bad spots including a few small bars."[54] Clarence was playing a four-hour gig in a sports bar on Friday nights, soon to be accompanied by Coleridge and his band. He told them, "There's nothin' better than a good piece of blues when you want to hear music," and he was persuaded to record an album, *Swamps the Word*, for Coleridge's Sidetrack label, backed by his friend Henry Gray among other younger players, with further songs from the sessions being issued in later years. Edwards died in Baton Rouge on May 20, 1993.

Henry Gray's career was in complete contrast to that of his friend Clarence, whom he had known since the 1930s. He had been born in Kenner outside New Orleans on January 15, 1925, but he was raised in Alsen, just north of Baton Rouge. He learned piano when he was nine, and within a few years was playing organ in his local Baptist church. He started playing secular music at house suppers and the like, and he said he enjoyed the Bluebird label recordings of Bill Broonzy and Sonny Boy Williamson, but he particularly liked what he heard from pianist Roosevelt Sykes. After spending part of World War II in the Army in the Philippines, he gravitated to Chicago, where he had previously sampled the blues scene and was mentored by pianist Big Maceo Merriweather, rather than back to Baton Rouge. He worked in several bands, including that of fellow Louisianian Little Walter. In 1956 he took a step up into the Howlin' Wolf band, where he remained for a dozen years, recording sessions with Wolf, Jimmy Rogers, Jimmy Reed, and other stars of the Chicago blues scene. He tired of the schedule, though, and moved back to Baton Rouge in 1968 to look after his sick father. He became a roofer for the parish school board by day and an occasional musician by night. He formed the Cats, whose early struggles were described to the *Advocate* in 1987 by their long-time drummer, Zack "the Cat" Gaines: "We'd play at Alsen, then wind up at Jackson at Miz Scott's place. We'd play when there be water all over the place, wading in water at Miz Scott's. . . . We'd play one Saturday and the next Saturday I'd ask, 'where's Henry?' Oh Henry gone to Chicago. Then a couple weeks, there'd be Henry back again. Next couple of weeks he'd be gone again."[55]

When things stabilized for Gray in Baton Rouge, he took to playing organ as often as piano. In 1970 he recorded for Jay Miller's Blues Unlimited label and for Arhoolie and started to appear at all the local jazz and blues festivals. In February 1978, Gray talked to Ed Cullen of the *Advocate* about why he had returned home—"I stayed on the road 26 years and I just got tired. It's that simple"—and how he found the blues scene on his return home. He emphasized that family ties were overriding the disadvantages of the local music scene: "What sustains us is our kids. We're still working, still scratching. . . . until about 15 years ago a black man couldn't get into [musicians' union] Local 10, all you had was the black local."[56] The musicians registered with the black section of the union had limited employment options in comparison with white union members up until the mid-1960s when unions merged. Slim Harpo was a member of the union for some years, William Gambler confirming, "he was a member of the union for a while, for certain."[57]

From 1977, Gray started to accept offers to tour in Germany and other parts of Europe on the back of recordings for a German label, Bluebeat. Since then, he has been in demand at festivals across the United States and Europe and has recorded albums for specialist labels like Blind Pig, Wolf, Telarc, Blue House, Lucky Cat, and Hightone. At one point during a hectic tour in Europe he lost track of his schedule, telling Steve Coleridge: "You say we're in Belfast? I thought we were in Belgium." He appeared in Martin Scorsese's PBS series *The Blues*, and in 2006 he was awarded the National Heritage Fellowship Award by the National Endowment for the Arts. At the time of this writing, he is still playing.

Schoolboy Cleve had moved to Los Angeles in 1959 and largely retired from music for ten years, although he returned briefly at some point to make one fine rocking blues single, "New Kind of Loving" and "Leaving You Baby," issued in 1963 on Lloyd Renaud's Opelousas-based Renaud Records. In 1970 he moved to San Francisco and was inspired to restart a musical career in the local nightclubs and college venues. In 1972 he played at the Bay Area Blues Festival and was also persuaded to record for blues enthusiast Don Lindenau, who ran the small Blues Connoisseur label. Those discs, including "My Heart Is Crying," led him to start his own label, Cherrie Records, and to write new songs, including "Bicentennial Blues." In all, his records are among the best of the down-home blues by Baton Rouge artists. He died on February 5, 2008, in Daly City, California, half a continent away from his hometown and light years away from the days when he was a regular arrestee in the small print of the *Advocate*.

Matthew "Boogie Jake" Jacobs also spent much of his later life in California, moving to Berkeley in the early 1960s. He was discovered there a few years later by Tom Mazzolini, who persuaded Jake to appear at his San Francisco Blues Festivals in the late 1960s. In the 1970s he too saw a disc, "Automobile Blues," out on Blues Connoisseur, having contacted the label about releasing a session he had recorded himself backed by Mark Hummel and the Blues Survivors. Eventually Jake returned to Louisiana, playing music just for himself and serving as a deacon in his church. Boogie Jake died in December 2013.

Through the 1960s, pianist Robert Milburn had continued to play at clubs in the Baton Rouge area, although his set became less and less linked to the blues or even R&B. He took to playing the organ in a soul and pop-rock style, saying, "Black people don't care for the blues. If I go in a black club and do the blues they want me out the back door. . . . they want the latest up to date stuff."[58] Milburn never saw himself as a frontline recording artist, and in the post-Harpo period he recorded little, principally a 1982 session for Sunland Records of Val Rico, Florida, that yielded a single, "Money Hustlin' Woman," and a various-artists LP that featured Raful Neal, Henry Gray, Tabby Thomas, and Whispering Smith. Robert Milburn died in October 1983 in Baton Rouge.

Tabby Thomas was never actually a bluesman at all, but an R&B enthusiast who also embraced rock 'n' roll and soul music during his recording career. Then, when the blues was almost gone in the post-Harpo decade, Tabby reinvented himself as the front man for revival of the blues in Baton Rouge. His bar and music venue, Tabby's Blues Box, was a focus for old and new musicians and visiting blues fans for over twenty years after it opened in 1980. Visiting musician Steve Coleridge said:

> I think most musicians would agree about Tabby's limited musical abilities, though his singing was pretty good despite his trying to model himself on Johnny Mathis, and I remember the scorn some of them injected when they said his name. But Tabby did have drive, and the Blues Box as an institution certainly had an immense influence and led to a lot of careers getting a second wind. As well as Clarence Edwards, Silas Hogan and Arthur Kelley, I remember seeing Chicago Bob Nelson there and the vastly underrated Jimmy Dotson, not to mention all the New Orleans people who would always stop by there. We often had long chats, and he gave me good advice that saved several awkward situations. He could certainly talk his way into or out of anything, and I have a soft spot for the old rogue.[59]

Tabby was quite a hustler and had remained one of the most active of the Baton Rouge musicians even before he established his Blues Box. As early as 1961, he got himself a short-lived music column in the *News Leader* and— following his 1950s discs on Delta, Feature, Zynn, Rocko, and Excello, which were mainly in a rocking R&B style—he made more soul-sounding discs in the 1960s on labels including Tic-Toc, 3 Stars, Vedette, Soul Int., Jin, Hip, Bullseye, and Sunland. He remained in touch with Slim Harpo all through the 1960s, and on a couple of occasions he accompanied Harpo on recording trips to Nashville.

Lovell Moore spoke about Harpo taking Tabby up there to try to get him onto records, and how they all shared one motel room to save money, but it is not clear whether Tabby went as a prospective artist or just as a companion with an interest in certain songs. Tabby said, "I went to Nashville, and wrote a couple of things for Slim. I wrote 'My Baby She's Got It' and 'I'm Sorry Baby.'" Thomas had recorded a similarly titled but different song, "My Baby's Got It," for Jay Miller's Zynn label some years before, and Harpo's session came early in 1968. Tabby continued, "I was in Nashville, went up there with him and his wife, and I stepped out of the studio to get some water—they had a studio at Excello's main office—and I saw Slim and a man in there and they was arguing. Slim was saying, 'Whyncha give the man the credits for the song, 'cause he's a good writer, we're gonna need him up the road.' [The man] said, 'No we ain't gonna let him in on this,' and when the record came out they didn't put my name on it and that really hurt me." But Tabby was grateful for Slim's efforts to promote him: "I had a lot of respect for Slim Harpo. He always used to come by and tell me, 'don't give up, just keep on man, one of these days somethin' gonna shake.'"[60]

Eventually, Tabby decided to make things shake himself. In 1969 he set up his own Blue Beat label to record his own band and friends like Silas Hogan. The first single by his son, Chris Thomas (King), was on Blue Beat, too. Tabby made his recordings locally, and they were pressed a few hundred copies at a time to sell in local stores and at gigs. He would mail them to clubs as a kind of calling card to drum up bookings. However, in the late 1970s he was persuaded by Mark Miller, J. D.'s son, to make an LP for the Miller family's Blues Unlimited label. The resultant 25 Years with the Blues was, at best, described by reviewers as having "honest merit."[61] Multi-instrumentalist Otis Johnson had played with both Harpo and Thomas and had no doubt that "Harpo and Tabby, they were two totally different kinds of musicians. Tabby was a showman. But Harpo was so bluesy, he really played the blues."[62]

All this time, Thomas was working at a chemical plant by day, playing music when he could. He was finding new music venues hard to come by. Then in 1979 he took the decision to open his own venue, and a blues club at that, Tabby's Blues Box. His father had owned nightclubs in the past, and in his youth Tabby had seen a vibrant black entertainment scene around the Temple Roof Garden and North Boulevard generally. He still went to eat at Rose and Thomas's Café on North Boulevard, and one day he saw the building next door was empty. Rose gave him the address of the owner, who ran Griffon's Drug Store on Government Street. Tabby took the chance to rent one of the iconic buildings of his past, 1314 North Boulevard, for his Blues Box, gaining the required planning permissions when he developed the line that this was not just a nightclub or bar but a "Heritage Center" with the aim of promoting the music of Baton Rouge. He said, "When I opened the Blues Box I was [union] supervisor at a plant. . . . I was doing fine." But this was what he wanted to do, and he persevered despite his not knowing anything about the business. He had not acquired a liquor license by opening night, so "I had to give the stuff away, and the place was like that [packed]." He later said, "The Blues Box was really the first club in Baton Rouge where blacks and whites could listen to blues and mingle. . . . When the kids from LSU discovered us, we couldn't keep them out of there." In contrast to many venues from his past, he emphasized to visiting blues fans that "we never had an incident there—we never had no fights,"[63] although the court records show otherwise.

In 1980 a legendary star of New Orleans R&B, Huey "Piano" Smith, somewhat down from the peak of his career with memorable songs like "Rockin' Pneumonia and the Boogie Woogie Flu," moved to Baton Rouge. His biographer John Wirt has cataloged some of the difficulties Huey encountered adjusting to the more staid atmosphere there. One problem was unexpected; when Huey talked to Tabby Thomas about playing at the new Blues Box, Thomas advised him that it was for Baton Rouge talent only. Smith rarely played in Baton Rouge despite living there over thirty-five years. At about the same time, nationally famous soul-singer Percy Sledge moved to Baton Rouge, and he too kept a fairly low profile locally.

In the late 1980s, Tabby Thomas at last joined the list of performers persuaded to bring their wares to Europe, and he was generally well received for his entertaining and eclectic shows. However, back at home the live music scene was deteriorating again. Several blues fans, musicians, and writers who visited at that time found the town full of boarded-up clubs and Tabby's enterprise barely surviving.[64] In 1999, another round of urban improvement saw the Blues Box demolished for road widening. Thomas moved it to Lafayette Street, and it survived there until Tabby had a stroke in 2004. He had already had a bad automobile accident in 2002. Tabby Thomas died on January 1, 2014. One of his seven children, Chris Thomas King, said, "People who knew my dad well knew that he could be a little bit ornery. His stubbornness was that he loved his music. He was a champion for Louisiana's blues music during times when a lot of people turned away from it. He carried it on and passed it on."[65] Tabby himself described his limitations and his purpose to the *Philadelphia Inquirer* when he played a show in Atlanta in 1991: "I want to add to (the blues). I can't be Muddy Waters. I can't be Howlin' Wolf. I don't play like B. B. King. I don't want to be them people, I'm just myself. But I want to add something to it for my legacy, for my children, for my grandchildren. . . . I can get up there and play with a band and I don't even know them. That's what they call art, when you take nothing and make something. That's artistic."[66]

Tabby's long-time comrade in the Baton Rouge music scene, Buddy Stewart, founded a different type of music venue around the same time Tabby opened his club. This was Buddy's Rock Shop, a record store he operated in the years after he gave up his Top Notchers band. The store continued for many years, and when Stewart died in 1997, it was kept going by his daughter, Philliper, who now runs it as the Rhythm Museum and Rock Shop, selling collectibles in memory of Buddy's passion for playing, singing, writing, and promoting music. The Buddy Stewart Music Foundation also helps young musicians to keep live music going in Baton Rouge.

Harmonica player Raful Neal became one of Slim Harpo's closest friends and disciples during the 1960s. Characterized as "a large, burly man with a perpetual twinkle in his eye,"[67] Neal could and probably should have recorded for Excello like Harpo. However, he knew enough about Harpo's problems with Jay Miller to be wary that he might not get his due. He did go to Crowley with Harpo on one occasion, but Miller did not find him sufficiently interesting to record. Neal said, "Me and Jay Miller never could get together on a recording session. I just wouldn't cooperate the way Slim said I should'a." Raful's son, Kenny Neal, told *Living Blues* magazine's founding coeditor Jim O'Neal that he recalled Slim Harpo from when he was a child: "I can remember him and my dad being real close. I remember him telling my dad one time about a song called 'Scratch My Back.' And after Slim left, my dad said, 'That's got to be the most ridiculous thing I ever heard. Scratch my back. Who would want to hear that?' I had a chance to meet Slim Harpo, Lazy Lester, and all of the guys like that [when] my dad was in his twenties and really up on his instrument and it was prime time for him. And I got a chance to play on WXOK with my dad. Slim would play, Dad would play. That was a cool time."[68]

Raful Neal had a growing family by the early 1960s, eventually extending into double figures, and a maintenance job at the Baton Rouge Housing Authority. All this had to be weighed alongside his interest in a career in music, which he found increasingly difficult to maintain. He said that desegregation and civil rights brought their own problems at that time. "It was hard. Things got bad for musicians. They [white businesses] didn't want to face integration so, in about '63, they stopped hiring black bands for about ten years. We lost our regular gig at the Bentley hotel. . . . I was living in Port Allen. They didn't want integration there."[69] From time to time, Neal would drive a scrap-iron or cane truck for Harpo, but occasionally he would find that doing Slim a favor was almost at his own expense. On February 19, 1966, the *Advocate* described how "four persons escaped serious injury in a traffic collision here today. . . . officers said the incident occurred when a vehicle driven by Kenneth Weaver collided with a vehicle operated by Raful Neal Jr., 29, Port Allen negro. . . . Weaver failed to yield the right of way to Neal."

Ray Moore, Harpo's nephew, described another connection between the Moore and Neal families in the mid-1960s: "I recall my uncle taking me to Raful Neal's house a few times. Raful Neal's nephew and I went to high school together. We would both brag on our uncles, who has the latest hit and all that stuff. My uncle was the reason I started a local group. We would jam at each other houses on weekends. I start out playing lead guitar and later switch to keyboard because we had too many guitar players in the group. The group consist of my schoolmates which included the Jackson brothers, Oray on bass, Johnell on lead guitar, Gano on drums, along with Patrick Williams on lead guitar, Anaray Neal on sax, nephew of Raful, and Kenny Neal on trumpet, son of Raful. My uncle gave me my first microphone that we used in my group."[70]

Raful Neal did make the occasional recording session during the 1960s. In 1965 he recorded "It's Getting Late in the Evening" for Carol Rachou's La Louisianne Records of Lafayette, and soon after he recorded for Lionel Whitfield's Whit Records. Lionel was related to Gilbert Whitfield, who ran the Dew Drop Inn on Scotland Avenue, and he worked as a musician at that club and at the Bellemont Hotel. In the 1960s, Whit was run from Whitfield's house on Myrtle Avenue in Baton Rouge. Whitfield recorded his own band and various former members and associates, including Bobby Powell, his biggest artist, who also had an LP issued by Excello; Larry Seibert; Merle Spears; and Whispering Smith. The Whit label had some degree of national profile in the mid-1960s with Bobby Powell's hits, and it provided an outlet for truck-driver Merle Spears, born in Baton Rouge in 1939, who was brought up with gospel music and R&B, his father being both a Baptist minister and owner of a nightclub. By the time Raful Neal recorded for the label with "Let's Work Together," Whitfield had a manufacturing-and-distribution deal as an offshoot of Stan Lewis's Jewel label in Shreveport, Louisiana, following a deal with Cosimo Matassa's Dover Records in New Orleans. Raful Neal was accompanied on his Whit sessions by James Johnson and Rudy Richard, late of the Harpo band, and Roy Lee Shepherd and Murdock Stewart. After Whit, Raful recorded for the local Tic-Toc label of Tabby Thomas.

Although Raful Neal largely gave up playing live gigs in the late 1960s, whenever he did play, he tried to include Harpo's ex-bandsmen because they were very familiar with the down-home style he wanted to play. In 1972, blues collector Hasse Andreasson reported a trip to Baton Rouge, visiting "the American Legion on 13th South Street where Raful Neal was playing. Backed by Slim Harpo's former band including guitarist Rudolph Richard, Neal performed a mix of blues and soul . . . fine versions of 'Drivin' Wheel,' 'Let's Work Together' and 'Jody's Got Your Girl and Gone.'"[71] Increasingly, Neal started to involve his own sons in his band, and later in the 1970s things turned around when he found himself a member of *their* band, the Neal Brothers Funk Band. In 1977 the Neal brothers—Kenny Ray, Noel, Larry, and Little Ray—spent some time working with Buddy Guy in the North and touring in Canada. Kenny Neal remembered being involved with music as early as 1969 or 1970: "By age 12 or 13 I would fill in on any instrument Raful needed. . . . He had Rudolph Richard on guitar, Murdock Stewart on drums, and [my brother] Ray Neal on bass." Kenny grew up in Erwinville before the family moved into Baton Rouge, and he was familiar with the musicians living there. "Lonesome Sundown was one of the guys around, and Mose Smith, and this guy named 'Chewing Gum.' And the William Wolfolk band was there, called the Silver Spoons."[72]

In 1982 and 1983, Raful made some singles in Baton Rouge for Sunland Records of Val Rico, Florida, after a disc jockey saw him play in Baton Rouge while recording Henry Gray and others for Sunland's anthology of Louisiana blues. By 1987 Raful had traveled to the King Snake studio in Sanford, Florida, to record an entire album, *Louisiana Legend,* for Sunland's sister label,

Fantastic. One reviewer called it "raw, pure blues, without any apologies" and that was not far off the mark for that time. Kenny Neal recorded an LP, *Bio on the Bayou*, the next year for the associated King Snake label. By now, Raful was a regular at the New Orleans and Baton Rouge blues festivals. A report in 1990 found, "Every weekend Raful plays the Turning Point, the best club in Baton Rouge, on Choctaw and Acadian. His band includes James Johnson, a big, cheerful man with an afro and a Frank Zappa beard who plays sitting down because of a back injury."[73] In the 1990s Neal saw albums issued by Alligator, Ichiban, and La Louisianne.

Raful Neal died on September 1, 2004, after a battle with cancer. He was one of the last authentic bluesmen of the Harpo era, but he also left the legacy of the various blues and funk sounds created by members of his family, and in particular by Kenny Neal, who, like his father, has worked to keep not only a blues band together but the sound and spirit of the blues in Baton Rouge. Kenny said he first got a harmonica of his own when he went into one of Slim Harpo's trailers: "Slim was playing a joke on me. He said, 'Go inside, son, and see if any more equipment left in there.' And when I went inside he closed the doors and it got pitch black dark, and I freaked out. And he was saying, 'Oh I'm sorry, son, I'm so sorry.' He was trying to chill me out and he gave me a harmonica. And that soothes me out man. I went around the back of the house blowing on that thing. I was maybe nine, ten years old." Kenny was helped by Rudy Richard, too—"[he] taught me so much because he would tell me where the A was, the B flat, the C chord. And it wasn't around the house; it was on the gig. I learned on the job; played with Dad's band around age 12 or 13."[74]

HARPO'S MUSICIANS

Very few members of the several incarnations of Harpo's King Bees are still playing. James Johnson is the main man standing, but enough of the others continued playing off and on through the forty-six years since Harpo's passing that together their efforts have ingrained his songs, and to some extent his style, in the communal memory of the blues world.

The first to pick up Slim's music, and even his guitar, was his main lead man down the years, Rudy Richard. "I sold, practically gave, James' guitar to Rudy," remembered Lovell.[75] Richard's initial plan was to re-form Slim's band, even though he himself had left during Slim's later years, but he couldn't get the project off the ground. James Johnson had already given up playing with Harpo, as had Willie Parker and Sammy K. Brown. Boe Melvin had his own band, as did Simmie and Jesse Kinchen. Richard said later, "About a month after he died . . . I said, 'I'm gonna take this band and we're gonna play some music.' They all turned it down, 'Oh no, I'm not playing no more.' So everything was that."[76]

On leaving Harpo's band, Rudy had kept his base in Baton Rouge, where he worked for about twenty years as a handyman at a local insurance company. He had met his wife, Willie Belle, at a show at the Streamline in west Baton Rouge, and he always continued to play the blues at least part-time. He played with Raful Neal for a while, and then he was touted in the *Advocate* of August 16, 1985, as "the new heavyweight addition to Major Handy's band." Joseph Major Handy had formed a zydeco band called the Wolf Couchon, but he was an R&B guitarist before he switched to zydeco accordion after working with Rockin' Dopsie, one of the masters of that idiom. Handy was born in Lafayette in 1947 and joined Jerry Thomas and his Rhythm Rockers in St. Martinville in his teens. Thomas was his cousin's husband. After service in the Marines, Handy joined Dopsie, another cousin by marriage, until he formed his own Louisiana Blues Band and recorded for Collier Records and Maison De Soul. The Wolf Couchon band made an LP for Crescendo Records in 1985, produced by Johnny Palazzotto of Baton Rouge, and toured locally and as far as California and Canada. Rudy Richard said, "I played with the Wolf Couchons in Los Angeles; that's where I learned to play more accordion—I started to learn the accordion from Clifton Chenier [years before]. Clifton Chenier played at the Richard's club. Chenier and Sundown played together and Lonesome Sundown used to call me up on stage. 'Come on Rudy, do a song, man'; and I'd go up and do it."[77]

In 1990, Rudy was playing what Steve Coleridge called "blues and zydeco guitar" with Coleridge's band, Short Fuse, then based in Baton Rouge, and with Harpo's last drummer, Jesse Kinchen. They played locally and as far away as Florida, Georgia, and South Carolina. In Coleridge's view, "Richard's picking is perhaps the most influential amongst Baton Rouge players and he has been credited as an influence by Kenny Neal and Troy Turner." Richard said that he had inherited some of Slim Harpo's approach to the musical life: "I think that if you go out there and play for the public you should be ready to see that they enjoy themselves. You can't go up there and stand like a statue and act like you're mad. The best way to meet the people is to be happy and

I'm a very happy guitar player."[78] Lynn Ourso agreed, saying, "Rudy was a very good guitar man. I first met him at the Glass Hat and noticed he had no heels on his shoes; I thought that was a look he wanted. Years later he would come in to my family's retail operation and I would wait on him and talk music. He had become a zydeco artist in his own right and was playing accordion and Cajun squeeze box rather than guitar."[79]

Richard sometimes led his own band, Rudy Richard and the Zydeco Express, until diabetes complications made it difficult. He played an acclaimed laid-back swamp-blues set with Lazy Lester at the Ponderosa Stomp Festival in New Orleans in 2011; James Johnson also appeared at the same event. Both of them appeared occasionally at the annual River City Blues Festival in Baton Rouge, as did Big Boe Melvin through the 1980s and 1990s, along with many of Slim's contemporaries. In his later years, Rudy became a celebrated conduit from Baton Rouge's blues past, playing with Kenny Neal and others keen to keep the music going. He still played occasional gigs until 2014, when his illnesses caught up with him. Rudy Richard died on September 22, 2014. "He was truly a blues legend in this town," said Johnny Palazzotto. "Two weeks before he died more than a thousand people showed up for his benefit at Phil Brady's Bar and Grill. Every musician adored Rudy Richard."[80]

At the time Slim Harpo died, James Johnson was largely out of the music scene. He had first quit the band in 1966, but he continued to play gigs with Harpo occasionally. They had a slightly stormy relationship, which Johnson summed up with the philosophy, "It's hard playing the blues. Sometimes it's fun, sometimes it isn't. But that's just like anything else." Johnson worked shows with Harpo on and off until 1968, by which time the recent death of his mother had, he said, "kind of slowed me down. And then they came out with this disco stuff. So the blues just dropped. I didn't play for about 14 years. I just hung myself up. I couldn't see no future in the guitar." He worked as a mechanic on the LSU campus and played at local jam sessions occasionally. Following this self-imposed retirement, Raful Neal persuaded James to return in the 1980s, first on bass and then on guitar. Johnson says, "I told Raful, 'I'll help you out, till you find somebody, but I don't really want to get back in it again.' But he wouldn't look for nobody. I stayed with him till he was gone." They played together almost until Neal died in 2004 and had a relationship Johnson enjoyed better than the one with Harpo. "[Raful] was a good guy to work with, kept you laughing all the time, always had a joke to tell or something."[81]

Since 2004, Johnson has appeared occasionally at blues events and jam sessions, and one of these led to his being seen by a movie crew and recruited to appear as the blues guitar player in the 2007 film *A Good Man Is Hard to Find*. James recalls this, and his old touring days, with modesty, telling local reporters, "I did music because I liked it, not to try to be a star. I guess it's because of my parents. They were kind of laid back, so they kind of had me laid back. That's about it." Only in 2014 did James Johnson release his first CD as a lead artist, *Stingin' & Buzzin'*, after a local musician, Miguel Hernandez, called him and proposed they make a CD. "I said yes. I thought I should leave a little legacy of my own." Two blues fans living in Baton Rouge, Gordon Mese and Arnaud Staib, funded the CD after hearing Johnson play at Tabby's Blues Box for many years. Apart from the title, there's some of Harpo in the CD, but Johnson feels strongly about other local artists and about the music he plays: "I'm a bluesman, that's what I like. Everybody talks about Slim. Alright. But there's been a lot of good players from Baton Rouge and I think others like Lightnin' Slim and Big Papa should get more credit for the music too."[82]

Apart from Johnson and Richard, several other guitarists worked with Harpo down the years. None more so than Big Boe Melvin, who recorded with Harpo both before and after the King Bees of the Richard and Johnson period. Melvin remained one of the mainstays of the local black music scene after Harpo died, even if he often wandered some way away from Harpo's traditional blues-based style. Melvin had learned his music in the Clinton area, where he first worked as a teenager with Papa Tilley after Buddy and Phil Guy left that band. Phil Guy said: "He used to sing but something happened to his voice."[83] He worked with guitarist Boogie Jake, too, and Jake remembers, "Yeah, Boogie Jake and the Houserockers—I had an old boy named Melvin and he was my lead guitar man. I taught him to play and I'd have to hit him on the fingers. And that rascal got to playing so good, it made me look bad! He was good."[84]

By the time Harpo died, Boe had already left to form his own group, the Nighthawks. Given the changing nature of black music and the youth of many of Boe's musicians, the Nighthawks provided an up-to-date revue show that ranged from R&B to soul to pop. Their exploits were tracked by the *News Leader* in its "On the Avenue" feature, a throwback to the days when every city had a thriving black area where all the newest sights and sounds were to be found. On December 13, 1970, the paper gave a rundown of the members of the Nighthawks as well as the entertainment available that day:

"Playboy Club, 1526 Terrace—big dance every Weds night featuring Big Bo Melvin and the Nighthawks comprising James Robinson, vocal, Low Down Sammy, bass, Herman Jackson drums, Reginald Hardesty and Napoleon Martin, saxes." Other Baton Rouge venues that week included Byrd's Satellite Lounge, where Chuck Mitchell played on Fridays and the Nighthawks on Saturdays; the Golden Bull at 2500 North Boulevard, where the Herculoids and Chuck Mitchell were to be found on Thursdays; and the Five Crown Social Club on Thirteenth Street, where the Herculoids and Chuck Mitchell came in on Saturdays. Eighteen months later, on August 6, 1972, the *News Leader* confirmed: "Bo Melvin and Nighthawks still appearing Saturdays at Wilson and Henry Byrd's Satellite Lounge on the west side, Highway 190. On Sundays, Simmie and the Dynamics with Larry Washington, vocal."

A year later, on August 26, 1973, it was reported, "The Nighthawks, one of Baton Rouge's foremost entertainment acts, along with vocalist James Robertson, opened an indefinite engagement at the posh Jaguar Lounge in Scotlandville last Saturday. . . . The group has for a number of years been a mainstay at Byrd's Satellite Lounge. Most recent recording is on the Big Boe label, a subsidiary of Montel. It's 'Do The Best I Can' featuring James Robertson on vocal. See the Nighthawks for unparalleled showmanship and wide range of musical artistry." Around this time, Melvin also issued an LP of his family band, *Boe Melvin and the Night Hawks,* featuring songs written by his daughter and keyboards played by Little Boe (Boe Melvin Hill Jr.). Big Boe was on guitar with other support by Noel Neal, Roy Johnson, Danny Johnson, James Bell, and singer Janet Johnson. Phil Guy remembered in the 1980s, "The Nighthawks didn't really get caught up in the blues, but they *can* play the blues like crazy." Sammy Thornton, Boe's bass player, used to be Buddy Guy's bass player. In March 1986, when the *News Leader* was advertising shows by Bobby Bland and Millie Jackson at Southern University, their backing band was furnished by Big Boe Melvin's Nighthawks. Kenny Neal remembered Boe's days at Byrd's Satellite Lounge: "At the time Boe was trying to keep up with the top 40. . . . he covered every Bobby Bland and Johnny Taylor record that was out, [but] Boe is really a hard core bluesman. When I sit in with him now [1988], you better be ready to ride. He's one of those guys can hit a note and make your hundred notes look like, y'know, half a note."[85] Boe Melvin Hill continued to play locally at music festivals until he died, like Harpo, at a relatively young age. He died on the day before Christmas 1995 in Baton Rouge.

Among Harpo's other musicians, the Kinchen family figured throughout his career. The best known, Jessie C. "Little Jesse" Kinchen, joined Harpo on drums toward the end of his recording and touring career. He was the only one who went to both New York and California with Slim. His father, Joseph Kinchen, born in 1926 in the Denham Springs area just to the east of Baton Rouge, played guitar with Big Papa and the Country Boys and then with Harpo in the days when Slim first formed a group in the wake of his first records. At some point Joseph, known by some musicians as "T. J.," moved to New York, where he died in 1997. His brother, Simmie Kinchen, played with Harpo and Boe Melvin at times before he formed his group Simmie and the Uptighters. Little Jesse continued in music off and on, including at Baton Rouge music festivals, where he became increasingly in demand as "Slim Harpo's drummer," surfacing and apparently disappearing on and off down the years. In 1990 he was interviewed by Steve Coleridge while playing with Coleridge's band on a tour from Alabama up to Illinois. In 2010 he spoke to Johnny Palazzotto about Harpo: "After Slim, I stopped playing for a while. Then I played with Bobby Powell and started to get back. But Slim, that was the man that helped me, and brought me out. Every time I go in a club, I think about him. Always. Slim never got so high as he could have got [in the business,] but Slim made the kind of blues that everybody could get. Like that 'Mailbox Blues,' haven't you gone to the box for something you didn't get? And Slim didn't care what color you was, if you could play the blues." Jesse added that, when Harpo's songs were taken up by rock groups, "he loved it."

Harpo used several drummers before Kinchen. As far as Slim's various relations and musicians recall, these were Pee Wee Johnson, a man named Ernest who was possibly one of Slim's relatives, and Wilbert Byrd, who was part of the family who ran Byrd's Satellite Lounge, motel, and restaurant. Harpo's best-known drummer, Sammy K. Brown, was from Woodville, Mississippi, not far over the Louisiana state line, born in 1943 to Jake and Carrie Brown. It is not clear when he came to Baton Rouge, but he joined Harpo's group around 1960 and certainly made many of Harpo's regular gigs and tours as well as most of his recording sessions in the early 1960s. "He lived on the other side of town, on the south side," William Gambler remembers, though sometimes Brown and James Johnson would stay with Rudy Richard in his house opposite Harpo's own. Like Rudy Richard and James Johnson, Brown has in the past been credited with even more appearances on Harpo's discs than he actually made, but he was definitely the man who made Harpo's beat for some years. Known to his family as "Teedy," Brown was used by Jay Miller on recording sessions with other singers as well. Beyond that, little is known of his musical career. He died, also quite young, in a Baton Rouge hospital on February 7, 1989. James Johnson confirmed, "Sammy died young. He was some drummer, though."[86]

And then we come to Harpo's horn section, often just Willie "Pro" Parker, who also operated pretty much under the radar after Harpo died. He was originally recruited, William Gambler recalls, when Harpo realized that he needed more variety to his sound on live gigs, particularly those played before white teenagers who were weaned on R&B and rock 'n' roll. "There was a time when saxophones were popular, so Slim found Pro some way, just to add that to his sound. Slim used to have just drums and guitars before that." Gambler remembers Pro as "a fun-loving person. He liked a drink."[87] It seems that Parker had left Harpo by the time he started recording in Memphis and taking more gigs a long way from home. Pro was just forty-three years old and living on Van Buren Street in Baton Rouge when he died on July 30, 1977, at the Earl K. Long Memorial Hospital. He was survived by his parents, Charlie Parker and Christine Adams, his sister Gertie Mae, and his brother Louis. How could he not have been a saxophonist with a father of that name?

THE LAST OF THE OLD-TIME RECORD MEN

The record men who brought Harpo's music to the marketplace both outlived him. Ernie Young, who came late in life to his twenty-year career selling records and whose role in promoting both gospel and blues music is often undervalued, died in June 1977 in Nashville at the age of eighty-four. After his gradual retirement in the late 1960s, Young remained at 1031 Overton Lea Drive in the Nashville suburb of Oak Hill, where he had lived since the 1950s, an address celebrated on an Excello disc as an instrumental title. He still played an extensive collection of easy-listening music that he had built up at home while he was recording Nashville's finest roots sounds at work and helping turn Jay Miller's recordings into discs and the careers of Louisiana artists like Slim Harpo into names that would endure.

Jay Miller died in March 1996 at Lourdes Hospital in Lafayette, Louisiana, aged seventy-three, from complications following heart-bypass surgery. His passing was noted not just locally but in the general and specialist music press alike, who acknowledged his role in capturing the Cajun, hillbilly, and blues music of Louisiana as well as playing a major part in the creation of swamp-pop music. He had continued in and out of the record business for some years after losing his Excello deal, running Modern Sound Studios and later Master-Trak Studios in Crowley with his son, Mark, an engineer who still runs the studio today. The Ford Building that housed his late-1960s studio was purchased in 2000 from his family and since 2006 has housed Crowley City Hall, the History of Crowley Museum, the Rice Interpretive Center, and the J. D. Miller Recording Studio Museum, showcasing the original recording equipment and musical instruments from historic Miller recording sessions. Mark Miller runs the center, now called Master-Trak Enterprises, where Cajun, zydeco, and swamp-pop bands continue to record. Although J. D. Miller's relationship with Harpo was often strained, Slim's musicians say that he did always acknowledge Miller's expertise and role in developing the recordings they made together. Other musicians involved in the Harpo sessions agreed. Pianist Katie Webster told interviewer Paul Harris: "I always admired Miller, always had the greatest of respect for him because he was a good producer back in those swamps. You had to do it over until you got it right, that's just the way he was—J. D. had a very keen ear and if something didn't sound right—'stop, start all over again'—cause we didn't have the electronics that we do now." Saxophonist Lionel Torrance concurred: "J. D. Miller's a businessman [but] in the studio he knew what he wanted. . . . he had him something going."[88]

And what of that other kind of record man, Ray "Diggie Doo" Meaders, who played a leading part in exposing R&B and blues music locally and in connecting bluesmen with Jay Miller? After leaving Baton Rouge for Memphis, he wound up in 1964 in Dayton, Ohio, and during the late 1960s he was also regional president of the National Association of Television and Radio Announcers. There he helped pass a resolution that NATRA was "appalled at the lack of black ownership or management of broadcast stations or record companies."[89] As "Big Ray" Meaders, he was part of the formation of WDAO as the first all-R&B-formatted FM station, and which became black-owned, in the country. He covered civic events and ball games as well as music programs. After retiring from radio, he stayed in Ohio and died in Dayton in July 1988. As a war veteran of six months' service in 1945, he had been treated at the Veterans Administration Center of the Good Samaritan in Dayton.

ALL ABOUT THE MUSIC

Rudy Richard, James Johnson, and Jesse Kinchen were among the best placed to see Harpo at work with various record men, including Jay Miller, and they all described traits and an approach to recording in Slim Harpo that others have seen in Jay Miller when it came to the business of making records. Harpo's band mates remembered Slim as an easygoing, relaxed man. But when it was time to make music, they said, it was different and he was very exacting. Johnson reflected, "You had to do what Slim say. He wasn't a real hard guy to get along with, but he had his ways. If he told you to do something he'd expect you to do it, as simple as that. . . . When you got to the gig you had to step on it, because he didn't want no mess."[90] Even talking about their early times together, "He wasn't making money then. We just wanted to play, so we fell right in with Slim. He was all about the music."[91] To Rudy Richard, "He was a nice, nice guy, but he really meant business. He wanted everybody trying to do it right."[92] Looking back, Kinchen said, "If you're into the blues, like Slim, it's going to be all right. Anytime we do it, if we do it with Slim, it's gonna be all right. Slim always had a good feeling."[93]

All of Slim's focus on his music and his sometimes hard-tasking approach were for a purpose, though. As William Gambler described, "When he did get success, that was what he wanted. It was what he'd worked for. It wasn't a surprise."[94] Just before Harpo died, he and Lovell had gone to get passports for a trip to England, and Gambler later said, "In all probability, I would have had the house to myself, because if he got over there, he was going to stay there and enjoy that. He did like entertaining. Entertainers get it in their minds, 'I'm a star. I'm a celebrity. Look at me.' He had the same attitude. It is an experience to think that you came from nothing to where you got millions of people that know who you are."[95]

8. THE HERITAGE BLUES

FESTIVAL TIME

There came a time in the early 1970s when Slim Harpo had died, players like
James Johnson had "hung myself up," the nightclubs were promoting the
newer sounds of soulful R&B and rock music, and urban renewal had pretty
much done in the clubs and commerce on North Boulevard. The rise of black
awareness had pushed the old music to the background of black history, and
there was little sign that the jukebox blues of Lightnin' Slim or Slim Harpo
or anyone else of their generation might survive the devastation of the soul
era and the LP-driven market of rock music.

By 1978, the blues was becoming a forgotten music, a curiosity, when
the *Sunday Advocate* sent reporter Ed Cullen to meet and explain the city's
bluesmen to their fellow residents. Cullen dropped by at a regular home jam
session organized by Tabby Thomas in the days before his Blues Box existed:

> They start arriving at a house on East Harrison Street shortly before 7 on a week-
> day night. Their dress—the younger men wear dark three piece suits, the older
> men, magenta coat and slacks—belies their occupations. By day they are roofers,
> plasterers, maintenance men. Tabby is a union steward. Come the night, they are
> blues men, members of an elite, dwindling fraternity. They say when they go they'll
> take a piece of the blues with them, a unique bit of blues—Baton Rouge blues.
> There are less than 20 of them, virtually unknown in their native city, known only
> by blues lovers in cities like Chicago, New Orleans, St. Louis, Memphis. Ironically

their records get better play on radio stations in Europe and the Far East than they do in Baton Rouge.[1]

Cullen listed that night's bluesmen of Baton Rouge. They included Henry Gray, Wilbert Byrd, Lionel Whitfield, William "Nature Boy" Ross, Roosevelt Sample, Guitar Kelley, Silas Hogan, Moses "Whispering" Smith, Guitar Jap [Keys], Big Boe Melvin, Sammy Thornton, and Clarence Edwards. They begin to play. Cullen says, "It is a kind of blues in which four instruments predominate—piano, guitar, harmonica and drums. No horns. Most songs consist of three-chord progressions, misery and hope and celebration in four-four time." It's a nice description and Cullen's is a warmly written piece, but there's no indication he's describing any kind of unique blues.

Nevertheless, there was a way in which this music could survive—whether it be a style *unique to* Baton Rouge or at least some form of "real" blues *played in* Baton Rouge. The first signs came with the notion of blues as a part of black heritage, and this became linked to the gradual development of the themed music festival. In New Orleans, the first Jazz and Heritage Festival was held just after Slim Harpo died in 1970, and it attracted some Baton Rouge artists. It was small scale, catering to fans in the hundreds rather than the half-millions of today, but gradually it prospered, as did the hotels and motels that sponsored the event. It took a while, but eventually it became clear that some kind of festival could work in Baton Rouge, too. This led in turn to the blues heritage becoming a part of Baton Rouge tourism in the same way as jazz in New Orleans, blues and rockabilly in Memphis, or the Grand Ole Opry in Nashville.

The first concerted attempt to bring hometown blues music into the consciousness of local people as a performing art that was part of their heritage—not to mention a potential source of fame for performers and income for the city's tourism business—came with the Louisiana State Division of the Arts and their appointment of a folklore director. This was Nick Spitzer, a folklorist trained in Philadelphia who was now creating films, festivals, and recordings of Louisiana's regional culture and who helped bring Cajun music and zydeco to a wider audience, later working with the Smithsonian Institute, National Public Radio, and Tulane University. In 1979, Spitzer approached a local former LSU student and radio producer, Jimmy Beyer, with a project to "establish a data file on Baton Rouge area musicians" before it was too late and "to document the contributions of ageing musicians." Beyer spent some eighteen months talking with musicians and drafting a booklet for publication, *The Baton Rouge Blues*. His work was launched through an article in the *Advocate* on August 15, 1980, where it was also made clear that by now Spitzer and Beyer realized that blues concerts should also be held to keep the music live and relevant to local people. Beyer made it clear that "some of these guys have toured Europe and influenced famous white rock bands . . . but they can't even draw a crowd in their home town." This was something he vowed to change, and in May 1981 the first Baton Rouge Blues Festival was arranged on the campus of Southern University.

The first of a few preliminary festivals was held in June 1980, the *Advocate* reporting "a free jazz and blues concert outside Clinton's East Feliciana Parish courthouse," given as part of the Jazz and Blues Project of the Arts and Humanities Council of Greater Baton Rouge. "This and other concerts are an effort to give living blues men the recognition they deserve. Tabby Thomas's House Rockers will feature Moses Smith and Rudy Richard. . . . Henry Gray will play. . . . Silas Hogan from Devils Swamp north of Baton Rouge will play with Arthur Kelley from Clinton and a drummer."

The first full-fledged festival, titled the "River City Blues Festival," featured the same local artists as at Clinton, along with the Raful Neal band and Ernie K-Doe from New Orleans. By then Tabby Thomas had opened his Blues Box and would soon develop the "Heritage Hall" tag that sat well with the arts council and the city government. In 1982 and 1983 the annual festival continued to feature bands led by Henry Gray, Tabby Thomas, Robert Milburn, and Boe Melvin of the local old guard, Mississippi Delta bluesman Scott Dunbar, and a sprinkling of newer artists, including white musician Kenny Acosta, whose performance style, he now says, includes "a hint of bluesy jazz mixed with the New Orleans street beat and Caribbean rhythms sautéed in a funky mixture of soulful growl." It was already clear that if the blues tradition were to survive, it would do so alongside sounds that would be alien to the likes of Slim Harpo.

By 1984, the River City Blues Festival, then held at the Old State Capitol, rated a full review in the *Advocate* of April 27. Performers included some "new" old-timers including William Wolfolk, described as "a singer, drummer, and trumpeter who has played with Lightnin' Slim and Slim Harpo." Another band included Clarence Edwards, Buddy Stewart, Slim Powell, and Otis Johnson, "who has played with Slim Harpo." A white group from Austin, the Fabulous Thunderbirds, were in town that month, too, and making some waves in the rock-music world. Their first LP had included Harpo's song "Baby Scratch My Back," and their leader, Jimmie Vaughan, was at pains to tell the newspaper that "basically, we're a 1980s version of Slim Harpo."

The 1985 music festival was linked to a Louisiana Folklife Festival that July. It again featured old and new blues alongside different sounds ranging from Lawrence Ardoin's French music to Percy Sledge's soul. Nick Spitzer said the Arts and Humanities Council was "trying to encourage people to preserve their own culture. . . . I like to see people closer to home being recognized by their own public," as well as by people from outside Louisiana. The same month, LPB-TV aired a "unique program featuring the blues heritage of Baton Rouge, 'Rainin in My Heart,' a musical special not a documentary," according to producer Carol Leslie. "The performers through their own styles and language give us a good idea of where the blues has been, where it is today, and hint at some of the possibilities of where it is headed."[2] Those performers included Whispering Smith, Silas Hogan, Guitar Kelley, and Raful Neal.

Gradually, the blues festivals expanded, and by 1986 the lineup included the Blue Notes—"founded by the late Robert Milburn, perhaps Baton Rouge's oldest blues band, now led by Ed Johnson"; William Wolfolk and the Blues Boys—"playing memories from way back, members have played with Slim Harpo and Lightnin' Slim previously"; Silas Hogan—"it's obvious that his style is the starting point for all [today's] Baton Rouge musicians"; Arthur Kelley; Jap (Marion Keys) and the Jet Set—"taking up old local styles like Harpo as well as B. B. King"; Boe Melvin and the Nighthawks—"one of the most popular attractions at local blues festivals—electric blues with strong vocals by Luchus Brown"; the Kenny Neal R&B band; Raful Neal and the Neal brothers; Rockin' Tabby Thomas and the Mighty House Rockers; and Chris Thomas—"a gifted guitarist with blues insight few others can have." All these local bluesmen were joined at the festival by the Zion Travelers gospel group of Rev. Burnell Offlee—"local radio singers 37 years, most bluesmen learned music in church," and by a number of white bands, among which the local ones were the Nitetimers—"local club favorites, playing blue eyed soul and blues"; the Circuit Breakers—"led by Bruce Lamb, known as Neckbone Slim, mixing Baton Rouge and Texas and Chicago blues"; and Eyewitness Blues—"a young white band playing rocking blues for the '80s."[3]

In 1987 the festival was expanded, and performers played on a number of different stages. By now there was the added involvement of several more of Harpo's close associates. James Johnson led a band for the first time, and

Rudy Richard was present as part of the band of Major Handy. Jesse Kinchen was in Michael Wolfe's band. Lazy Lester was in town, too. Publicity for the festival extended out to promotion and awareness of other blues-listening opportunities.

BATON ROUGE BLUES JAMS

On March 29, 1987, *Sunday Advocate* feature writer Charles Hunt summarized the story of the blues in general and welcomed the survival of Tabby's Blues Box, "which opened in 1980 at 1314 North Boulevard." Tabby was now described as "an impresario and preservationist. . . . At his club, frat types sit at tables with down-home bluesmen, Belgian visitors, country music fans, and as unpretentious an assortment of people as can be imagined." At another venue, Buddy's Snack Shop on Acadian Thruway, owned by Buddy Stewart, there is:

> a bar at back for special parties. Here are seven musicians seated on motel surplus chairs. They include Harpo's guitarist, James Johnson, Roy Shepperd on bass and drummer Larry Neal. Someone calls for the key of G and says, "OK Nose, hit it, man." Clyde Causey, known as "Harmonica Nose," a withered man of indeterminate age, until now recumbent in his chair, bolts up, tapping with, yes, both feet at once to a rhythm only he hears. "Nose" works the harmonica above his head, then he kneels and plays . . . Then he plays to the carpet for a while. . . . Someone calls, "Do it Nose, you getting it now," as he hits a note heard clear to Brusly. . . . Next, Black Diamond aka Sterling Collins takes his turn, singing to the balcony even when he's in the back room at Buddy's Snack Shop.

Born in April 1939, Clyde Causey was from Clinton but moved to Baton Rouge. He was related to the man who lived next door to James Moore back in 1943 and may have been an important player in James's early jam-session days. He appeared briefly on the recordings made by Smoky Babe for Harry Oster in 1960.

Stumbling on such local jam sessions as these inspired some European musicians to settle in Baton Rouge for a time. In 1987, Julian Piper, who had formed the Junkyard Angels band back in England, spent a year playing at Tabby's with a number of the old-time players before persuading Tabby, Kenny Neal, and others to tour in Europe. In 1990 another English musician and blues fan, Steve Coleridge, was so inspired he extended his planned two-week stay in Baton Rouge, started playing with local musicians, began to record them, and documented the scene he found there. Coleridge had discovered the music of Slim Harpo in Paris, of all places, a few years before. He had moved to Paris on a whim after he read a book about the bohemian scene of the 1950s. He taught English, did portraits in the street, sold newspapers, "the usual Henry Miller, Jack Kerouac type of thing," and enrolled at Université Paris 8. A Peruvian poet named Elias Duran gave him some music cassettes in return for a translation of some of his poems; one was by Slim Harpo and another by Excello artists generally. Coleridge then moved to Spain, met two American musicians who said they would teach him to play bass, and "I was still crazy about the Excello cassette and said that was what I wanted to learn . . . so time went by and my ex and I formed a band . . . and played Lonesome Sundown and Slim Harpo, and our drummer suggested if we wanted to do it right the best way would be to go to Baton Rouge and see the real thing. When I got there, and realized there was a unique blues scene there, I persuaded my girlfriend to sell the car and rent the house and come there too, and we started playing at Tabby's on Mondays."

Coleridge started a weekly round of what he told *Folk Roots* magazine was "blues jam heaven," Tabby's jam on Saturday, Larry Garner's on Sunday, Estelle's on Monday, Raful Neal's on Tuesday, and Phil Brady's on Thursday. Coleridge met many local musicians, including Bruce Lamb, who guided him around and, importantly to Steve, "had possession of Slim Harpo's guitar, the 335, the brown one, at least someone had painted it brown, 'baby shit brown' as he described it, but he had restored it to its original color." Then Coleridge met Clarence Edwards playing at Tabby's Blues Box, and "I couldn't understand why he wasn't making records—so, enthusiast turns into businessman." Coleridge started booking gigs for his band with Edwards, and then he started Sidetrack Records with the help of Lamb, issuing LPs by Edwards (*Swamps the Word*), T. Bone Singleton (*Living with the Blues*), and other artists (*Chemical City Shakedown*). He recorded an artist called "Battlerack Scatter" who couldn't make his mind up about his songs being released—"which was a tragedy because he was by far the most talented songwriter." Soon, though, Coleridge started to find things were not as straightforward as he wanted. "A lot of these people had just as much talent [as Clarence Edwards] but they were just very hard to deal with . . . and then I started to feel really obliged to people. It was always 'lend me ten dollars' etc." Then, too, there was the little matter of a work permit, a green card, which had been overlooked in the rush to change a two-week holiday into a Baton Rouge business. He found people started to work against him: "So, Clarence and I just got our gigs outside of Baton Rouge itself. Clarence said, 'Look, let's stay out of this place because as soon as you start succeeding they'll do everything they can to drag you down again,' and he was right. I should not have created such a stir in Baton Rouge. I could see trouble coming and that's why I had to stop." Although he loved the blues scene, Coleridge was amazed at how "racism continued to permeate everything." Coleridge returned to Spain and "started bringing Mohammed to the mountain," touring with Henry Gray and others in Europe "for decent money, whereas Tabby was paying Henry and Clarence 20 dollars."[4]

Before he left Baton Rouge, Coleridge took time to summarize what he had seen there for *Blues & Rhythm* magazine. He was quick to point out that the city has very diverse neighborhoods. The lush parks and scenic lakes surrounding the capitol and the university and the ranch-type houses and plantation buildings in the country were at the far end of a spectrum from the houses of the black communities off North Acadian Thruway and in Scotland-ville, but to Coleridge "the concrete reality of modern industrial Baton Rouge is that the DJs all announce they are broadcasting from Chemical Alley," a phrase coined after well over 100 chemical and industrial plants located along the river between New Orleans and Baton Rouge, forming a "petrochemical corridor." Coleridge made the rounds of the blues clubs, favoring Phil Brady's blues jam on Thursdays, noting that Tabby's "is OK but, be careful, the walk to the car could be your last." Clarence Edwards played at Tabby's on Saturdays while Henry Gray occasionally played at Vibes & Visions in Port Allen on Sundays, a "middle class" club with "expensive decor and an R&B band, not blues," often featuring Larry Garner. Other places purveying some real blues were the Turning Point, Protocol, the Vineyard, Estelle's, and Otis Bell's in Clinton.

As far as records went, Buddy Stewart's Rock Shop was "still flourishing—a few blocks from Slim Harpo's house—a survivor of the local stores that used to be the mainstay of record distribution in the black communities." Coleridge reckoned there were nineteen active singers/guitarists in town in 1990, including eight he considered "in the Baton Rouge tradition." These were Guitar Kelley and Silas Hogan, Clarence Edwards, Tabby Thomas, Rudy Richard, James Johnson, Boe Melvin, and Ray Neal. Among the few harmonica players he found locally, he felt Raful and Kenny Neal and Oscar Davis were in the local tradition. Oscar Davis led the Blues Boys, "the only authentic swamp-blues band still playing. . . . they perform in places where people in their 50s and 60s get up and dance to what they've danced to since the days of Big Papa." Born in 1943, Davis was influenced by Harpo and by Raful Neal and went on to play with many of the town's best players. By 1990, Coleridge found, "Oscar Davis played 'Caress Me Baby,' 'Scratch My Back' and 'Rainin'' better than anyone else. He was mainly in the black clubs like the Elks, and had a big female following; nine children, eight different women." Davis went on to be a regular attraction at Phil Brady's club and still plays the Harpo blues. Davis told Coleridge, "I liked Slim Harpo. I used to sneak out to see him at the Streamline."[5]

Coleridge enjoyed several local players who were not of "the tradition" but who had something to say. These included "Richard Pettis, a semi-blind bass player with a swamp sound, Alfred Jackson, a bizarre almost African rapid-rhythm guitarist, and Troy Turner," a twenty-two-year-old rising blues star of Cherokee and black descent and with rock roots. Raised musically with the Neal brothers, "he is definitely a blues player but he could go shooting off in any direction and still be a blues player." Bass player A. G. Hardesty was then playing with Troy Turner. From Baton Rouge, Hardesty had toured with blues bands from elsewhere, including those of Fenton Robinson and James Cotton. He told Coleridge about his early days playing with a make-shift neighborhood band: "Slim Harpo was my neighbor. He saw us play one time—almost died laughing. My bass only had one string. Later my dad got me a real one. I didn't know they had four strings."[6]

Coleridge was instrumental in helping another local artist, Larry Garner, to get a recording contract, shopping him around to European labels until JSP in England took a chance with him. Garner was born in New Orleans but came to Baton Rouge at age nine. He had a comfortable family life and started playing R&B with his cousins, the Twisters, in the 1960s, and had played rock music, too. After high school and the military, he worked for nineteen years at a chemical plant back home and only really started playing blues after Tabby's Blues Box opened. He remembered hearing the old blues as a child, years before, the sounds carrying across the fields from Henry Holmes's Juke Joint at Scot-bar Road in Slaughter, near Clinton. He could even hear the music from Mattie Bee's joint about five miles away in the woods. As well as Harpo, he heard Robert Milburn, Chuck Mitchell, and his own cousins' band. Garner was taught to play guitar by his uncle George Lathers, who played Jimmy Reed style, and Garner was influenced too by Elder Utah Smith and other traveling gospel singers.[7] One of the best preachers in Louisiana, the Rev. Charlie Jackson, lived in Baton Rouge. "That's why my stuff comes off preachin' the blues," says Garner, who writes a lot of his own material and often performs a long and spontaneous preaching blues about whatever irritates him at the time, often including local people. "People winced when they heard him starting that," remembers Coleridge. Garner won a blues contest at the 1988 Blues Foundation festival, but his first recordings were rejected as "too blues" before he got with JSP. Garner makes what *Blues Revue* called "extremely musical and eminently listenable blues."

Garner puts in the miles at home but also plays regularly abroad, getting the sort of plaudits that might have been Slim Harpo's had he lived: "I go to Europe and England a few times a year. Over there they hear guys playing the blues, but when I come in, they come right up and say, 'Thank God—a real blues band.'" He told *Living Blues* in 1999, "Steve Coleridge came here to Baton Rouge. He was hanging out and looking for that old black bluesman who lived in a shotgun house with a washtub hanging on the side. But that's not here. It don't exist anymore. So he found Clarence Edwards, and they came over one night to a jam I was hosting in Port Allen. . . . he liked me and said he was shopping out Clarence's music and he could do so with mine."[8] After JSP launched his recording career, Garner made albums for Verve, Ruf, Dixiefrog, and other labels.

By the time Coleridge left town, Baton Rouge blues venues were into another period of depression, despite the continued presence of Tabby's Blues Box. In 1994 the Baton Rouge Blues Festival "took a hiatus" in the words of the organizers, and it did not reappear until 2008. When it came back, the headliners were now of a younger generation, including Larry Garner, Kenny Neal, and Tab Benoit. The Harpo band did make an appearance too, though, in the form of Rudy Richard and James Johnson working with Lazy Lester.

TWENTY-FIRST-CENTURY BLUES

Today, Baton Rouge houses just under a quarter of a million people, and double that in the surrounding area, about 54 percent of whom are of African American descent. The city's publicity machine tells us that government and business have begun a move back to the central district following many years when the petrochemical boom caused expansion away from the river and the city center and left the historic downtown areas stranded. The famous

Temple building is still there on the Strip, though hidden under a concrete overpass, as is a new blues venue, the Blue Room, reopened in 2013 on the site of Tabby's Blues Box. North Boulevard is still a major access road into downtown Baton Rouge but is largely barren if not dilapidated. On the waterfront at Port Allen, where James Moore would have caught the ferries in his younger days, there is now the new leisure area of Old Ferry Landing Park, the last ferry having crossed in 1971. Not far downstream, the Port of Greater Baton Rouge, rebuilt on the west bank in 1954, is the nation's fifth largest and employs some three thousand people.

Baton Rouge remains something of a tourist attraction. Apart from its arts, science, and history museums, government buildings, Capitol Park, riverfront, universities, and the like, there is still the continuing annual blues festival. The 2015 lineup included Lazy Lester alongside artists with styles and sounds Slim Harpo could never have imagined: rockers, rappers, blacks, whites, and blues. The annual festival was followed by a separate show in honor of Slim Harpo and a festival in Port Allen organized by and featuring Kenny Neal. And outside of festival time, as the New York Times travel section reported in 2015, "for the curious traveler—and music fan—there are still places in the city that hark back to Baton Rouge's blues heyday. With a mix of the old and the new, in some places, the blues are quietly thriving."[9] The paper found the spare and no-frills Blues Room hosting live music Friday through Sunday as the only blues-dedicated bar in downtown Baton Rouge. Half an hour's drive took them to one of the area's oldest and most authentic live-music locations, Teddy's Juke Joint in Zachary, "a rustic place in the middle of nowhere [with] as much of an old-time, down-home feel as any venue in the South." Lloyd Johnson, known as Teddy, has run the bar for the last thirty-five years with its dark and cluttered inside, green and gold Mardi Gras masks hanging from the ceiling, and flashing neon lights. Back in the heart of Baton Rouge is an anonymous green building on Government Street, Phil Brady's bar, opened in 1979 by a Vietnam veteran who is committed to live music. Brady has been hosting a Thursday-night blues jam every week since 1986.

When the New York Times visited, they found a regular clientele, young and old, rich and poor, black and white. Those playing included drummer Jo Monk, "a short, wiry man with a charming smile and the most in-the-pocket drum chops in town"; Zach Korth, "a young science graduate and talented guitarist"; Miguel Hernandez, "one of the most solid bass players in

Baton Rouge"; and ex-Harpo guitarist James Johnson, who "takes the vocals and punctuates proceedings with his scratchy, rapid-fire leads." The *Times* concluded that "when you find yourself in one of the city's smoky, dirty bars late at night, with a loud band loosely belting out an old Slim Harpo number, it's hard not to feel a spark of what used to be. And, often, that's more than enough."[10]

Since Slim Harpo's day, many of the players and promoters of blues in Baton Rouge, and elsewhere, have been white people motivated, certainly, by their love of the music. It's debatable, though, how far many of them go toward fitting the picture promoted by the Dialogue on Race organization founded in 2012 as a local educational movement with the view that "the time is now for transforming the image of Baton Rouge from being a racially divided community to becoming a city known for being open and non-exploitative." Maxine Crump's view is that "this is often overlooked by those who love, revere, and follow the great blues geniuses" like Slim Harpo. She points to such academics and orators as Princeton professor Cornel West, who has long promoted the view that black people "don't want to enslave others; we want freedom for everybody." West calls himself "a bluesman in the life of the mind; a jazzman in the world of ideas, forever on the move." Maybe Slim Harpo had a little of this approach too, or generated such an approach among some of his white following.[11]

THE SLIM HARPO AWARDS

Slim Harpo lived in the days before halls of fame, preservation foundations, or the awards industry really took hold in music. The first large-scale Grammy Awards ceremony took place the year after he died. However, in 2008, Harpo received a posthumous Grammy Hall of Fame Award for "I'm a King Bee," categorized as "a recording of lasting qualitative or historical significance." Today, he has an awards ceremony in his own name in his hometown and is named in the Louisiana Music Hall of Fame, a growing "online multi-media virtual museum."

In 2002, a new group was formed with the aim of promoting, preserving, and celebrating the blues culture. The Baton Rouge Blues Foundation is a nonprofit organization that sponsors a Blues Education Program, the Blues Music History Project, the annual Blue Carpet Blues Gala, and, of course, the annual Baton Rouge Blues Festival, free and open to the public. In 2003 the festival was used as a vehicle for a new awards event, the Slim Harpo Blues Awards. Since then, the annual Slim Harpo Awards ceremony has attracted performers and honorees from all over the music world. It was the idea of local music publisher, producer, and promoter Johnny Palazzotto, a founder and until recently a director of the Baton Rouge Blues Foundation. He said:

> In 2000, I was doing a radio interview with Rob Payer on WBRH 90.3 in Baton Rouge. We were talking about local music legends and naturally Slim Harpo was mentioned—when you hear a Slim Harpo song, you know it's Slim Harpo. Slim's stepson William was listening and called in and we decided to meet. He brought me to Ms. Lovell [by then remarried as Mrs. Lovell Casey] and an immediate friendship began. I had the idea of doing some sort of music awards program and after months of discussions Ms. Lovell granted me exclusive representation of the name and likeness of Slim Harpo and I asked permission to start the Slim Harpo Music Awards, and she approved. Proceeds from the Slim Harpo Music Awards benefit the Music in the Schools outreach program.[12]

In 2003, the first Harpo Awards went to James Johnson, Rudy Richard, and Raful Neal. Gradually the net was widened, and by 2012 awards were given to producer J. D. Miller, posthumously, and Rolling Stones guitarist Keith Richards. In 2013, swamp-pop musicians Warren Storm, Gabriel "Guitar Gable" Perrodin, and Clarence "Jockey" Etienne of the Musical Kings received "legends" awards. David Kearns of Mobile, Alabama, was also honored as an "ambassador." In 2014, honorees included Irish rocker Van Morrison and C. C. Adcock, a guitarist, music consultant, and producer whose bands, Lil Band of Gold and Lafayette Marquis, both perform Harpo tracks such as "Strange Love" and "Shake Your Hips." Adcock has said, challengingly, "If you don't know Slim Harpo, I don't think I'd care to know you," underscoring his feeling that Harpo is "up there with Louis Armstrong, Hank Williams, and Fats Domino. It's not a stretch to say that his musical legacy contains the DNA for just about everything that has happened since in popular music. So many of Slim's records transcend the blues or any style or era. It's why so many others through the years have been inspired by them and found success covering and copying them."[13]

The Harpo Awards recognize homegrown and outside talent, just as Baton Rouge's annual music festival has gradually widened its remit to include more and more blues from outside the city. Through the first decade of the new millennium, the festival continued to feature Harpo men like Rudy Richard and James Johnson, August Ranson and Jesse Kinchen, and other local artists, but as the publicity reads, "expanding outside our backyard, the festival has brought in nationally and internationally recognized names like Bobby Blue Bland, Marcia Ball, Phil Guy, Larry Garner and Charlie Musselwhite. In 2013, the Baton Rouge Blues Festival saw over 10,000 guests ranging from 18 to 65 years old. Of those attendees, the largest percentage (31%) was between the ages of 18 and 34, and over 80% were from the city of Baton Rouge."[14]

In 2014 the festival was headlined by New Orleans music legend Dr. John, when the organizers tallied nearly 30 percent of attendees as newcomers. While the majority of those in attendance were from south Louisiana, nearly 13 percent apparently traveled to Baton Rouge for the festival from cities like Houston and Philadelphia and other countries such as Scotland and France. In 2015 the Harpo Awards, given at a show separate from the annual festival, featured performances by new honorees Jimmie Vaughan and Lou Ann Barton. They were joined on stage for some Harpo numbers by James Johnson, who had already sung along enthusiastically at the back as the band played "Rainin' in My Heart."

THE HISTORIC MARKER AT MULATTO BEND

The 2014 Harpo Awards coincided with the placing of a State of Louisiana Historic Marker at the intersection of US Highway 190 and Mulatto Bend Road, near Slim's grave in Mulatto Bend Cemetery. The event on June 21 was organized by David Couvillon, a member of the West Baton Rouge Historical Association. Couvillon grew up in the area and became interested in the blues when passing the White Owl Inn while driving his grandfather's tractor. He stopped to listen to music coming through the door, played by Slim Harpo. "That's how I got turned on to the blues," Couvillon told the local paper. "Later on, it really hit home for me that somebody as influential as Slim Harpo, James Moore, was right out of my backyard. Slim Harpo influenced a tremendous number of people, but even though 'Rainin' in My Heart' is played at almost every Louisiana wedding reception, people in Europe know more about him than people in his own parish do."[15] Nevertheless, Couvillon said, some longtime residents of the area attended the marker dedication and offered remembrances of their famous neighbor. One of those locals was Barbara Ross Carter, who remembered trips to Crowley and singing with James Moore and Otis Hicks way back—"they used to play and we wouldn't miss it for nothing in the world. We had a good time with Slim Harpo. He was a nice young man. We missed him after he was gone."[16]

William Gambler is amazed that his stepfather's music has remained popular throughout the four and a half decades since his death. Slim's popularity is "probably greater now than it was then," he told local reporters when the historical marker was placed. "He would be overjoyed, but he would still be humble."[17]

MY LITTLE QUEEN BEE

Those who knew James Moore personally have looked on while there has been continued worldwide interest in the music of Slim Harpo, along with a sustained and developing culture of music-heritage festivals. Some have been involved with the action, others have not; some have been happy with these developments, some have been bemused. All of them, including those who remain unknown to fans and promoters of Slim Harpo's music, have lived with this as at least some small part of their continuing daily life.

Lovell Moore continued to live at 906 North Thirty-Sixth Street after James Moore's death. Her son, William, moved back into her house temporarily until she was ready to go to work. She became a cook at the Illinois Central Railroad. She became the recipient of royalties due to Harpo, but she took little further interest in music, other than church music. At some point she took an interest in a younger churchgoer, Willie Casey Jr., who had featured in the local paper in May 1966 as one of "22 members of Mt. Zion Baptist church graduating from Baton Rouge high schools this month and to be presented with bibles at a special ceremony by Rev. Jemison."[18] Lovell had taken a job with Montgomery Ward, and she met Casey there sometime in the 1970s. Casey moved in with Lovell, and on June 16, 1980, a marriage license was granted to Willie Casey Jr. and Lovell Moore Jones, both of 906 North Thirty-Sixth Street. In May 1993, Aaron, the last of Lovell's three brothers, died, and in March 1997 her daughter, Harpo's stepdaughter, Betty Gambler Sewell, a postal worker, died at the young age of fifty-two, having suffered with diabetes from the age of seventeen. Lovell Moore Casey died in Baton Rouge on May 15, 2004, at the age of eighty. There were services at Elm Grove Baptist Church on North Thirty-Eighth Street before she was taken to Dorseyville Cemetery. She was noted to have been a high-school graduate, a retired cook, a keen gardener, and a member of the Elm Grove Church choir. She was survived by a sister, a son, and three grandchildren. Two other brothers and four sisters had died before her. Interestingly, her obituary in the *Advocate* made no mention whatsoever of James Moore or Slim Harpo.

Verna Mae Vaughn, Slim's first wife, died in New Orleans on February 5, 2003. She was born on June 2, 1922, and had three children, Carol Jean Vaughn, born on August 9, 1949, and twins Cheryl Ann and Shannon Marie Vaughn, born in 1950, all in New Orleans.

James Moore's sisters all survived him by some years. Lillie E. Collins was still living at Mulatto Bend before she died at Earl K. Long Memorial Hospital in Baton Rouge on December 25, 1981, aged sixty-nine, just three months after her husband, Dan Collins, was killed in an automobile accident in Port Allen. Matilda Murray died in Pontiac, Michigan, on October 18, 1985, in her sixties, leaving a son, Willie Murray Jr., Harpo's nephew. Doris Moore Robertson died on December 6, 1989, in Port Allen, where she had retired from her work as a housekeeper at Earl K. Long Hospital. She was survived by three sons, Harpo's nephews, Otis Kelly, Ray Moore, and Herbert Moore.

Otis Kelly, Slim's eldest nephew, still lives in Mulatto Bend at this writing. Ray Moore went to college in Baton Rouge before moving to Arizona to work for Honeywell as a software engineer. He did not pursue the musical career that his uncle inspired back in his school days. He lives in Arizona today. The youngest nephew, Herbert Moore, was at the 2014 historic marker ceremony but has since been very ill. He is a deacon of a church in the Jackson area, north of Baton Rouge. According to Ray Moore, "My brother Herbert started taking up band in junior high school. He was learning to play the sax, but for some reason after my uncle died, my mother make him quit."

William Gambler, James Moore's stepson, lives in Baker with his wife, Dorothy, and daughter, Chandra. They live near their two other children and four grandchildren, many of whom were at the historic marker ceremony along with relations and friends of the Moore family. After he left the Air Force, William studied for another year and a half before going to work for the US Postal Service. He retired in 2000. His late sister, Betty, had also worked for the Postal Service before her disability and early death. William is the guardian of the Harpo estate. He is joined on the board of the annual Slim Harpo Awards by his son, Alonzo Gambler, and his daughter, Tynita Howard, who is chief executive of the local postal credit union.[19]

James and Lovell's house at 906 Thirty-Sixth Street has been occupied by members of the Moore/Gambler/Casey family since Lovell's death. Over the river in Mulatto Bend, the house where James Moore's sister, Lillie, lived still stands and is occupied by James's nephew Otis Kelly. The house next door, once occupied by James's mother and where James also lived, and was probably born, is now a vacant lot.

THE BATON ROUGE BLUES?

It is probably not a question that much exercised Slim Harpo, but it is a serious question today because much of the festival publicity of the past four decades has been predicated on an affirmative answer. The question is: Did the Baton Rouge blues exist? Did it ever exist? And, not completely flippantly, was it a coincidence that, when Kris Kristofferson and Bobby McGee hitched a ride out of Baton Rouge in 1969, it was the blues that Bobby chose to sing— and to a harp accompaniment? Certainly, some forty-six years after Slim Harpo left us, his name remains to the fore as "sponsor" of the annual music awards, and through the Baton Rouge Blues Festival the blues continues to be played and promoted in Baton Rouge. Whether this is a continuation of a specific form of identifiably *Baton Rouge* blues, though, is a different issue.

Kenny Neal told *Louisiana Life* magazine in 2010 that he realized early on that one musician, perhaps more than anyone else, came to personify the spirit of the music and the city that produced the swamp-blues sound: Slim Harpo. "Coming from the little town of Baton Rouge, I saw that he really made a big name for himself. He made his mark coming from the Deep South and swamp-blues. He put a style out there that gave us all an identity."[20] Neal also said, "His harmonica playing is so simple, but to get somebody to play that simple is really hard to do, and . . . he's just got something special. It's a mixture between the blues, the country and the gospel."[21]

In 2010, *Louisiana Life* noted that contemporary musicians such as Kenny Neal, Chris Thomas King, and Tab Benoit were leading the dozens, if not hundreds, of modern blues stylists who have been directly influenced and inspired by Slim Harpo, and who keep alive the distinctive musical tradition Harpo helped develop and eventually embodied. In carrying the swamp-blues banner originally planted by Harpo, Tab Benoit, variously hailed as a Cajun, a Houma native, and a wetlands defender, was quoted saying practically any blues or rock band rooted in the Baton Rouge area features a Harpo song in its repertoire. "It's not like Chicago blues or Texas blues," according to Benoit, but "it's a very laid-back, bayou style of playing, like someone's just playing on his porch."[22]

Away from Baton Rouge, Harpo's music has been promoted in Chicago and Atlanta and other places where Robert Lee "Chicago Bob" Nelson played after he left Louisiana in 1966. Despite his nickname, Nelson was a devotee of Harpo—his bands were variously called the King Bees or the Heart Fixers. Born in Bogalusa, Louisiana, in 1944, he always said that he took up the harp at age eight when playing with his father, Versie Nelson, and Versie's jam-session friends, including Harpo and Lazy Lester. Chris Thomas King has been part of both the traditional and the new blues scenes. He learned some blues at Tabby Thomas's feet but was also growing up in the hip-hop and rap era. He had his first album released by Arhoolie in 1986 when a teenager, and in 1994, to Tabby's dismay, he developed a new take on the blues for his fourth album, *21st Century Blues . . . From da 'Hood*. In contrast, he played the part of a 1920s bluesman in the 2001 movie *Oh Brother Where Art Thou?* and has made an album about old-time bluesman Tommy Johnson.

But while pioneering a form of blues fusion, Chris Thomas King has developed an interesting take on the Baton Rouge blues, telling people that blues never left Baton Rouge, but people in Europe and elsewhere took it away and defined what blues should be: "I can't relate to a lot of this stuff that people put out and they say that this is the blues. It's not the blues that I know. . . . It doesn't speak to the culture like it once did."[23] He meant the black culture of the moment, but that includes the shadow of the past within it, whether embraced or rejected.

So what was the culture? In the absence of any recordings of blues from Baton Rouge performers prior to the Harpo era, it is very difficult to say whether there ever really was a precisely definable form of *Baton Rouge* blues to be continued. Named elders, like the Meddy brothers, played music that is long gone now, as is the music of Butch Cage and Willie Thomas or Robert Pete Williams, though we have their recordings to remind us what it was. The bottom line is that before the 1950s, there were indeed people playing the blues in Baton Rouge, in their own homes or at local gatherings at a house party or a social event or nightclub, but in the main these were songs learned by individuals from other individuals or from commercial records, jukeboxes, or radio. As far as anyone knows, they were not making any particular form of consistently different or distinctive Baton Rouge blues.

Then, in the days after the Second World War, there was a time when small, independent, regional record companies started to affect local music scenes. When Jay Miller and Excello Records recorded Lightnin' Slim, Slim Harpo, and other musicians from the Baton Rouge area, for a time there did certainly appear an identifiable sound known today as the "swamp-blues." But Lightnin' and Harpo and the others were largely giving their own takes on blues styles created originally in Texas, Mississippi, and Chicago. So the swamp sound they made was not a direct descendant from some earlier local musicians; it was a whole new amalgam of blues. That was particularly so in the case of Slim Harpo, who somehow had the talent, vision, and temperament to create and adapt to new songs, new rhythms, and new session musicians without losing the essence of his original style.

Even taking the Excello sound as one and the same as the Baton Rouge blues, it is difficult to say that this lasted much beyond the Harpo era. Just as the unrecorded folk-blues of the days before Harpo was, surely, changed beyond measure by the bluesmen of Harpo's generation, the music of Harpo and his contemporaries could not survive unadulterated. As musicologist David Evans, who worked with Harry Oster at LSU in the early 1960s, said, some years after Harpo died, "There is almost no purely traditional music left. All American music now is in some way influenced by commercial music and popular forms. We have a total interplay of folk and pop. . . . Records can be used profitably to enhance an artist's career. However they do alter the product and can be negative. A record is different from a recording. The blues scene in Baton Rouge didn't come into its own until the 1950s and that was through commercial recordings."[24]

Projecting this line forward beyond the Harpo era, when the music started to change again later in the 1960s, the change was toward a ubiquitous take on the music of Chicago and other blues towns as much as that of Baton Rouge, part of the developing "global blues" played by black and white musicians, American and European and beyond, young and old, traditional and modern.

If you talk to musicians from New Orleans, they will tell you about the unique conditions that spawned the music called jazz and about the "lazy" style of playing associated with what is normally characterized as "hot" music. If you talk to musicians from Memphis, they will also talk about their unique style of "playing behind the beat." If you go to Muscle Shoals or Atlanta or some other places, they'll have another version of their own inimitable regional style. So on one level, the defining of a kind of swamp-blues from

Baton Rouge is just another example of southern musicians explaining what they are doing and how they believe it's unique to them.

People have continued playing the blues in Baton Rouge and, at some point after the festival culture took hold, it became a "tradition" to do so, but in truth, apart from a few of the direct descendants of the Harpo-era bluesmen, most of the music made after Slim Harpo died in 1970 was back to being *blues in Baton Rouge* rather than the *Baton Rouge blues*. Effectively, there was only one heyday of swamp-blues, of Baton Rouge blues—and that came when the likes of Slim Harpo and Lightnin' Slim were making records of it.

WHEN ALL'S SAID AND DONE

There's a final question. What, really, were Slim Harpo's, James Moore's, achievements? Apart from his innate and learned abilities to play, sing, and compose songs, I think this is what he achieved: he had the inspiration and tenacity to keep at his hobby and to start a career in music relatively late in life; he had the ability together with Jay Miller to forge a distinctive sound and style; his talent to create new takes on known blues themes was considerable; his ability to roll with the flow through his career was evident; his capacity to adapt to the new requirements of his record label and booking agents while retaining his basic blues style, format, and identity was admirable; and lastly, he was able to inspire others throughout his life and beyond.

A parallel with New Orleans jazz would see unrecorded bluesmen like the Meddy brothers in the role of Buddy Bolden, Lightnin' Slim in the place reserved for King Oliver, and Slim Harpo playing the part of Louis Armstrong, no less. Those who came after Harpo are either in the equivalent of Preservation Hall or are working in the brave new world of stylistic change. Or, in a rock 'n' roll analogy, Cage and Thomas might be seen as the obscure roots men, Lightnin' Slim as the pioneer Bill Haley, and Harpo as the talisman Elvis Presley taking the music further forward to where it never expected to go.

Just as innate music played live and local—think Robert Pete Williams—comes out sounding different from commercially planned and motivated music—think Harpo and Jay Miller—all music lives differently, too, in the memories of those involved and in the reminiscences of those who knew the players. Those memories of Slim Harpo, his music, and his life are evaporating and becoming fewer by the day. It's not been possible to collect as many

memories as I'd have liked, but I hope there are enough here, woven within
the facts of Harpo's life and times and his legacy, to justify my offering this
as my own record of Slim Harpo and the blues in Baton Rouge.

WHEN THE BLUES COMES IN

It's now 2015, and I'm in Baton Rouge when there is yet another blues-event
weekend. At a mid-scale hotel built on a lot that once was home to many
poor local folks and supported several blues bars and clubs, near a highway
once traversed regularly by James Moore in his scrap-iron truck, some of the
fans have flown or driven in early and are being checked in by the smart and
efficient young lady at the desk. Outside in the parking lot, various musicians,
black and white, are off-loading their personal and musical gear, including
some ominously large amps. Other people are trying to inquire about rooms
and restaurant facilities, fussing about the trappings of modern life. They're
told, "Well you need to book in soon, 'cause when the blues comes in it's gon'
get real busy then."

Roll over, Slim Harpo—and come in the front door.

NOTES

PREFACE

1. John Broven, email to the author, 2014; Paul Jones, liner note to *The Best of Slim Harpo* (Ace CDCHM 410); Jeff Hannusch, liner note to Bear Family CD *Slim Harpo Rocks* (BCD 17129); Peter Guralnick, *Listener's Guide to the Blues* (New York: Facts on File Inc., 1982); Pete Welding, liner note to *Rural Blues* (Imperial LP LM94001); Hank Davis, email to the author, 2014; Stephen Coleridge, *Blues & Rhythm* 52 (1990); Sam Charters, liner note to *He Knew The Blues* (Excello LP 8013); Jim Delehant, "Tempo" column, *Hit Parader*, June 1969.

2. Mick Jagger, interview by Jonathan Cott, *Rolling Stone*, October 12, 1968.

3. *Rolling Stone*, March 19, 1970.

4. Jimmy Beyer, *Baton Rouge Blues* (Baton Rouge: Arts Council of Greater Baton Rouge, 1980).

5. The spelling of Lightning Slim's name in this book varies, largely reflecting the two main spellings used by record companies. Jay Miller named him "Lightning" initially, and he appeared that way on Feature Records. Excello changed this spelling to "Lightnin'" on their record labels, and gradually this became the more accepted spelling on records and promotional materials.

6. As John Broven notes in his Foreword, some of the trade-paper descriptions of discs by South Louisiana artists occasionally used terms like "straight from the swamps" to indicate the nature of the music being reviewed. However, the contemporary trade papers and record companies did not use the phrase "swamp-blues" or "swamp-pop" to explain or describe this genre of music. "Swamp-blues" did not come into frequent use until after the Excello/Blue Horizon LP *Swamp Blues* was issued in 1970. "Swamp-pop" was first used as a deliberate stylistic name by the peerless rock enthusiast and writer Bill Millar in an article titled "Swamp Pop—Music from Cajun Country" in the British weekly pop-music paper *Record Mirror* on June 12, 1971.

1. SOMETHING INSIDE ME

1. Connie Dents, interview by the author, 2013.

2. Pearline's birth surname was recorded as "Brown" and her state of origin as Louisiana when she reported the death of a son in Texas in the 1920s. Her name was recorded as "Pearlie Brown"

and her place of birth Port Hudson on the birth certificate of Isiah Moore in 1924, when she was thirty years old. There is no public record of her being born in 1889 as per her gravestone. She might be the Pearl Brown noted in the US Census of 1900 as born in December 1894, an adopted child living in Ward Five of West Baton Rouge with a woman named Emma Jackson, a farm laborer.

3. Pearline was variously recorded as "Pearl B Emmerson" or "Poline Emerson" in census documents.

4. Mark Twain, *Life on the Mississippi* (Boston: James Osgood, 1883), chapter 40.

5. Ibid., chapter 11.

6. I have standardized the spelling of "Bellmont." In public documents it has variously been given as "Bellemont," "Bellmont," and more latterly "Belmont."

7. Tilda was probably named "Matilda" but reported to the census as Tilda and was known to most people as Tillie. Her Social Security records show her birth date as July 27, 1920, while other public records show February 12, 1922. "Dorris" was spelled with a double *r* in census returns, but she was normally known as Doris.

8. At various points one or more uncles or uncles-in-law lived with James's family. In census returns they were named Zuke Emerson, Felix Emerson, Felix Amos, and other spellings.

9. *State-Times Advocate*, January 11, 1924.

10. Ibid., February 9, 1924.

11. Ibid., March 3, 1928.

12. Delehant, "Tempo" column, June 1969.

13. Buddy Guy, *When I Left Home* (New York: Da Capo Press, 2012), 13.

14. Robert Pete Williams, quoted by Peter Guralnick, *Feel Like Going Home* (New York: Outerbridge/Vintage Books, 1971), 131.

15. April 11, 1923.

16. *State-Times Advocate*, July 30, 1934.

17. Ibid., October 7, 1932.

18. Delehant, "Tempo" column, June 1969.

19. Connie Dents, interview by the author, 2013.

20. Guy, *When I Left Home*, 4.

21. *Morning Advocate*, February 26, 1938.

22. Ibid., May 22, 1940.

23. There were two Matilda/Mathilda Moores listed in Baton Rouge that year in the city directory. A week after the sentencing, the *Baton Rouge Advocate* carried this item: "Explanation: The Mathilda Moore sentenced a week ago for larceny is not the Mathilda Moore living on South Thirteenth Street."

24. Delehant, "Tempo" column, June 1969.

25. James Moore interview, probably November 1968, from the collection of Sue Cassidy Clark held by the Center for Black Music Research, Columbia College, Chicago.

26. Delehant, "Tempo" column, June 1969.

27. Baton Rouge city directories, 1937–43.

28. All Humphrey quotations are from Robert Mann, "Hubert Humphrey's Year in Baton Rouge," *New Orleans Times-Picayune*, June 23, 2014.

29. Internet site, all-that-is-interesting.com/voting-history-america (accessed December 18, 2015).

30. Nicholas Spitzer, *Louisiana Folklife: A Guide to the State* (Baton Rouge: Louisiana Office of Cultural Development, 1985), www.louisianafolklife.org/LT/Virtual_Books/Guide_to_State/creole_book_guide_to_state.html.

31. This property was owned by a woman listed as "Sedonia Lewis, colored," in the city directories.

32. Delehant, "Tempo" column, June 1969.

33. Writer Jeff Hannusch learned from Boogie Bill Webb, a Mississippian living in New Orleans, that he recalled going to work as a stevedore, unloading freight on the riverfront, in 1957, he thought, and "there he met future blues legends Slim Harpo and Buddy Guy, who were also stevedoring." This seems unlikely in 1957, the year Guy moved to Chicago and Harpo started making records. It was more likely ten years earlier, although Buddy Guy would then have been much too young to have been with Harpo. Webb lived in a boarding house on Harmony Street, which makes sense because one of the major docks was the Harmony Street Wharf.

34. City directories show Robert Causey at 167 Mary Street in 1942.

35. James Moore is listed in the city directory at number 745 in the alphabetical list of Baton Rouge area residents. In the house-by-house listings of occupants, the primary occupants of number 745 are listed as being Percy Davis, a laborer with the Aluminum Company of America, and Pearl Davis. The possibility that James's widowed mother, Pearl, was now living with Davis has not been pursued. If she was, she soon after returned to the family's house at Mulatto Bend.

36. Promotion sheet to prospective booking agents from Universal Attractions, New York, late 1960s (undated), in author's possession.

37. Divorce petition to the Civil District Court of Orleans Parish, dated March 8, 1949.

38. *Morning Advocate,* unrecorded date, 1940.

39. Bill Webb, interview by Jeff Hannusch, unknown date, forwarded by email to the author, 2014.

40. Justin Nystrom, "The Vanished World of the New Orleans Longshoreman," *Southern Spaces,* southernspaces.org/2014/vanished-world-new-orleans-longshoreman (accessed November 8, 2015).

41. Ibid.

42. Ibid.

43. Divorce petition to the Civil District Court of Orleans Parish, dated March 8, 1949, and judgment, dated April 18, 1949.

44. Carol was born on August 9, 1949. Her twin sisters were Cheryl and Shannon. There is no evidence that James Moore had children with Verna or anyone else, but this is an area that has not been explored to a final conclusion.

45. The 1940 Selective Training and Service Act instituted national conscription in peacetime, requiring registration of all men between twenty-one and forty-five, later amended to men aged eighteen to sixty-four, with selection for service by a national lottery or a local selection process. The World War II draft operated from 1940 until 1947, when its legislative authorization expired. From 1940, the black induction rate was lower than that for whites, and during World War II most African American soldiers served only as truck drivers and as stevedores. There is

no obvious recorded registration for James Moore but, if he was not exempt from service, then the most closely identifiable serviceman is the black civilian farmhand named James Moore born in 1924 who was enlisted by the Army at Camp Beauregard, Louisiana, on April 5, 1944, although he gave his county as Iberia Parish, some forty miles to the southwest of Baton Rouge.

46. Delehant, "Tempo" column, June 1969.

47. "Boogie Chillun" led immediately to discs by artists like Country Jim, Stick Horse Hammond, Country Paul, and even Lightnin' Hopkins. It was adapted regularly by Chicago-based artists and in recordings in Memphis at the Sun studio. The same "groove" reappeared in 1957 on Ace Records as a popular blues disc by Frankie Lee Sims, "Walking with Frankie."

48. Leslie Johnson, interview by the author, 2013.

49. For more on early field recordings, see Joshua Clegg Caffery, *Traditional Music in Coastal Louisiana* (Baton Rouge: Louisiana State University Press, 2013), and Marybeth Hamilton, *In Search of the Blues* (London: Jonathan Cape, 2007).

50. Paul Oliver, *Conversation with the Blues* (London: Cassell Books, 1965), 44.

51. Oster, liner note to *Country Negro Jam Sessions*, Folk-Lyric LP FL 111.

52. Quotations from Harry Oster's liner notes to various Folk-Lyric LPs.

53. Report of court decisions, *Morning Advocate*, August 13, 1956.

54. Quotations from Harry Oster's liner notes to various Folk-Lyric LPs.

55. Al Wilson, "Robert Pete Williams: His Life and Music," *Little Sandy Review* (Minneapolis), July 1966, 19.

56. Quotations from Harry Oster's liner notes to various Folk-Lyric LPs.

57. Hogan quotations from interviews in *Blues Unlimited* 71: 15, and vol. 74 (1990): 5; *Blues & Rhythm* 46 (1990): 18, and vol. 48 (1991): 14; *Juke Blues* 30 (1994): 26; *Living Blues* 114 (1993): 75, and vol. 115 (1994): 62.

58. Army call-up records for March 28, 1941, Silas Hogan of Scotlandville, reported in the *Morning Advocate*.

59. *Advocate*, January 1, 1944.

60. Hogan quotations from interviews in *Blues Unlimited* 71: 15, and vol. 74 (1990): 5; *Blues & Rhythm* 46 (1990): 18, and vol. 48 (1991): 14; *Juke Blues* 30 (1994): 26; *Living Blues* 114 (1993): 75, and vol. 115 (1994): 62.

61. Brett Bonner, Silas Hogan obituary, *Living Blues* 115 (1994): 62.

62. From his US Army registration card, signed February 18, 1942. Other birth dates have been given, ranging from 1917 in an *Advocate* obituary from 2001, giving his age as eighty-three, to 1924 in Beyer's *Baton Rouge Blues*.

63. Kelley interviews in *Blues & Rhythm* 64 (1990): 11, and vol. 164 (2001): 20.

64. Interviews quoted in *Living Blues* 179: 12, and vol. 198 (2005): 67; *Blues & Rhythm* 33 (1987), vol. 44 (1989): 22, and vol. 233 (2009): 13.

65. James Johnson, interview by the author, April 2015.

66. According to the 1950 city directory for Baton Rouge, where she is listed as Mrs. "Lovell Gamble."

67. William Gambler, interview by the author, 2012.

68. Lovell Moore Casey, interview by Johnny Palazzotto, 2002.

69. Lovell Moore Casey, interview by Steve Coleridge, 1990.

70. Reed and Jemison quotes from the East Baton Rouge Public Library's Louisiana Black History Hall of Fame Collection, batonrougedigitalarchive.contentdm.oclc.org/cdm/landing-page/collection/.

71. Ibid.

72. Interviews from McKinley High School project, accessed via LSU Libraries Special Collections, www.lib.lsu.edu/sites/all/files/sc/exhibits/e-exhibits/boycott/johnson.html.

73. Maxine Crump interview, July 8, 1992, by Pamela Dean, LSU Oral History Program, LSU Libraries, crdl.usg.edu/export/html/luu/ibe/crdl_luu_ibe_ibe40.html.

74. Delehant, "Tempo" column, June 1969.

75. Lovell Moore Casey, interview by Coleridge.

76. Scott Dirks, Tony Glover, and Ward Gaines, *Blues with a Feeling: The Little Walter Story* (New York: Routledge Press, 2002), 48.

77. John Broven, email correspondence with author, March 2015.

78. Dirks, Glover, and Gaines, *Blues with a Feeling*, 10.

79. All court reports from the *Morning Advocate*.

80. William Gambler, interviews by the author, 2014–16.

81. Ibid.

82. Arlene Batiste, interview by the author, 2014.

83. Ray Moore, interview by the author, 2014.

84. William Gambler, interview by Ruth Laney, *Country Roads* (Baton Rouge), June 2015, 54.

85. Lovell Moore Casey, interview by Coleridge.

86. James Moore interview, probably November 1968, from the collection of Sue Cassidy Clark held by the Center for Black Music Research.

87. Several writers have referred to Otis Hicks's parents, Jerry Lee Hicks and Sylvana Hicks, living at 302 South Jefferson Avenue in St. Louis, saying Otis was born there. There is no apparent documentary evidence for this. There are Army and prison documents stating his birthplace as Good Pine, Louisiana.

88. Liner note to Lightnin' Slim, *Rooster Blues*, Excello LP 8000.

89. Delehant, "Tempo" column, June 1969.

90. Otis Hicks, Lightnin' Slim, quoted by Mike Leadbitter, "Slim '72," *Blues Unlimited* 91 (1972): 16.

91. Leadbitter, "Slim '72," 16. There are uncertainties surrounding the identities of both Doddy and Charlie. The spelling of Monro Doddy's name is the phonetic usage by Leadbitter. In the case of the "local guitarist" known as "Left Hand" Charlie, his surname was not divulged at all, and at times writers have confused "Left Hand" Charlie with other musicians. Eddie Shuler of Goldband Records in Lake Charles, Louisiana, recorded a "Left Hand Charlie" whose songs had the songwriting credit "Morris" and who Shuler said came from Lafayette. There was an artist recorded by Jay Miller for the Excello subsidiary, Nasco Records, known as "Blue Charlie," who may also have lived in Lafayette but originated in Florida, and there was a singer and right-handed guitarist with Buddy Stewart's band in Baton Rouge named Charlie Morris who, along with another band member, Sonny Martin, recorded for Jay Miller (as Morris Charles), who leased their songs to Felsted Records. There is no certain evidence that any of these men was the guitarist described by Lightnin' Slim.

92. This and other Lightning Slim quotes in *Blues Unlimited* 52 (1968): 7, vol. 69 (1969): 5, vol. 71 (1970): 9, vol. 81 (1971): 4, and vol. 90 (1972): 17; in *Living Blues* 17 (1974): 3; and in *Blues & Rhythm* 34 (1989): 4, vol. 276 (2013): 4, and vol. 277 (2013): 15.

93. Galen Gart, *First Pressings* (Milford, NH: Big Nickel Publications, 1989), vol. 2: 21.

94. Like the expression "swamp-pop," the term "swamp-blues" was inspired by the phraseology of record reviewers in *Cash Box* and *Billboard*, but it was really coined by *Blues Unlimited* magazine and particularly Mike Leadbitter. The publication of John Broven's *South to Louisiana* in 1983 helped spread both of the terms locally.

95. Guy, *When I Left Home.*

96. Syndicated story, *Pittsburgh Courier,* December 15, 1956.

97. Lovell Moore Casey, interview by Johnny Palazzotto, 2002.

98. Quoted in John Broven, *South to Louisiana: The Music of the Cajun Bayous* (Gretna, LA: Pelican Publishing, 1983).

99. Dennis Detheridge, "Lightnin' Slim Talkin'," *Melody Maker,* June 24, 1972.

100. Guralnick, *Feel like Going Home,* 134.

2. SWAMP RECORDS AND RADIO SALES

1. Broven, *South to Louisiana,* 37.

2. Ibid., 36.

3. Dave Booth interview of Jay Miller, unpublished, broadcast on CHYM and CFNY radio, Ontario, Canada, unknown dates.

4. Broven, *South to Louisiana,* 169.

5. John Broven, *Record Makers and Breakers* (Champaign: University of Illinois Press, 2009), 169.

6. Booth radio interview of Miller.

7. Ibid.

8. Broven, *South to Louisiana,* 120.

9. Booth radio interview of Miller.

10. Ibid.

11. Broven, *South to Louisiana,* 124.

12. Bill Dahl, *Goldmine* 386 (May 12, 1995): 16.

13. Martin Hawkins, *A Shot in the Dark: Making Records in Nashville, 1945–1955* (Nashville: Country Music Foundation Press–Vanderbilt Press, 2006), 180.

14. Booth radio interview of Miller.

15. Ernie Young, interview by Shannon Williams for the author, 1999.

16. Both quotes in this paragraph are from Hawkins, *A Shot in the Dark,* 186.

17. Booth radio interview of Miller.

18. Broven, *Record Makers and Breakers,* 171.

19. *Blues Unlimited* 75 (1970).

20. Tom Mazzolini in *Living Blues* 31 (1977): 26.

21. Quoted by Tony Russell, *Melody Maker,* February 12, 1972.

22. Arnold Shaw, *Honkers and Shouters* (New York: Macmillan Books, 1978), 490.

3. I'M A KING BEE

1. James Moore interview, probably November 1968, from the collection of Sue Cassidy Clark held by the Center for Black Music Research.

2. Booth radio interview of Miller.

3. Ibid.

4. Leslie Johnson, interview with Larry Benicewicz, Baltimore Blues Society, *Westcoast Blues Review* 11 (1995): 26.

5. Delehant, "Tempo" column, June 1969.

6. Miller quoted in *Blues Unlimited* 47 (1967): 5; Gable in interview with Gene Tomko, 2012, reported in email to the author.

7. Gene Tomko, "Boogie Jake: We Used to Make 'Em Talk," *Living Blues* 231 (2013): 9.

8. Leslie Johnson, interview with author, 2014, unpublished.

9. James Johnson, interview by the author, 2014, unpublished.

10. Jay Miller, interview by Becky Shexnayder Owens, 2014, unpublished.

11. Jimmy Dotson, email to the author, 2015.

12. Delehant, "Tempo" column, June 1969.

13. Will Romano, *Big Boss Man* (San Francisco: Backbeat Books, 2006), 99–101.

14. Jay Miller, interview with Steve Coleridge, 1990.

15. James Moore, interview with Steve Coleridge, 1990.

16. Delehant, "Tempo" column, June 1969.

17. Jennifer Searcy, "The Voice of the Negro: African American Radio, WVON, and the Struggle for Civil Rights in Chicago," PhD diss., Loyola University Chicago, 2012, Dissertations, Paper 688, page 203, ecommons.luc.edu/luc_diss/688 (accessed November 12, 2015).

18. William Gambler, interview by the author, 2014; Lovell Moore Casey, interview by Coleridge, 1990.

19. Tabby Thomas, interview by Mark Jackson, *Riverside Reader* (Erwinville, LA), April 27, 1998.

20. *Still Singing the Blues,* radio documentary, Louisiana Endowment for the Humanities, 2010.

21. *Baton Rouge News Leader,* January 14, 1956.

22. Ibid., February 4, 1956.

23. Ibid., July 21–July 5, 1956.

24. Ibid.

25. Ibid.

26. Johnny Palazzotto, email to the author, 2013.

27. Jay Miller, interview by Coleridge, 1990.

28. Blues Art Studio, Larry Benicewicz, "Remembering King Karl and Guitar Gable," February 2006, www.bluesartstudio.at/NeueSeiten/King+KarlRemembering%20.html.

29. Jay Miller, interview by Mike Leadbitter, in *Crowley, Louisiana Blues* (Bexhill, UK: Blues Unlimited Publications, 1968), 9.

30. Leslie Johnson, interview by the author, 2014.

31. Booth radio interview of Miller.

32. *Advocate,* April 5, 1957.

33. *Morning Advocate,* July 17, 1958.

34. Barbara Sims, email to the author, 2015.

35. Cleveland White discussed in *Blues Unlimited* 65 (1969); *Juke Blues* 69 (2009); *Blues & Rhythm* 170 (2002), and vol. 228 (2008); and quoted in an obituary by John Wirt in the *Advocate,* February 9, 2008, 21.

36. *Morning Advocate,* March 17, 1954.

37. Ibid.

38. Clarence Edwards, interview by Terry Pattison in *Blues Unlimited* 75 (1970): 6.

39. *Morning Advocate,* January 23, 1954.

40. Clarence Edwards, interview by Coleridge, 1990.

41. Steve Coleridge, "Welcome to Chemical City USA," *Blues & Rhythm* 52 (1990): 5.

42. Guy, *When I Left Home,* 38.

43. Big Papa's band was known as the Country Boys. Dotson is not alone in mentioning "the Cane Cutters" as a band name, probably confusing the two names. If Papa Tilley used the "Cane Cutters" name as well, his musicians, such as James Johnson, have no recollection of it.

44. Jimmy Dotson, quoted in Broven, *South to Louisiana,* 142.

45. James Johnson, interview by the author, 2014.

46. "Phil Guy: Down in Louisiana," interview by Norman Darwen, *Blues & Rhythm* 33 (December 1987): 4.

47. Phil Guy, interview by Justin O'Brien in "Just One of the Guys," *Living Blues* 179 (2005): 12.

48. Guy, *When I Left Home,* 15–32.

49. Phil Guy, interview by Justin O'Brien, *Living Blues* 179 (2005): 12.

50. Kenny Neal quoted in *Blues Access* 30 (1997), www.bluesaccess.com/No_30/neals.html (last accessed December 21, 2015).

51. Raful Neal, interview by Steve Coleridge, 1990; see also *Living Blues* 91 (1990): 21–24.

52. Raful Neal, interview by Justin O'Brien, *Living Blues* 176 (2005): 80.

53. Kenny Neal quoted in *Blues Access* 30 (1997), www.bluesaccess.com/No_30/neals.html (last accessed December 21, 2015).

54. Ibid.

55. Leslie Johnson, interview by Scott Bock, *Living Blues* 163 (2002): 14.

56. Ibid.

57. Leslie Johnson, interview by the author, 2014.

58. Jeff Hannusch, "Masters of Louisiana Music," *Offbeat,* September 21, 2003, www.offbeat.com/articles/cornelius-green-lonesome-sundown/.

59. Broven, *South to Louisiana,* 135.

60. Gene Tomko, *Living Blues* 231 (December 2013): 8–9.

61. Kalamu Ya Salaam, "Dave Bartholomew: Music Legend," *Offbeat,* June 1, 1990, www.offbeat.com/articles/dave-bartholomew-music-legend/.

62. Peter Lee and David Nelson, *Living Blues* 91 (1990): 10.

63. Ernest Joseph Thomas, interview by Julian Piper, *Blues & Rhythm* 40 (1989): 4.

64. *State-Times Advocate,* December 19, 1990.

65. Chris Thomas King, "Memories of My Beloved Dad, Tabby Thomas," *Offbeat,* February 4, 2014, www.offbeat.com/news/memories-my-beloved-dad-ernest-rocking-tabby-thomas/.

66. *State-Times Advocate,* December 19, 1990.

67. Leslie Johnson, interview by the author, 2013.

68. William Gambler, telephone interview by the author, 2013.

69. William Gambler, interview by the author, January 2015.

70. The documents refer to a Joe Carl. This was either the man who booked the show or singer Joe Carl who had a band called the Dukes of Rhythm who played frequently in Baton Rouge and recorded for Jay Miller.

71. John Wirt, from a 1993 interview for the *Advocate* quoted in Rudy Richard's obituary, *Advocate,* September 25, 2014.

72. Rudy Richard, interview with Steve Coleridge, 1990, and quoted by Coleridge in "Rudy Richard and the Slim Harpo Legacy," *Wavelength,* August 1990, 21.

73. Lovell Moore Casey, interview by Coleridge, 1990.

74. John Broven, email to the author, 2012.

75. James Johnson, interview by the author, 2014.

76. Ibid.

77. Ibid.

78. "Down in Louisiana," *Blues & Rhythm* 33 (1987): 6.

79. Lynn Ourso, email to author, 2013.

80. James Johnson, interviews by the author, 2013, 2014.

81. *Morning Advocate,* March 15, 1960.

82. Ibid., April 10, 1960.

83. *State-Times Advocate,* May 5, 1960.

84. Johnny Palazzotto, email interviews by the author, 2013.

85. Liner note to Slim Harpo, *I'm a King Bee,* Ace Records, CDCHD 510.

86. Hannusch, quoting Rudy Richard in liner note to *Slim Harpo Rocks* CD.

87. Shannon Williams, in email to the author, 1999.

88. *Morning Advocate,* June 23, 1960.

89. Coleridge, "Welcome to Chemical City," 4.

90. *News Leader,* January 25, 1962.

91. Jeff Hannusch, *I Hear You Knockin': The Sound of New Orleans Rhythm and Blues* (Ville Platte, LA: Swallow Publications, 1985), 259–66.

4. RAININ' IN MY HEART

1. Mike Leadbitter, *Blues Unlimited* 91 (1992): 17.

2. Booth radio interview of Miller.

3. Larry Garner, interview by Cilla Huggins, *Juke Blues* 35 (1996): 12.

4. William Gambler, interview by the author, 2014.

5. Chelsea Brasted, *Times-Picayune,* October 12, 2013.

6. Rudy Richard, interview by Coleridge, 1990.

7. Ibid.

8. William Gambler, interview by the author, 2014.

9. "Phil Guy: Down in Louisiana," interview by Darwen, 6.

10. Lovell Moore Casey, interview by Coleridge, 1990.

11. Lovell Moore and Jesse Kinchen, both interviewed by Steve Coleridge, 1990; William Gambler, interview by the author, 2013.

12. William Gambler recalls being at a funeral in 2010 attended by Clara, but I have not sought to contact her or any of Harpo's lady friends directly, nor the descendants of his first wife, preferring just to make it clear that there were these other elements in his life.

13. Jesse Kinchen, interview by Steve Coleridge, 1990, unpublished.

14. James Moore, interview, probably November 1968, from the collection of Sue Cassidy Clark held by the Center for Black Music Research.

15. William Gambler, interview by the author, 2015.

16. Hank Davis, email to the author, 2015.

17. Broven, *South to Louisiana*, 131.

18. Ibid.

19. William Gambler, interview by the author, 2014.

20. Paul Jones, liner note to Slim Harpo, *I'm a King Bee* CD.

21. Q, 2011, "Keith Richards Record Collection," www.fiorellavaldesolo.com/index.php?/mtf/keith-richards-record-collection/ (accessed December 21 2015).

22. James Johnson, interview by the author, 2012.

23. William Gambler, interview by the author, 2014.

24. Shannon Williams, email interview by the author, 2013.

25. Publicity sheet, Dick Alen Promotions, 1968, from the archives of Bill Millar.

26. Johnny Palazzotto, email to the author 2012, based on Palazzotto's interview with Lovell Moore Casey, 2002.

27. Booth radio interview of Miller.

28. Jay Miller interview by Coleridge, 1990.

29. Lovell Moore Casey, interview by Coleridge, 1990.

30. Broven, *Record Makers and Breakers*, 167.

31. Lovell Moore Casey, interview by Coleridge, 1990.

32. Johnny Palazzotto, email to the author, 2012, based on Palazzotto's interview with Lovell Moore Casey, 2002.

33. Broven, *South to Louisiana*, 132.

34. Jay Miller, interview by Coleridge, 1990.

35. Booth radio interview of Miller.

36. William Gambler, interview by the author, 2014.

37. Jay Miller, interview by Coleridge, 1990.

38. James Johnson, interview by the author, 2013.

39. Two titles were issued in the Imperial Legendary Masters LP series, and the complete Imperial session was issued subsequently by Ace Records.

40. David Kearns, email interview by the author, 2012.

41. John Broven, email to the author, 2013.

42. David Kearns, email interview by the author, 2012.

43. David Kearns, email to the author, 2013.

44. Ibid.

45. Ibid.

46. Ibid.

47. James Johnson, interview by the author, 2013.

48. *Sting It Then,* Ace CD, 1997; *Buzzin' The Blues: The Complete Slim Harpo,* boxed set, Bear Family Records, BCD 17339 EK.

49. Steve Coleridge, email to the author, 2013.

50. Rudy Richard, interview by Steve Coleridge, 1990.

51. Lovell Moore Casey, interview by Coleridge, 1990.

52. "The Neals—First Family of the Blues," *Blues Access* 30 (1997).

53. In the song "Rednecks" in 1974, containing the lyrics "We're rednecks . . . college men from LSU / Went in dumb—come out dumb too," and the explanation that southerners are too ignorant to realize "the North has set the nigger free." The twist, though, is that in the rest of the country the freedom is "to be put in a cage" in the city ghettos.

54. David Kearns, email to the author, 2013.

55. *Louisiana Weekly,* March 11, 1961.

56. *Advocate,* March 21, 1961.

57. Ibid., June 9, 1961.

58. Ibid., June 1, 1961.

59. Otis Johnson, interview by the author, 2015.

5. BUZZIN', SCRATCHIN', HIP SHAKIN', BREAD MAKIN'

1. Peter Lee and David Nelson, "Rockin' Tabby Thomas," *Living Blues* 91 (1990): 12.

2. Shannon Williams, email to the author, 1999.

3. *Blues Unlimited* 1 (1963): 3.

4. Connie Dents, interview by the author, 2014.

5. Arlene Batiste, interview by the author, 2015.

6. Connie Dents, interview by the author, 2014.

7. Steve Coleridge, "Goin' Crazy over Jimmy," *Blues & Rhythm* 84 (1993): 17.

8. *Juke Blues* 25 (1992).

9. Coleridge, "Goin' Crazy over Jimmy," 17.

10. John Broven, *Juke Blues* 25 (1982): 8.

11. Ibid.

12. John Broven, "Here's Jimmy Anderson" *Juke Blues* 25 (1982): 9.

13. Silas Hogan, interview by Julian Piper, *Blues & Rhythm* 46 (1989): 20.

14. Beyer, *Baton Rouge Blues,* 29.

15. Leslie Johnson, interview by the author, 2014.

16. Jay Miller, interview by Steve Coleridge, 1990.

17. *Living Blues* 163 (2002): 14.

18. Jay Miller, quoted to Lynn Ourso and described in an email to the author, 2013.

19. Broven, *South to Louisiana,* 125.

20. Arlene Batiste, interview by the author, 2015.

21. Jimmy Dotson, quoted in sundayblues.org/archives/tag/jimmy-dotson (last accessed December 17, 2015).

22. Oliver, *Conversation with the Blues,* 118.

23. Gerard Herzhaft, *Encyclopedia of the Blues* (Fayetteville: University of Arkansas Press, 1992), 245.

24. Richard Allen founded the New Orleans Jazz Archive in 1958 and later became curator of the Hogan Jazz Archive at Tulane University in New Orleans.

25. Allen quoted in *Advocate,* April 17, 1983.

26. "Some Got Six Months," from the LP *Angola Prisoners' Blues,* 1959, Louisiana Folklore Society LFS A3.

27. Oliver, *Conversation with the Blues.*

28. Guralnick, *Listener's Guide to the Blues.*

29. *Still Singing the Blues.*

30. Simon Napier in *Blues Unlimited* 33 (1966): 17, writes, "The fact that so much of Oster's material is derivative is interesting insofar as it would seem from his earlier notes that he himself was unaware of this." He quotes examples of Butch Cage and Willie Thomas, Clarence Edwards, and Robert Pete Williams recording songs from discs by Peg Leg Howell, Howlin' Wolf, Barbecue Bob, and others, which Oster took to be originals.

31. Jay Miller, interview by Coleridge, 1990.

32. William Gambler, interview by the author, 2014.

33. Mike Leadbitter, "Crowley, Louisiana Blues," *Blues Unlimited* (1968): 6.

34. Broven, *South to Louisiana,* 249.

35. Hank Davis, email to the author, 2015.

36. William Gambler, interview by the author, 2013.

37. Ibid., 2015.

38. Lovell Moore Casey, interview by Coleridge, 1990.

39. Jesse Kinchen, interview by Coleridge, 1990.

40. William Gambler, interview by the author, 2015.

41. *Advocate,* October 12, 1962.

42. James Segrest and Mark Hoffman: *Moanin' at Midnight: The Life and Times of Howlin' Wolf* (New York: Thunder's Mouth Press, 2005), 75.

43. James Johnson, interview by the author, 2014.

44. John Wirt, "Blues Community Mourns Death of Rudy Richard," *Advocate,* September 26, 2014.

45. David Kearns, email interviews by the author, 2014 and April 2015.

46. Bill Wyman, *Blues Odyssey* (London: Dorling Kindersley Press, 2001), 309.

47. Hannusch, liner notes, *Slim Harpo Rocks* CD.

48. Broven, *South to Louisiana,* 133.

49. Ibid., 134.

50. Lynn Ourso, email interview by the author, 2014.

51. Broven, *South to Louisiana,* 249.

52. Rick Milne, *Down South Blues* (London: Hanover Books, 1971), 134.

53. Maxine Crump interview, July 8, 1992, by Pamela Dean, LSU Oral History Program, LSU Libraries, crdl.usg.edu/export/html/luu/ibe/crdl_luu_ibe_ibe40.html.

54. Lee and Nelson, "Rockin' Tabby Thomas," 12.

55. James Moore, interview, probably November 1968, from the collection of Sue Cassidy Clark held by the Center for Black Music Research.

56. Delehant, "Tempo" column, June 1969.

57. James Moore interview, probably November 1968, from the collection of Sue Cassidy Clark held by the Center for Black Music Research.

58. John Fred Gourrier, interview by John Broven for *South to Louisiana*.

59. James Johnson, interview by the author, 2014.

60. Etienne, interview by Becky Owens at request of the author, 2014.

61. James Johnson, interview by the author, 2014.

62. Lee and Nelson, "Rockin' Tabby Thomas," 12.

63. *Advocate,* September 25, 2014.

64. James Brown with Bruce Tucker, *The Godfather of Soul: An Autobiography* (New York: Da Capo Press, 2003).

65. Lester Kinsey, interview by Jim O'Neal, *Living Blues* 75 (1987): 16.

66. Lovell Moore Casey, interview by Coleridge, 1990.

67. James Johnson, interview by the author, 2014.

68. Delehant, "Tempo" column, June 1969.

69. Jim Delehant, "The King Bee," *Blues Unlimited* 33 (1966): 8.

70. Ray Moore, interview by the author, 2014.

71. Rick Milne, *Blues Unlimited* 33 (1966): 9.

72. David Kearns, email interview by the author, 2014.

73. David Kearns, emails to the author, 2013 and 2015.

74. James Johnson, interview by the author, 2014.

75. Ibid.

76. Kirk Beasley, interview by the author, 2014.

77. Greenville, Mississippi, *Delta Democrat Times,* October 4, 1966.

78. Broven, *Record Makers and Breakers,* 111.

79. William Gambler, interview by the author, 2015.

80. Arlene Batiste, interview by the author, 2015.

81. Ibid.

82. William Gambler, interview by the author, 2015.

83. Frank Scott, "Baton Rouge Blues," *Blues Unlimited* 87 (1971): 16.

84. James Johnson, interview by Steve Coleridge, 1990.

85. Lovell Moore Casey, interview by Coleridge, 1990.

86. Broven, *Record Makers and Breakers,* 171.

87. Booth radio interview of Miller.

88. Shannon Williams, interview by John Broven, unpublished.

89. "Crowley, Louisiana Blues," *Blues Unlimited* (1968): 6.

90. Jay Miller, interview by Coleridge, 1990.

6. THE MUSIC'S HOT

1. Confusingly, Lazy Lester has said, "I made percussion on 'Tip on In,' it was in two parts. That was recorded at the Jay Miller studio with Jesse Kinchen on drums" (interview by the author, 2014). On aural and circumstantial evidence, this is not possible in the case of the surviving, issued recording.

2. John Broven, email to author with extracts from his interviews with Shannon Williams, various dates.

3. Jesse Kinchen, interview by the author, 2014.

4. Barney Hoskyns, *Say It One Time for the Broken Hearted: Country Soul in the American South* (London: Fontana Press, 1987), 129.

5. Ted Jarrett, *You Can Make It if You Try: The Ted Jarrett Story of R&B in Nashville* (Franklin, TN: Hillsboro Press, 2005), 134.

6. Kirk Beasley, interview by the author, 2015.

7. Shannon Williams, interview by John Broven, unpublished.

8. Colin Escott, email discussion with the author, 2014.

9. Shannon Williams, interview by John Broven, unpublished.

10. Lovell Moore Casey, interview by Coleridge, 1990.

11. *New York Amsterdam Times,* January 13, 1968.

12. Rudy Richard, interview by Coleridge, 1990.

13. "Phil Guy: Down in Louisiana," interview by Darwen, 6.

14. Phil Guy, interview by Justin O'Brien, *Living Blues* 179 (2005):18.

15. Mike Stephenson, "An Interview with Sheffield Walker,"*Magic City Blues News* 257 (December 2014): 7.

16. According to Charles Cross in *Room Full of Mirrors* (New York: Hyperion Books, 2005), 90, "Most band members of the King Kasuals took day jobs to survive. Jimi toured during this time as backup for Carla Thomas, Tommy Tucker, Slim Harpo, Jerry Butler. . . . most were just a few dates on the Chitlin Circuit."

17. Lovell Moore Casey, interview by Coleridge, 1990.

18. Rudy Richard, interview by Coleridge, 1990.

19. *News Leader,* April 27, 1968.

20. Slim Harpo, interview, probably November 1968, from the collection of Sue Cassidy Clark held by the Center for Black Music Research.

21. Ray Moore, interview by the author, 2014.

22. *News Leader,* October 27, 1968.

23. *Blues Unlimited,* unrecorded date, late 1960s.

24. Lovell Moore Casey, interview by Coleridge, 1990.

25. *New York Times,* November 29, 1968.

26. Peter Guralnick, email correspondence with the author, 2015.

27. Slim Harpo, interview, probably November 1968, from the collection of Sue Cassidy Clark held by the Center for Black Music Research.

28. Ibid.

29. Delehant, "Tempo" column, June 1969.

30. *Record World,* December 14, 1968.

31. Slim Harpo, interview by Bob Austin, *Record World,* December 1968.

32. Lovell Moore Casey, interview by Coleridge, 1990.

33. *Blues Unlimited* 69 (January 1970): 3.

34. Jesse Kinchen, interviews by Coleridge, 1990, and Johnny Palazzotto, 2002.

35. Leslie Johnson, interview by the author, 2014.

36. James Moore, interview, probably November 1968, from the collection of Sue Cassidy Clark held by the Center for Black Music Research.

37. Ibid.

38. Slim Harpo, interview, probably November 1968, from the collection of Sue Cassidy Clark held by the Center for Black Music Research.

39. Lovell Moore Casey, interview by Coleridge, 1990.

40. Press release, Universal Attractions, 1969.

41. *Billboard,* March 15, 1969, 12.

42. Andy Schwarz on "The Hound" blog, thehoundblog.blogspot.co.uk/ (last accessed December 23, 2015).

43. Tony Forte, in powerpop.blogspot.co.uk/2010/09/compare-and-contrast-blues-came-down.html.

44. Lovell Moore Casey, interview by Coleridge, 1990.

45. Jesse Kinchen, interview by Coleridge, 1990.

46. Otis Johnson, interview by the author, 2015. Johnson also recalled that King Lloyd moved to near Woodville, Mississippi. Lloyd died in Centreville, Mississippi, in 2010.

47. *News Leader,* May 4, 1969.

48. William Gambler, interview by the author, 2015.

49. Jesse Kinchen, interview by Johnny Palazzotto, 2010. The name of the bass player mentioned is difficult to hear but may have been Frank Kinchen, or "Geacher."

50. Lovell Moore Casey, interview by Coleridge, 1990.

51. For more context, see Jeff Hannusch, "The Legend of Jody Ryder," *Living Blues* 163 (2002): 21.

52. Quoted by Hannusch in "The Legend of Jody Ryder," 21.

53. Bob Wilson, email interviews by the author, 2013.

54. Hoskyns, *Say It One Time for the Broken Hearted,* 133.

55. Michael J Fairchild, liner notes for *Jimi Hendrix: Blues* (MCAD-11060), MCA CD, 1994.

56. Bob Wilson, email interviews by the author, 2013.

57. Ibid.

58. Ibid.

59. *News Leader,* September 14, 1969.

60. Lynn Ourso, email interviews by the author, 2013, 2014.

61. Lynn Ourso, email to the author, 2013.

62. Roy Hayes, telephone interview by the author, 2014.

63. Steve Coleridge, commenting to the author on the Bear Family boxed set, 2015.

64. Roy Hayes, telephone interview by the author, 2014.

7. GOODBYE, SLIM HARPO

1. Ike Brown, born 1881, may have been James Moore's uncle, his mother's brother. He lived in Port Allen and was a sugarcane worker.

2. William Gambler, interview by the author, 2013.

3. Leslie Johnson, interview by the author, 2014.

4. Ibid.

5. Tabby Thomas interview, *Living Blues* 91 (1990): 15.

6. Hannusch, liner notes, *Slim Harpo Rocks* CD.

7. *Goldmine,* March 11, 1988, page unrecorded.

8. William Gambler, interviews by the author, 2013 and 2014.

9. Otis Johnson, interview by the author, 2015.

10. "Slim Harpo Dead of Heart Attack," *Rolling Stone,* March 19, 1970.

11. Ibid.

12. Lynn Ourso, interview by the author, 2013.

13. Ibid.

14. Mike Vernon, email to the author, 2014.

15. Mike Vernon, "Slim Harpo: A Tribute," *Melody Maker,* February 28, 1970, 14.

16. Lovell Moore Casey, interview by Coleridge, 1990.

17. Lovell Moore Casey, interview by Johnny Palazzotto, 2003.

18. William Gambler, interview by the author, 2014; Harris Copenhaver, correspondence from letters to David Kearns, seen by the author.

19. Bruce Bastin, "Jay Miller's Blues," *Blues Unlimited* 122 (1976): 16, 17.

20. Bruce Bastin, conversations with the author, 2013, 2014.

21. *Blues Unlimited* 74 (1970): 6.

22. Delehant, "Tempo" column, June 1969.

23. *News Leader,* April 13, 1969.

24. Ibid., January 31, 1970.

25. From city directories. For a summary, see Jonathan Olivier in Dig Baton Rouge, dig batonrouge.com/the-strip-baton-rouge-blues-history/ (last accessed December 23, 2015).

26. Ibid.

27. Ibid.

28. Steve Coleridge, "The Swamp Blues Trail," *Folk Roots,* February 1991.

29. Ibid.

30. Chris Thomas King, *Living Blues* 168 (2003): 26–41.

31. *Advocate,* December 17, 1970, quoting Harry Oster, *Living Country Blues* (Farmington Hills, MI: Gale Research Publications, 1970).

32. *Louisiana Blues,* Arhoolie 1054, LP, 1970.

33. Mike Vernon, email to the author, 2014.

34. Allen quoted in *Advocate,* April 17, 1983.

35. David Evans, interview by Alan Wilson, *Little Sandy Review* (Minneapolis), July 1966, 1–19.

36. David Evans, email to the author, 2015.

37. *Advocate,* August 20, 1968.

38. *Blues & Rhythm* 46 (1989): 18.

39. *Living Blues* 115 (1994): 62.

40. Terry Pattison, "Behind the Sun," *Blues Unlimited* 75 (1970): 7.

41. Quoted in Beyer, *Baton Rouge Blues,* 33.

42. *Advocate,* September 20, 2001.

43. Mike Leadbitter, *Nothing but the Blues* (London: Hanover Books, 1971), 153.

44. Tony Russell, "Gone Fishin'," *Melody Maker,* February 1972.

45. Fred Reif, email interview by the author, 2014.

46. *Blues Unlimited* 91 (May 1972): 15.

47. Broven, *South to Louisiana*, 127.

48. Leadbitter, *Crowley, Louisiana Blues.*

49. Leslie Johnson, interview by the author, 2014.

50. Fred Reif, email to the author, 2014.

51. Otis Johnson, interview by the author, 2015.

52. "Phil Guy: Down in Louisiana," interview by Darwen, 4.

53. Clarence Edwards, quoted in Beyer, *Baton Rouge Blues,* 42.

54. Coleridge, "Welcome to Chemical City," 5.

55. *Advocate,* April 3, 1987.

56. Ibid., February 26, 1978.

57. William Gambler, interview by the author, 2014.

58. Robert Milburn, quoted in Beyer, *Baton Rouge Blues,* 45.

59. Steve Coleridge, email to the author, 2015.

60. Lee and Nelson, "Rockin' Tabby Thomas," 10–15.

61. Broven, *South to Louisiana*, 145.

62. Otis Johnson, interview by the author, 2015. Otis Johnson went on to play with Johnnie Jackson, and Rev and the Deacons, and still plays as of October 2015.

63. Lee and Nelson, "Rockin' Tabby Thomas," 10–15.

64. Julian Piper, *Blues & Rhythm* 40 (1988): 4–7.

65. *Advocate,* January 5, 2014.

66. David Rotenstein, "A Blues Singer Coming into his Own," *Philadelphia Inquirer,* July 20, 1991, 1-D.

67. Steve Coleridge, "Raful Neal," *Living Blues* 91 (1990): 21.

68. *Blues & Rhythm* 51 (1988): 21.

69. *Advocate,* April 20, 1984.

70. Ray Moore, interview by the author, 2014.

71. *Blues Unlimited* 87 (1972): 16.

72. *Living Blues* 225 (2013): 12.

73. Coleridge, "Welcome to Chemical City," 5.

74. *Living Blues* 225 (2013): 12.

75. Lovell Moore Casey, interview by Coleridge, 1990.

76. Chelsea Brasted, *New Orleans Times-Picayune,* October 12, 2013.

77. Rudy Richard, interview by Coleridge, 1990.

78. Ibid.

79. Lynn Ourso, email to the author, 2014.

80. Johnny Palazzotto, email to the author, 2014.

81. James Johnson, interview by the author, 2014.

82. Ibid.

83. "Phil Guy: Down in Louisiana," interview by Darwen, 4.

84. Gene Tomko, *Living Blues,* December 2013, 8.

85. *Blues & Rhythm* 41 (1988): 75.

86. James Johnson, interview by the author, 2014.

87. William Gambler, interview by the author, 2014.

88. *Juke Blues* 45 (1999): 68.

89. *Broadcasting,* March 31, 1969.

90. Jack Barlow, "Chicken Scratch," *Living Blues* 234 (2010): 27.

91. James Johnson, interview by the author, 2014.

92. Quoted in Ryan Whirty, "Requiem for Slim Harpo," *Louisiana Life* (Metairie, LA), January 2010.

93. Jesse Kinchen, interview by Coleridge, 1990.

94. William Gambler, interview by the author, 2013.

95. *Advocate,* June 21, 2014.

8. THE HERITAGE BLUES

1. *Sunday Advocate,* February 26, 1978.

2. *Advocate,* July 22, 1985.

3. All quoted descriptions from *Advocate,* April 11, 1986, Fun supplement.

4. Steve Coleridge, emails to the author 2013, 2014.

5. *Living Blues* 91 (1990): 33.

6. Ibid.

7. *Juke Blues* 35 (1996).

8. *Living Blues* 143 (1999): 24.

9. Jack Barlow, "In Baton Rouge, They're Still Singing the Blues," *New York Times,* January 18, 2015, TR6.

10. Ibid.

11. Maxine Crump, email correspondence with the author, 2015; Cornel West, *The Cornel West Reader* (New York: Civitas Books, 1999), 1.

12. Johnny Palazzotto, email to the author, 2013.

13. Adcock quoted in 225 magazine, June 10, 2014, www.225batonrouge.com/entertainment/slim-harpo-music-awards-announces-2014-recipients-van-morrison-david-couvillon-and-c-c-adcock-to-be-honored.

14. Festival attendance statistics from the Baton Rouge Blues Foundation, www.batonrouge bluesfestival.org/home.

15. *Advocate,* June 21, 2014

16. Ibid.

17. Ibid.

18. Ibid., May 28, 1966.

19. William Gambler, interview by the author, 2015.

20. Whirty, quoting Kenny Neal and others, "Requiem for Slim Harpo."

21. Ibid.

22. Quoted in Whirty, "Requiem for Slim Harpo."

23. John Sinclair, *Living Blues* 168 (2003): 37.

24. *Sunday Advocate,* April 17, 1983.

DISCOGRAPHY

SLIM HARPO

All previously published Harpo discographies have started from the pioneering version published in *Blues Records, 1943–1966,* by Mike Leadbitter and Neil Slaven, as amended by subsequent editions of the *Blues Discography,* by Les Fancourt and Bob McGrath. Since then, the work of Bruce Bastin, John Broven, Rob Santos, and latterly Bill Millar has also been important in assessing and analyzing original session tapes and in making sense of the original sequence of the tapes held by the successive owners of Excello Records and by Jay Miller's family. Fortunately, Miller kept a log of song titles he recorded, by artist.

Nevertheless, the original paperwork pertaining to virtually every recording session Slim Harpo made has not survived, even for the union-registered sessions made in his later years. Harpo's session discography therefore relies to an unusually high extent on the memories of those who were present at the time. I have hoovered up their various statements made down the years and have been back to as many as I could to try to clarify their previous statements and to dig for more information. Those who knew Slim Harpo well, like James Johnson, Rudy Richard, and Lazy Lester, agree that the record needs to be put straight, and Lester is adamant that much of the session information published down the years is "as wrong as two left shoes." However, although Harpo's musicians and associates have provided much valuable information, still on occasions their memories conflict with each other or with other evidence in the recorded tapes or elsewhere. Counting everyone who has ever told an interviewer they played on "Rainin' in My Heart," for instance, would yield about five guitarists and ten drummers!

I have used what appear to be the most reliable available sources to build this picture of Harpo's sessions, and have made decisions taking into account new evidence and interviews. Within each session are listed the musicians known or most likely to have been present, but I have not attempted to specify which musicians were playing on each individual track. Some "sessions" were in fact recorded over several days or more, and the basic tracks were often added to after the event.

The studios in which Harpo recorded have never been fully documented, either. He recorded in several different studios both before and after his split with Jay Miller. Because the venues of the Miller sessions were not logged, I have drawn on the unpublished information about the dates and locations of Miller's several studios put together by John Broven along with Becky Schexnayder Owens of Lafayette in discussion with the Miller family and artists. For the post-Miller sessions, I have listed the recording studios known to have been used or most likely to have been used, based on the memories of the participants, in each case. Strangely, the few sessions made toward the end in Nashville and Baton Rouge are among the least well documented.

The record numbers given below refer to the first issue of each song, either as a single or as an LP or CD track.

Every issued song listed here is included on the CD boxed set *Buzzin' The Blues: The Complete Slim Harpo,* issued by Bear Family Records in 2015, BCD 17339.

SESSION, POSSIBLY MARCH 1957

J. D. Miller Recording Studio, 118 North Parkerson Ave., Crowley, La.; producer: Jay Miller

James (Slim Harpo) Moore: vocal, harmonica; possibly Otis Hicks: guitar; unidentified: bass; unidentified: drums

One of These Days (J. Moore)   Flyright LP 558

SESSION, PROBABLY MARCH 1957

J. D. Miller Recording Studio, 118 North Parkerson Ave., Crowley, La.; producer: Jay Miller

James (Slim Harpo) Moore: vocal, harmonica; James Taylor: guitar; Matthew Jacobs: guitar; Pee Wee Johnson: drums; Leslie Johnson (Lazy Lester): overdubbed percussion

I'm a King Bee (J. Moore)   Excello single 2113
I'm a King Bee (Alt) (J. Moore)   Flyright LP 520
This Ain't No Place for Me (J. Moore–J. West)   Flyright LP 520
I Got Love if You Want It (J. Moore)   Excello single 2113
I Got Love if You Want It (Alt) (J. Moore)   Flyright LP 558

SESSION, UNKNOWN DATE, 1957

J. D. Miller Recording Studio, 118 North Parkerson Ave., Crowley, La.; producer: Jay Miller

James (Slim Harpo) Moore: vocal, harmonica; possibly Matthew Jacobs: guitar; James Taylor: guitar; Pee Wee Johnson: drums; Sonny Martin: piano

That Ain't Your Business (J. Moore–J. West)	Flyright LP 520
Things Gonna Change (J. Moore–J. West)	Flyright LP 520

SESSION, NOVEMBER 5, 1957

J. D. Miller Recording Studio, 118 North Parkerson Ave., Crowley, La.; producer: Jay Miller

James (Slim Harpo) Moore: vocal, harmonica; possibly Leroy Washington: guitar; Gabriel Perrodin (Guitar Gable): guitar; John Clinton Perrodin: bass guitar; Clarence "Jockey" Etienne: drums; possibly Leslie Johnson (Lazy Lester): percussion

Wondering and Worryin' (J. West–J. Moore)	Excello single 2138
Wondering and Worryin' (Alt) (J. West–J. Moore)	Flyright LP 520
Wondering and Worryin' (Alt) (J. West–J. Moore)	Ace CD CHD 510
Strange Love (J. Moore–J. D. Miller)	Excello single 2138
Strange Love (Alt) (J. Moore–J. D. Miller)	Flyright LP 558

SESSION, MAY 1959

J. D. Miller Recording Studio, 118 North Parkerson Ave., Crowley, La.; producer: Jay Miller

James (Slim Harpo) Moore: vocal, harmonica; possibly Leroy Washington: guitar; Boe Melvin: guitar; possibly T. J. Kinchen: bass guitar; Wilbert Byrd: drums; possibly Leslie Johnson (Lazy Lester): percussion/guitar

You'll Be Sorry One Day (J. West)	Excello single 2162
One More Day (J. West)	Excello single 2162
One More Day (Alt) (J. West)	Flyright LP 520
One More Day (Alt) (J. West)	Flyright LP 614
Late Last Night (J. Moore–J. West)	Flyright LP 520
Cigarettes (J. Moore)	Flyright LP 607

SESSION, NOVEMBER/DECEMBER 1959

Probably J. D. Miller Recording Studio, 118 North Parkerson Ave., Crowley, La.; producer: Jay Miller

James (Slim Harpo) Moore: vocal, harmonica; probably Rudolph Richard: guitar; James Johnson: guitar; possibly Boe Melvin: guitar; Sammy K. Brown: drums; Sonny Martin or Katie Webster: piano; Willie Parker: saxophone

Bobby Sox Baby (J. Moore–J. West)	Excello LP 8003
Bobby Sox Baby (Alt) (J. Moore–J. West)	Ace CD CHD 510
Buzz Me Babe (J. Moore–J. West)	Excello single 2171
Buzz Me Babe (Alt) (J. Moore–J. West)	Ace CD CHD 510
Late Last Night (J. Moore–J. West)	Excello single 2171
Late Last Night (Alt) (J. Moore–J. West)	Excello CD 3015
That Ain't Your Business (J. Moore–J. West)	Flyright LP 558
Things Gonna Change (J. Moore–J. West)	Flyright LP 558
Talking Blues (J. Moore–J. West)	Flyright LP 558
What's Goin' On (J. Moore)	Flyright LP 520
You Ain't Never Had to Cry (J. Moore–J. West)	Flyright LP 520
That's Alright (You'll Be Sorry One Day) (J. West)	Flyright LP 520
That's Alright (You'll Be Sorry One Day) (J. West)	Ace CD CHD 1368
Rainin' in My Heart (Alt) (J. Moore–J. West)	Excello LP 8005

SESSION, JUNE 1960

Probably Jay Miller Productions Studio, North Highway 13, Crowley, La.; producer: Jay Miller

James (Slim Harpo) Moore: vocal, harmonica; probably Rudolph Richard: guitar; James Johnson: guitar; Boe Melvin: bass; Sammy K. Brown: drums; Sonny Martin: piano; Willie Parker: tenor sax

Yeah Yeah Baby (J. Moore–J. West)	Excello CD 2001
Dream Girl (J. Moore–J. West)	Excello LP 8003
Dream Girl (Alt) (J. Moore–J. West)	Flyright LP 558
Don't Start Cryin' Now (J. Moore–J. West)	Excello single 2194
Don't Start Cryin' Now (Alt) (J. Moore–J. West)	Flyright LP 558
What a Dream (J. Moore–J. West)	Excello single 2184
Blues Hang-over (J. Moore–J. West)	Excello single 2184
Blues Hang-over (Alt) (J. Moore–J. West)	Flyright LP 520

SESSION, NOVEMBER 1960

Jay Miller Productions Studio, North Highway 13, Crowley, La.; producer: Jay Miller

James (Slim Harpo) Moore: vocal, harmonica; Rudolph Richard: guitar; James Johnson: bass; Sammy K. Brown or Joe Percell: drums; Sonny Martin: piano; possibly Leslie Johnson (Lazy Lester): harmonica on "My Home Is a Prison," percussion; Willie Parker: tenor sax

My Home Is a Prison (J. D. Miller–C. Green)	Excello LP 8003
Please Don't Turn Me Down (J. Moore)	Excello single 2265

Moody Blues (Inst) (J. Moore–J. West)	Excello LP 8003
Moody Blues (Inst) (Alt) (J. Moore–J. West)	Flyright CD 05
Rainin' in My Heart (Alt) (J. Moore–J. West)	Ace CD CHD 510
Rainin' in My Heart (J. Moore–J. West)	Excello single 2194
Snoopin' Around (Instr) (J. Moore–J. West)	Excello LP 8003
Wild about My Baby (J. Moore)	Blues Unlimited single 2015
That's Alright Baby (J. Moore)	Ace CD CHD 510
Lover's Confession (J. Moore)	Excello CD 2001

SESSION, JUNE 27, 1961

Cosimo Recording Studio, 521 Governor Nicholls St., New Orleans, La.; producer: unknown

James (Slim Harpo) Moore: vocal, harmonica; probably Rudolph Richard: guitar; James Johnson: guitar; Sammy K Brown: drums; Willie Parker: tenor saxophone

Something inside Me (J. Moore)	Imperial LP LM 94001
Still Rainin' in My Heart (J. Moore)	Ace CD CHD 558
A Man Is Crying (J. Moore)	Imperial LP LM 94001
Tonite I'm Lonely (J. Moore)	Ace CD CHD 558

LIVE RECORDINGS, JUNE 30, 1961

National Guard Armory, Sage Ave., Mobile, Ala.; recorded by David Kearns and Joe Drago

James (Slim Harpo) Moore: vocal, harmonica except * and **; Rudolph Richard: guitar; James Johnson: bass guitar; Sammy K. Brown: drums; Willie Parker: tenor sax; "Tomcat": vocal* and introductions; unknown: vocal**

Star Time Theme (Instr) (J. Moore)	Bear Family CD box BCD 17339
Hold Me Tenderly (D. Malone)	AVI CD 3015
Little Liza Jane (Trad. arr. J. Moore)	Bear Family CD box BCD 17339
I'm a King Bee (J. Moore)	Ace CD CHD 658
Buzzin' (Cha Cha Cha in Blue) (J. Moore–J. West)	Ace CD CHD 658
I Got Love if You Want It (J. Moore)	Ace CD CHD 658
You Know I Love You (J. Reed)	Ace CD CHD 658
Lottie Mo (L. Dorsey–R Richard)	Ace CD CHD 658

Everybody Needs Somebody (W. Jacobs)	Ace CD CHD 658
Big Boss Man (A. Smith–W. Dixon)	Ace CD CHD 658
I'll Take Care of You (B. Benton)	Ace CD CHD 658
Boogie Chillun (J. L. Hooker)	Ace CD CHD 658
Moody Blues (Instr) (J. Moore–J. West)	Ace CD CHD 658
Sugar Coated Love (J. D. Miller)	Ace CD CHD 658
Last Night (Instr) (Mar-Keys)	Bear Family CD box BCD 17339
Mathilda* (G. Khoury–H. Thierry)	Bear Family CD box BCD 17339
Talk to Me Baby** (W. Dixon)	Bear Family CD box BCD 17339
Star Time Theme—2 (Instr) (J. Moore)	Bear Family CD box BCD 17339
I'm a King Bee—2 (J. Moore)	Ace CD CHD 658
I Don't Play (W. Dixon)	Ace CD CHD 658
I Got Love if You Want It—2 (J. Moore)	Ace CD CHD 658
Little Liza Jane—2 (Trad. arr. J. Moore)	Ace CD CHD 658
When the Saints Go Marchin' In—2 (Trad. arr. J. Moore)	Ace CD CHD 658
Rainin' in My Heart—2 (J. Moore–J. West)	AVI CD 3015

There remain from the live recordings some unissued songs, unissued band instrumentals, and unissued songs by an unknown vocalist, but these all have sound quality below the standard acceptable for release.

SESSION, SEPTEMBER 1963

Jay Miller Productions Studio, North Highway 13, Crowley, La.; producer: Jay Miller

James (Slim Harpo) Moore: vocal, harmonica; Al Foreman: guitar; Rufus Thibodeaux: bass; Austin Broussard: drums; Boo Boo Guidry, Harry Simoneaux, Peter Gunter or Bobby Fran: saxes

I Love the Life I'm Living (J. Moore)	Excello single 2239
I Love the Life I'm Living (Alt) (J. Moore)	Flyright LP 558
I Love the Life I'm Living (Alt) (J. Moore)	Ace CD CHD 510
Buzzin' (Instr) (J. Moore)	Excello single 2239
Buzzin' (Instr) (Alt) (J. Moore)	Flyright LP 558
Harpo's Blues (J. Moore)	Excello single 2265
My Little Queen Bee (Got a Brand New King) (J. West)	Excello single 2246

| My Little Queen Bee (Alt) (J. West) | Flyright LP 558 |
| Little Sally Walker (S. Thompson–S. Johnson) | Ace CD CHD 558 |

SESSION, JANUARY 1964

Jay Miller Productions Studio, North Highway 13, Crowley, La.; producer: Jay Miller

James (Slim Harpo) Moore: vocal, harmonica, possibly guitar; Rudolph Richard: guitar; James Johnson: guitar; August Ranson: bass; Sammy K. Brown: drums; Willie Parker: saxophone; unknown: saxophone

Boogie Chillun (J. L. Hooker)	Ace CD CHD 510
What's Goin' On Baby (J. Moore)	Excello single 2261
I Need Money (Keep Your Alibis) (J. Moore)	Excello single 2246
Blueberry Hill (Lewis-Stock-Rose)	Ace CD CHD 558

"What's Goin' On Baby" may be an overdub of a bed track recorded at a 1959 session.

SESSION, JUNE 1964

Jay Miller Productions Studio, North Highway 13, Crowley, La.; producer: Jay Miller

James (Slim Harpo) Moore: vocal, harmonica; Rudolph Richard: guitar; James Johnson: guitar; August Ranson: bass; Sammy K. Brown: drums; Willie Parker: tenor sax; unknown: tenor sax; unknown: piano; possibly Leslie Johnson (Lazy Lester): percussion

Sittin' Here Wondering (Wondering Blues) (J. Moore)	Excello single 2261
We're Two of a Kind (J. Moore)	Excello single 2253
We're Two of a Kind (Alt) (J. Moore)	Flyright LP 558
Still Rainin' in My Heart (J. Moore)	Excello single 2253
I'm Waiting on You Baby (Alt 1) (J. Moore)	Ace CD CHD 558
I'm Waiting on You Baby (Alt 2) (J. Moore)	Ace CD CHD 558

SESSION, JANUARY 1965

Jay Miller Productions Studio, North Highway 13, Crowley, La.; producer: Jay Miller

James (Slim Harpo) Moore: vocal, harmonica; Rudolph Richard: guitar; James Johnson: guitar; August Ranson: bass; Sammy K. Brown: drums; Willie Parker: tenor sax; unknown: tenor sax; probable overdubs—Katie Webster: organ; Lazy Lester: percussion

You'll Never Find a Love (As True as Mine) (J. Moore)	Ace CD CHD 558
Midnight Blues (J. Moore)	Excello single 2278
Loving You (The Way I Do) (J. Moore)	Excello single 2282

SESSION, OCTOBER 1965

Jay Miller Studio, Jay Miller Productions Studio, North Highway 13, Crowley, La.; producer: Jay Miller

James (Slim Harpo) Moore: vocal, harmonica; James Johnson: guitar; possibly Boe Melvin: guitar; August Ranson: bass; probably Jockey Etienne: drums; Lazy Lester: percussion

Baby Scratch My Back (J. Moore)	Excello single 2273
Baby Scratch My Back (The Scratch) (Alt) (J. Moore)	Ace CD CHD 558
I Don't Want No One (To Take Me Away from You) —1 (J. Moore)	Ace CD CHD 558
I Don't Want No One (To Take Me Away from You) —2 (J. Moore)	Ace CD CHD 558
I'm Gonna Miss You (Like the Devil) (J. Moore)	Excello single 2273

SESSION, FEBRUARY 1966

Probably Jay Miller Productions Studio, North Highway 13, Crowley, La.; producer: Jay Miller

James (Slim Harpo) Moore: vocal, harmonica, possibly guitar; James Johnson: guitar; August Ranson: bass; unknown: drums; Willie Parker: tenor sax; probable overdubs—Katie Webster: organ; Lazy Lester: percussion

Shake Your Hips (J. Moore)	Excello single 2278
Baby You Got What I Want (J. Moore)	Ace CD CHD 558
Your Love for Me Is Gone (J. Moore)	Ace CD CHD 558

SESSION, SEPTEMBER 1966

Probably Jay Miller Productions Studio, North Highway 13, Crowley, La.; producer: Jay Miller

James (Slim Harpo) Moore: vocal, harmonica, guitar; James Johnson: guitar; Boe Melvin: guitar; August Ranson: bass; possibly Jesse Kinchen: drums

I'm Your Bread Maker, Baby (J. Moore)	Excello single 2282
I Gotta Stop Loving You (J. Moore)	Ace CD CHD 558
Stop Working Blues (J. Moore)	Ace CD CHD 558

SESSION, EARLY 1967

Royal Recording, 1320 South Lauderdale, Memphis, Tenn.; producer: Ray Harris, with Bob Holmes and Shannon Williams

James (Slim Harpo) Moore: vocal, harmonica, probably guitar; probably Charles Hodges: organ; Mabon "Teenie" Hodges: guitar; Leroy Hodges: bass; possibly Jesse Kinchen: drums

Tip on In (Part 1) (J. Moore–R. Holmes)	Excello single 2285
Tip on In (Part 2) (J. Moore–R. Holmes)	Excello single 2285
I'm Gonna Keep What I've Got (J. Moore)	Excello single 2289
I've Got to Be with You Tonight (J. Moore)	Excello single 2289
Hey Little Lee (J. Moore)	Excello LP 8008

SESSION, LATE 1967/EARLY 1968

Probably Woodland Sound Studio, 1011 Woodland St., Nashville, Tenn.; producer: Bob Holmes

James (Slim Harpo) Moore: vocal, harmonica, possibly guitar; probably Frank Smith: guitar; Sheffield Walker: guitar; Billy Cox: bass; Freeman Brown: drums; Bob Holmes: organ; unknown: second vocal on *Stick Your Chest Out Baby*

Mailbox Blues (J. Moore–R. Stuart)	Excello single 2294
Te-Ni-Nee-Ni-Nu (J. Moore)	Excello single 2294
Stick Your Chest Out Baby (J. Moore)	Excello LP 28030

SESSION, EARLY SUMMER 1968

Woodland Sound Studio, 1011 Woodland St., Nashville, Tenn.; producer: Bob Holmes

James (Slim Harpo) Moore: vocal, harmonica, guitar; Frank Smith: guitar; Sheffield Walker: guitar; Billy Cox: bass; possibly Freeman Brown: drums; Bob Holmes: organ

My Baby She's Got It (J. Moore)	Excello LP 8008
I'm So Sorry (J. Moore)	Excello LP 8008
I've Been a Good Thing for You (J. Moore)	Excello LP 8008

SESSION, LATE 1968

Fame Recording Studios, 603 East Avalon Ave., Muscle Shoals, Ala.; producer: Aaron Varnell

James (Slim Harpo) Moore: vocal, harmonica; Jimmy Johnson: guitar; unknown: guitar; probably Billy Cox: bass; Roger Hawkins: drums; unknown: organ, piano; unknown: horns

Mohair Sam (D. Frazier)	Excello single 2301
Mohair Sam (Alt) (D. Frazier)	Unissued re-mix
I Just Can't Leave You (J. Moore)	Excello single 2301
I Just Can't Leave You (Alt) (J. Moore)	Excello LP 8008

SESSION, PROBABLY EARLY 1969

Brill Building, New York City

Demo session

James (Slim Harpo) Moore: vocal, harmonica; unknown: guitar; unknown: bass; unknown: drums; unknown: piano

Big Black Car (T. Forte)	Unissued
Other titles unknown	

SESSION, PROBABLY JANUARY/FEBRUARY 1969

Woodland Sound Studio, 1011 Woodland St., Nashville, Tenn.; producer: Bob Holmes

James (Slim Harpo) Moore: vocal, harmonica, guitar; possibly Frank Smith: guitar; possibly Sheffield Walker: guitar; Billy Cox: bass; possibly Freeman Brown: drums; Bob Holmes

That's Why I Love You (J. Moore)	Excello single 2305
Just for You (J. Moore)	Excello single 2305
Mutual Friend (J. Moore)	Excello single 2306
The Price Is Too High (T. Jarrett)	Excello single 2309

A horn section was overdubbed onto "The Price Is Too High" by Pee Wee Ellis after the session of April 1969, below.

SESSION, MARCH 1969

Probably Audio Arts Studio, 5607 Melrose Ave., Los Angeles, Calif.; producer: Slim Harpo

James (Slim Harpo) Moore: vocal, harmonica, possibly guitar; probably Simmie Kinchen: guitar; probably Lloyd Palmer: bass; probably Jesse Kinchen: drums

Jody Man (J. Moore)	Excello single 2316
The Hippy Song (J. Moore)	Excello LP 8013
Dynamite (J. Moore)	Excello LP 8013
Got My Mojo Working (Arr. Harpo)	Incomplete/unissued
Probably:	
I'm All Mixed Up	
and other unknown titles	

SESSION, PROBABLY APRIL 1969

Woodland Sound Studio, 1011 Woodland St., Nashville, Tenn.; producer: Bob Wilson, Ben Keith

James (Slim Harpo) Moore: vocal, harmonica; Bob Wilson: keyboards; Ben Keith: dobro; Mac Gayden: guitar; Billy Cox: bass; Karl Himmel: drums; Pee Wee Ellis: alto saxophone; Norm Ray: baritone saxophone

Folsom Prison Blues (J. Cash)	Excello single 2306
I've Got My Finger on Your Trigger	
(B. Keith–B. Wilson–B. Cox)	Excello single 2309

SESSION, DECEMBER 1969

Deep South Recording Studio, 100 Government St., Baton Rouge, La.; producer: Lynn Ourso

James (Slim Harpo) Moore: vocal, harmonica, guitar; unknown: guitar; Lynn Ourso: guitar; unknown: bass; Chuck Mitchell: drums; unknown: piano

The Music's Hot (J. Moore–R. Hayes)	Excello LP 8013
You Can't Make It (J. Moore–R. Hayes)	Excello LP 8013
Boogie Chillun (J. L. Hooker)	Excello LP 8013
Rock Me Baby (King-Josea)	Excello LP 8013
Baby Please Come Home (J. Moore)	Excello LP 8013

SESSION, JANUARY 1970

Possibly home demo, Thirty-Sixth St., Baton Rouge, La.; producer: Slim Harpo

James (Slim Harpo) Moore: vocal, harmonica, probably guitar; unidentified vocal chorus

There's Nothing as Sweet as Making Up	
(J. Moore–R. Hayes)	Bear Family CD box BCD 17339

I have excluded from this discography several tracks issued on AVI, Ace, P-Vine, and other labels that purport to be different versions of some of the songs listed above, but which are not in fact different. Neither have I included a song called "Bought Me a Ticket," issued in 2014 on an Ace CD, because the artist is quite clearly not Slim Harpo.

BATON ROUGE BLUES

The following is a summary of the commercial singles issued as 45-rpm or 78-rpm discs by blues or blues/R&B-related singers associated with Baton Rouge during and just before and after the years Slim Harpo was recording. There could be differing views on what discs are blues and what are R&B, and who was a Baton Rouge artist and who wasn't, but I have aimed to be inclusive rather than exclusive. Other discs on these labels that have no relevance to Baton Rouge blues or R&B are excluded. The list is set out by record label rather than by artist, and roughly chronologically, with the year of issue of the first and last discs listed being indicated in parentheses.

The singles lists are followed by details of the original Excello long-playing albums, and by a selection of albums issued on other labels during Slim Harpo's lifetime or by his contemporaries.

HOLLYWOOD RECORDS

Los Angeles; owner John Dolphin

237   Tabby Thomas, *Midnight Is Calling / I'll Make the Trip* (1952)

DELTA

Jackson, Miss.; owner Jimmie Ammons

415   Buddy Stewart, *Wheeling and Dealing / Tired of Your Putting Down*
416   Tabby Thomas, *Thinking Blues / Church Members Ball* (1953)

FEATURE

Crowley, La.; owner Jay Miller

3006   Lightning Slim, *Bad Luck / Rock Me Mama* (1954)
3007   Tabby Thomas with Bob Johnson Orchestra, *Tomorrow / Mmmmm I Don't Care*
3008   Lightning Slim, *I Can't Live Happy / New Orleans Bound*
3012   Lightning Slim, *Bugger Bugger Boy / Ethel Mae*
3013   Schoolboy Cleve, *She's Gone / Strange Letter Blues* (1955)

ACE

Jackson, Miss.; owner Johnny Vincent Imbragulio

505   Lightning Slim, *Bad Feelin' Blues / Lightning Slim Blues* (1955)

Ace also issued discs by white rock and ballad singers Jimmy Clanton, Ike Clanton, the Rockets, and by R&B artists Sugar Boy Crawford, Big Boy Myles, and Joe Tex who had links with Baton Rouge. Ace had major hits with Clanton following "Just a Dream" in 1957 and with New Orleans group Huey "Piano" Smith and the Clowns. Johnny Vincent issued country, R&B, and rock 'n' roll on other labels, including Champion and Vin, but no Baton Rouge bluesmen.

EXCELLO

Nashville, Tenn.; owner Ernie Young

2066	Lightnin' Slim, *Lightnin' Blues / I Can't Be Successful* (1955)
2075	Lightnin' Slim, *Sugar Plum / Just Made Twenty-One*
2080	Lightnin' Slim, *Goin' Home / Wonderin' and Goin'*
2092	Lonesome Sundown, *Leave My Money Alone / Lost without Love*
2095	Lazy Lester, *I'm Gonna Leave You Baby / Lester's Stomp*
2096	Lightnin' Slim, *Bad Luck and Trouble / Have Your Way*
2102	Lonesome Sundown, *My Home Is a Prison / Lonesome Whistler*
2106	Lightnin' Slim, *Mean Ole Lonesome Train / I'm Grown*
2107	Lazy Lester, *They Call Me Lazy / Go Ahead*
2112	Joe Hudson and the Rocking Dukes, *Baby Give Me a Chance / Ooh Wee Pretty Baby*
2113	Slim Harpo, *I'm a King Bee / I Got Love if You Want It*
2116	Lightnin' Slim, *I'm a Rollin' Stone / Love Me Mama*
2117	Lonesome Sundown, *I've Got the Blues / Don't Say a Word*
2129	Lazy Lester, *I Told My Little Woman / Tell Me Pretty Baby*
2131	Lightnin' Slim, *Hoo Doo Blues / It's Mighty Crazy*
2132	Lonesome Sundown, *Lonely Lonely Me / I'm a Mojo Man*
2135	Eddie Hudson, *That Long Lost Baby / She's Sugar Sweet*
2138	Slim Harpo, *Wondering and Worryin' / Strange Love*
2142	Lightnin' Slim, *My Starter Won't Work / Long Leanie Mama*
2143	Lazy Lester, *I'm a Lover, Not a Fighter / Sugar Coated Love*
2145	Lonesome Sundown, *Don't Go / I Stood By*
2150	Lightnin' Slim, *I'm Leavin' You / Feelin' Awful Blue*
2154	Lonesome Sundown, *You Know I Love You / No Use to Worry*
2155	Lazy Lester, *I Hear You Knockin' / Through the Goodness of My Heart*
2160	Lightnin' Slim, *Sweet Little Woman / Lightnin's Troubles*
2162	Slim Harpo, *You'll Be Sorry One Day / One More Day*
2163	Lonesome Sundown, *If You See My Baby / Gonna Stick to You Baby*
2166	Lazy Lester, *I Love You, I Need You / Late, Late in the Evening*
2169	Lightnin' Slim, *Rooster Blues / G.I. Slim*
2171	Slim Harpo, *Buzz Me Babe / Late Last Night*

2173   Lightnin' Slim, *Tom Cat Blues/Bed Bug Blues*
2174   Lonesome Sundown, *Love Me Now/Learn to Treat Me Better*
2179   Lightnin' Slim, *Too Close Blues/My Little Angel Chile*
2182   Lazy Lester, *Bye Bye Baby (Gonna Call It Gone)/A Real Combination for Love*
2184   Slim Harpo, *Blues Hang-over/What a Dream*
2186   Lightnin' Slim, *Cool Down Baby/Nothin' But the Devil*
2194   Slim Harpo, *Rainin' in My Heart/Don't Start Cryin' Now*
2195   Lightnin' Slim, *I Just Don't Know/Somebody Knockin'*
2197   Lazy Lester, *Patrol Blues/You Got Me Where You Want Me*
2202   Lonesome Sundown, *Lonesome Lonely Blues/I'm Glad She's Mine*
2203   Lightnin' Slim, *I'm Tired Waitin' Baby/Hello Mary Lee*
2206   Lazy Lester, *I'm So Glad/Whoah Now*
2207   Sonny Martin, *Air Force–U.S. Navy/Life Will Be So Hard to Bear*
2212   Tabby Thomas, *Hoodo Party/Roll on Ole Mule*
2213   Lonesome Sundown, *My Home Ain't Here/I Woke Up Cryin'*
2215   Lightnin' Slim, *Mind Your Own Business/You're Old Enough to Understand*
2219   Lazy Lester, *If You Think I've Lost You/I'm So Tired*
2220   Jimmy Anderson, *Naggin'/Nothing in This World*
2221   Silas Hogan, *You're Too Late Baby/Trouble at Home Blues*
2222   Tabby Thomas, *He's Got the Whole World in His Hands/Popeye Train*
2224   Lightnin' Slim, *I'm Warning You Baby/Winter Time Blues*
2227   Jimmy Anderson, *Going through the Park/I'm a King Bee*
2228   Lightnin' Slim, *I'm Evil/If You Ever Need Me*
2230   Lazy Lester, *Lonesome Highway Blues/I Made Up My Mind*
2231   Silas Hogan, *Airport Blues/I'm Gonna Quit You Pretty Baby*
2232   Whispering Smith, *Mean Woman Blues/Hound Dog Twist*
2234   Lightnin' Slim, *You Know You're So Fine/Lovin' around the Clock*
2235   Lazy Lester, *You're Gonna Ruin Me Baby/Strange Things Happen*
2236   Lonesome Sundown, *When I Had, I Didn't Need/I'm a Samplin' Man*
2237   Whispering Smith, *Don't Leave Me Baby/Live Jive*
2239   Slim Harpo, *I Love the Life I'm Livin'/Buzzin'*
2240   Lightnin' Slim, *Blues at Night/Don't Mistreat Me Baby*
2241   Silas Hogan, *I'm Goin' in the Valley/Lonesome La La*
2242   Lonesome Sundown, *Guardian Angel/I Wanta Know Why*
2243   Lazy Lester, *A Word about a Woman/The Same Thing Could Happen to You*
2245   Lightnin' Slim, *The Strangest Feelin'/You Give Me the Blues*
2246   Slim Harpo, *Little Queen Bee/I Need Money*
2249   Lonesome Sundown, *I Had a Dream Last Night/Got a Broken Heart*

2250	Whispering Smith, *Cryin' Blues/I Tried So Hard*
2251	Silas Hogan, *Dark Clouds Rollin'/I'm in Love with You Baby*
2252	Lightnin' Slim, *Greyhound Blues/She's My Crazy Little Baby*
2253	Slim Harpo, *Still Rainin' in My Heart/We're Two of a Kind*
2254	Lonesome Sundown, *You're Playin' Hookey/Please Be on That 519*
2255	Silas Hogan, *Everybody Needs Somebody/Just Give Me a Chance*
2257	Jimmy Anderson, *Goin' Crazy Over T.V./Love Me Babe*
2258	Lightnin' Slim, *Baby Please Come Home/You Move Me Baby*
2259	Lonesome Sundown, *Hoo Doo Woman Blues/I'm Gonna Cut Out on You*
2260	Whispering Smith, *I Can't Take It No More/Baby You're Mine*
2261	Slim Harpo, *Sittin' Here Wondering/What's Goin' On Baby*
2262	Lightnin' Slim, *Have Mercy on Me Baby/I've Been a Fool for You Darling*
2264	Lonesome Sundown, *It's Easy When You Know How/Gonna Miss You When You're Gone*
2265	Slim Harpo, *Harpo's Blues/Please Don't Turn Me Down*
2266	Silas Hogan, *Baby Please Come Back/Out and Down Blues*
2267	Lightnin' Slim, *Can't Live This Life No More/Bad Luck Blues*
2269	Lightnin' Slim, *Don't Start Me to Talkin'/Darling You're the One*
2270	Silas Hogan, *Every Saturday Night/So Long Blues*
2271	Silas Hogan, *Early One Morning/If I Ever Needed You Baby*
2272	Lightnin' Slim, *Love Is a Gamble/I Hate to See You Leave*
2273	Slim Harpo, *Baby Scratch My Back/I'm Gonna Miss You (Like the Devil)*
2274	Lazy Lester, *Take Me in Your Arms/You Better Listen*
2276	Lightnin' Slim, *Just a Lonely Stranger/Goin' Away Blues*
2277	Lazy Lester, *Because She's Gone/Ponderosa Stomp*
2278	Slim Harpo, *Shake Your Hips/Midnight Blues*
2281	Tab Thomas, *Play Girl/Keep On Trying*
2282	Slim Harpo, *I'm Your Bread Maker, Baby/Loving You*
2285	Slim Harpo, *Tip on In—Part 1/Tip on In—Part 2*
2289	Slim Harpo, *I'm Gonna Keep What I've Got/I've Got to Be with You Tonight*
2294	Slim Harpo, *Te-Ni-Nee-Ni-Nu/Mailbox Blues*
2301	Slim Harpo, *Mohair Sam/I Just Can't Leave You*
2305	Slim Harpo, *That's Why I Love You/Just for You*
2306	Slim Harpo, *Folsom Prison Blues/Mutual Friend*
2309	Slim Harpo, *The Price Is Too High/I've Got My Finger on Your Trigger*
2315	Arthur Guitar Kelley, *Number Ten at the Station (and Number 12 Is on the Road)/How Can I Stay*
2316	Slim Harpo, *Jody Man/Raining in My Heart*

2320   Lightnin' Slim, *Good Morning Heartaches/My Babe*
2326   Bobby Powell, *Your Good, Good Loving/All These Things Made You Mine*
2331   Bobby Powell, *Nothing Takes the Place of You/Wake Up People*
2338   Whispering Smith, *Why Am I Treated So Bad/It's All Over*
2339   Bobby Powell, *Your Good, Good Loving/I'm Going to Win Her Love*
2341   Bobby Powell, *Thank You/C.C. Rider*
2343   Bobby Powell, *Crazy Love/Her Love Is All I Need* (1974)

ZYNN

Crowley, La.; owner Jay Miller

503   Henry Clement, *I'm So in Love with You/Please Please Darling* (1957)
504   The Gay Notes, *Plea of Love/Waiting in the Chapel*
511   Jimmy Dotson and the Blue Boys, *I Wanna Know/Looking for My Baby*
513   Little Henry and the Dew Drops, *What Have I Done Wrong/Jenny Jenny Jenny* [Henry Clement]
1002   Tabby Thomas, *My Baby's Got It/Tomorrow I'll Be Gone*
1006   Henry Clement, *I'll Be Waiting/Trojan's Walla*
1014   Jimmy Anderson, *Angel Please/I Wanna Boogie* (1962)

ROCKO

Crowley, La.; owner Jay Miller

511   Tabby Thomas, *Too Late Blues/Don't Say* (1958)
516   Jimmy Dotson, *Oh Baby/I Need Your Love*
518   Sonny Martin, *When True Love Is Gone/How to Win Your Love* (1959)

PEACOCK

Houston; owner Don Robey

1686   Raful Neal, *Sunny Side of Love/Crying Hard* (1958)

MONTEL

Baton Rouge, La.; owner Sam Montalbano

1001   Lester Robertson and the Upsetters, *My Girl across Town/Take It on Home to Grandma* (1958)

1003 James "Sugar Boy" Crawford and His Cane Cutters, *Danny Boy / White Christmas*

1003 [also] James "Sugar Boy" Crawford and His Cane Cutters, *Danny Boy / Round and Round*

1004 James "Sugar Boy" Crawford, *My Heart Forever Yearning / Oh Babe*

903 Lester Robertson and the Upsetters, *My Girl across Town / My Heart Forever Yearns* (1961)

905 Lester Robertson, *Send for Me / Everybody Wants to Know*

913 The Nitehawks, *Big Bo and the Arrows, Boogie Chillun / Well, Get It*

913 [also] The Nitehawks, *Big Bo and the Arrows, Boogie Chillun / Record Machine* (1963)

MICHELLE

Baton Rouge, La.; owners Sam and Mickey Montalbano

916 Miss Ann and the Nitehawks, *I'm Calling on You / Muddy* (1963)

929 Lee Tillman, *All These Things / One More Time*

931 James "Sugar Boy" Crawford and His Cane Cutters, *Danny Boy / Round and Round*

934 Joe Tex, *The Next Time She's Mine / I've Got a Song*

935 Lee Tillman, *Fortune Teller / One Kind of Love*

938 Lee Tillman, *Have Love Will Travel / If I Ever*

948 Tabby Thomas, *Closer to My Heart / Let Me Have Two* (1965)

MONTEL-MICHELLE

Baton Rouge, La.; owners Sam and Mickey Montalbano

953 Lee Tillman, *Kiss Tomorrow Goodbye / One Kind of Love* (1964)

963 Lee Tillman, *Tossin' and Turnin' / I Can't Forget Your Love* (1965)

Montel Records and the associated Michelle and Montel-Michelle labels issued a number of records by rock 'n' roll groups from the Baton Rouge area and the top-selling white swamp-pop duo Dale and Grace, notably "I'm Making It All Up to You" in 1963.

AMA

New Orleans, La.; owner unknown

503 Robert Pete Williams, *Letter from the Penitentiary / Part Two* (possibly 1959)

MINIT

New Orleans, La.; owner Joe Banashak

   601/2   Boogie Jake, *Bad Luck and Trouble/Early Morning Blues* (1959)
   608   Mathew Jacobs, *Chance for Your Love/Loaded Down* (1960)

SPOT

Crowley, La.; owner Jay Miller

   1000   Henry Clement, *Late Hour Blues/Trojan Walla* (1961)

HOME OF THE BLUES

Memphis, Tenn.; owners Celia Camp and Ruben Cherry

   244   Jimmy Dotson, *Search No More/Feel Alright* (1962)

ALON

New Orleans, La.; owner Joe Banashak

   9001   The Night Hawks, *Rockin' Hawk/Your Somethin' Else* (1962)

REYNAUD

Opelousas, La.; owner Lloyd Renaud

   1017   Schoolboy Cleve, *Leaving You Baby/New Kind of Loving* (1963)

WHIT

Baton Rouge, La.; owner Lionel Whitfield

   1   Larry Seibert and the Jaguars, *Never Come Back/You Said* (1965)
   711   Merle Spears, *I Want to Know/I'm Gonna Move to the Outskirts of Town*
   712   Bobby Powell, *What Are You Trying to Do to Me/Red Sails in the Sunset*
   713   Merle Spears, *Ain't No Need/It's Just a Matter of Time*
   714   Bobby Powell, *That Little Girl of Mine/C. C. Rider*
   715   Bobby Powell, *Do Something for Yourself/It's Getting Late in the Evening*
   716   Bobby Powell, *I'm Gonna Leave You/Hold My Hand*
   717   Bobby Powell with Jackie Johnson, *I'm Gonna Leave You/Done Got Over*

718   Lee Tillman and the Secrets, *She's the One I Love / Trash*
729   Bobby Powell, *Have a Good Time / I Care*
730   Bobby Powell, *Thank You / Why Am I Treated So Bad*
731   Bobby Powell, *Just a Matter of Time / Question*
732   Bobby Powell, *I've Been Waiting / Stay in Bed*
6900   Bobby Powell, *Who Is Your Lover / I'm Not Going to Cry over Spilled Milk*
6901   Raful Neal, *Blues on the Moon / Let's Work Together*
6902   Bobby Powell, *Funky Broadway 1969 / In Time*
6903   Bobby Powell, *Cry to Me / There Is Something in a Man*
6904   Raful Neal, *You Don't Love Me No More / It's Been So Long*
6905   Bobby Powell, *Have a Heart / They Don't Know*
6907   Bobby Powell, *The Bells (Vocal) / The Bells* (Instr)
6908   Bobby Powell, *Peace Begins Within / Question*
6909   Bobby Powell, *Into My Own Thing / Love Man* (1970s)

EL-TEE RECORDS

Baton Rouge, La.; probable owner Lionel Whitfield

101   Charles Dixon, *Come to Me / One of These Days* (mid-1960s)

BUDIX

Baton Rouge, La.; owners Buddy Stewart and Charles Dixon

133   Chuck Mitchell with Buddy Stewart's Top Notchers, *Her Precious Love / Your Good Loving* (1965)

J-MER

New Orleans, La.; owner Cosimo Matassa

101   Merle Spears with Johnnie Jackson and the Blazers, *What You Gonna Do / Wisdom of a Fool* (1966)

HERCULOIDS

Baton Rouge, La.; owner Roy Stewart

1001/1002   The Herculoids, *Get Back / When Something Is Wrong with My Baby* (1967)

LA LOUISIANNE

Lafayette, La.; owner Carol Rachou

8116   Raful Neal, *Change My Way of Livin'/Getting Late in the Evening* (1969)

BLUES UNLIMITED

Crowley, La.; owner Jay Miller

1001   Henry Gray, *A Lucky Lucky Man/You're My Midnight Dream* (1970)
2015   Slim Harpo, *Wild about My Baby/Rainin in My Heart* (1979)
2019   Tabby Thomas, *Where You're Shackin' At/Mean and Evil Woman*
2022   Tabby Thomas, *Nose Wide Open/Candy* (1981)

AHURA MAZDA

New Orleans, La.; owner Parker Dinkins

101   Robert Pete Williams, *Goodbye Slim Harpo/Vietnam Blues* (1971)

BLUES CONNOISSEUR

San Francisco, Calif.; owner Don Lindenau

1002   Schoolboy Cleve, *My Heart Is Crying/If It's Love You Want,
          Come to Me* (1972)

CHERRIE

San Francisco, Calif.; owner Cleveland White

2372   School Boy Cleve, *Here I Go Again/Really, I Apologize* (1973)
2400   School Boy Cleve, *Don't Thread on Me/I Saw the Blues* (1977)

SUNLAND

Val Rico, Fla.; owners Bob Snow and Bob Scheir

101   Tabby Thomas, *My Special Plea/Got My Eye on You* (1982)
102   Whispering Smith and the Mighty House Rockers, *Just Like a
          Woman/Hound Dog Crawl* (Instr)
107   Robert Milburn and His Blue Notes, *Money Hustlin' Woman/
          We Gonna Party Tonight*
??? #   Lazy Lester, *Tell Me Baby/Night Time Is the Right Time*

FANTASTIC

Val Rico, Fla.; owners Bob Snow and Bob Scheir

102   Raful Neal, *Hard Times/Down Home Blues* (1985)

103   Raful Neal, *Man Watch Your Woman/Baby Scratch My Back* (1985)

BIG BOE

Baton Rouge, La.; owner Boe Melvin Hill

101   Big Boe and the Night Hawks, *My Thing/Do the Best You Can* (1980s)

102   Big Boe Melvin and the Night Hawks, *You Don't Know Like I Know/ Thank You Falletin Me Be Miceelf Again*

103   Big Boe Melvin and the Night Hawks, *Country Funk/Country Funk— Part Two* (1983)

There is a fine cut-off point between black music tending toward blues, and that tending toward soul music. I have left out the details of many Baton Rouge discs at the soul end of the spectrum, but the following summary gives an indication of the artists and labels concerned.

Joe Johnson, who may have been from the Baton Rouge area, saw many singles issued in the late 1960s and 1970s, starting with a Jay Miller label, Cry, and a subsidiary of Excello, A-Bet.

In the same time period, Walter Boulingy from Baton Rouge saw discs issued as Dynamic Walter B on labels in Baton Rouge, New Orleans, and California.

In the 1970s, George Perkins from Denham Springs, close to Baton Rouge, had discs issued on the local Golden, Second Line, 3 Stars, Red Stick, Soul Power, Royal Shield, and Cryin' in the Streets labels, owned variously by Ebb Harrison and himself.

Ernest Jackson from Baton Rouge recorded for the Bofuz and Stone labels in Baton Rouge in the 1960s and 1970s.

Finally, in the period after Slim Harpo died in 1970, Tabby Thomas recorded with other local artists in a range of R&B and soul styles, with an occasional blues, on labels including Tic Toc, Hartco-Golden, Hip, Jin, Jay-J3, 3 Stars, Vedette, Soul International, Bullseye, Blue Beat, and Maison de Soul, many of them local to Baton Rouge and some self-owned. He also recorded Silas Hogan on Blue Beat 1002, Bad Little Puppy/Hairy Leg Woman, in 1986.

Those with an interest in the soul end of the spectrum will enjoy the Baton Rouge aspects of the website Deep Soul Heaven: www.sirshambling.com/

EXCELLO LPS

LP-8000	Lightnin' Slim, *Rooster Blues* (1960)
LPS-8003	Slim Harpo, *Raining in My Heart* (1961)
LPS-8004	Lightnin' Slim, *Bell Ringer* (1965)
LPS-8005	Slim Harpo, *Baby Scratch My Back* (1966)
LPS-8006	Lazy Lester, *True Blues* (1967)
LPS-8008	Slim Harpo, *Tip on In* (1968)
LPS-8010	Slim Harpo, *The Best of Slim Harpo* (1969)
LPS-8011	Various Artists, *The Real Blues* (1969)
LPS-8012	Lonesome Sundown, *Lonesome Lonely Blues* (1970)
LPS-8013	Slim Harpo, *Slim Harpo Knew the Blues* (1970)
LPS-8015	Various Artists, *Swamp Blues, Volume 1* (1970)
LPS-8016	Various Artists, *Swamp Blues, Volume 2* (1970)
LPS-8018	Lightnin' Slim, *High and Low Down* (1971)
LPS-8019	Silas Hogan, *Trouble at Home* (1972)
EX-8020	Whispering Smith, *Over Easy* (1972)
LPS-8021	Various Artists, *Blues Live in Baton Rouge* (1971)
LPS-8023	Lightnin' Slim, *London Gumbo* (1972)
LPS-8025	Various Artists, *The Excello Story* (1972)
LPS-8028	Bobby Powell, *Thank You* (1972)

SELECTED OTHER BLUES LPS

Louisiana Folklore Society

LFS A-3	Robert Pete Williams et al., *Angola Prisoners' Blues* (1959)
LFS A-5	Robert Pete Williams et al., *Prison Worksongs*
LFS A-6	Robert Pete Williams et al., *Angola Prison Spirituals*

Folk-Lyric

FL 109	Robert Pete Williams, *Those Prison Blues*
FL 111	Various Artists, *Country Negro Jam Sessions*
FL 118	Smoky Babe and Friends, *Hot Blues* (1961)

Bluesville

1026	Robert Pete Williams, *Free Again* (1961)

Storyville

SLP 129   Butch Cage, Willie Thomas, Clarence Edwards et al., *The Country Blues* (1962)

Takoma

1011   Robert Pete Williams, *Louisiana Blues* (1966)

Ahura Mazda

AMS 2002   Robert Pete Williams, *Robert Pete Williams* (1971)

The Harry Oster artists and especially Robert Pete Williams were also included on other various-artists LPs during the 1960s and beyond.

Big Boe

LP 102   Boe Melvin and the Night Hawks, *Night Hawks* (1980s)

Sunland

LP 2001   Various Artists [Henry Gray, Raful Neal, Robert Milburn, Whispering Smith, Tabby Thomas], *Louisiana Blues Anthology* (1984)

Fantastic

LP 1001   Raful Neal, *Louisiana Legend* (1987)

RECOMMENDED LISTENING

For those with a deep interest in Slim Harpo, the Bear Family boxed set of five CDs contains in its 153 tracks all the music you need to hear—both sides of each of the original Excello 45-rpm singles; all tracks issued on LPs; all tracks not originally issued but appearing on LP and CD since Harpo's death, including all alternative versions of songs; and an extended version of a live show by Slim Harpo and his King Bees from 1961.

Slim Harpo: Buzzin' The Blues (Bear Family Records BCD 17339 EK, issued in 2015)

For those seeking a shorter overview, try:

The Excello Singles Anthology (Hip-O 000058302)
The Best of Slim Harpo (Ace CDCHM 410)
I'm a King Bee (Ace CD CHD 510)

For those interested in other Baton Rouge bluesmen of Harpo's era, try:

Lightnin' Slim, Rooster Blues / Bell Ringer (Ace CD CHD 517)
Robert Pete Williams, I'm Blue as a Man Can Be (Arhoolie CD 394)
Robert Pete Williams, Robert Pete Williams (Fat Possum CD 80349)
Herman E. Johnson / Smoky Babe, Louisiana Country Blues (Arhoolie CD 440)
Silas Hogan, So Long Blues (Ace CD CHD 523)
Various Artists, Swamp Blues (Ace CD CHD 661)
Various Artists, Country Negro Jam Session (Arhoolie CD 372)

This is a very short and to-the-point list. The Internet will reveal dozens more CDs containing blues-related music by Baton Rouge musicians made in the years since Slim Harpo died.

RECOMMENDED READING

Rather than direct the reader to the multitude of books, newspapers, magazine articles, Web sites and other sources I have spent years looking through in connection with Slim Harpo, and hopefully have distilled sufficiently in this book, I am listing a few major books by some of the key writers who have written about Harpo, his musical colleagues, music in Louisiana generally, and the community in which Harpo was raised.

There are three groundbreaking books by the acknowledged expert on the recorded music of Louisiana:

Broven, John. *Record Makers and Breakers.* Champaign: University of Illinois Press, 2011.
———. *Rhythm and Blues in New Orleans.* 3rd ed., Gretna, LA: Pelican Publishing, 1983. Formerly published as *Walking to New Orleans* (1974).
———. *South to Louisiana: The Music of the Cajun Bayous.* Gretna, LA: Pelican Publishing, 1983.

These two books are by an expert on the music of nearby New Orleans:

Hannusch, Jeff. *I Hear You Knockin'.* Ville Platte, LA: Swallow Publications, 1985.
———. *The Soul of New Orleans.* Ville Platte, LA: Swallow Publications, 2001.

A Baton Rouge journalist who has written often about local blues topics is author of the biography of a fascinating musician from New Orleans who later moved to Baton Rouge:

Wirt, John. *Huey "Piano" Smith and the Rocking Pneumonia Blues.* Baton Rouge: Louisiana State University Press, 2014.

One of the few bluesmen ever to have written an autobiography came from Louisiana:

Guy, Buddy, with David Ritz. *When I Left Home.* New York: Da Capo, 2012.

The biographies of other bluesmen are a fascinating corroboration of Harpo's times and an interesting contrast to his life:

Coleman, Rick. *Blue Monday: Fats Domino and the Lost Dawn of Rock 'n' Roll.* New York: Da Capo, 2006.

Guralnick, Peter. *Feel like Going Home: Portraits in Blues and Rock 'n' Roll* (with a chapter on Robert Pete Williams). 1971. New York: Vintage Books, 1981.

Lauterbach, Preston. *The Chitlin' Circuit and the Road to Rock 'n' Roll.* New York: W. W. Norton and Co., 2011.

O'Brien, Timothy, and David Ensminger. *Mojo Hand: The Life and Music of Lightnin' Hopkins.* Austin: University of Texas Press, 2013.

Oliver, Paul. *Conversation with the Blues* (including Butch Cage and Willie Thomas). London: Cassell, 1965.

Romano, Will. *Big Boss Man: The Life and Music of Bluesman Jimmy Reed.* San Francisco: Backbeat Books, 2006.

Segrest, James, and Mark Hoffman. *Moanin' at Midnight: The Life and Times of Howlin' Wolf.* New York: Thunder's Mouth Press, 2005.

The West Baton Rouge Museum and Historical Society has produced a fascinating general account of life in that parish down the years:

Rose, Julie, ed. *History of West Baton Rouge Parish.* St. Louis, MO: Reedy Press, 2012.

A MUSICAL APPRECIATION
STEPHEN COLERIDGE

[The issue of Slim Harpo's music in full boxed-set form in 2015 rekindled the burning interest musician Steve Coleridge had developed for Harpo's music some thirty years earlier. Steve began to send me comments and insights into Slim's music that, as a non-musician, I found fascinating. I decided to ask whether I could edit those comments into a commentary to sit alongside the Harpo discography in this book. Steve agreed, and that is so appropriate because he had moved his life from Europe to Baton Rouge in 1990 purely for the purpose of writing a book about Slim Harpo. The book didn't happen. He became distracted by the live-music scene in Baton Rouge, and instead he played and worked with the musicians who were still there, including Rudy Richard and other members of Harpo's King Bees. He is exceptionally well equipped to have a view on the music of Harpo in the context of the bluesmen of Baton Rouge, and his knowledge and enthusiasm come through loud and clear.]

Listening to the whole Slim canon again, taking a few notes, I'm hearing what I loved from before and picking up a lot of things I hadn't noticed, which you only really notice if you're playing along, which I am.

I look at Slim's career in three phases, really. First was the Deep Blues phase, which ended with "Rainin in My Heart" and the dry spell (sorry) that followed it. Then after the live show came a second Miller phase in Crowley. Third came the recordings not made in Crowley, the post-Miller phase.

DEEP BLUES

Lightnin' Slim's favorite key is D on his early Miller recordings, playing in open E with the guitar tuned down a step, and Harpo's early "One of These Days" is likewise. But "I'm A King Bee" is in F. If Slim picked up the guitar and started strumming an idea for a song, using the E position, it would come out in F if he used a capo. His later publicity photos almost always show him using a guitar capoed on the first fret, what Rudy Richard always referred to disparagingly as "a cheater." So, Harpo's slow numbers favor F, but there are of course many exceptions, and he also used A, D, E, G and C, even Bb capped on the sixth fret. Like "King Bee," "Got Love if You Want It" is in F, as is the superb doomy "Things Gonna Change" with its insistent bass drum, and "That Ain't Your Business," one of his greatest rockers. My feeling is that, when Miller and Harpo went for the nasal singing, Miller suggested F, as D would be too low, and Slim made F his favorite key from then on. All the instrumentals are in F too, though using a chromatic harp would account for that, and various ballads. He does use Bb, which is a jazz key, favored by bands that have a sax player, like the King Bees. The musicians on the early discs set the bar high for subsequent recordings. Rudy liked Bb, as did B. B. King.

But Harpo was famous for the harp, not the guitar. And he certainly is underrated as a harp player. Some people said Slim was influenced by Jimmy Reed's harp playing. Hmm—I can only find two examples of Jimmy Reed–style, position-one harmonica. Slim's most overtly Reedian tracks were "What's Goin On" and "Dream Girl." When playing first-position harp, he preferred an A harp like Reed. As for Slim's actual harp-playing technique, he plays both with pursed lips and tongue blocking, in "Baby, Scratch My Back," for example, where he also likes to bend a note and then play it straight, a technique often referred to as scooping and favored by Sonny Boy Williamson and Little Walter.

Many have inferred an overall Jimmy Reed influence in "King Bee," but I don't hear it. Lightnin' Slim's "Rock Me Mama" seems to me the closest thing. It became something of a standard, derived from the version recorded by Blind Lemon Jefferson that's at the root of the B. B. King version—but Lightnin' Slim's "Rock Me Mama" only resembles the Blind Lemon version lyrically. The I to minor 3rd to IV being a favorite, almost trademark, lick of Lightnin' Slim's and almost an archetype of what makes swamp-blues. As far as the influence of Blind Lemon Jefferson is concerned, I would not wish to underestimate it. I don't believe there is any one person more influential. When playing on one's own there is the luxury of using as many bars, or as few, as seem appropriate—Lightnin' Slim, Lightnin' Hopkins, and Muddy Waters all do this on recordings rather than being constrained by the twelve-bar format that's essential when playing with other people. On "King Bee," Slim changes early, in fact sometimes on those first sessions in the middle of a bar. Some call it pushing the beat, but this is done in a very exaggerated way. Then there's that bass line, even though it's played on guitar, AA DC AA CD if you're in the key of A, which is almost the definitive swamp-blues line, used in Harpo's "Buzz Me Babe," "Queen Bee," and others.

Slim ventures into A on "Wondering and Worryin'," with its call-and-response guitar and vocal interplay, but I suspect the band insisted on a change of key—not many guitarists like playing in F. The same session produced "Strange Love" in G, not a favorite key for Slim, but a song that shows Miller's keen ear for a gimmick or quirk as there is a little slide up to the high tonic on the 12th fret a la "sting it then," something that would make the song stand out a little when heard on a cheap radio. At the next session, F was again avoided in favor of the more conventional E for "One More Day," where the reverbed guitar gives a rainy night feel. I can hear Miller in the last verse lyrics—"there's one thing 'bout you women"—it's very polished and somehow does not seem like a Slim-Lovell line.

Slim's timing was bad in Rudy Richard's opinion. Rudy didn't like to do things that weren't "right." Blind Lemon and all those country blues guys didn't give a damn about the twelve bars, and they changed when they felt like it, and that is wrong to the classical mind of Rudy, though maybe not wrong to you and me.

"One of These Days" was a thinly disguised homage to Muddy Waters since Slim's first verse is the second verse of "Long Distance Call." The theme of the telephone call to the relative who'd made the Great Migration to Chicago would be a familiar one. From the point of view of a non-American writing in a different century, one can often underestimate the immediate power of lyrics in blues songs, but the lyrics were what sold the song to the public.

"Buzz Me Babe" is more uptempo and has a more threatening atmosphere than "King Bee" thanks to the vast echo and the aggressive bass buzz, and sharper sting. The elements were all in place for the arrival of Slim's classic road band, the King Bees. When Slim took his King Bees band to record with him, the sound changed, especially as far as lead guitar was concerned. Rudy Richard was happy to play in any key although he eschewed reverb and distortion, preferring a more B. B. King–like clean tone. Rudy was one of those musicians who seemed born with a guitar in their hands and who heard details in the music and put in little flourishes that normal mortals fail to pick up on. They seem to dominate their instrument effortlessly and sometimes find it strange that others have to struggle. A great deal of credit should be given to him, because these little details made some of the Miller-era tracks unique in the mixture of simple melodies with some sophisticated guitar that never goes over the taste barrier.

Rudy's character gave him superhuman abilities on the guitar, and when I was in Baton Rouge he was head and shoulders above every other guitar player—and the town was stuffed with class-A musicians. He was one of the great players ever in blues, putting chords in solos and doing little runs that repeat that I've not heard anyone else do. He was very neat in his personal appearance, and somehow that fitted in with the precision in his playing. He was almost always in a good mood and was very popular and likeable, though I think he had an inner world with fairly strict views that he kept to himself, and was certainly a very complex character and much harder to convey in print than James Johnson who, while the silent type, was more straightforward.

Had "Rainin in My Heart" not been a hit, it's possible to surmise that Slim Harpo would have continued to record mainly swamp-blues like his contemporaries. The origins of that song no doubt lay in Slim's subconscious where the I-to-V Louisiana ballad changes are a form as set in stone as a twelve-bar blues. But identifying where the great producers make their mark and where the artist is responsible is like trying to analyze what makes the taste in a good stew, and with the great producers like Miller it's very hard to tell what their artists would have sounded like without their input. If one wanted to assess the importance of Miller's input, nothing could be clearer proof than the mediocrity of the Imperial sessions. "A Man Is Cryin'" is of course "What's Goin' On," but the intro is absolutely conventional on the lower strings of the guitar and the harp sound has vanished, Rudy's guitar is way down in the mix, the snare is producing the shuffle feel instead of emphasizing the offbeat. "Something inside Me," in G unusually for an original, is quite interesting for an almost zydeco beat and has some nice harmonica playing, but Miller could have found its essence and extracted it.

It's hard to be grateful enough to the people who recorded the King Bees that hot night at the Armory in Mobile. The first thing that struck me was the number of slow tracks, easily explained by the temperature. Rudy's guitar work is striking, too, and the solidity of the band. The most significant cover was Little Walter's "I Don't Play" as Walter's influence is obvious in Slim's use of chromatic harp, though he never attempted to emulate Walter's distorted tones, unmistakably urban in their aggression. The solo on Walter's version was clearly influential for Slim, melody-wise. If you care to sing "I'm a Bread Maker, Baby" over "I Don't Play" it fits perfectly. The Armory show indicated how in tune with current trends the band was, and not limited to being a pure blues band. The constant gigging had produced a superb road band.

POST-RAININ' CROWLEY

Slim Harpo's voice had a warmth that could cross into other genres. Miller realized this after "Rainin'" and saw that the same comfortable feelings that Fats Domino produced in people could be created by Slim. Hopes for pop-ballad crossover hits led to such numbers as "We're Two of a Kind," "I'm Waiting on You Baby," and "You'll Never Find a Love (As True as Mine)," none of which can be considered Slim's finest hour.

But after the hiatus Miller also began experimenting, not only with rhythms but in the use of Latin percussion as well. From the shuffle and 12/8 rhythms the band had used up to now, which are the basis of what Miller would call down-home gutbucket blues, in would come the Latin beats and pop ballads. "Snoopin' Around" was the first time he'd used woodblocks, but soon they'd become more noticeable by their absence. Many rhythmic experiments produced satisfactory results, "I Need Money," "Buzzin'," and "Midnight Blues." The more obvious rumbas could be heard in "Scratch My Back" and "Breadmaker," and later in "Mailbox Blues."

Jay Miller has been quoted as saying the British Invasion of the early 1960s tore a hole in black music, but I think it is more a question of eclectic experimentation tearing a hole in traditional black-music scenes. Some of the blame for the decline in fortunes of the independent producers must be laid at their own door, for their lack of imagination and failure to see what was happening in the outside world. In fact the white youth market was consuming black product in quantities previously unimagined—ask Berry Gordy if he had any complaints. By 1961, Jay Miller was already trying to move away from down-home, gutbucket blues to a crossover, as "Rainin in My Heart" proved, and at that time the Beatles were still scuffling in Hamburg.

POST-MILLER PERIOD

In the post-Miller period we come to the genius rhythm guitar of Teenie Hodges, and whoever played on the Nashville tracks—well, the good ones—

deserves a statue, too. It's funny that when I listen to the early Miller stuff I'm thinking this is Slim's finest hour, and then I get to these later sessions and think, no, this is their best stuff, it's that good. There aren't many artists who make one think like that.

It took Slim's move to Memphis to show the potential of a new R&B mixture that hasn't got a label because it was, and remains, unique. It was not surprising that Slim felt comfortable with his new studio band as they were among the greatest that existed. Fortune smiled on the new sound from the word go, and "Tip on In" has since become a standard and almost started a genre of its own in Austin and Dallas some two decades later.

"I'm Gonna Keep What I've Got" in the new key of F sharp was very clearly a Lovell-Slim collaboration and lyrically was outside normal blues territory. Slim went for a cross between blues and country harp, the intro and solo being played on the middle of a B harp, with few bends or trills or other Walteresque gymnastics, and in so doing seemed to be starting on a path of more melodic cozy-sounding harp. The rhythm section let the bass take care of holding the groove together while Hodges improvised behind the vocal but held a solid pattern beneath the harp solo. If one were to teach rhythm guitar, this would be the "How To" track. As the saying goes, you should only notice the vanilla in ice cream when it ain't there. How many guitarists live by this maxim? About 3 percent, I'd say.

In the wider world the times they were a-changing, and had been for some time; however, if one were living in Memphis in 1967 and working in music, there was little reason to imagine things had any way to go but up. It was the musical equivalent of Renaissance Florence, and this optimism comes across in the productions.

"Mailbox Blues" seems at first hearing to be a cover, but is in fact original, though because Slim and Lovell were seldom apart for very long it rings less true than such songs as "That's Why I Love You." There's little to say about "Stick Your Chest Out," except I find it hard to believe Slim or especially Lovell had any part in these seriously embarrassing lyrics. It sounds to me like the sort of thing someone might record late at night when the engineer might say: my nephew wrote this, will you have a crack at it? Wisely it was not released in Slim's lifetime.

The mysterious Nashville sessions followed with "My Baby She's Got It," which lyrically is in the soul style, and "I'm So Sorry," a gently wistful slow blues possibly autobiographical with the scratch guitar way down in the mix and the other guitar, presumably Slim, playing sliding chords twice in each bar. The Memphis sound permeates these Nashville sides.

"Hey Little Lee," a bouncy piece of R&B, has an infectious groove that's down to a great bass player, and the rhythm guitar is locked into a three-note pattern with a little flourish. That follows the I, IV, V, does not vary, and could well be Slim. The lead player has a fair amount of reverb, and the solo could be overdubbed as he's not doing much the rest of the time. In fact as there's a muffled rake in the solo, it could be Slim. This has to be in my Slim Harpo top five. It was not a single, maybe because it had no middle eight. I can't think of any other reasonable explanation.

"I've Got to Be with You Tonight" could have been composed on the harmonica. One thing that Slim almost never did was to put fills in between vocal lines, and I'm not sure why as its almost reflexive to sing a line and then respond on harp, unless of course you a have a guitar player to do the fill for you. B. B. King is the obvious person who answers his vocal with guitar, and in the harp field you can cite Rice Miller, who almost converses with himself.

"That's Why I Love You" is possibly the peak of the Lovell-Slim Nashville paeans to married bliss, the keyboard and guitar playing a compound riff and then, after the second verse, a double guitar solo, two guitarists soloing independently, maybe with a view to choosing the best solo later, but they forgot, or it's an overdub, or they just kind of liked it that way. Whatever, it's a great song with a tremendous riff, and there were a series in this category of riff-based songs with the harmonica coming in after the last verse. This one is almost the archetype of the latter-period Slim Harpo, happy, groovy, contented R&B over a solid riff, with a harp fadeout.

Slim recorded just five slow blues in the post-Miller era: "I Just Can't Leave You," "I'm So Sorry," "I've Been a Good Thing for You" and the almost identical "Just for You," and the superb "Mutual Friend"—how many Dickensian titles are there in blues? And as for standard twelve-bar shuffles, then "Jody Man" stands out.

One of the great if-onlys is what would have happened if Slim had gone to London and made an album with Mike Vernon? I surmise that it would have probably followed the line laid down by the first side of *Slim Harpo Knew the Blues*—if I had a desert-island compilation, those songs would be on it.

GENERAL INDEX

INDEX OF SONG TITLES